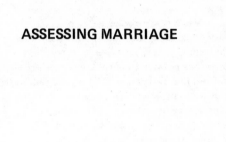

SAGE FOCUS EDITIONS

1. **POLICE AND SOCIETY,** edited by David H. Bayley
2. **WHY NATIONS ACT,** edited by Maurice A. East, Stephen A. Salmore, and Charles F. Hermann
3. **EVALUATION RESEARCH METHODS,** edited by Leonard Rutman
4. **SOCIAL SCIENTISTS AS ADVOCATES,** edited by George H. Weber and George J. McCall
5. **DYNAMICS OF GROUP DECISIONS,** edited by Hermann Brandstätter, James H. Davis, and Heinz Schuler
6. **NATURAL ORDER,** edited by Barry Barnes and Steven Shapin
7. **CONFLICT AND CONTROL,** edited by Arthur J. Vidich and Ronald M. Glassman
8. **CONTROVERSY,** edited by Dorothy Nelkin
9. **BATTERED WOMEN,** edited by Donna M. Moore
10. **CRIMINOLOGY,** edited by Edward Sagarin
11. **TO AUGUR WELL,** edited by J. David Singer and Michael D. Wallace
12. **IMPROVING EVALUATIONS,** edited by Lois-ellin Datta and Robert Perloff
13. **IMAGES OF INFORMATION,** edited by Jon Wagner
14. **CHURCHES AND POLITICS IN LATIN AMERICA,** edited by Daniel H. Levine
15. **EDUCATIONAL TESTING AND EVALUATION,** edited by Eva L. Baker and Edys S. Quellmalz
16. **IMPROVING POLICY ANALYSIS,** edited by Stuart S. Nagel
17. **POWER STRUCTURE RESEARCH,** edited by G. William Domhoff
18. **AGING AND SOCIETY,** edited by Edgar F. Borgatta and Neil G. McCluskey
19. **CENTRE AND PERIPHERY,** edited by Jean Gottmann
20. **THE ELECTORATE RECONSIDERED,** edited by John C. Pierce and John L. Sullivan
21. **THE BLACK WOMAN,** edited by La Frances Rodgers-Rose
22. **MAKING BUREAUCRACIES WORK,** edited by Carol H. Weiss and Allen H. Barton
23. **RADICAL CRIMINOLOGY,** edited by James A. Inciardi
24. **DUAL-CAREER COUPLES,** edited by Fran Pepitone-Rockwell
25. **POLICY IMPLEMENTATION,** edited by John Brigham and Don W. Brown
26. **CONTEMPORARY BLACK THOUGHT,** edited by Molefi Kete Asante and Abdulai S. Vandi
27. **HISTORY AND CRIME,** edited by James A. Inciardi and Charles E. Faupel
28. **THE FUTURE OF EDUCATION,** edited by Kathryn Cirincione-Coles
29. **IMPROVING SCHOOLS,** edited by Rolf Lehming and Michael Kane
30. **KNOWLEDGE AND POWER IN A GLOBAL SOCIETY,** edited by William M. Evan
31. **BLACK MEN,** edited by Lawrence E. Gary
32. **MAJOR CRIMINAL JUSTICE SYSTEMS,** edited by George F. Cole, Stanislaw J. Frankowski, and Marc G. Gertz
33. **ANALYZING ELECTORAL HISTORY,** edited by Jerome M. Clubb, William H. Flanigan, and Nancy H. Zingale
34. **ASSESSING MARRIAGE,** edited by Erik E. Filsinger and Robert A. Lewis
35. **THE KNOWLEDGE CYCLE,** edited by Robert F. Rich
36. **IMPACTS OF RACISM ON WHITE AMERICANS,** edited by Benjamin P. Bowser and Raymond G. Hunt
37. **WORLD SYSTEM STRUCTURE,** edited by W. Ladd Hollist and James N. Rosenau
38. **WOMEN AND WORLD CHANGE,** edited by Naomi Black and Ann B. Cottrell

ASSESSING MARRIAGE

New Behavioral Approaches

Edited by
ERIK E. FILSINGER
and ROBERT A. LEWIS

Published in cooperation with the
National Council on Family Relations

 SAGE PUBLICATIONS   Beverly Hills   London

For information address:

SAGE Publications, Inc.
275 South Beverly Drive
Beverly Hills, California 90212

SAGE Publications Ltd
28 Banner Street
London EC1Y 8QE, England

Printed in the United States of America

Library of Congress Cataloging in Publication Data

Main entry under title:

Assessing marriage.

   (Sage focus editions ; 34)
   Includes bibliographies.
   1. Marriage—Addresses, essays, lectures.
2. Behavioral assessment—Addresses, essays,
lectures. I. Filsinger, Erik E. II. Lewis,
Robert A. (Robert Alan), 1932-
HQ734.A76   306.8   81-13625
ISBN 0-8039-1570-5   AACR2
ISBN 0-8039-1571-3 (pbk.)

FIRST PRINTING

CONTENTS

SERIES EDITOR'S PREFACE

It is with extreme pleasure that I welcome this, my first volume as general editor, into the series of books sponsored by the *National Council on Family Relations*.

Our goal is to make this series the publication vehicle for the most significant books in family studies, significant in the sense that they deal with "cutting-edge" issues—whether the issues be theoretical, methodological, substantive, or applied. Moreover, we want the series to encompass a broad range of work styles—including quantitative or qualitative research, or purely theoretical efforts.

Keeping with those objectives, Erik Filsinger and Bob Lewis have put together what I believe to be the finest collection of papers available on the increasingly important topic of marriage behavioral assessment. This work is clearly on the "cutting edge" of methodological approaches to the family. Anyone (whether theorist, researcher, or therapist) interested in keeping abreast of research trends that are likely to become increasingly important during the next 5 to 10 years will need to read this stimulating and provocative collection. The implications of their work stretch far beyond the explication of a particular style of research. To the degree that behavioral observation becomes an ever more common means of gathering data about marriages/families, traditional methodologies will come under closer scrutiny and be open to more severe critiques. Similarly, the "behaviorist" implications of this approach will force us to reexamine our theoretical assumptions and frameworks more carefully as well. In short, I expect the book to be a long-remembered contribution to the field of family studies, and we are proud to have it in the NCFR-Sage book series.

John Scanzoni

PREFACE

In February of 1980, a conference entitled "Marital Observation and Behavioral Assessment" was held at Arizona State University. While the conference was noteworthy for the raging floodwaters of the Salt River, it was also significant to the extent that a cross section of sociologists, psychologists, anthropologists, family therapists, and home economists were brought together on the same platform, many for the first time. That forum represented a significant step in the communication among those various disciplines concerning the fundamental issues of marital assessment.

At the suggestion of John Scanzoni, Monograph Series Editor for the National Council on Family Relations, a proposal for a monograph dealing with marital observation techniques was submitted. With an eye on the specific focus of marital observation, we solicited certain of the papers presented at the conference to form the nucleus of the book. These papers were augmented by contacts made to other scholars in the field.

After several months of writing and rewriting, an initial draft was submitted to Dr. Scanzoni. The services of Robert Ryder were sought in reviewing the work, and his helpful suggestions and criticisms are reflected in the following pages, as is the managing focus of Dr. Scanzoni. It is our hope that this book will stimulate thought and provide the basis for continued effort, and that, rather than being viewed as a definitive end product, the book will be seen as a steppingstone to amplification and extension in the future.

It would be unfair not to mention the help of others. Mrs. Dottie DeWitt and Ms. Kathi Buechler provided secretarial assistance. Ms. Terri Mann helped with clerical tasks. Appreciation should also be expressed to the College of Liberal Arts and the Center for Family Studies of the Department of Home Economics at Arizona State University, for support in the preparation of the manuscript.

Erik E. Filsinger
Robert A. Lewis

1

INTRODUCTION:
TRENDS AND PROSPECTS
FOR OBSERVING MARRIAGE

Erik E. Filsinger
Robert A. Lewis
Philip McAvoy

A book usually has a purpose. This one's purpose is to give the reader an overview of research developments in *marital behavioral assessment*. The chapters of this volume represent a cross section of observational research issues in the study of marriage. The forum is interdisciplinary and includes the work of psychologists, sociologists, home economists, and anthropologists. Indeed, one of its unique features is that it brings together the work of researchers from quite different traditions who previously may not have shared the same platform.

It is perhaps noteworthy that the *National Council of Family Relations* devotes a book in its monograph series to this topic. It indicates that in the development of family-related literature, a point has been reached at which it is thought necessary to take a closer look at husband-wife interaction as it unfolds in real life behavior. This concern grows out of the long-term interest of researchers and therapists in assessing marriage and in finding ever more secure data on which to base theory and practice.

Consistent with the purpose of this book, we have attempted to maintain the primary focus on marital behavioral assessment. That limitation has determined, directly and indirectly, the topics and authors included.

As a result of the primary focus on the behavioral assessment of marriage, several implications and ramifications should be noted. First, marital dyads are being studied. This is consistent with the belief that there are significant issues to be addressed within the system of the husband and the wife without necessarily having to deal with other members of the couple's environment (see Weiss, 1978). Certainly not all of the authors whose works are contained herein would adhere to this viewpoint, but they have been asked to take this as their focus.

The behavioral emphasis is twofold. Regardless of theoretical framework, the predominant data collection mode is observation by a trained other of husband-wife interaction. In fact, it appears that, despite conceptual differences, researchers from the various theoretical perspectives are advocating behavioral methods of data collection (see Jacobson & Margolin, 1979).

Behaviorism as a theoretical perspective is also strongly represented in the work, both because of its central place in the development of the methods and because of the bias of the principal editor (E. F.). However, it is a newer variant of the species which includes the study of a number of cognitive behaviors as central to understanding human existence.

In addition, rather than having only this perspective, the book contains other ideas and frameworks. Several chapters are included precisely because of their divergent perspectives. For example, Lowman (Chapter 4) makes the case for a self-report measure of family affectivity. Other chapters clearly call for multi-method assessment (for example, Cromwell & Peterson, Chapter 3). Clearly, the reader should be warned that behavioral techniques and observational data are not cure-alls.

The term *assessment* further delimits the scope of the work. Specifically, the primary interest is in the clinically relevant task of distinguishing distressed from nondistressed relationships. Techniques are offered which can be used to diagnose marital distress and can also be used to assess the progress or effectiveness of the treatment.

ANTECEDENTS AND PRECURSORS

While we are attempting in many ways to paint the picture of an exciting new art, it would be somewhat false not to give acknowledgment to the contributions made in the past in the area of observational research (for example, Mishler & Waxler, 1968; Raush, 1972; Ryder, 1968; Tallman & Miller, 1974). A modern-day behaviorist's (Jacobson, 1980) use of affectionate, interactive, and instrumental categories of behaviors reminds the reader of Bales's original scheme for assessing the behavior within small groups (Bales & Strodtbeck, 1951). Similarly, the Allred Interaction Code (Chapter 10) bears resemblance to Bales's work, although Allred also draws heavily on Adlerian principles.

In what sense, then, is there a reason for the renewed interest in behavioral methods? Our answer is that the time appears ripe. We would suggest that a number of historical developments have lead to the renewed interest in observational techniques.

For one thing, several factors may have inhibited the development of behavioral techniques among family researchers. By and large, the researchers studying marriage have been sociologists, a breed of scholars never particularly reliant on behavioral conceptualization or methodology. Instead, sociologists have tended to rely on the questionnaire approach to marital studies.

Moreover, sociologically oriented family researchers have most frequently used concepts such as power, which lends itself quite easily to win scores. While a behavioral interchange may have been used as the situation which produced the win scores, the specific characteristics of the behavior itself were not often coded and used as data.

Exceptions do exist in the area of small group research. However, in the cases where behavioral measures were used, the research issue was most often theoretical. A couple of examples can be cited. Ryder (1968) used the Color Matching Test to provide behavioral data which could distinguish husband-wife dyads from married strangers. In a later study, Tallman and Miller (1974) used observational data on family decision making. In each case, the hope was to further our understanding of theoretically significant phenomena, not to generate data for application.

Another factor involves the disenchantment among family scholars with the ability of traditional questionnaire measures to provide the data base upon which to build theory and practice (Raush et al., 1974). This disenchantment created a void of sorts, which was ripe for alternative techniques, specifically behavioral observation.

Outside of marital studies directly, but still having a significant impact, is the work of the ethologists. Their work has most directly influenced researchers in child development, but its influence on social psychology through scholars such as Argyle and Mehrabian has set the stage for further fine-tuned analysis of intimate human relationships. Also, the ethologists have given rise to some of the more sophisticated developments of recording devices (Holm, 1978).

Another historical precursor is the work done under family systems theory. Because of their close usage of communication theory and attempts to formalize the interdependencies within the family, family systems therapists have led in the development of some of the more sophisticated observational projects (Mishler & Waxler, 1968). While also influenced by psychoanalytic frameworks, Raush and his colleagues (Raush, 1972; Raush et al., 1974) have presented some of the more sophisticated studies, in terms of observational data analysis strategies, using Markovian approximations that test some of those interdependencies. Raush's work also represents the commitment to behavioral methods, "Studying what people say about themselves is no substitute for studying how they behave. Self-reports, particularly those given in brief questionnaires, are subject to massive distortion. Questionnaires and scales of marital satisfaction and dissatisfaction have yielded very little" (Raush et al., 1974, p. 5).

But perhaps the two most important forces that bring observational techniques to the forefront in marital studies are the arrival of the empirical clinician and the continued success of behaviorism.

The future will probably see more and more emphasis placed on making clinical decisions with the aid of data collected, rather than solely on subjective judgments. For example, the theme of the 1980 Convention of the Association for the Advancement of Behavior Therapy was "The Decade of the Empirical Clinician." It was argued that data will be used in the diagnosis of the problem, the selection of treatment, and the evaluation of the success of the treatment. Indeed, with behavioral approaches data collection itself is often thought to be therapeutic (see Jacobson & Margolin, 1979). It should be noted that with this increased emphasis on data collection and usage in the clinical setting, therapists are becoming more involved in designing assessment packages.

It has been a hallmark of behavioral assessment that behavioral measures are gathered before, during, and after treatment. The result has been that behaviorists have generated a large amount of literature from this data, indicating its success. Being hard-nosed about objective data, behaviorists have come to the fore with an impressive array of empirical evidence (Kazdin, 1975). Of importance here is that much of it is observational, in line with the behaviorist principles.

It should not be overlooked that similar thoughts about the close relationship between research and practice also exist elsewhere. In stating the case for bridging clinical and research questions, Olson (Chapter 5) suggests several contributions that researchers can make to therapists. These include clarifying treatment goals, developing diagnostic instruments, and providing normative data in traditional assessment.

Nevertheless, there is a greater isomorphism between assessment and treatment in behavioral approaches than there is under traditional assessment procedures. Behavioral assessment involves both treatment selection and treatment evaluation, and the assessment is continuous with treatment. In traditional assessment, the diagnostic labeling occurs prior to treatment and has few treatment-specific implications. These factors make behavioral assessment attractive to many researchers and therapists.

CURRENT BEHAVIORISM

As Steinglass (1978) has recently discussed in his review of systems theory, there is really no such thing as *the* systems theory perspective. Instead, there are many different perspectives which share some basic commonalities. Similarly, behaviorism comes in a variety of forms. Weiss (1978) implores readers not to reject offhand a behaviorist perspective because of some objections to certain beliefs about behaviorists. As Weiss indicates, the entrance of behaviorism into the field of marital studies has not been received enthusiastically. He argues that there are a variety of behaviorist models and that the current emphasis in behaviorism incorporates many forms of cognitive processes. These include expectations, self-talk, mental rehearsal, self-reinforcement, and attributions (Bandura, 1977; Mahoney, 1974; Meichenbaum, 1977). Indeed, some of the most reliable findings supporting a behavioral definition of marital distress come from studies that use the spouse's reaction to a behavior as defining it as rewarding or punishing (see Jacobson, 1980).

Behaviorism has characteristically been atheoretical, often functioning as a therapeutic technology used to bring about desired changes. However, without theory, it is difficult to choose the aspects of the couple's relationship on which to focus. Weiss (Chapter 2) states the need for a theory of couple relationship to guide research and practice and to define the characteristics of marital distress. In addition to Weiss, there are a number of others developing theories (for example, Gottman, 1979).

It should be noted that new concepts may become critical to the understanding of marriage because they will be able to be measured more effectively through behavioral techniques. That is, the assessment of some aspects of marital relationships may actually be improved through behavioral measures because of the nature of the concept. Whereas marital satisfaction can be reasonably assessed by a self-report—individuals should know whether they are happy or not—other concepts may not lend themselves as easily to self-report because their referents may not be as available to the individual. For example, a husband would probably have problems accurately evaluating the competence of his behaviors directed to his wife. It would be quite reasonable to expect the husband to feel that he is quite effective, when actually his competence may be more alleged than real. While interpersonal competence has a rich conceptual tradition in family studies (for example, Foote & Cottrell, 1955), the measurement of the concept has been primarily through self-report (see Farber, 1962; Filsinger, 1980). In contrast, social skills have been central to behaviorist conceptualizations because they are accessed as observables. Behavioral skills may be used more frequently in studying marriage. Our current knowledge of the importance of communication between partners suggests the validity of a focus on skills.

Similarly, concepts such as equity and reciprocity take on new meaning when measured behaviorally (see Gottman, 1979). Conger and Smith (Chapter 14) provide an insightful discussion of the interplay between data analysis strategy and these concepts.

RECENT DEVELOPMENTS

A number of current trends in the areas of marital observation and behavioral assessment can be identified in order to further understand the context of this book. For one, researchers in different disciplines or schools of thought are becoming increasingly aware of the work of others. The present anthology, for example, brings together some current, innovative thoughts of psychologists, sociologists, psychiatrists, and anthropologists.

There is also some convergence between schools in the conceptualization of what constitute the important features of marital and family relationships. One specific illustration of this is the dialogue between behaviorists and systems theorists. Birchler and Spinks (1980) attempted a conceptual integration of social learning and family systems perspectives. They suggest, for example, that family rules are patterns of behavior shaped by reinforcement and punishment. These contingencies also account for the homeostatic effect of the rules. Weiss (1978) has provided a theoretical framework, which he calls the Behavioral Systems Perspective (see also Chapter 2). His central effort, as with that of Birchler and Spinks, is to translate communication processes of the family into behavioral principles. In so doing, the behavioral framework is expanded beyond its original emphasis.

As has already been suggested, another central feature of current behavioral conceptualizations is the role given to cognitive behaviors. Gottman and his colleagues (1976) have provided evidence that a great deal of interpretation of behaviors goes on in husband-wife interaction and that the intended message may be quite different from that received. That which is received may be more important than that which is sent. Distressed couples can be distinguished from nondistressed couples in that they may have a greater communication deficit (Gottman et al., 1976). Margolin (Chapter 6) devotes a section of her contribution to an overview of the role of cognitions in behavioral assessment, as do Weiss (Chapter 2) and Olson (Chapter 5).

However, cognitive behaviors involve more than just the attribution of meanings. Filsinger (Note 1) has offered a model of social competence in marital relationships which draws heavily on the concepts of efficacy expectations, self-systems, and reciprocal causation. Essentially, he argues that the functioning of the individual in the dyad is the result of a complex network of interacting factors, including the individual's behavior, the input from the spouse and from the larger environment, and the control of the self-system. A large component of the self-system governance is the individual's self-efficacy. Performances that obtain desired goals enhance self-efficacy, which will make it more likely that the individual will select successful situations and scenarios in the future. Weiss (Chapter 2) also draws on Bandura's (1977) model of efficacy expectations, suggesting that a couple possesses a theory or collective expectation about their relationship and that these beliefs function to facilitate or inhibit change in the relationship.

It may be that future work will be able to identify some of the cognitions that accompany marital dysfunction. A possible list, for starters, comes from the area of heterosexual-social anxiety. Arkowitz (1977) cites overly negative self-evaluations, negative covert self-statements, excessively high standards for performance, selective attention to negative aspects of performance, and pathological patterns of attribution for social success or failure as cognitive processes which may be dysfunctional for social interaction. The same cognitions may account for dysfunctions in marital interaction as well.

Given the complexity of levels of individual and dyadic processes in relationships, perhaps it is not surprising that there is also an increased emphasis on *multimethod measurement*. Margolin (Chapter 6) suggests that the therapist must be aware of behaviors, cognitions, and general relationship characteristics. Cromwell and Peterson (Chapter 3) present an argument for selecting multiple measurements on the basis of the particular levels of systems involved in one's conceptualization of a research or therapy, such as individual, family, and society. Allred and his colleagues (Chapter 10) provide an elaborate assessment framework which incorporates even physiological measurements—a step consistent with earlier suggestions in the general behavioral assessment literature (for example, Hersen & Bellack, 1977).

Another significant trend is the concern that has been generated over the comparative validity of the traditional and behavioral assessment procedures (Goldfried & Linehan, 1977). Two chapters in the present volume address this issue (Lewis, Filsinger, Conger, & McAvoy, Chapter 16; Markman, Notarius, Stephen, & Smith, Chapter 15). These chapters suggest that progress is being made in answering this question.

A final trend in the literature which may be particularly useful for maturation of the science is the development of some standard research paradigms. For example, Olson and Ryder's (1970) vignettes in the Inventory of Marital Conflict have been used frequently as a basis for stimulating husband-wife interaction (see Filsinger, Chapter 9; Gottman, 1979; Olson, Chapter 5). The standardization of this and other research paradigms greatly increases the comparability of studies and facilitates the integration of findings. The use of behavioral assessment procedures in behavioral marital therapy has also led to the use of similar procedures and situations as aids in therapy (Margolin, Chapter 6).

RECENT TECHNIQUES

One development—a topic in itself—is the increased sophistication of data collection techniques being employed in marital studies. This is paralleled by developments in the area of establishing reliability and sophisticated data analysis procedures (see chapters by Hartmann and Notarius). The present volume contains presentations and discussions of a number of the most common and the latest coding systems: the Marital and Family Interaction Coding System (MFICS; Olson, Chapter 5); the Couples Interaction Scoring System (CISS; Notarius & Markman, Chapter 7); the Home Observation Assessment Method (HOAM; Steinglass & Tislenko, Chapter 8); the Dyadic Interaction Scoring Code (DISC; Filsinger, Chapter 9); the Allred Interaction Analysis (AIA; Allred et al., Chapter 10); and the Social Interaction Scoring System (SISS; Conger & Smith, Chapter 14).

Some efforts in the last few years have been devoted also to establishing the validity of coding systems. For example, validity studies on the Marital Interaction Coding System have shown behavioral differences between distressed and nondistressed couples (Birchler et al., 1975; Vincent et al., 1975). Gottman (1979) has reported sophisticated analyses which group specific behaviors of the CISS on the basis of how similarly they function in sequential analysis. Both the MICS and the CISS have been subjected to generalizability studies which support their psychometric properties (Wieder & Weiss, 1980; Gottman, 1979). Finally, Markman and his colleagues (Chapter 15) discuss the comparative findings of a number of the coding systems. Additional outside work has investigated the particular behavioral components that are associated with the prediction of marital satisfaction and marital distress (Koren et al., 1980; Royce & Weiss, 1975).

The last few years have also been characterized by the increased sophistication and increased usage of digital data acquisition systems. Filsinger (Chapter 9) has developed a coding system built around the Datamyte 900 from Data General Corporation. Holm (Chapter 11) reviews a number of data acquisition machines, including the MORE from Observational Systems Incorporated. Allred and his colleagues (Chapter 10) also employ machine-aided data collection. These various machines allow for rapid data collection, storage, and computer interface, thus saving many person-hours of data preparation and processing. The comparative validity of machine-aided versus other coding procedures has not yet been established. The machines do facilitate data acquisition and are quite flexible as to location of usage.

The application of Markovian and lag sequential analyses to behavioral data has also become more prevalent in the last few years (Gottman & Notarius, 1978; Sackett, 1978) and has greatly improved the ability of researchers to identify patterns of marital interactions (Gottman et al., 1977). Of particular theoretical interest to behavioral researchers are those specific patterns of certain behaviors which are likely to follow other specific behaviors. For example, by examining the immediate consequences of behaviors on spouses' behaviors, Gottman (1979) was able to identify a "behavioral rigidity" in distressed couples wherein patterning of behaviors was very tight, predictable, and immediate. Finally, Notarius and his colleagues (Chapter 13) review some possible applications of spectral time series analysis to behavioral data.

STRUCTURE OF THE BOOK

Part I contains five differing statements on major issues concerning frameworks for behavioral assessment. Weiss (Chapter 2) outlines a behaviorist theoretical perspective into which behavioral techniques may be plugged. The chapter also represents a bridging of behaviorist and systemic conceptual frameworks. Cromwell and Peterson (Chapter 3) take a different approach and argue for the use of multimethod assessment designed to match the level of the family system being assessed. Lowman (Chapter 4) argues that behavioral and cognitive components are important, but he also suggests that it all really comes down to the affective relations in the family. He provides data to support his position.

The interface between clinical and research issues is addressed directly in the last two chapters of Part I. Olson (Chapter 5) outlines what the researcher can offer the clinician and what the clinician can offer the researcher. He suggests that family typologies serve a useful function in bridging their respective interests. Margolin (Chapter 6) makes the case for the clinician even stronger by outlining techniques whereby the clinician can adapt assessment strategies to meet his or her clinical needs.

As such, Part I begins on a theoretical note and moves through to practicality. It is our hope that the reader will leave Part I with a feeling of the diversity of perspectives and a notion that techniques must be fitted to the research problem.

The second part of the book contains chapters outlining different techniques for collecting observational data on marital interaction. These are the tools researchers and practitioners can use to suit their individual purposes. The chapters range from descriptions of coding systems to a discussion of machine hardware as it can be used to operationalize coding systems. In many ways, these chapters are the heart of the book.

Part III presents discussions of data analysis techniques as they apply to determining reliability (Hartmann & Gardner, Chapter 12), to optimally analyzing sequential data (Notarius and colleagues, Chapter 13), and to an in-depth example of operationalizing the single concept of equity (Conger & Smith, Chapter 14).

The fourth part of the book presents two chapters dealing with the current status of marital behavioral assessment. Markman and his colleagues (Chapter 15) provide an intensive overview of the current research findings resulting from observational techniques. In a slightly different vein, Lewis and his colleagues (Chapter 16) offer data on the convergent validity of traditional self-report and behavioral assessment techniques.

The fifth and final section offers a number of divergent concerns on the use and current status of behavioral assessment. Straus (Chapter 17) addresses the critical issue of ethical concerns in the use of marital behavioral assessment. Research must be conducted within the socio-political-legal milieu of the larger society. Restrictions on the use of human subjects is no small stumbling block to continuing research. Straus provides an insightful discussion of the ethics of behavioral and observational research.

In the concluding chapter, Arkowitz and his colleagues present a critical overview of the book and suggest weaknesses in the current status of behavioral assessment. Issues for future efforts are designated.

While each section, or even each chapter, could fruitfully be read by itself, the reader is encouraged to look on the book as a whole, integrated effort. The divergent positions and approaches offered are designed to stimulate the reader's own unique ideas as to what is right and proper. We hope to develop a general appreciation of the complexities of the issues involved and the overall validity of marital behavioral assessment.

REFERENCE NOTE

1. FILSINGER, E. E. *Social competence in short- and long-term relationships.* Paper presented at the Theory Construction and Methods Workshop, Portland, Oregon, October 1980.

REFERENCES

ARKOWITZ, H. Measurement and modification of minimal dating behavior. In M. Hersen (Ed.), *Progress in behavior modification* (Vol. 5). New York: Academic, 1977.

BALES, R. F., & STRODTBECK, F. L. Phases in group problem solving. *Journal of Abnormal and Social Psychology,* 1951, *46,* 485-495.

BANDURA, A. Self-efficacy: Toward a unifying theory of behavioral change. *Psychological Review,* 1977, *84,* 191-215.

BIRCHLER, G. R., & SPINKS, S. H. Behavioral-systems marital and family therapy: Integration and clinical application. *American Journal of Family Therapy,* 1980, *8,* 6-28.

BIRCHLER, G. R., WEISS, R. L., & VINCENT, J. P. A multimethod analysis of social reinforcement exchange between maritally distressed and nondistressed spouse and stranger dyads. *Journal of Personality and Social Psychology,* 1975, *31,* 349-360.

FARBER, B. Elements of competence in interpersonal relations: A factor analysis. *Sociometry,* 1962, *25,* 30-47.

Erik E. Filsinger et al.   **19**

FILSINGER, E. E. Social competence and marital adjustment. *Home Economics Research Journal*, 1980, *9*, 158-162.

FOOTE, N. N., & COTTRELL, L. S., Jr. *Identity and interpersonal competence*. Chicago: University of Chicago Press, 1955.

GOLDFRIED, M. R., & LINEHAN, M. M. Basic issues in behavioral assessment. In A. R. Ciminero, K. S. Calhoun, & H. E. Adams (Eds.), *Handbook of behavioral assessment*. New York: John Wiley, 1977.

GOTTMAN, J. M. *Marital interaction: Experimental investigations*. New York: Academic, 1979.

GOTTMAN, J. M., MARKMAN, H., & NOTARIUS, C. The topography of marital conflict: A study of verbal and nonverbal behavior. *Journal of Marriage and the Family*, 1977, *39*, 461-477.

GOTTMAN, J. M., & NOTARIUS, C. Sequential analysis of observational data using Markov chains. In T. Kratochwill (Ed.), *Strategies to evaluate change in single-subject research*. New York: Academic, 1978.

GOTTMAN, J. M., NOTARIUS, C., MARKMAN, H., BANK, S., YOPPI, B., & RUBIN, M. E. Behavior exchange theory and marital decision making. *Journal of Personality and Social Psychology*, 1976, *34*, 14-23.

HERSEN, M., & BELLACK, A. S. Assessment of social skills. In A. R. Ciminero, K. S. Calhoun, & H. E. Adams (Eds.), *Handbook of behavioral assessment*. New York: John Wiley, 1977.

HOLM, R. A. Techniques of recording observational data. In G. P. Sackett (Ed.), *Observing behavior* (Vol. 2): *Data collection and analysis methods*. Baltimore: University Park Press, 1978.

JACOBSON, N. S. Behavioral treatments for marital discord: A critical appraisal. In M. Hersen, R. Eisler, & P. Miller (Eds.), *Progress in behavior modification* (Vol. 8). New York: Academic, 1980.

JACOBSON, N. S., & MARGOLIN, G. *Marital therapy: Strategies based on social learning and behavior exchange principles*. New York: Brunner/Mazel, 1979.

KAZDIN, A. E. *Behavior modification in applied settings*. Homewood, Il: Dorsey, 1975.

KOREN, P., CARLTON, K., & SHAW, D. Marital conflict: Relations among behaviors, outcomes, and distress. *Journal of Consulting and Clinical Psychology*, 1980, *48*, 460-468.

MAHONEY, M. J. *Cognition and behavior modification*. Cambridge, MA: Ballinger, 1974.

MEICHENBAUM, D. *Cognitive-behavior modification: An integrative approach*. New York: Plenum, 1977.

MISHLER, E. G., & WAXLER, N. E. *Interaction in families: An experimental study of family process in schizophrenia*. New York: John Wiley, 1968.

OLSON, D. H., & RYDER, R. G. Inventory of Marital Conflicts (IMC): An experimental interaction procedure. *Journal of Marriage and the Family*, 1970, *32*, 443-448.

RAUSH, H. L. Process and change—A Markov model for interaction. *Family Process*, 1970, *11*, 275-298.

RAUSH, H. L., BARRY, W. A., HERTEL, R. K., & SWAIN, M. A. *Communication conflict and marriage*. San Francisco: Jossey-Bass, 1974.

ROYCE, W. S., & WEISS, R. L. Behavior cues in the judgment of marital satisfaction: A linear regression analysis. *Journal of Consulting and Clinical Psychology*, 1975, *43*, 816-824.

RYDER, R. G. Husband-wife dyads versus married strangers. *Family Process*, 1968, *7*, 233-238.

SACKETT, G. P. The lag sequential analysis of contingency and cyclicity in behavioral interaction research. In J. Osofsky (Ed.), *Handbook of infant development*. New York: John Wiley, 1978.

STEINGLASS, P. The conceptualization of marriage from a systems theory perspective. In T. J. Paolino & B. S. McCrady (Eds.), *Marriage and marital therapy: Psychoanalytic, behavioral and system theory perspectives*. New York: Brunner/Mazel, 1978.

TALLMAN, I., & MILLER, G. Class differences in family problem solving: The effects of verbal ability, hierarchical structure, and role expectations. *Sociometry*, 1974, *37*, 13-37.

VINCENT, J. P., WEISS, R. L., & BIRCHLER, G. R. A behavioral analysis of problem-solving in distressed and nondistressed married and stranger dyads. *Behavior Therapy*, 1975, *6*, 475-487.

WEISS, R. L. The conceptualization of marriage from a behavioral perspective. In T. J. Paolino & B. S. McCrady (Eds.), *Marriage and marital therapy: Psychoanalytic, behavioral and systems theory perspectives*. New York: Brunner/Mazel, 1978.

WIEDER, G. B., & WEISS, R. L. Generalizability theory and the coding of marital interactions. *Journal of Consulting and Clinical Psychology*, 1980, *48*, 469-477.

PART I

FRAMEWORKS FOR BEHAVIORAL ASSESSMENT

2

THE NEW KID ON THE BLOCK:
BEHAVIORAL SYSTEMS APPROACH

Robert L. Weiss

Interest in couples' therapy, evidenced by the number of articles and books published on the subject, might appear to be growing geometrically. Olson (1970) reported finding 25 articles prior to 1950; in the decade of the 1950s he found 50 articles; over 100 articles were found in the 1960s. Gurman and Kniskern (1978) found some 200 studies in the literature. In that portion of the field represented by Behavioral Marital Therapy (BMT) alone, there has been considerable activity. Yet, it is doubtful whether clinical interest in couples' therapy, per se, has changed substantially during these years. Depending upon how one makes the estimate, as many as 75% of the cases reporting for therapeutic assistance will involve marital and family-related problems (Gurman & Kniskern, 1970; Overall, 1971; Overall et al., 1974). The costs of separation and divorce in terms of physical health alone is considerable (see Bloom et al., 1978). The progressive increase in public self-consciousness about intimate relationships, notably the problems typical of such relationships, reflects in large measure the ability of technology to outrun the contribution of theory. The need for couples' therapy techniques no doubt has existed for some time; in all likelihood the appearance of a systematic, empirically based technology would be welcomed by many practitioners. Behavioral Marital Therapy, as it has become known, began in the mid-1960s and has been like the new kid on the block. It was characterized by a set of teachable techniques, an optimism about relationships, and an arrogance often seen in the behavioral camp. The mid-

1960s also spawned an influential transactional point of view regarding adult intimacy: the clinical work of the early Palo Alto group of family therapists summarized by Lederer and Jackson (1968). It represented a systems point of view which focused on the context of intimate relationships rather than the intrapsychic determinants of the individual partners. Unlike BMT, it emphasized the design of larger schemes over the teaching of specific skills. Whatever the systems approach may have lacked in empirical rigor, it made up for with an intuitively appealing conception of how intimates interact. Patterning and the persistence of dysfunctional (symptomatic) transactions were described cogently within this framework (for example, see Haley, 1963).

The aim of this chapter is to propose the basis for an amalgam of BMT and systems model conceptions, which, as we shall argue here, is necessary partly because of the effectiveness of earlier forms of BMT. Although Gurman (1978) has provided the most noteworthy attempt to integrate the three prominent approaches to marital therapy—psychodynamic, behavioral, and systems theory—this discussion will be more narrowly focused on the behavioral conception. This decision was dictated by two reasons: (a) BMT offers the most systematic *empirical* approach to marital therapy and therefore it should be evaluated on its own ground; and (b) suggesting new directions is useful only after limitations within a single system are encountered. In an earlier conceptual paper (Weiss, 1978), I have introduced the reasoning behind a behavioral systems approach to BMT. Birchler and Spinks (1980) have published a more clinically focused account of such a behavioral systems integration. I will briefly summarize some of the conceptual and technological advances made by BMT, survey its current status and problems encountered within this approach, and then present some implications of the behavioral systems integration.

CONCEPTUAL AND TECHNOLOGICAL ADVANCES

BMT began in a series of fits and starts with the arrogance of the new kid on the block. Some behavior therapists, and those identified with behavior modification, employed behavioral techniques with individuals who happened to be married. The relationship, per se, was not the target of change in these early treatment efforts. Thus, Goldiamond (1965) taught a husband self-control procedures for dealing with his obsessive thoughts about his wife's fidelity; Goldstein and Francis (Note 1) taught wives operant reinforcement techniques for use with their own husbands. Stuart (1969) described a social psychological cum behavioral psychology blend which he used as the conceptual basis for treating seven couples. Drawing from exchange theory (Thibaut & Kelley, 1959), systems theory (Haley, 1963; Jackson, 1965), and early behavioral notions of the coercion process (Patterson & Reid, 1970), Stuart provided a

conceptual basis for the use of a form of contingency control with adult intimates: Husbands and wives were taught contracting skills which made a specific target (problem) behavior of one contingent upon the occurrence of a target
behavior of the other. In this quid pro quo arrangement, the frequency of some
desired behavior was made contingent upon the frequency of a complementary
behavior in the other person.

The late 1960s saw the original Oregon group (consisting of Patterson,
Weiss, and Ziller, together with their students) developing a social learning
approach to marital conflict and accord. The early model, which was explicitly
modular in design, was described by Weiss et al. (1973) the same year that
Azrin et al. (1973) published their model for "reciprocity counseling." (The
latter also stressed a kind of quid pro quo contingency control of desired
behaviors.) With the publication of Stuart's paper and thereafter, there developed a more or less explicit concern with the relationship rather than with
bringing about changes in the behavior of individuals. Yet during this period it
seemed that even the simplest (lowest level) empirical generalization had to be
established de novo. As others have observed (Laws, 1971; Olson, 1970), the
marriage literature was generally of poor quality methodologically and seldom
dealt with interactions. Marital satisfaction, a primary concept, was itself
poorly understood and measured solely by retrospective self-reporting. Much
of our own early effort was devoted to developing measures for assessing
intimate relationships, especially laboratory interactions of distressed couples.
(These efforts have been summarized in Weiss & Margolin, 1977.) Not surpris-
ingly, the development of assessment technology has gone along hand in hand
with the development of couples' therapy.

Conceptually, BMT focuses on the process of contemporaneous marital
interactions and suggests certain mechanisms to account for the persistance of
marital distress; in one sense these mechanisms provide the structural elements
of relationship transactions. Intimate partners are seen as providing beneficial
exchanges for one another; each is said to have control of reinforcing contingencies for the other. Either the withholding of a reward (positive consequences) or
the application of aversiveness (criticism, nagging, and so on) provides the
partners with ways of manipulating *costs* associated with their exchanges.
Distressed marital interactions are said to be characterized by low rates of
exchanged positive and high rates of exchanged negative consequences. Although it is expected that low rates of exchange of positive reinforcers within a
relationship predict to subjective reports of marital distress, Jacobson (1979)
has argued that the fact of such low rates may either *describe* distressed relationships or they may be the *cause* (etiology) of such distressed relationships.
For example, the marital distress we observe at any given time shows a relatively low level of exchange of positive reinforcers, but it may be that the low
level of positive exchange caused the distress.

A number of studies have been reported which pertain to this issue of positive versus negative exchanges (see Jacobson, 1979; Weiss, 1978; Weiss & Wieder, in press). Using both spouse observational techniques and behavioral coding of spouse problem-solving interactions (typically coded by the MICS— Marital Interaction Coding System), the results support the increased rate of negative exchanges, whereas the picture for positive exchanges is mixed; some studies find support while others do not, over a variety of methods. The descriptive versus etiological hypothesis has not been tested directly, although Markman (1979) has reported a significant effect for impact ratings of partner's communication: Those unmarried who rated the impact of their partner's communication highly satisfactory tended to have more satisfying relationships some two and one-half years later.

A second issue in the behavioral model goes beyond the rates of exchanged positive-negative consequences and involves the reciprocal relationship between these types of events. Earlier views (for example, Stuart, 1969) stressed the importance of reciprocity in relationships, based largely on the work of Patterson and Reid (1970), who found base rate evidence for exchange parities. *Overall,* family members tended to exchange rewards at about equal levels. However, further elaboration of the reciprocity idea (Wills et al., 1974) distinguished between short- and long-term reciprocity. Gottman and his associates (Gottman, 1979) provided a microanalysis of reciprocity by looking at specific sequences of reward-punishment exchanges. Thus reciprocity could be interpreted to mean overall parity of exchange (base rate similarity) or a tit-for-tat, tightly controlled reciprocity. The escalation that one sees in distressed interactions is typical of negative reciprocity: "You wouldn't care what I did!" "You *never* want to do anything with me anyway." "See if I'll stand around taking care of you!" The base rate type of reciprocity is described best as the "bank account" model (Gottman et al., 1976); couples invest by presenting rewards to each other which accumulate, thereby making it possible for any individual partner to withdraw from the "account" without having to make an immediate deposit to cover the withdrawal. Over time both partners receive rewards that "equal out" so that no one person is either greatly advantaged or disadvantaged. The tit-for-tat reciprocity is sequentially controlled: A given negative response is the stimulus for a similar negative response from the other.

Evidence has been presented for both forms of reciprocity (see reviews by Jacobson, 1979; Weiss & Wieder, in press), suggesting that distressed couples rely more heavily than nondistressed couples on reciprocal exchanges of aversive exchanges and that for distressed couples tit-for-tat or sequential reciprocity characterizes their aversively controlled interactions.

The behavioral model has also been explicit in its statements about the components of satisfaction. Starting with the earlier work of Wills et al. (1974) there have been numerous studies of the specific classes of behavior which covary with daily reported marital satisfaction. When specific behaviors are tracked daily, it is possible to account for 25% to 40% of the variance in daily satisfaction ratings (DSR); when judgments about the prior day's events are made, the percentage of DSR variance account for goes up substantially (e.g., 95% of the DSR variance). What is most significant about this type of study is the attempt to pin satisfaction down to events that occur within a relationship, rather than relying upon global retrospective judgments.

Finally, in this review of the behavioral model, we need to mention the emphasis on the technology of teaching relationship skills. BMT has a stock in trade, so to speak; couples are taught communication skills, problem-solving skills, and many behavior management techniques. In this sense BMT has provided practitioners with performance criteria of relationship effectiveness.

It is fair to say that overall BMT has provided an explicit testable model for adult intimacy. BMT has provided a breath of fresh air in the marital field— some empirical substance about relationships. We turn next to a consideration of BMT in its current context, noting problems within the model.

THE CURRENT CONTEXT OF BMT

BMT has not been without its vocal critics (see Gurman & Kniskern, 1978). In an earlier paper, Olson (Note 2) asked: Are frequencies all that count? The notion that discrete behaviors could be added together to produce "love" or "affection" seemed shortsighted to that critic. We begin our inquiry about the current content of BMT by noting that any conception of marital intimacy must address itself to three facets: Emotion, Epistemology, and Effectiveness—the three Es. By *emotion* we mean the affective component of adult intimacy—affection, joy, anger, and so on. Epistemology presents a different problem: How to partners utilize information about their transactions? What constitutes information? Epistemology is the study of how we know; how do partners draw knowledge from the behavioral events of their relationship? Effectiveness refers to the ways in which behaviors are organized in a planned way to accomplish ends. There is work to be accomplished in ongoing committed relationships, the unit of which we facetiously can call the *Merg* (Merg = unit of marital work expenditure).

It is my thesis that BMT has succeeded on two out of three facets; it has done poorly with regard to the third, notably epistemology. The background for this claim is as follows:

(1) We often encounter consumer resistance to BMT technology. Clients (and often colleagues!) frequently are put off by BMT, as conception and practice. Certainly part of this is a carry-over from difficulties people have had with behavior modification itself.

(2) Marital therapy often begins with illicit contracts. Setting aside the issue of whether anyone ever truly seeks change, it becomes readily apparent in couples' work that what is sought from therapy does not always square with what the therapist is prepared to offer. Part of the problem is that many therapists are unprepared to maintain a dyadic focus, that is, they are not adept at stating issues *as relationship problems* rather than individual problems. But a large part is attributable to the patterning of coercive behavior transactions. Therapeutic attempts to change the balance of exchanges often produces "symptoms" in the nonsymptomatic partner. This is less an example of "symptom substitution" than it is an illustration of the importance of patterning in relationships. Dealing with a symptom-free partner may be extremely frightening to someone who has organized his or her marital life around those very symptom behaviors. It is not surprising then to learn (eventually) that one of the partners actually sees no need for change.

(3) Shaping takes forever. An important behavioral tenet is that one shapes (through successive approximations) the behavior that is desired. With adult couples it is possible to spend considerable time on minute components of a skill. To be sure, there are often clear instances when a couple simply lacks the necessary skills, as in listening, turn taking, paraphrasing, and so on, and shaping is essential. But many other times it becomes apparent that a change in context is needed, that is, the values of the behaviors themselves need to be changed. Gurman has made this point using the systems notions of Level I- and Level II-type change: Level I changes are brought about *within* the system itself, for example, the couple learns a new communication skill. Level II change refers not to responses, but to change in the rules of organization of the systems, such as context changes.

In similar fashion, BMT clients often show what in other quarters has been called "resistance" (Weiss, 1979; Birchler & Spinks, 1980). Using such devices as penalty deposits, to ensure completion of homework assignments, is often of limited value. These and other forms of response shaping may produce as much therapist frustration as they do little change in clients. Interestingly enough, BMT often provides the content for resistance: "She is only doing this because the *program* makes her do it." It is easy to question the sincerity of an act when it is highly programmed.

The epistemology issue is summarized best through the medium of a George Price *New Yorker* cartoon: A hawkish wife, standing large over her inept husband, who is seated in front of a TV set, says: "You say you're sorry. You look sorry. You act sorry. But *I* know you are not sorry!" Whatever the behavioral data, the wife *knows best,* calling upon some noncorporeal transmission of information. The problem for modern BMT is a better understanding of the interface between cognitions and behavioral events. Olson's question about whether frequencies count should be rephrased: For *whom* do frequencies count? Couples left to their own devices do not track behavioral events. A considerable amount of time and effort goes into teaching tracking skills and maintaining compliance once taught. Even more interesting, there is now some evidence to suggest that marital distress status interacts with the tracking and/or reporting of spouse observations (for example, see Robinson & Price, 1980). The conclusion to be drawn from these considerations is that the behavioral data base, provided from BMT activities, may not be the data (knowledge) base used by the couples themselves.

An important clarification is needed before going on. The argument here is not that the language (model) of effective intervention (treatment) and the language of client experience must be one and the same. The final product that derives from the ways in which couples symbolize their own experiences may be quite different from that arrived at by BMT therapists using their own language system. Rather, the point being argued here is that we may have ignored the importance of the cognitive-behavioral event interface in favor of a technological emphasis on performance change, that is, inducing behavior change through skills training may not be sufficient. It is as though the BMT practitioner breaks down a couple's pattern of transactions into skill components (deficits), and hopes that, by teaching them remedial skills, relationship change will occur. But it is also as though the couple's *beliefs about themselves in their relationships* are relegated to the back burner. The BMT technology deals with performance change and not with cognitions about one's relationship.

I have tried to organize this choice of options by borrowing from Bandura's (1977) model of efficacy expectation, recasting his schema to fit relationships rather than individuals. This is illustrated in Figure 2.1. I am suggesting that BMT currently focuses on the Transaction → Outcome segment of the three-unit relationship of Dyad, Transaction, and Outcome; the terms used originally by Bandura were Person, Behavior, and Outcome. By teaching couples what to do, we affect their outcome expectations. The latter represent the cognitive component of performance, that is, knowing that behavior X will produce outcome X'. On the cognitive level, it is learning about what leads to what, for example, learning about contingency control (talking about the day's problems in bed at night reduces the probability of having mutual sex). At the behavioral level, it means learning how to make the appropriate response; knowing that being nice to another is a good idea does not necessarily instruct one about which behaviors to emit, unless, of course, these are already in the repertoire.

For purposes of this discussion, the A segment of Figure 2.1 is of particular importance, since this segment (Dyad—Transaction) really captures those factors associated with *initiation* of behaviors. By "efficacy expectations," Bandura was referring to the collective cognitions one holds about the likelihood

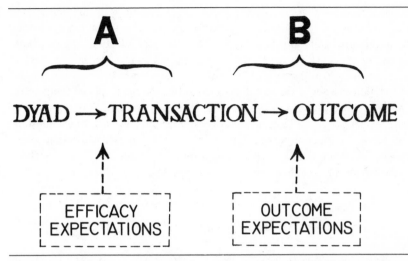

Figure 2.1   Efficacy and Outcome Expectations Related to BMT Interventions

that one *could* engage in certain behaviors. The issue is not whether the person has knowledge that some act produces some outcome (performance expectations), but rather whether persons could see themselves actually engaging in that behavior: "Is it possible for me (us) to do this?" The A segment, dealing with efficacy expectations, comprehends what I call the "theory of relationship" held by a couple. By this I mean the collective wisdom about intentionality, good or bad faith, voluntary versus compelled acts, and so on. The theory one holds about a relationship also provides needed explanations as to why something cannot occur, such as why wife cannot drive a stick shift car, why husband will not stop drinking, why sex cannot be mutually initiated, and so on. Once again, the validity of these ideas is not at issue here, that is, whether wife truly could never drive a stick shift car; such cognitions serve either as facilitators or belief barriers to subsequent change.

To summarize briefly: The current status of BMT is reflected by the B segment of Figure 2.1. BMT is largely a performance-based theory and technology of marital interaction, and while attempts have been made to understand the behavioral correlates of something as important as marital satisfaction—the behaviors which provide the basis for the judgment of satisfaction—we are still relatively ignorant of the A segment of Figure 2.1, that is, the ways in which efficacy expectations can be changed to facilitate relationship change within a BMT framework. The performance-based model of BMT has been described in detail elsewhere (Weiss, 1978; Weiss & Birchler, 1978) and will be mentioned here only in passing. The model is essentially a competency-based model which defines 4 generic competencies, 12 content areas of interaction, and stages of the family life cycle. Depending upon the specific number of stages defined in the family life cycle, we have a 4 × 12 × N cell cube. Ignoring stage of family life cycle, we have a 48-cell matrix, which provides both an assessment and intervention map. A relationship can be viewed in terms of its ability to function in each of the 48 cells, which define the intercepts of competency (such as Objectification, Support/Understanding, Problem Solving, and Behavior Change) by the 12 content areas of interaction (such as Companionship, Affection, Consideration, and Sex). BMT currently provides a couple assistance in any of these cells (see also Jacobson & Margolin, 1979). We turn next to the proposal for a behavioral systems integration.

COGNITIONS AND COMPETENCIES

We arrive at a place where the particular strength of BMT, its performance-based technology, can be at odds with the efficacy expectations held by partners in distressed relationships. (See Note 3.) Changing efficacy expectations—in the sense of relationship theory used here—requires therapist skill in changing contexts. It is as though *the attributions of causality that partners make about one another's behavior actually set the reward value of the behaviors they exchange.* In distressed relationships, there is an observable erosion of the generalized reward value of partner's behaviors. Systems points of view, especially those represented by the communications writers (Haley, 1963; Watzlawick et al., 1974; Sluzki, 1978), focus to a great extent on the context and patterning of transactions, as we noted earlier. Context refers to efficacy expectations in this formulation. The meanings given to each other's behaviors— "cognitive appraisals" (Jacobson & Margolin, 1979)—become ritualized in distressed relationships; couples endorse highly linear models of causality. Many forms of strategic therapy deal explicitly with techniques for changing the context or explanation of transactional events, such as use of reframes, predicting failures, and so on. These are based upon nonlinear or circular models of causality. What therapists run into as resistance are the implicit quid pro quo expectations, such as: "How can I be loving when he doesn't do such and so." The context can be changed by creating a different, higher order problem for the couple to solve. As Watzlawick et al. (1974) observe, the solution adopted by the couple is *the problem.* Thus, rather than attempting to deal with specific accusations of this or that shortcoming of the partners (abundantly offered in early sessions), the marital therapist can raise a new issue that they must grapple with, for example, "Since all relationships have an obligation that the partners make themselves attractive to one another, I wonder how you folks handle that?" Note, this is not the problem that the couple came with, but it does provide a puzzle that has high relevance to them.

Interactional behaviors become patterned in one of two ways: On the basis of reinforcing contingencies ("response control") and stimulus control ("rule control; Weiss, 1978). As we noted above, tit-for-tat or short-term reciprocity operates on the basis of response consequences—for example, the chaining of aversive exchanges fit this model. Exchanges can be patterned (routinized) by virtue of their being under a complex form of stimulus control, namely, rule control. Efficacy expectations are one form of rule control. As such, they tend to be more or less explicitly cognitively elaborated, that is, persons can verbalize something about the rules. But we also evolve such controlling statements about others, and like the Price cartoon, we see ourselves as experts on the motivation—intentionality—of others, especially an intimate other. The situation is further complicated, since, as we have noted, there may be wholesale disregard for the data base of the cognitions held about another. I have referred to this as a case of "sentiment override"—that is, a partner may be viewed noncontingently favorably or unfavorably. In fact, in extreme cases the mere presence of the partner is aversive; reward values are set by sentiment.

There are some data to support these hypotheses. Distressed couples have been shown to operate on short-term reciprocity and their daily marital satisfaction ratings are more highly dependent upon specific relationship events than is true for nondistressed couples; the latter seem to operate more on a bank account paradigm (see Jacobson et al., 1980; Williams, 1979).

In an attempt to integrate the more explicitly cognitive elements with the more typical competency-based notions of reciprocity and exchange, it is possible to create a two-factor space as a theoretical factor solution. The axes are defined by two continua: Response Control—Rule Control, and High- and Low-Cognitive elaboration. Figure 2.2 illustrates this arrangement and the placement of the 12 content areas of interaction defined within the competency-based model discussed above. Focusing on the axes themselves, the resulting four quadrants provide a guide for defining the kinds of attributions couples are likely to make as joint function of how much verbal discrimination has been made about some behavior, *and* whether the behavior is more under response (contingency) or rule (stimulus) control. That is to say, some behaviors are clearly discriminated while others occur with little cognitive elaboration, such as ritualized transactions. As noted above, some behaviors are under tit-for-tat reciprocity (high response control), whereas others are organized by rule control.

Each of the four quadrants thus defined by this selection of axes is likely to give rise to a unique set of attributions about behaviors. In Figure 2.3, I have attempted to spell out (a) the most likely attribution of behavior appearing in

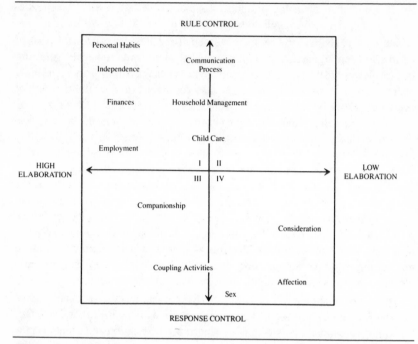

Figure 2.2   Theoretical Typology for Generating Attributions about Behavioral
Transactions

each quadrant, (b) the classes of behaviors therapists would seek to include or exclude based upon this model, and (c) examples of attributional failures for each quadrant, such as what happens whenever "inappropriate" behaviors are included in each quadrant.

Focusing first on "most likely attribution," it may be seen that each quadrant defines a different set of conditions for judgments about spontaneity, volitional choice, and perhaps "genuineness" of an act. Contrasting I and IV will help with the discriminations involved: Behaviors in quadrant I are under explicit rule control, that is, a high degree of verbal discrimination *and* dependent upon prior agreement or prior planning. In contrast to this we find that quadrant IV behaviors are defined by implicit response control, that is, low verbal discrimination *and* largely under reinforcing contingency control. Attributions in quadrant I must be based upon the *lack* of voluntary control, or highly planned or premeditated nature of the behavior, whereas those in IV would be viewed in terms of *most* voluntary (person chose to do it) or at least highly spontaneous in the sense of being least controlled by reason.

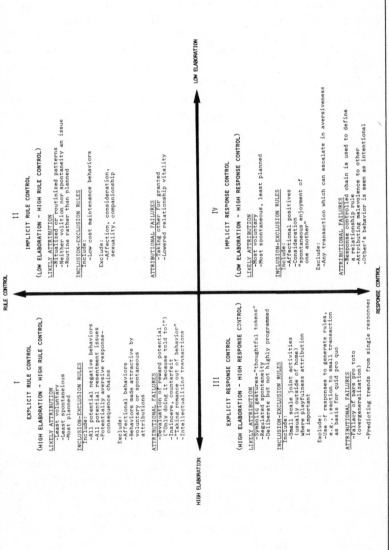

RULE CONTROL

HIGH ELABORATION ← → LOW ELABORATION

RESPONSE CONTROL

I

EXPLICIT RULE CONTROL

(HIGH ELABORATION - HIGH RULE CONTROL)

LIKELY ATTRIBUTION
-Least voluntary
-Least spontaneous
-Most planned

INCLUSION-EXCLUSION RULES
Include:
-All potential negative behaviors
-All potential resentment issues
-Potentially aversive response-consequence chains

Exclude:
-Affectional behaviors
-Behaviors made attractive by voluntary or spontaneous attributions

ATTRIBUTIONAL FAILURES
-Devaluation of reward potential ("Only doing it because told to:")
-"Inadvertent" counter-control
-"Taking romance out of behavior"
-Intellectualizing transactions

II

IMPLICIT RULE CONTROL

(LOW ELABORATION - HIGH RULE CONTROL)

LIKELY ATTRIBUTION
-Ritualized or routinized patterns
-Neither volition nor spontaneity an issue
-Routine rather than planned

INCLUSION-EXCLUSION RULES
Include:
-Low cost maintenance behaviors

Exclude:
-Affection, consideration, sexuality, companionship

ATTRIBUTIONAL FAILURES
-Taking other for granted
-Lowered relationship vitality

III

EXPLICIT RESPONSE CONTROL

(HIGH ELABORATION - HIGH RESPONSE CONTROL)

LIKELY ATTRIBUTION
-Symbolic gestures-"thoughtful tokens"
-Regulated spontaneity
-Deliberate but not highly programmed

INCLUSION-EXCLUSION RULES
Include:
-Small scale joint activities
-Usually outside of home) where playfulness attribution is important

Exclude:
-Use of responses to generate rules, use reaction to small transaction as basis for quid pro quo

ATTRIBUTIONAL FAILURES
-Fallacy of pars toto (overgeneralization)
-Predicting trends from single responses

IV

IMPLICIT RESPONSE CONTROL

(LOW ELABORATION - HIGH RESPONSE CONTROL)

LIKELY ATTRIBUTION
-Most voluntary
-Most spontaneous, least planned

INCLUSION-EXCLUSION RULES
Include:
-Affectional positives
-Consideration
-"spontaneous enjoyment of one another"

Exclude:
-Any transaction which can escalate in aversiveness

ATTRIBUTIONAL FAILURES
-Response controlled chain is used to define a relationship rule
-Attributing malevolence to other
-Other's behavior is seen as intentional

Figure 2.3 Examples of Attributions Made on Basic Two-Factor Typology

Contrasting II and IV, we see a case of implicit rule control (implicit because of low verbal discrimination) and explicit response control (high elaboration of small behaviors), respectively. Behaviors in quadrant II would be seen as ritualized, lacking spontaneity transactions, whereas those in quadrant IV would be seen symbolic gestures; symbolic in the sense that more is being made of the small (token) behavior than might be warranted otherwise.

When we consider which type of behavior to include (exclude) from each of the categories, the placement of the content category labels in Figure 2.3 provides a convenient reference point. Taking the quadrants in sequence, starting with the first: The high degree of elaboration of rule-controlled behaviors suggests that potentially aversive transactions belong here. A "failure" is thus a noncompliance with a prior agreement, not an indication of bad faith, "meanness," or other trait designation. Similarly, because of the high degree of structure and lack of spontaneity, we would exclude affectional behaviors—a planned kiss loses its value. The implicit rule control of II suggests that only low-cost routines be placed here. Behaviors associated with consideration, affection, or self-worth items would be excluded. The major significance of II is the balance between planning and spontaneity of temporal short-term behaviors. The inclusion dangers (or behavior to be excluded) include any possibility for generating a "rule" from a single episode. Thus, any specific response failure should not be allowed to "support" a theory of the relationship. Finally, the behaviors in IV should include all those that are to be experienced as genuine, loving acknowledgments of the other's importance as a lovable person. Any aversive exchange should be excluded, since in this quadrant the tendency is to see behavior as "just happening" and not under rational control. In fact, as already noted, aversive chains are best brought under rule control, as in quadrant I.

What we have attempted here is to make explicit for therapists how various BMT interventions can be viewed by clients. The definition of quadrants should facilitate understanding the importance of context in the attributional process. Thus, while many BMT techniques involve fairly explicit exchanges of rewards (for example, contracting procedures), it is also possible to become alert to unintended attributional failures. Programmed affection is not likely to be received happily. Conversely, couples often use a minute event as the basis for a full-blown generalization about their relationship. This arrangement of axes also helps guide the therapist in determining which techniques should be made explicit and which are better left undiscriminated for the couple. In some instances, the therapist will want to increase the range of client choices to enhance the illusion of control.

In sum, efficacy expectations, as used here, alert BMT practitioners to the kinds of cognitive restructuring that is necessary with couples. As part of this, we seek opportunities to change context by creating different dyadically focused problems—different from the well-practiced solutions brought to therapy. At this stage the behavioral systems integration emphasizes ways for conceptualizing cognitive variables in BMT applications. The systems contribution is how we conceptualize cognitions in transactional terms in work with couples.

SUMMARY

A brief review of Behavioral Marital Therapy (BMT) was presented to set the stage for a consideration of what might be called a "behavioral systems approach" to couples' therapy. BMT has been, up to now, a performance-based technology for treating intimate distress; it has relied heavily upon providing couples with skills designed to alter the what-leads-to-what segment of the total transactional sequence. In that sense we have focused on outcome expectations, teaching which outcomes can be expected from which actions. For a number of reasons, couple "resistance" to behavioral technology among them, it is suggested that BMT conceptualize and develop techniques for the more avowedly cognitive elements of the total transactional sequence, namely, the efficacy expectations a couple may hold about their relationship, that is, their theories as to why such and so cannot ever change. The argument was not to supplant the empirically accredited aspects of BMT with a new wave of the cognitive *Zeitgeist*, but rather to find a common ground between the cognitive and performance aspects of couples' assessment and intervention.

It was suggested that some aspects of systems approaches might be useful to a broadened behavioral understanding of couples' interactional distress. Systems points of view often emphasize transactional patterning, which in turn is seen as dysfunctional to relationship change. Patterning can be viewed behaviorally in terms of stimulus or "response" controlled behavioral enactments. Stimulus control refers to the cue functions provided by the context of the interaction and especially by verbalizations persons make to themselves. "Response" control refers to behavioral patterning largely under the control of consequences, a kind of tit-for-tat exchange.

Using these notions we have proposed a typology (theoretical factor space) making stimulus-response control and degree of cognitive elaboration (crudely, awareness) as orthogonal dimensions which provide four quadrants involving either high or low values of each dimension. The different kinds of attributions couples are likely to make about transactions (exchanges) were posited using this framework. The advantage of this approach is focusing more on *process* implications of behavioral exchanges while also taking account of a major cognitive mode for construing relationship events, or attributions partners make about their own and therapist-induced behavior changes. At this point the behavioral systems approach is offered as a heuristic for workers in this field.

REFERENCE NOTES

1. GOLDSTEIN, M. K., & FRANCIS, B. *Behavior modification of husbands' wives.* Paper presented at the annual meeting of the National Council of Family Relations, Washington, D.C., October 1969.
2. OLSON, D. H. *Review and critique of behavior modification research with couples and families: Or are frequency counts all that really count?* Paper presented at the annual meeting of the Association for the Advancement of Behavior Therapy, New York, October 1972.
3. Material for this section was drawn from Weiss (1980) and from a symposium paper entitled *Toward a Model of Strategic Marital Therapy,* presented at the meetings of the Western Psychological Association, Honolulu, May 1980.

REFERENCES

AZRIN, N., NASTER, B., & JONES, R. Reciprocity counseling: A rapid learning-based procedure for marital counseling. *Behavior Research and Therapy,* 1973, *11,* 365-382.

BANDURA, A. Self-efficacy: Toward a unifying theory of behavior change. *Psychological Review.* 1977, *84,* 191-215.

BIRCHLER, G. R., & SPINKS, S. H. Behavioral-systems marital and family therapy: Integration and clinical application. *American Journal of Family Therapy,* 1980, *8,* 6-28.

BLOOM, B. L., ASHER, S. J., & WHITE, S. W. Marital disruption as a stressor: A review and analysis. *Psychological Bulletin,* 1978, *85,* 867-894.

GOLDIAMOND, I. Self-control procedures in personal behavior problems. *Psychological Reports,* 1965, *17,* 851-868.

GOTTMAN, J. M. *Marital interaction: Experimental investigations.* New York: Academic, 1979.

GOTTMAN, J. M., NOTARIUS, C., MARKMAN, H., BANK, S., YOPPI, B., & RUBIN, M. Behavior exchange theory and marital decision making. *Journal of Personality and Social Psychology,* 1976, *34,* 14-23.

GURMAN, A. S. Contemporary marital therapies: A critique and comparative analysis of psychoanalytic, behavioral and systems theory approaches. In T. J. Paolino, Jr., & B. S. McCrady (Eds.), *Marriage and marital therapy.* New York: Brunner/Mazel, 1978.

GURMAN, A. S., & KNISKERN, D. P. Research on marital and family therapy: Progress, perspective and prospect. In S. L. Garfield & A. E. Bergin (Eds.), *Handbook of psychotherapy and behavior change: An empirical analysis* (2nd ed.). New York: John Wiley, 1978.

HALEY, J. *Strategies of psychotherapy.* New York: Grune and Stratton, 1963.

JACKSON, D. D. Family rules: Marital quid pro quo. *Archives of General Psychiatry,* 1965, *12,* 589-594.

JACOBSON, N. S. Behavioral treatments for marital discord: A critical appraisal. In M. Hersen, R. M. Eisler, & P. M. Miller (Eds.), *Progress in behavior modification.* New York: Academic, 1979.

JACOBSON, N. S., & MARGOLIN, G. *Marital therapy: Strategies based on social learning and behavior exchange principles.* New York: Brunner/Mazel, 1979.

JACOBSON, N. S., WALDRON, H., & MOORE, D. Toward a behavioral profile of marital distress. *Journal of Consulting and Clinical Psychology,* 1980, *48,* 696-703.

LAWS, J. L. A feminist review of marital adjustment literature: The rape of the locke. *Journal of Marriage and the Family,* 1971, *33,* 483-515.

LEDERER, W., & JACKSON, D. *Mirages of marriage.* New York: Norton, 1968.

MARKMAN, H. J. The application of a behavioral model of marriage in predicting relationship satisfaction of couples planning marriage. *Journal of Consulting and Clinical Psychology,* 1979, *47,* 743-749.

OLSON, D. H. Marital and family therapy: Integrative review and critique. *Journal of Marriage and the Family*, 1970, *32*, 501-538.

OVERALL, J. E. Associations between marital history and the nature of manifest psychopathology. *Journal of Abnormal Psychology*, 1971, *78*, 213-221.

OVERALL, J. E., HENRY, B. W., & WOODWARD, A. Dependence of marital problems on parental family history. *Journal of Abnormal Psychology*, 1974, *83*, 446-450.

PATTERSON, G. R., & REID, J. B. Reciprocity and coercion: Two facts of social systems. In C. Neuringer & J. Michael (Eds.), *Behavior modification in clinical psychology*. Englewood Cliffs, NJ: Prentice-Hall, 1970.

ROBINSON, E. A., & PRICE, M. G. Pleasurable behavior in marital interaction: An observational study. *Journal of Consulting and Clinical Psychology*, 1980, *48*, 117-118.

SLUZKI, C. E. Marital therapy from a systems perspective. In T. J. Paolino, Jr., & B. S. McCrady (Eds.), *Marriage and marital therapy*. New York: Brunner/Mazel, 1978.

STUART, R. B. Operant interpersonal treatment for marital discord. *Journal of Consulting and Clinical Psychology*, 1969, *33*, 675-682.

THIBAUT, J., & KELLEY, H. H. *The social psychology of groups*. New York: John Wiley, 1959.

WATZLAWICK, P., WEAKLAND, J., & FISCH, R. *Change: Principles of problem formation and problem resolution*. New York: Norton, 1974.

WEISS, R. L. The conceptualization of marriage and marriage disorders from a behavioral perspective. In T. J. Paolino & B. S. McCrady (Eds.), *Marriage and marital therapy: Psychoanalytic, behavioral, and systems theory perspectives*. New York: Brunner/Mazel, 1978.

WEISS, R. L. Resistance in behavioral marriage therapy. *American Journal of Family Therapy*, 1979, *7*, 3-6.

WEISS, R. L. Strategic behavioral marital therapy: Toward a model for assessment and intervention. In J. P. Vincent (Ed.), *Advances in family intervention, assessment, and theory*. Greenwich: Jai, 1980.

WEISS, R. L., & BIRCHLER, G. R. Adults with marital dysfunction. In M. Hersen & A. Bellack (Eds.), *Behavior therapy in the psychiatric setting*. Baltimore: Williams & Williams, 1978.

WEISS, R. L., HOPS, H., & PATTERSON, G. R. A framework for conceptualizing marital conflict, a technology for altering it, some data for evaluating it. In F. W. Clark & L. A. Hamerlynck (Eds.), *Critical issues in research and practice: Proceedings of the Fourth Banff International Conference on Behavior Modification*. Champaign, IL: Research Press, 1973.

WEISS, R. L., & MARGOLIN, G. Marital conflict and accord. In A. R. Ciminero, K. S. Calhoun, & H. E. Adams (Eds.), *Handbook for behavioral assessment*. New York: John Wiley, 1977.

WEISS, R. L., & WIEDER, G. B. Marital and family distress. In A. Bellack, M. Hersen, & A. Kazdin (Eds.), *International handbook of behavior modification*. New York: Plenum, in press.

WILLIAMS, A. M. The quantity and quality of marital interaction related to marital satisfaction: A behavioral analysis. *Journal of Applied Behavior Analysis*, 1979, *12*, 665-678.

WILLS, T. A., WEISS, R. L., & PATTERSON, G. R. A Behavioral analysis of the determinants of marital satisfaction. *Journal of Consulting and Clinical Psychology*, 1974, *42*, 802-811.

3

MULTISYSTEM-MULTIMETHOD ASSESSMENT: A FRAMEWORK

Ronald E. Cromwell
Gary W. Peterson

Recent developments in family studies have emphasized the formalization of linkages among theory, research, and practice (Burr et al., 1979; Cromwell & Olson, 1975; Olson, 1976; Sprenkle, 1976; Thomas & Keber, Note 1). In most cases, however, the realization of such ties is the exception rather than the rule. This is particularly the case when considering the theoretical concepts, research process, and methods of application which are components of, or derived from, family systems theory.

Certain principles of systems theory, such as the emphases upon the complex interdependencies and organization among system components, are particularly problematic in the assessment process. In practice, most theorists, researchers, and practitioners oversimplify the complexity of systems by focusing exclusively on only one level of the whole. For example, some scholars rely exclusively on individual self-reports of a higher level of the family system (marriage, parent-child relationships, or the family) and thereby ignore the

AUTHORS' NOTE: The work on which this chapter is based was made possible by NIMH Biomedical Support Grant R01-121008 "Diagnostic Tools for Relationship Therapy: Review and Research." Appreciation is expressed to David M. Klein, Bradford P. Keeney, and Erik E. Filsinger, who made critical comments on earlier drafts of this chapter.

essence of systems theory. In contrast, the approach proposed here calls for multiple assessments of multiple levels of the family system to gain a more holistic view of the entire family system and the relationships among component parts. Three interrelated issues guide the development of the assessment framework posited in this chapter. First, the concepts of *wholeness* and the *hierarchical structure* of systems are discussed. A second consideration is the issue of *problems of fit* (or correspondence). This concerns the match between the phenomenon of interest at a specific level of the family system and the choice of an appropriate assessment tool or technique to measure that phenomenon.

A third issue focuses on *multiple indicator measurement*, with special emphasis on the utility of multiple assessment techniques to assess the unique aspects of different system levels as well as the issues that the entire family shares in common. This use of multiple indicators, therefore, provides divergent information about system components, while simultaneously converging upon the unifying elements of the whole.

WHOLENESS AND HIERARCHICAL STRUCTURE OF SYSTEMS

A basic notion in systems theory acknowledges the interrelationship and interdependency among subsystem components within the overall system (Hill, 1971). The framework introduced here considers the individual, marital dyad, and the family unit to be distinctive, but also interdependent, levels (or subsystems) of the family system (see Cromwell et al., 1976; Keeney & Cromwell, 1977; Steinglass, 1978; Skynner, 1976).

In the most fundamental sense, systems theory proposes that all components of the family system are related in a dynamic, mutual, and circular manner rather than in a static, linear, cause-effect fashion (Bateson, 1972; Buckley, 1967; Keeney, 1979; Bertalanffy, 1968). Moreover, each component operates as an integral part of the system. This configuration of interrelated and interdependent components combines to produce a dynamic process of wholeness; a social system greater than the additive sums of the separate parts. Assessment of the family from a systems perspective, therefore, requires the potential use of a wide range of measurements geared to specific subsystem levels or units of assessment. This approach is sensitive to the wholeness of a system while being attentive to component subsystems.

The integral nature of family systems is further characterized by a hierarchical pattern of organization. Central to this issue is the idea that systems are organized in a series of hierarchical levels, like a succession of Chinese boxes (Keeney & Cromwell, 1977; Keeney, 1979; Steinglass, 1978; Skynner, 1976).

According to this notion, each system is composed of smaller component subsystems which, in turn, are elements of a larger suprasystem (in this case the family). Each component part is complex and different from other components. Furthermore, each of the levels within the family system maintain boundaries which are variably permeable to information from the outside environment.

From this perspective, the individual is conceptualized as a psychological and biological system level that functions as the basic unit of the larger family suprasystem. The marital relationship, in turn, includes both the husband and wife (individual) subsystems, which structure a second, more encompassing dyadic relationship level between marital partners. A more extensive system level circumscribing the marital, parent-child, and sibling subsystems is the family unit level. Each of these levels of the family system would require assessment techniques appropriately fitted to its distinctive organization and structure.

For purposes of illustration, consider the substantive focus on power in families. Contemporary scholarly accounts on the "state of the field" consider power to be a systemic and dynamic process of the family system (Cromwell & Olson, 1975; McDonald, 1980; Scanzoni, 1979), yet many, if not most, re-searchers continue to focus on individual self-reports which concern the out-come of a process (Cromwell & Olson, 1975; McDonald, 1980). To rely only on individual self-reports of power represents a blatant confoundment of sys-tem levels and an inappropriate selection of measurement tools or techniques to assess the phenomenon of interest. A further point of illustration is the now classic study on conjugal decision making by Blood and Wolfe (1960). These scholars relied on the self-report of wives to assess husband/wife decision-making structure in marriage, and referred to it as the "dynamics of family living" or family power. Their unit of assessment was the individual.

THE PROBLEM OF FIT

The above illustration points to the inappropriate selection of an assessment approach. In the case of Blood and Wolfe's research, individual self-reports on the outcome of conjugal decision making were assumed to address the "dy-namics of family living." A more appropriate assessment approach to studying family power would be to use measures designed to tap interaction levels or power dynamics of the system beyond the individual. These issues reflect the problem of fit or the appropriate match between a particular measurement technique and the level of system for which it was originally designed.

Observers of the scientific process often note that a fundamental epistemo-logical issue concerns the correspondence between the symbols or concepts carried in our minds and the empirical reality outside the observers' perception (Popper, 1963; Thomas et al., Note 2). In the case of marital and family assessment, it is crucial that the researcher select a measurement approach designed to measure the phenomenon of interest at a specific system level. For example, use of intrapsychic personality measures, or other forms of individual self-reports to assess larger social contexts are potentially invalid and only serve to confound the assessment of system levels (Cromwell et al., 1976; Cromwell & Keeney, 1980). This is an obvious issue, but one that is routinely violated by family researchers and clinicians alike.

This "multisystem" orientation provides a perspective on the integral nature of family situations by viewing the system from different perspectives through multiple methods. The unique structure and organization of each level will provide more complete insight into subsystem phenomena, and will also converge on common issues across the semipermeable boundaries of successive levels of the system. This perspective then, is sensitive to the qualitative differences between intrapersonal and interpersonal levels of a system. At the same time, it is recognized that efforts to focus exclusively on only one level of a system are contrary to the concepts of "complementarity" and "synthesis" within family systems theory (Vassiliou, cited in Jackson, 1967, p. 151). These concepts acknowledge that each level of a system has qualities that are simultaneously similar and different, interrelated and interdependent.

Consistent with systems theory is the notion that multiple methods of assessment will be required to simultaneously capture the unique qualities within the boundary of each subsystem and the holistic character of the family. The requirement for the use of several different measures in systemic assessment is supported by Broderick (1976) who argues that couples and families are uniquely different and that each level requires procedures which specifically address its special qualities. A thorough assessment procedure, therefore, would first scan the system from different levels and then integrate the information from the entire system hierarchy. This procedure would also be sensitive to the correspondence or fit between the level of system assessed and an appropriate tool or technique matched to that level.

The collected data from each system level can provide a holistic picture of the interrelationships among system levels when juxtaposed, examined, and evaluated. These notions are consistent with the viewpoint expressed by Ackerman (1958), who proposed, more than two decades ago, that a complete family assessment would take into account the individual, role, marital dyad, family group, and their interrelationships.

MULTIPLE INDICATOR MEASUREMENT

This proposal for a variety of measurement techniques in marriage and family assessment corresponds with developments in several social science fields. Mischel (1977), for example, argues that a variety of measures are necessary to adequately assess the "multiple determinants of behavior" and "contextualism" relevant to the measurement of personality. Elsewhere, the most thorough example of a multiple assessment strategy is presented as part of an analysis procedure developed by Campbell & Fiske (1959) in the field of psychometics. The method of analysis that they introduced is referred to as "Multitrait-Multimethod (MT-MM) Matrix Analysis" and is used to assess reliability and validity of measures. Since its original introduction, this method of analysis has been widely applied in the social sciences, including psychology, sociology, child development, and family studies (Althauser & Heberlein, 1979; Cromwell et al., 1975; Cromwell & Kenney, 1979, 1980; Thomas et al., Note 2; Wylie, 1974; Bentler & McClain, 1976; Kavanaugh et al., 1971; Russell, 1980; Sullivan & Feldman, 1979; Straus, 1964).

Specifically, the MT-MM addresses the correlations between measures representing at least two different traits, assessed by at least two different methods. Examination of the MT-MM allows an investigator to evaluate both the adequacy of a conceptualization and the measurement of a desired dimension. It can be employed as a tool in the process of deciding what to rework or discard, either in terms of the instrumentation involved or the particular construct being assessed. The MT-MM focuses both upon the degree to which different methods "converge" (convergent validity) to measure the same construct, as well as the degree to which the same methods produce "divergent" (discriminant validity) results when assessing different constructs.

This simultaneous emphasis by the MT-MM upon divergence and convergence in measurement is conceptually analogous to the framework proposed here; hence, the descriptor Multisystem-Multimethod (MS-MM) assessment. In this measurement strategy, different assessment methodologies are employed which fit the divergent qualities of each system level. Furthermore, these measures can be used to converge upon the holistic character of the family system as the data from each level of the system are juxtaposed and examined for similar phenomena, viewed from different levels of the system. In short, the MS-MM seeks divergent information from separate and distinct levels of the family system in order to converge on its holistic character, both within and across system levels.

PROCEDURAL GUIDELINES

The procedural guidelines for pursuing a MS-MM strategy initially requires the examiner to specify an appropriate conceptual focus. This entails viewing assessment from a multisystem perspective and conceptualizing family phenomena in terms of various systems levels. For example, an examiner would view "personality issues" as part of the individual system level, "discrepancies in marital roles" as a facet of the marital subsystem, and "family cohesiveness" as a component of the family unit level. The basic idea is that different assessment procedures provide different types of information which can be classified by a particular level of the total system.

A second step is to select assessment tools and techniques that fit the appropriate system level, while at the same time addressing the particular phenomenon the examiner desires to know more about. In making these decisions, one must be aware of various complexities of assessment techniques which will influence their choices. As previously emphasized, an initial concern is *the system focus of an assessment method*. For example, such measures as the Inventory of Marital Conflict (Olson & Ryder, 1970), the Marital Roles Inventory (Hurvitz, 1965), and the Ravich Train Game (Ravich, 1969) focus on the marital subsystem, whereas the Kvebaek Family Sculpture Technique (Cromwell et al., 1981) and the Family Adaptability and Cohesion Evaluation Scales (Olson et al., Note 3) focus on the family system level.

A second complicating factor is that assessment techniques and tools vary in terms of *the level of the family system which is being observed or providing information about* an aspect of the system. In the case of the Marital Roles Inventory, for example, the individual level of the family system (a person) provides information about the marital subsystem. The Inventory of Marital Conflict, on the other hand, assesses both the individual's perceptions of, and the couple's joint resolution of, marital conflict within the marital subsystem. These multiple assessments acquire convergent and divergent information from different subsystem components (that is, individual marital partners and the dyad itself) about the same level of system (in this case, the marital dyad).

AN ILLUSTRATION OF
MULTISYSTEM-MULTIMETHOD ASSESSMENT

A point of clarification is in order before proceeding to illustrate the MS-MM approach to assessment. The approach advocates selection of specific tools designed to gather information about system phenomena of interest. If a researcher's primary interest focuses on "role strain" within the family, then tools and techniques designed to measure that phenomenon at different levels of the system (units of assessment) should be selected. Another substantive focus would require different assessment tools.

The following approach to MS-MM assessment is a modest attempt to outline one means of implementation. The tools chosen in this investigation were intended to provide a general overview of several different variables and were not specific to any single phenomenon within the family. Various patterns and themes emerged from the interpretation of assessment data within and across divergent system levels in the following illustration.

The Smith family. The Smith family contains five positions: husband/father, David, age 42; wife/mother, Judy, age 41; son/brother, Jason, age 17; daughter/sister, Nancy, age 16; and son/brother, Pete, age 9. The husband works in a skilled trade and the wife is employed as a sales clerk. All of the children attend public school.

The Smith family entered family therapy after Jason, their oldest son was earlier referred to individual therapy. The presenting problems included a number of symptoms which Jason began exhibiting when he was 15 years old. Jason had been involved in serious problems at school, which, in addition to poor academic performance and disruptive classroom behavior, included stealing and fighting. He had stolen a car and was subsequently involved in a wreck with the vehicle which resulted in two adolescent passengers being seriously injured. Consequently, Jason was placed on probation by the juvenile court system, referred to therapy, and informed by the court that further trouble would result in some form of institutionalization.

The initial family therapy contact with the Smith family occurred within the context of multiple family therapy with three other families with delinquent adolescents. During the multiple family therapy sessions, Jason and both parents attended. Subsequently, Jason's siblings became involved in group therapy. After one of the multiple family therapy sessions, the Smith family was invited and agreed to participate in the MS-MM procedure. Implementation of the MS-MM approach to assessment was conducted in two sessions. The first session involved the husband-wife (dyadic) system level and the second session included the total family system (husband-wife and their three children).

Prior to implementation of the MS-MM assessment approach, Jason completed the Minnesota Multiphasic Personality Inventory (MMPI). The interpretation of the MMPI, by a licensed clinical psychologist, indicated Jason was borderline schizophrenic. No other individual personality assessments were made, although Jason's response to the MMPI provided important information about the individual level of the family system. For future reference, it is important to note that several of the other assessment procedures characterize the marital and family situation of the Smiths as being one in which schizophrenia develops. Additional implications from these data will be made in the summary following intrepretation of the findings from assessments made at the marital and family system level.

SESSION I—HUSBAND/WIFE DYADIC SUBSYSTEM

Several instruments were employed to assess the marital subsystem level, including the Marital History Supplement, Personal Assessment of Intimacy in Relationships (PAIR), and the Inventory of Marital Conflict (IMC). Each of these methods potentially provides convergent and divergent information about the same level of the family system (the marital subsystem).

Marital History Supplement. The initial assessment tool was the Marital History Supplement: Form DD (MHS), originally used in the NIMH intramural "Courtship and Marriage Study" by Ryder and Olson in 1968. It contains a thorough demographic profile, a marital problems checklist, items on marital satisfaction, and open-ended questions. In this case, the individual level of the family system responds both about themselves and about the marital subsystem.

On the open-ended questions, both identified "problems at work" as one individual issue they did not talk to their spouse about, while Judy added "money and bills" to this category. David listed "social obligations/time" as the thing he liked least about being married, whereas Judy indicated that her major dislike was an absence of a social life with David (unless it involved something that he was interested in). Judy perceived social isolation to be an issue in their marriage; she reported feeling cut off from her husband's leisure time activities and other outside contacts. On the other hand, David wanted her to become more socially involved and to pursue leisure activities without him. David indicated that he enjoys the pursuit of a variety of hobbies and recreational activities with a network of friends independent of his wife and family. Both Judy and David independently listed "security" as the aspect of being married that they liked the most.

These data begin to illuminate potential problems within the marital dyad. Especially noticeable is the fact that this couple tended to present their marital relationship as being more satisfying than it probably is. Their differences and/or dissatisfaction with jealousies, social, and recreational issues were indicative of potential marital difficulties, despite the attempt to portray a lack of conflict. Judy appeared to be trapped within the home in traditional or sex-role stereotyped functions. David, on the other hand, maintained active or instrumental roles outside their relationship. Their lives were separate in many ways.

PAIR. A second assessment procedure involved administration of the PAIR Inventory (Personal Assessment of Intimacy in Relationships), recently published by Schaefer and Olson (1981). PAIR is a self-report instrument specifically designed to assess five types of intimacy in relationships, including emotional, social, sexual, intellectual, and recreational intimacy. The PAIR also assesses the extent to which each member of the relationship is "faking good" or responding in a conventional or socially desirable manner.

A substantial amount of the information obtained from the PAIR converges with that obtained from the Marital History Supplement (MHS). In so doing, it verifies the previous information revealed about the individual and marital subsystems of the Smiths. Two important facets of the data are the Conventionality values for Judy and David, which are 64 and 52, respectively. Because scores higher than 55 reflect high social desirability (Schaefer & Olson, 1981), the results on the five intimacy areas should be interpreted with caution. This corroborates the information on the MHS which indicated that the couple seemed to be masking potential conflicts in their relationship in order to exhibit the facade of a united front.

Other information from the PAIR also corresponded with information from the MHS. For example, both perceive low social intimacy while exhibiting high expectations for the future. Furthermore, David and Judy reported low recreational scores, indicating that they perceived shared hobbies and pastimes as being minimal. The expectation scores on this dimension however, are substantially higher.

The PAIR also provided some new information about the marital subsystem within the Smith family. The emotional intimacy dimension, for example, revealed above-average scores for the couple, with David perceiving a higher level of emotional intimacy in the marriage than Judy perceived. Both David and Judy appeared to have high expectations for future emotional intimacy. In the area of sexual intimacy, the scores denoted a highly satisfying sexual life. Given that Schaefer and Olson (1981) identify the average range on this dimension to be 42-58, David's score of 96 (the maximum possible) and Judy's score of 84 were extremely high. A large discrepancy between David's and Judy's intellectual intimacy scores was also apparent.

Inventory of Marital Conflict. A third assessment procedure, focused on the marital subsystem level of the Smith family, utilized a combined self-report and behavioral observation instrument referred to as the *Inventory of Marital Conflict* (IMC.) (Olson & Ryder, 1970). The IMC consists of 18 short vignettes presenting various types of marital conflicts (nine are represented on Form A and nine on Form B). In the interest of conserving time, only Form B was administered. The IMC format includes four questions about each of the conflict situations, which consist of (1) "Who is most responsible" for the conflict?; (2) A two-category forced-choice item as to "What they should do?"; (3) "Is this situation relevant to you?"; and (4) "Is this situation relevant to other relationships you know?"

In 6 of the 9 vignettes the husband received information which made the wife appear responsible, while the wife received information which made the husband appear at fault. After the partners had individually completed their self-reports, the couple was brought together and asked to discuss each conflict situation and jointly decide "who is most responsible" and "what should they do?" The interaction was tape-recorded for coding as specified by IMC procedures (Olson & Ryder, 1970).

The individual responses at the marital subsystem level revealed that David and Judy exhibited disagreement on whether specific descriptions or vignettes were relevant either to his/her relationship or other relationships. Judy reported that none of the situations applied to her marriage or other relationships that she was aware of. In contrast, David reported that three were relevant to his relationship (whether to seek professional help for marital difficulties, Judy's conversations with men at parties, and conflicts over televison football games) and one was relevant to other relationships he knows (conflict over wife's lateness for a dinner engagement). These results tended to converge with information provided by the MHS and the PAIR, indicating this couple experiences low social intimacy and insufficient recognition of conflict in their relationship.

In the case in which the marital dyad is the level of the system providing information (during the behavioral observation), some of these data acquired on the IMC also converge with previous information acquired about the Smith marriage within the marital level. For instance, the process of conflict resolution between the couple can be characterized as avoidance rather than resolution. On two of the disagreement items, the husband and wife actually reversed their initial positions as to who was responsible, cancelling out the potential conflict. During those conflict situations, where they did not reverse the outcome, one partner would change his or her initial response to accommodate the other, thereby avoiding conflict resolution altogether. In this case there was not a winner, but no one lost, either.

This conflict-avoidance strategy was further represented by the codes for the Conflict Dimension from the interaction codes. There was little "self-disclosure," no "process disagreement," and minimal "outcome disagreement" (frequency of 3 each). For the Affect Dimension of the interaction codes, a high frequency of "laughter" was present for this couple, which may be another type of conflict avoidance. The conflict avoidance and superficial closeness of this couple appeared to be consistent with Wynne's (1958) concept of "pseudomutuality." These measures reveal a structurally fused marital dyad.

Results on the Task Leadership Dimension from the interaction codes also supported earlier information from the MHS indicating that David occupies an instrumental role relative to Judy. For example, David initiated 6 of 9 vignette discussions, and read instructions to Judy 15 of 25 times.

SESSION II—THE FAMILY SYSTEM

The second assessment session included the husband-wife dyad and the three Smith children. The assessment of the family level of the system involved the administration of three measurement techniques: a family interaction game (FIG); a self-report instrument, referred to as FACES (Family Adaptability and Cohesion Evaluation Scales); and the Kvebaek Family Sculpture Technique (KFST). These methods of assessment provided convergent and discriminant information about the family level of the system. In addition, some of the information acquired at the family level was found to converge with data acquired earlier from dyadic self-reports and interaction.

Family interaction game. The family interaction game (FIG) involved the family working together for 30 minutes on a common task. In this case, the family provided information about the family unit level of a system and their interaction was observed and coded.

At the beginning of the FIG, the family is "given" $85,000 for the purpose of accomplishing the task of "creating an ideal home." Construction paper, precut rooms of varying sizes, scissors, a pen, and a price list for each room are provided. The family is then requested to reach consensus, make decisions, and create a floor plan with these materials. The family is also asked to label each room and specify who can use it.

Summaries of the observed family interaction provided information about the family unit level that converged across system levels with the individual and marital subsystems. For example, the marital dyad was fused in a strong coalition in relation to the children. This tended to correspond with earlier data from the marital subsystem indicating that the parents have a *structurally* close marital relationship. The parents dominated the process and any attempts by the children to enter the coalition were denied. During the FIG, Jason and Nancy did not participate in the verbal interaction or decision-making process. Pete attempted to become involved several times by suggesting where rooms should go, but was either ignored or rejected by his parents.

Consistent with the findings for the marital subsystem which indicated that David assumed an instrumental role, this measure for the entire family portrayed the father as an unquestioned authority. David took charge from the beginning, while Judy made occasional suggestions about the number of bedrooms and bathrooms required, without challenging David's authority. The only time advice was sought from the children was on the placement of each child's room. The authority structure is hierarchical, with the husband/father having the greatest authority.

FACES. A second assessment procedure at the family level of the system involved administering FACES, a self-report instrument designed to assess 16 different dimensions of "Cohesion" and "Adaptability" (Olson et al., Note 3). FACES required the individual level of the system (a person) separately to provide information about the family suprasystem by responding to 111 forced-choice items about his or her family.

The Cohesion dimension of FACES contains nine subscales: emotional bonding, independence, family boundaries, coalitions, time, space, friends, decision making, interests, and recreation. The Adaptability dimension contains seven subscales: assertiveness, control, discipline, negotiation, rules, and system feedback. Composite scores on the Cohesion and Adaptability dimensions are classified into four levels (very low, low to moderate, moderate to high, and very high) and translated into descriptive types of families. The Adaptability dimension is partitioned into the rigid, structured, flexible, and chaotic types, while the Cohesion dimension is broken down into the disengaged, separated, connected, and enmeshed types of families. When each of the four family varieties on the Cohesion dimension are paired with each of the four categories on the Adaptability dimension, then, sixteen family types are possible. The Smith family was classified as *Rigidly Separated,* based on their cohesion and adaptability scores. This description converged with the information acquired at individual, dyadic, and family levels of the system which reflected a rigid authoritarian family characterized by structural rather than emotional closeness.

Each family member's subscale scores of the Adaptability dimension further indicated that the family was morphostatic and inflexible. For example, David had low scores for control, discipline, negotiation, and rules, while Judy was low in such areas as control, discipline, rules, and system feedback. Jason scored low on control, discipline, rules, and system feedback, while Nancy's scores were quite inconsiderable on assertiveness, control, negotiation, rules, and system feedback. Pete's scores on control and discipline were also quite low. The members of the family, therefore, seemed to agree in their morphostatic perception of the family.

Moderate scores on the Cohesion subscale provided additional important information about the Smith family. Noteworthy were Judy's low scores on the subscales of time, family boundaries and friends. These were consistent with the dissatisfactions she expressed in the dyadic assessments. Also consistent with earlier assessments were David's low scores on time and space. Jason's scores on these same two dimensions were also quite low, while Nancy and Pete's scores are all within the moderate range on these subscales.

Some divergent information about the Smith family was also provided by the scores on the Cohesion subscales. While assessment of the marital subsystem revealed the Smith marriage to be moderately cohesive on certain external qualities, it might seem somewhat surprising that the entire Smith family was classified as *Separate* on FACES. This description, on the other hand, may also reflect the existing distance in this couple's relationship, which they frequently attempted to disguise. This finding also reflected the clear structural boundary that David and Judy have established between themselves and their children.

The Kvebaek Family Sculpture Technique. A final family assessment procedure administered was the Kvebaek Family Sculpture Technique (KFST). This technique was developed originally in Norway as a diagnostic tool by the family therapist, David Kvebaek, and was modified as a research tool by Cromwell et al. (1981).

The KFST consists of a 1×1 meter board visually divided into a 10×10 square grid. It was designed to be used on a table approximately the same size. Family members are asked to place a set of wooden sculptures or figurines (depicting family members) on the board in a manner that represents how they view the relationship structure in their family. There are 13 figurines in Kvebaek's original set: 4 grandparents, 2 parents, 4 children, 2 "third persons," and 1 family pet. These allow sculptures of the extended family and the relevant social network, if so desired. In this clinical application, only figurines representing the nuclear family of 5 were utilized.

The overall procedure consisted of two separate tasks, each with two subdivisions. The first task involved an individual family member as a respondent about the family unit level of the system, while the second task concerned the responses of the entire family about the family level of the system. For the first task, individual family members were asked to independently sculpt both their real and ideal family relationship. The real perception of their family relationship is a representation of the "here and now," while the second provided a picture of how each would like to change the present situation. Individual sculptures were completed independently in different rooms, and both the real and ideal sculptures were recorded on a score sheet which depicted the 10 × 10 grid. Each family member was encouraged to explain his or her placement of the figurines. Final placements, order of placement, and movement of each figurine were recorded on the recording form.

The second task required the family to work together to provide a family consensus on real and ideal sculptures of family relationships. This situation provided an opportunity to view family interaction structured by a task now familiar to the participants. Family members were encouraged to discuss their placements and resolve differences in reaching consensus on their group perception of both the real and ideal family relationships. Final placements, order of placement, and movement of figurines for both tasks were recorded on score sheets and the verbal interaction was tape-recorded for analysis.

The information acquired about the Smith family on the KFST tended to correspond with earlier assessments at the individual, dyadic, and family levels. The clear generational boundary indicated by other methods was also evident during the KFST. The figurines representing father and mother were placed first by all family members, often as one unit. During the family consensus trials, David assumed the leadership role, while Judy functioned in a supportive role. The children were minimally involved in this process and communication tended to be constrained, unemotional, formal, and indirect.

The family's "identified problem," Jason, was viewed as the most distant member of the family. All of the family members, except David, moved Jason's figurine closer to them during the ideal phase of the task. In contrast to other family members, however, David moved the figurine representing Jason further away in the ideal, with the comment that he needed independence. The father, therefore, seemed to send Jason mixed messages. On the KFST, he advocated independence, while other assessments had indicated that he strongly resisted this by demanding respect for his authority.

The surface-level closeness of this family also was revealed by the KFST. For example, Pete, the youngest child, was perceived by everyone to be close to them, but he did not share that perception. The children perceived the strength of the structural bond between parents, but that bond was not viewed as an emotional one. Nancy and Pete were both perceived to be somewhat closer to the parents than Jason. The KFST, therefore, portrayed the Smith family in a manner consistent with previous assessments, that is, as structurally cohesive, with definite generational boundaries and rigid interaction patterns.

SUMMARY

Ackerman (1958) indicated many years ago that the family can be thought of as a carrier of elements predisposing it to mental health and mental illness. Viewed in this context, the Smith family is potentially pathology-generating, characterized by: (1) a traditional (sex-role stereotyped) marriage; (2) conflict avoidance; (3) suppression of affect; (4) masked and indirect communication; (5) structural fusion between husband and wife with an absence of emotional bonding; (6) little social intimacy; and (7) rigid separation among members. These characteristics emerged clearly from examination of the multiple assessments reviewed in this chapter.

From a clinical perspective, the above family qualities seem characteristic of Wynne's (1958) concept of "pseudomutuality" which, in turn, is associated with schizophrenic development (Epstein et al., 1978; Goldberg & Goldberg, 1980). It is not surprising, therefore, that assessment of the individual subsystem indicated a borderline schizophrenic personality profile for Jason, following interpretation of his MMPI profile. In this case, it might be speculated that Jason's dysfunctional behavior serves a functional, albeit unhealthy, role in maintaining the family.

CONCLUSION

This chapter has proposed a strategy for mapping both specific subsystem components and the holistic qualities of family systems. In moving toward this complex task, an initial assumption was that an assessment strategy must have the capacity to assess the complex array of components within the family system, with special emphasis upon their interrelationship. This task is compounded by the hierarchical character of family systems. From this perspective, systems are composed of levels or subsystems which share common issues across their boundaries, while also possessing qualities which make each component unique.

These holistic and componential aspects of family systems have encouraged the proposal for a "Multisystem-Multimethod" assessment strategy. First, the MS-MM requires that measures be selected which appropriately address particular phenomena of interest within specific levels of the family system. Attention was also focused upon the fit between the phenomenon of interest (within a particular system level) and the selection of appropriate measurement techniques. More specifically, this problem concerns the correspondence among the assessment tool selected, the conceptual dimension in the mind of the investigator, and the empirical world. An appropriate strategy for selection of assessment tools that appropriately addresses all levels of a system will "converge" upon issues pervading the entire system. Furthermore, it will also provide divergent information from the separate subsystems. The result should be a composite, and detailed, portrait of the family system.

Future utilization of the MS-MM framework might include the application of this strategy with large samples of clinical and nonclinical families. One potential result of this utilization could be the identification of different typologies of families classified by level of system, unique subsystem components, and overall systemic quality. It is also anticipated that the MS-MM approach will lead to the development of new and improved assessment tools specifically designed to tap the different levels of family system, and geared to specific phenomena of interest.

REFERENCE NOTES

1. THOMAS, D. L., & KEBER, J. E. *Through the glass darkly: The new philosophy of science and hermeneutics.* Paper presented at the Theory Construction and Research Methodology Workshop, National Council on Family Relations, Portland, Oregon, October 1980.

2. THOMAS, D. L., PETERSON, G. W., & ROLLINS, B. C. *Validity in parent-child research: A comparison of self-report and behavioral observations.* Paper presented at the annual meeting of the National Council on Family Relations, San Diego, CA, October 1977.

3. OLSON, D. H., BELL, R., & PORTNER, J. *FACES: Family Adaptibility and Cohesion Evaluation Scales.* Unpublished technical report, Family Social Science, University of Minnesota, 1978.

REFERENCES

ACKERMAN, N. B. *The psychodynamics of family life.* New York: Basic Books, 1958.

ALTHAUSER, R. P. & HEBERLEIN, F. A. Validity and the multitrait-multimethod matrix. In E. F. Borgatta & G. W.Bohrnstedt (Eds.), *Sociological methodology.* San Francisco: Jossey-Bass, 1979.

BATESON, G. *Steps to an ecology of mind.* New York: Ballantine, 1972.

BENTLER, P. M., & McCLAIN, J. A multitrait-multimethod analysis of reflection-impulsivity. *Child Development,* 1976, *47,* 218-226.

BERTALANFFY, L. V. *General system theory.* New York: George Braziller, 1968.

BLOOD, R. O., & WOLFE, D. M. *Husbands and wives.* New York: Macmillan, 1960.

BRODERICK, C. Foreword. In D. H. Olson (Ed.), *Treating relationships.* Lake Mills, IA: Graphic, 1976.

BUCKLEY, W. *Sociology and modern systems theory.* Englewood Cliffs, NJ: Prentice-Hall, 1967.

BURR, W. R., HILL, R., NYE, F. I., & REISS, I. L. *Contemporary theories about the family: Research-based theories* (Vol. 1). New York: Macmillan, 1979.

CAMPBELL, D. T., & FISKE, D. W. Convergent and discriminate validation by the multitrait-multimethod matrix. *Psychological Bulletin,* 1959, *56,* 81-105.

CROMWELL, R. E., FOURNIER, D. G., & KVEBAEK, D. J. *The Kvebaek Family Sculpture Technique: A diagnostic and research tool in family therapy.* Jonesboro, TN: Pilgrimage, 1981.

CROMWELL, R. E., & KEENEY, B. P. Diagnosing marital and family systems: A training model. *Family Coordinator,* 1979, *28,* 101-108.

CROMWELL, R. E., & KEENEY, B. P. A systems approach to marital and family diagnosis. *Journal of Counseling and Psychotherapy,* 1980, *2,* 69-78.

CROMWELL, R. E., KLEIN, D. M., & WIETING, S. G. Family power: A multitrait-multi-method matrix analysis. In R. E. Cromwell & D. H. Olson (Eds.), *Power in families.* New York: Halsted, 1975.

CROMWELL, R. E., & OLSON, D. H. (Eds.). *Power and families.* New York: Halsted, 1975.

CROMWELL, R. E., OLSON, D. H., & FOURNIER, D. G. Tools and techniques for diagnosis and evaluation in marriage and family therapy. *Family Process,* 1976, *15,* 1-49.

EPSTEIN, N. B., BISHOP, D. S., & LEVIN, S. The McMaster model of family functioning. *Journal of Marriage and Family Counseling,* 1978, *4,* 19-31.

GOLDBERG, I., & GOLDBERG, H. *Family therapy: An overview.* Belmont, CA: Wadsworth, 1980.

HILL, R. Modern systems theory and the family: A confrontation. *Social Science Information,* 1976, *10,* 7-26.

HURVITZ, N. Marital Roles Inventory as a counseling instrument. *Journal of Marriage and the Family,* 1965, *27,* 492-501.

JACKSON, D. D. The individual and the larger contexts. *Family Process,* 1967, *6,* 139-154.

KAVANAUGH, M. J., MacKINNEY, A. C., & WOLIN, L. Issues in managerial performance: Multitrait-multimethod analyses of ratings. *Psychological Bulletin,* 1971, *75,* 34-49.

KEENEY, B. P. Ecosystemic epistemology: An alternative paradigm for diagnosis. *Family Process,* 1979, *18,* 117-129.

KEENEY, B. P., & CROMWELL, R. E. Toward systemic diagnosis. *Family Therapy,* 1977, *4,* 225-236.

McDONALD, G. W. Family power: The assessment of a decade of theory and research. *Journal of Marriage and the Family,* 1980, *42,* 841-854.

MISCHEL, W. On the future of personality measurement. *American Psychologist,* 1977, *32,* 246-254.

OLSON, D. H. Bridging research, theory and application: The triple threat in science. In D. H. Olson (Ed.), *Treating relationships.* Lake Mills, IA: Graphic, 1976.

OLSON, D. H., & RYDER, R. G. Inventory of Marital Conflict: An experimental interaction procedure. *Journal of Marriage and the Family,* 1970, *32,* 443-448.

OLSON, D. H., SPRENKLE, D. H., & RUSSELL, C. S. Circumplex model of marital and family systems I: Cohesion and adaptability dimensions, family types, and clinical applications. *Family Process,* 1979, *18,* 3-28.

POPPER, K. Science: Problems, aims, responsibilities. *Proceedings of the American Societies for Experimental Biology,* 1963, *1,* No. 4.

RAVICH, R. A. The use of the Interpersonal Game-Test in conjoint marital psychotherapy. *American Journal of Psychotherapy,* 1969, *23,* 217-229.

RUSSELL, C. S. A methodological study of family cohesion and adaptability. *Journal of Marital and Family Therapy,* 1980, *6,* 459-470.

SCANZONI, J. Social processes and power in families. In W. R. Burr, R. Hill, F. I. Nye, & I. L. Reiss (Eds.), *Contemporary theories about the family: Research-based theories* (Vol. 1). New York: Macmillan, 1979.

SCHAEFER, M. T., & OLSON, D. H. Assessing intimacy: The PAIR Inventory. *Journal of Marriage and Family Therapy,* 1981, *7,* 47-60.

SKYNNER, A. C. R. *Systems of family and marital psychotherapy.* New York: Brunner/Mazel, 1976.

SPRENKLE, D. H. The need for integration among theory, research and practice in the family field. *Family Coordinator,* 1976, *24,* 261-263.

STEINGLASS, P. The conceptualization of marriage from a systems theory perspective. In T. Paolino & B. McCrady (Eds.), *Marriage and marital therapy.* New York: Brunner/Mazel, 1978.

STRAUS, M. A. Measuring families. In H. T. Christensen (Ed.), *Handbook of marriage and the family.* Skokie, IL: Rand McNally, 1964.

SULLIVAN, J. L., & FELDMAN, L. *Multiple indicators: An introduction.* Beverly Hills, CA: Sage, 1979.

WYLIE, R. C. *The self-concept* (Vol. 1). Lincoln: University of Nebraska Press, 1974.

WYNNE, L. C., RYCKOFF, I. J., DAY, J., & HIRSCH, S. Pseudomutuality in the family relations of schizophrenics. *Psychiatry,* 1958, *21,* 205-222.

4

LOVE, HATE, AND THE FAMILY: MEASURES OF EMOTION

Joseph Lowman

A history of marital and family measurement might aptly be titled "Search for the True Measure" as prevailing methodological paradigms have shifted over time. Self-report questionnaires directed toward individual personality characteristics or family concepts such as "solidarity" (Jansen, 1952) fell into disrepute as the emphasis shifted to observer ratings of family interaction in laboratory (for example, see Mishler & Waxler, 1968) and home (Steinglass & Tislenko, this volume) settings. The rise of behavioral applications to family (Patterson et al., 1968; Parsons & Alexander, 1973) and marital (Jacobson & Margolin, 1979; Weiss et al., 1973; Weiss, this volume) distress during the 1970s has shown an accompanying advocacy of behavioral assessment, and a number of behavior frequency checklists and rating systems have emerged (see review by Jacobson et al., in press). Heretofore these periods of paradigmatic shift have usually been characterized by polemics about not only what is the proper theoretical and therapeutic approach to take with families, but what are the correct methods of measuring the variables of special interest.

It is heartening at the beginning of the 1980s to observe strong signs of attempts to integrate psychoanalytic, systems, and behavioral perspectives on family and marital distress (for example, the special summer 1980 issue of the *American Journal of Family Therapy,* and Jacobson & Margolin, 1979). The illusion that there is in fact any *one* correct approach to family measurement has also weakened considerably. As Cromwell et al. (1976) argue in a comprehen-

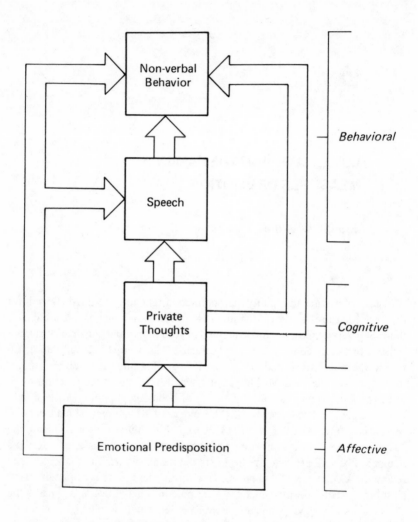

Figure 4.1   Multilevel Model of Determination

sive review, marital and family research should use methods of measurement assessing both subjective and objective data as perceived from within and without the phenomenology of the family members under study.

In this chapter, I will attempt to add to this growing rapprochement between previously contentious theoretical and measurement paradigms by arguing that the greatest *single source* of predictive variance in all family and marital measures is the affective or emotional predispositions (positive and negative feelings) existing between family members.[1] Simply put, it is my contention that *all family and marital measures are correlated with a common affective dimension and that it is this common dimension from which they derive the lion's share of their predictive variance*. A multilevel model of family functioning consisting of an affective substratum and successive cognitive and behavioral overlays will be presented in support of this argument. The *Inventory of Family Feelings* (IFF; Lowman, 1980), a sociogrammatic family measure based on this model, will also be described and its use in conjunction with other family measures outlined. The approach to be advocated here not only proposes that emotional predispositions are major determinants of an individual's thoughts and behavior, but that the *pattern* of affect as distributed among family members is also of critical importance in influencing observable and system-level phenomena.

MULTILEVEL MODEL OF FAMILY FUNCTIONING

Figure 4.1 presents a schematic outline of the proposed multilevel model with individuals as the unit of analysis. As can be seen, the *behavioral* or observational level consists of nonverbal behavior and speech. These are typically the items of interest in the family and marital interaction coding systems. The *cognitive* level consists of private thoughts or cognitive mediators known only to the family members in question, unless they choose to share them with us. Formal, well-structured thoughts that family members have about one another, as well as their more transitory and fragmented fantasies, would be included in this level; in effect, any conscious thoughts would be included. The *affective* level is the primary focus of this discussion and is seen as a powerful set of emotional investments each family member has toward each of the others and which are reflected indirectly. Although they cannot be easily measured directly,[2] the effects of these emotional predispositions can be seen in private thoughts and both classes of observable behavior. Research evidence will be presented below to show how the effects of the affective level on the behavioral one can be seen in observational measures of speech and in verbal behavior. Similarly, studies will be cited illustrating its influence on the cognitive level as manifested in subjective and objective self-report measures.

Figure 4.1 presents the proposed model as it applies just to single individuals. In fact, the total model consists of a group extension of the levels, especially the affective level. This is a critical point requiring some elucidation.

The position taken here is that the primary distinguishing factor between casual groups and more intimate human systems, especially families,[3] is the emotional interdependence of the members or the power of one member to stimulate emotional overreactions in others by actual acts or speech or by subtle innuendos. Students of group phenomena (see Shaffer & Galinsky's 1974 volume on various group models) universally report that as individuals interact with one another over time, there develops among them a powerful and emotional group life (Gibbard et al., 1974; Mann, 1967; Slatter, 1966). Because they are small and especially intense groups, families are even more prone to demonstrate behaviors that appear to have been produced by strong and irrational emotional reactions of a positive and a negative nature between specific family members or between one individual and the others symbolically as a group. For a demonstration of these phenomena, skeptics about the power of this nonrational motivational force need only observe almost any group of otherwise reasonable adult siblings as they try to settle their parents' estate. It is this collectivity of emotional experience that forms the basic phenomena of family systems theory and toward which most family interventions are directed. As will be seen, the IFF attempts to assess the emotional predispositions of every member of a family system toward every other member. Such comprehensiveness is needed to properly capture the affective level of the family system.

As the lines of influence in Figure 4.1 show, the direction of influence proposed in this model moves from unobservables to observables, from emotional predispositions to external behavior. It is acknowledged that much contemporary research (for example, Michel, 1979; Schacter & Singer, 1962), especially that influenced by attribution theory, assumes that the direction of causality is the opposite of what is shown. Following recent reformulations of this question (Zajonc, 1980), the position taken here is that the direction of influence portrayed is a viable option which should be tested empirically even though it may be inconsistent with the more prevailing and rational view of human behavior. The model also allows for multiple pathways of influence, the emotional predispositions of one family member toward another influencing their private thoughts about that person and, in turn, influencing the verbal and nonverbal behavior they show toward that person. Emotional predispositions can also directly influence speech and nonverbal behavior without necessarily influencing private thoughts. Finally, private thoughts are seen in this model to be capable of influencing nonverbal behavior directly without showing themselves in speech.

Family measurement research, especially that coming from the systems and behavioral perspectives, has, in recent years, focused heavily on observable interactions and has shied away from dealing with less observables. In that the important role cognitions play in psychopathology and therapy is now generally recognized by most behavioral theorists and therapists (for example, Beck,

1976), the position is taken here that we should also move one step further from observables to consider strong emotional predispositions, or what Gottman (Gottman et al., 1976) calls "hidden agendas" and Weiss (this volume) refers to as "sentiment overrides."

In sum, this multilevel model views the family as a complex and highly emotional set of positive and negative affective predispositions which influence many of the individuals' private thoughts, speech, and nonverbal communications toward one another. With this view in mind, comprehensive family measurement must, as Olson (Chapter 5, this volume) and Cromwell (Chapter 3, this volume) argue, assess as many of these levels and specific relationships as is possible. The IFF will be offered to you as a cost-effective and relatively pure measure of private thoughts about the affective substratum influencing a family's observable interactions.

SUPPORTING EVIDENCE

Research supporting the model proposed in Figure 4.1 will be presented, showing how family measures tapping cognitive, speech, and nonverbal levels consistently differentiate distressed from nondistressed families on affective dimensions. The underlying affective dimension reflected in many of these measures, including the more objective ones, will also be noted.

There is ample evidence for the preeminence of the affective dimension in self-report subjective measures and their ability to discriminate different groups. Martin's (1975) review of research on parent-child relationships indicates the affective dimension to show stronger and more consistent relationships than any other. In the psychiatric literature, van der Veen and Novak (1971) compared the affective ratings of identified patients (IPs), their siblings, and control children toward their parents and obtained results supporting an inverse relationship between affect and psychopathology. Factor analyses of subjective self-report inventories have almost always found a large first factor dealing with positive and negative affect (see Paitsch & Langevin, 1976; Schaeffer & Bell, 1958). In addition, the traditional self-report measures of marital distress, the Locke and Wallace (1959) and the Spanier (1976) scales, are also strongly directed toward spouse satisfaction and agreement. Snyder's (1979) multidimensional scale, the Marital Satisfaction Inventory, appears distinctly superior to the previous marital scales in focusing on a wider range of marital behaviors, but a factor analysis of all 280 items also produced a large first factor dealing with positive and negative affect (Snyder, Note 1). Thus, the preponderance of variance in instruments assessing family members' private thoughts about the other members of their families (or their spouses) appears to be associated with an underlying affective dimension. The ability of these scales to discriminate groups of families also appears to be associated with this affective variance.

Self-report measures focused toward specific observable behavior, instruments referred to as objective self-report in the schema proposed by Cromwell et al. (1976), can also be seen to be influenced by emotional predispositions, although it is not known to what degree such influence occurs independently of more subjective conscious thoughts. Stuart's Marital Pre-Counseling Inventory (Stuart & Stuart, 1972), for example, contains substantial sections dealing with subjective ratings of general satisfaction and with ratings of how rewarding each spouse feels the other's behavior to be. As additional examples, the Areas of Change Questionnaire (Patterson, 1976; Weiss & Margolin, 1977) and the Spouse Observation Checklist (Patterson et al., 1976) both commonly use behavioral checklists with couples, asking each spouse to rate the specific behaviors in question along scales assessing how pleased or displeased each is with his or her spouse's behavior or how much each wishes his or her partner would change his or her behavior. The position taken here is that *whenever these or other behavior checklists ask family members or marital pairs to rate others' behavior using concepts such as "rewardingness," or along a "pleasing-displeasing" continuum, the essential measurement as opposed to descriptive function occurring here is along an affective dimension regardless of how objective the rated behaviors may appear to be.*

Thus, self-report measures all assess the cognitive level of Figure 4.1 and whenever they deal with family members or relations they are most strongly influenced by an affective dimension. Incidentally, work in psycholinguistics and social psychology also shows the importance of the affective dimension in *all* cognitions. Osgood's (1964; Osgood et al., 1957) classic work on meaning found that the affective component accounted for twice as much variance as either secondary dimension of potency and activity. Insko and Schopler's (1967) reformulation of Heider's (1958) balance theory also stresses the importance of what are called "sentiment relations" in human phenomenology.

Reviews of family interaction literature (see Haley, 1972; Riskin & Faunce, 1972) demonstrate the large magnitude of effort that has gone into rating family interactions in laboratory situations. Such systems typically have confounded the speech and nonverbal levels of Figure 4.1, with little distinction made between them. Thus, the role of the affective stratum will be discussed in this chapter as an influence on both levels taken as a group. Jacob's (1975) review of this interaction data indicates family studies found predicted differences on dimensions of affect more often than on dimensions of conflict, dominance, or communication clarity. Studies using the two major behavioral systems for rating marital interactions, the Marital Interaction Coding System (MICS; Hops et al., 1971) and the Couple's Interaction Scoring System (CISS; Gottman, 1979; Notarius et al., this volume) have demonstrated that both are capable of discriminating distressed from nondistressed couples. In studies using these systems, distressed groups show significantly more negative affect and, to a lesser degree, less positive affect (Birchler et al., 1975; Vincent et al., 1975). In addition, both objective rating systems are typically used by combining the discrete behavioral categories (29 in the MICS and 27 in the CISS) into summary dimensions, such as problem solving, agreement, mind reading, or positive and negative verbal and nonverbal behaviors. In some studies with the MICS (Klier & Rothberg, Note 2), categories are combined into simply positive and negative behaviors. The objectivity of the rated marital behaviors in these systems does not obscure the fact that they produce scores which reflect *variation* along an affective dimension. The CISS system is more explicit in this regard in that every speech or act receives two codes, one a discrete content code, and the other a rating of whether the nonverbal aspect of the behavior was positive, neutral, or negative. Gottman and his colleagues report several studies in which the nonverbal scores account for the significant discrimination between groups. Gottman (1979) also reports the refinement of detailed systems for rating nonverbal facial and body expressions. These are also likely to be heavily dependent on the affective dimension.

Thus, there is clear and abundant evidence that the emotional predispositions of family members toward the other members of their families account for a substantial amount of the variance and discriminative validity of family measures directed toward cognitive and behavioral levels; in effect, there is reason to believe that all family measures share a great deal of common predictive variance due to the presence of this dimension. The following section of this chapter will describe a self-report measure focusing exclusively on this dimension, and the concluding section will propose how family and marital systems may be most appropriately and comprehensively assessed when the underlying affective dimension is given appropriate recognition.

THE INVENTORY OF FAMILY FEELINGS

DESCRIPTION AND SCORING

The IFF is a 38-item scale requiring approximately 20 minutes to complete, in which each member of a family answers "agree," "disagree," or "neutral" to each item in terms of his or her feelings at that moment toward every other member. Sample items are "I feel close to this family member," "This family member doesn't show a lot of consideration toward me," and "I feel very warm toward this family member." The items were selected, from a longer version containing 101 items, on the basis of a principal component analysis, and contain words written on a fifth-grade reading level. Thus, it can be completed by most children of at least 12 years of age or by persons with at least a sixth-grade reading ability.

Several kinds of affect scores are produced when the IFF is administered to every member of a family: *Individual Scores* reflect one member's affective rating of a given other member; *Dyad Scores* are an average of two members' individual scores toward each other; *Response Scores* represent an average of individual scores a member produces toward the members of his or her family as a group; *Reception Scores* refer to the average individual scores given to one member by the others as a group; and the *Family Unit Scores* are the average individual scores produced by an entire family.

IFF scores produce what is, in effect, a sensitive family sociogram. In this sense it is similar to the rating scale methods of sociogramatic measurement used with children (Oden & Asher, 1977), a method found to be more reliable with younger children than the standard peer nomination method (Asher et al., 1979). Although it can be argued that a family's various scores on the IFF may represent transient phenomena, the fact that sociogramatic measures of school children have been shown to be quite stable over time (Rolf et al., 1972) provides support for the position taken here that family sociograms represent relatively enduring emotional patterns as well.

Before summarizing the validational evidence on the IFF, illustrative data of clinic and control families will be presented.

ILLUSTRATIVE FAMILY DATA

IFF data from four families, each consisting of two children and with a marriage that has been intact for at least four years, are presented in Tables 4.1 through 4.4 and Figures 4.2 through 4.5. Of these families, 2 were selected from a group of 27 treatment families to illustrate the kinds of variability found in their affective structures, or the patterns with which their affect is distributed

TABLE 4.1   Family 1: Treatment Family

Family Member Responding to Item	Family Member Who Is Object of the Others' Responses				
	Father	Mother	Son	Daughter[a]	Response Scores[b]
Father		15	22	28	21.7
Mother	11		23	10	14.7
Son	20	11		15	15.3
Daughter[a]	30	7	13		16.7
Reception Scores[c]	20.3	11.0	19.3	17.7	
				Family Unit Score[d]	
				17.9	

NOTE: Mean = 26.3, S.D. = 4.51.
a. IP.
b. Each member's average score toward others.
c. Average score of others toward each person.
d. Average score within the family.

among the members. The remaining two families were randomly selected from 16 control families in which no marital separations, treatment for emotional problems, or serious legal or school problems had ever occurred. For each family, a Family Matrix showing each person's IFF scores toward every other person and summary scores will be presented, followed by a Dyadic Relation-

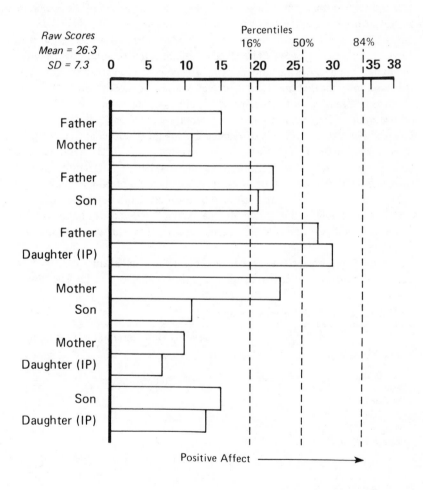

Figure 4.2   Dyadic Relationships Graph for Family 1

ships Graph comparing the reciprocal scores of each of the unique dyads of the family.

Table 4.1 and Figure 4.2 present IFF data from the first treatment family, a family with a 17-year-old daughter (the IP) and a 15-year-old son. The family had been in conjoint therapy for approximately two months when the IFF was completed, treatment being initiated after the daughter had been suspended from school following a fracas with a group of other girls. As can be seen in Table 4.1, the family's average score (Family Unit Score) of 17.9 was well below the mean for all families of 26.3. From an inspection of the Response Scores, it is clear that the father was more positive toward the others than was anyone else. The Reception Scores reveal that the mother was seen in the most negative light by the others. The Dyadic Relationships Graph as displayed in Figure 4.2 again shows the family's generally lower-than-average affect scores. It is also apparent that the father-daughter dyad is the most positive of the six separate relationships in the four-person family. In addition, it reveals that three of the relationships (the father-mother, mother-daughter, and son-daughter) are less positive than are typically encountered using this instrument. Incidentally, the son was described by the therapist as somewhat passive and withdrawn. The lack of reciprocity between the son and the mother in this family may be associated with his low degree of open communication of how he feels about her. The pattern of coalitions illustrated by this family is a commonly encountered one and might be dubbed an "oedipal pattern" in that the IP has a positive relationship with the opposite-sex parent and a negative one with the same-sex parent.

Family 2, as portrayed in Table 4.2 and Figure 4.3, and in contrast to the first treatment family, contains two daughters, aged 16 (the IP) and 15. The IP was

TABLE 4.2   Family 2: Treatment Family

Family Member Responding to Item	Family Member Who Is Object of the Others' Responses			
	Father	Mother	Daughter #1[a]	Daughter #2 Response Scores[b]
Father		36	18	19 24.3
Mother	32		20	27 26.3
Daughter #1[a]	2	3		38 14.3
Daughter #2	5	26	36	22.3
Reception Scores[c]	13.0	21.7	24.7	28.0
				Family Unit Score[d]
				21.8

NOTE: Mean = 26.3, S.D. = 4.51.
a. IP.
b. Each member's average score toward others.
c. Average score of others toward each person.
d. Average score within the family.

hospitalized briefly following an episode of drug abuse and a period of general unmanageability. The IP was perceived by staff working with the family as being very close to her mother until the onset of adolescence, when their relationship became more characterized by distance and conflict. The younger daughter was described as always looking up to her older sister and, in spite of a moderate degree of competitiveness, the two sisters were seen as very close.

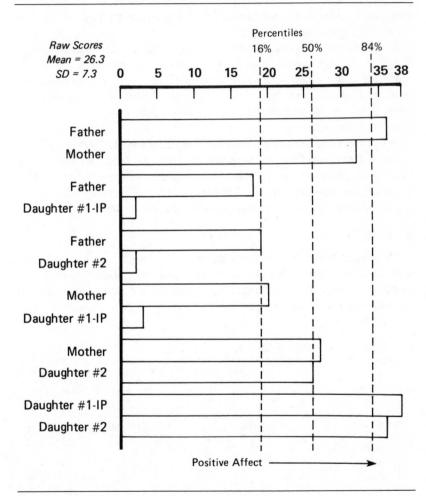

Figure 4.3   Dyadic Relationships Graph for Family 2

The Family Matrix presented in Table 4.2 shows this family's Family Unit Score also to be below the mean. It appears that the father received the lowest Reception Scores on responses from the others. As portrayed in Figure 4.3, the dyadic relationships in this family can be characterized as being allied within generations, the parents and the two girls having the most positive relationships and the other relationshps being typically less positive. The one exception to this is the moderately positive relationship between the mother and the younger daughter. It is unlikely that two adolescent siblings of opposite sexes could have allied in this strong a coalition because of anxiety stemming from their inevitable sexual feelings for one another.

These two treatment families illustrate rather different patterns of affect even though both are less positive than that typically found using the IFF. In one, the conflicted relationships were within the parental and specific child-parent and child-child relationships. In the other, however, the positive coalitions were between the parents and the siblings, and the conflict was shown between parents and children.

In contrast to these two treatment families, Tables 4.3 and 4.4 and Figures 4.4 and 4.5 present IFF data on two control families. Both families have Family Unit Scores almost a standard deviation above the mean and even though there are specific negative relationships within these "normal" families, they are less negative and there are fewer of them than was true for the treatment families.

SUMMARY OF VALIDATIONAL EVIDENCE

Three validational field studies using the IFF are reported elsewhere (Lowman, 1980) and their results will be summarized here. Studies involving 27 treatment families, 18 control families, 10 couples in marital therapy, and 10 control couples have demonstrated that IFF Response Scores have high reliabil-

TABLE 4.3   Family 3: Control Family

Family Member Responding to Item	Family Member Who Is Object of the Others' Responses				
	Father	Mother	Son	Daughter	Response Scores[a]
Father		37	36	32	35.0
Mother	38		33	24	31.7
Son	30	24		26	26.7
Daughter	32	10	35		25.7
Reception Scores[b]	33.3	23.7	34.7	27.3	
					Family Unit Score[c]
					29.8

NOTE: Mean = 26.3, S.D. = 4.51.
a. Each member's average score toward others.
b. Average score of others toward each person.
c. Average score within the family.

ity (.96 test-retest over two weeks' time), that families with IPs and couples in therapy score less positively toward each other than controls, and that most of the negative affect in distressed families centers on and emanates from the IPs. IFF affect scores and psychopathology indices on the MMPI were found to be negatively correlated to a significant degree ($r = -.33$, p less than .05) much as van der Veen and Novak (1971) reported. In one study (Fineberg & Lowman, 1975), trained raters made observational ratings of affect using a system based on Leary's system (1957; Terrill & Terrill, 1965). These externally observable

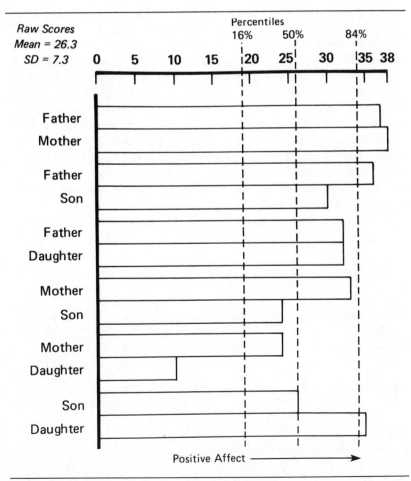

Figure 4.4   Dyadic Relationships Graph for Family 3

affect scores were correlated .49 with the IFF self-report Response Scores demonstrating that the self-report affect scores account for 24% of the variance in observer ratings. For the family data, reciprocity comparisons of dyadic relationships showed a moderate degree of association between actual relationships (r = .44, p less than .001), but no correlation between other nonreciprocal scores within the same families (r = .05, p less than .21).

COMPREHENSIVE FAMILY ASSESSMENT

The arguments presented thus far about the ubiquity of the affective dimension in family and marital research and the validational evidence for the IFF may seem to some to be rather obvious and not particularly useful. Admittedly, the conclusion that "distressed family members do not feel positively about one another" does appear at first blush to be at least simplistic, if not tautological. The implications of the model in Figure 4.1 for family assessment are more complex and useful, however, especially for research as opposed to clinical purposes. In fact, several of the following specific recommendations about family assessment are implied or explicitly argued in other chapters in this volume. Even though the studies reported thus far with the IFF do not exemplify fully the recommendations made below, studies are under way which are consistent, although they are not as ambitious as the multimethod approach advocated by Cromwell and Peterson in Chapter 3.

First of all, there can be no question that the cognitions of family members

TABLE 4.4   Family 4: Control Family

| Family Member Responding to Item | Family Member Who Is Object of the Others' Responses | | | | |
	Father	Mother	Son	Daughter	Response Scores[a]
Father		37	33	34	34.7
Mother	38		37	38	37.7
Son	15	27		17	19.7
Daughter	37	36	29		34.0
Reception Scores[b]	30.0	33.3	33	29.7	
					Family Unit Score[c]
					31.5

NOTE: Mean = 26.3, S.D. = 4.51.
a. Each member's average score toward others.
b. Average score of others toward each person.
c. Average score within the family.

about one another must be included in a comprehensive family assessment. In their recent volume on marital therapy, Jacobson and Margolin (1979) join researchers such as Olson (see Chapter 5, this volume) in stressing the assessment of cognitive as well as behavioral factors.

Second, there can be no question that assessment of as many aspects of a family system as possible must be made for a complete picture of that family as a unique social psychological unit to be gained (see Cromwell, Chapter 3, this volume). A sociometric approach searching for family patterns, as illustrated by the IFF with self-report data, should also be used with affective data collected using other methods.

Third, comprehensive assessment should include self-report subjective and

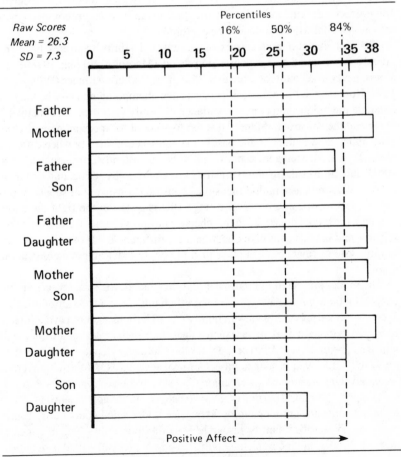

Figure 4.5   Dyadic Relationships Graph for Family 4

self-report objective measures as well as observer ratings of interaction collected in home or in laboratory settings.

Fourth, routine use of the IFF as the purest available measure of the affective dimension is recommended. With couples, having each spouse rate his or her parents and in-laws as well as each other has been found to be particularly revealing, although the IFF is best used with intact family units of more than one child. Comparing IFF scores to other cognitive and behavioral measures potentially can give an indication of the extent to which the affective level is reflected in them. Application or development of sophisticated statistical technology may be required to do so with confidence, especially given the statistical dependence of any data gathered from every member of a family system. Cromwell (see Chapter 3, this volume) proposes the application of the multimethod-multitrait approach, but the use of multivariate methods, especially when affect scores are treated as covariables and family roles are compared with orthogonal contrasts, should also be explored.

The fact that different classes of marital and family measures have frequently been found to be poorly correlated (Margolin, 1978a; 1978b) and almost never to account for more than 25% of each other's variance (Wills et al., 1974; Robinson & Price, Note 3) suggests that attempts should also be made to untangle the unique and common variance in family measures. One method is to expand the construct of family distress to account for measurement discrepancy, much as was done in the past to the construct of anxiety when different physiological measures were not found to be consistently correlated (Martin, 1961). Jacobson et al. (in press) illustrate this approach by advocating treatment of marital distress as a multidimensional construct consisting of spouse observation, self-report, and observer rating. This is a step in the right direction, although the model presented in this chapter may prove more useful in suggesting how and in what causative direction these different levels of individual and family systems relate to each other than in simply redefining the construct in question.

The model presented in Figure 4.1 and, in general, the stress placed in this chapter on the nonrational role of emotions in family phenomena are admittedly at odds with the prevailing view in family research (in fact, most psychological research) that rational processes (such as learning, social roles, or attributional) which can be understood will account for most human behavior. That may well prove to be true even in such highly emotional systems as families, but there is also a growing awareness, even among behaviorists (see Chapter 2, this volume), that a substantial portion of the variance may ultimately be attributable to more irrational and emotional processes. The fundamental goal of this chapter has been to sensitize family researchers to this possibility and to suggest, however briefly and incompletely, how they might proceed with this in mind.

NOTES

1. The concept of attitude can also accurately refer to such emotional bonds between family members, but because it has come to refer to such a large literature of experimental findings with undergraduates having little demonstrated generalizability to actual families, I prefer to use the term *emotional predisposition* instead.

2. It is an empirical issue as to whether autonomic nervous system measures could be used reliably to measure them more directly.

3. The word *families* will be used throughout the remainder of this chapter to refer to marital couples as well as to families with children or proximal extended members.

REFERENCE NOTES

1. SNYDER, D. K. Development of a multidimensional inventory of marital satisfaction. (Doctoral dissertation, University of North Carolina at Chapel Hill, 1978). *Dissertation Abstracts International*, 1978, *39*, 354OB. (University Microfilms No. 7900506)

2. KLIER, J. L., & ROTHBERG, M. *Characteristics of conflict resolution in couples*. Paper presented at the annual meeting of the Association for the Advancement of Behavior Therapy, Atlanta, December 1977.

3. ROBINSON, E. A., & PRICE, M. G. *Behavioral and self-report correlates of marital satisfaction*. Paper presented at the annual meeting of the Association for the Advancement of Behavior Therapy, New York, December 1976.

REFERENCES

ASHER, S. R., SINGLETON, L. C., TINSLEY, B. R., & HYMEL, L. A reliable sociometric measure for preschool children. *Developmental Psychology*, 1979, *15*, 443-444.

BECK, A. T. *Cognitive therapy and emotional disorders*. New York: International Universities Press, 1976.

BIRCHLER, G. R., & WEBB, L. J. Discriminating interaction in behaviors in happy and unhappy marriages. *Journal of Consulting and Clinical Psychology*, 1977, *45*, 494-495.

BIRCHLER, G. R., WEISS, R. L., & VINCENT, J. P. A multimethod analysis of social reinforcement exchange between maritally distressed and nondistressed spouse and stranger dyads. *Journal of Personality and Social Psychology*, 1975, *31*, 349-360.

CROMWELL, R. F., OLSON, D. H., & FOURNIER, D. G. Tools and techniques for diagnosis and evaluation in marital and family therapy. *Family Process*, 1976, *15*, 1-49.

FINEBERG, B., & LOWMAN, J. Affect and status dimensions of marital adjustment. *Journal of Marriage and the Family*, 1975, *37*, 155-160.

GIBBARD, G. S., HARTMANN, J. J., & MANN, R. D. *Analysis of groups*. San Francisco: Jossey-Bass, 1974.

GOTTMAN, J. M. *Marital interaction: Experimental investigations*. New York: Academic, 1979.

GOTTMAN, J. M., NOTARIUS, C., GONSO, J., & MARKMAN, H. *A couple's guide to communication*. Champaign, IL: Research Press, 1976.

HALEY, J. Critical overview of the present status of family interaction research. In J. L. Frano (Ed.), *Family interaction: A dialogue between family researchers and family therapists*. New York: Springer, 1972.

HEIDER, F. *The psychology of interpersonal relations*. New York: John Wiley, 1958.

HOPS, H., WILLS, T. A., PATTERSON, G. R., & WEISS, R. L. *Marital interaction coding system*. Eugene, OR: University of Oregon and Oregon Research Institute, 1971. (Order from ASIS/NAPS, c/o Microfiche Publications, 305 E. 46th Street, New York, NY 10017)

INSKO, C. A., & SCHOPLER, J. Triadic consistency: A statement of affective-cognitive-conative consistency. *Psychological Review*, 1967, *6*, 225-228.

JACOB, T. Family interaction in disturbed and normal families: A methodological and substantive review. *Psychological Bulletin*, 1975, *82*, 33-65.

JACOBSON, N. S., ELWOOD, R., & DALLAS, M. The behavioral assessment of marital dysfunction. In D. H. Barlow (Ed.), *Behavioral assessment of adult disorders*. New York: Guilford, in press.

JACOBSON, N. S., & MARGOLIN, G. *Marital therapy: Strategies based on social learning and behavior exchange principles*. New York: Brunner/Mazel, 1979.

JANSEN, L. T. Measuring family solidarity. *American Sociological Review*, 1952, *17*, 727-733.

LEARY, T. *Interpersonal diagnosis of personality*. New York: Ronald, 1957.

LOCKE, H. J., & WALLACE, K. M. Short-term marital adjustment and prediction tests: Their reliability and validity. *Journal of Marriage and Family Living*, 1959, *21*, 251-255.

LOWMAN, J. Measurement of family affective structure. *Journal of Personality Assessment*, 1980, *44*, 130-141.

MANN, R. D. *Interpersonal styles and group development*. New York: John Wiley, 1967.

MARGOLIN, G. The relationships among marital assessment procedures: A correlational study. *Journal of Consulting and Clinical Psychology*, 1978, *46*, 1556-1558. (a)

MARGOLIN, G. A multilevel approach to the assessment of communication positiveness in distressed marital couples. *International Journal of Family Counseling*, 1978, *6*, 81-89. (b)

MARTIN, B. The assessment of anxiety by physiological behavioral measures. *Psychological Bulletin*, 1961, *58*, 234-255.

MARTIN, B. Parent-child relations. In F. G. Horowitz (Ed.), *Review of child development research* (Vol. 4). Chicago: University of Chicago Press, 1975.

MICHEL, W. On the interface of cognition and personality: Beyond the person-situation debate. *American Psychologist*, 1979, *34*, 740-754.

MISHLER, E. G., & WAXLER, N. E. *Interaction in families: An experimental study of family process in schizophrenia*. New York: John Wiley, 1968.

ODEN, S., & ASHER, S. R. Coaching children in social skills for friendship making. *Child Development*, 1977, *48*, 495-506.

OSGOOD, C. E. Semantic differential. *American Anthropologist*, 1964, *66*, 171-201.

OSGOOD, C. E., SUCI, G. J., & TANNENBAUM, P. H. *The measurement of meaning*. Urbana: University of Illinois Press, 1957.

PAITSCH, D., & LANGEVIN, R. The Clarke Parent-Child Relations Questionnaire: A clinically useful test for adults. *Journal of Consulting and Clinical Psychology*, 1976, *44*, 428-436.

PARSONS, B. V., & ALEXANDER, J. F. Short-term family intervention: A therapy outcome study. *Journal of Consulting and Clinical Psychology*, 1973, *41*, 195-201.

PATTERSON, G. R. Some procedures for assessing changes in marital interaction patterns. *Oregon Research Institute Bulletin*, 1976, *16*(7).

PATTERSON, G. R., RAY, R. S., & SHAW, D. A. Direct intervention in families of deviant children. *Oregon Research Institute Bulletin*, 1968, *8*(9).

PATTERSON, G. R., WEISS, R. L., & HOPS, H. Training of marital skills: Some problems and concepts. In H. Leitenberg (Ed.), *Handbook of behavior modification*. New York: Prentice-Hall, 1976.

RISKIN, J. E., & FAUNCE, E. E. An evaluative review of family interaction research. *Family Process*, 1972, *11*, 365-456.

ROLF, M., SELLS, S. G., & GOLDEN, M. M. *Social adjustment and personality development in children*. Minneapolis: University of Minnesota Press, 1972.

SCHACHTER, S., & SINGER, J. Cognitive, social, and physiological determinants of emotional state. *Psychological Review*, 1962, *69*, 379-399.

SCHAEFFER, E. S., & BELL, R. Q. Development of a parental attitude research instrument. *Child Development*, 1958, *29*, 339-361.

SHAFFER, J. B., & GALINSKY, M. D. *Models of group therapy and sensitivity training*. Englewood Cliffs, NJ: Prentice-Hall, 1974.

SLATTER, P. E. *Microcosm: Structural, psychological, and religious evolution in groups*. New York: John Wiley, 1966.

SNYDER, D. K. Multidimensional assessment of marital satisfaction. *Journal of Marriage and the Family*, 1979, *41*, 813-823.

SPANIER, G. B. Measuring dyadic adjustment: New scales for assessing the quality of marriage and similar dyads. *Journal of Marriage and the Family*, 1976, *38*, 15-28.

STUART, R. B., & STUART, F. *Marital Pre-Counseling Inventory*. Champaign, IL: Research Press, 1972.

TERRILL, J. M., & TERRILL, R. E. A method for studying family communication. *Family Process*, 1965, *4*, 259-290.

VAN DER VEEN, F., & NOVAK, A. Perceived parental attitudes and family concepts of disturbed adolescents, normal siblings, and normal controls. *Family Process*, 1971, *10*, 327-342.

VINCENT, J. P., WEISS, R. L., & BIRCHLER, G. R. A behavioral analysis of problem-solving in distressed and nondistressed married and stranger dyads. *Behavior Therapy*, 1975, *6*, 475-487.

WEISS, R. L., HOPS, H., & PATTERSON, G. R. A framework for conceptualizing marital conflict, a technology for altering it, some data for evaluating it. In L. A. Hamerlynck, L. C. Handy, & E. J. Mash (Eds.), *Behavior change: Methodology, concepts, and practice*. Champaign, IL: Research Press, 1973.

WEISS, R. L., & MARGOLIN, G. Assessment of marital conflict and accord. In A. R. Ciminero, K. D. Calhoun, & H. E. Adams (Eds.), *Handbook of behavior assessment*. New York: John Wiley, 1977.

WILLS, T. A., WEISS, R. L., & PATTERSON, G. R. A behavioral analysis of the determinants of marital satisfaction. *Journal of Consulting and Clinical Psychology*, 1974, *42*, 802-811.

ZAJONC, R. B. Feeling and thinking: Preferences need no inferences. *American Psychologist*, 1980, *35*, 151-175.

5

FAMILY TYPOLOGIES:
BRIDGING FAMILY RESEARCH
AND FAMILY THERAPY

David H. Olson

Family research and family therapy are like two paths diverging in the woods; most family professionals choose one path or the other—only rare mavericks have tried to bridge the two fields. There is much, however, that family researchers and family therapists can learn from each other. In fact, both have suffered conceptually and methodologically from their mutual isolation.

This chapter will describe common issues confronting both family researchers and family therapists. It will identify their different orientations and solutions to these issues, and indicate the contributions they could make to each other and the family profession if they formed a more collaborative relationship. The advantages of bridging research, theory, and practice will be discussed and the usefulness of "insider" and "outsider" views of relationships will be described.

A major breakthrough that will help bridge the gap between family research and family therapy is that of typologies of couples and families. Typologies, whether developed theoretically or empirically, offer important conceptual and methodological advantages over traditional approaches used to describe and

AUTHOR'S NOTE: Work on this chapter was supported by a grant from the Agricultural Experiment Station, University of Minnesota, St. Paul, Minnesota.

analyze couples and families. This chapter will review recent developments regarding family typologies and will illustrate empirical and theoretical typologies developed by Olson and his colleagues.

COMMON ISSUES

The differences in training and orientation of family researchers and family therapists often obscure the common issues confronting them when they deal with couples and families. These common problems could provide a unifying direction that might facilitate more cooperation between them. The following are some of the common issues that both groups are continually struggling to resolve.

(1) How can the interaction in a marital or family system be most *effectively* and *efficiently described*?

(2) *What variables* are considered *most important* so that they can be accurately observed and assessed?

(3) *When* and *where* should the couple or family be *observed*—in an office, home, or laboratory setting?

(4) Should the interaction focus on *issues relevant* to the family or on some *standardized situations*?

(5) How can the observer (therapist or researcher) keep track of all the *important interactions* among all the subsystems within a family (dyads, triads, and so on)?

(6) To adequately understand a family system, *how many* and *which family members* should be observed?

(7) How can all the data on a family be *collapsed* or *summarized* so that the *total system* can be described rather than just individuals?

(8) How can we be sure that the final description of the family is *reliable, valid,* and *useful*—both clinically and theoretically?

What both groups fail to realize is that the family is one of the most complex systems to adequately describe and understand. As the late Margaret Mead (Note 1) once stated: "A family is tougher to work with than an individual and tougher than a whole culture. It is probably *the* toughest thing that you can prepare anybody to do therapy or research in." Because of the complexity of the family, it will take a more unified and cooperative approach to adequately understand these systems.

POTENTIAL MUTUAL CONTRIBUTIONS

Before family researchers and practitioners actually begin to work together in a more cooperative fashion, they both need to be aware of the benefits they will derive from such an endeavor. The following are some of the ways in which each could benefit from working more closely with the other. A more complete elaboration of these ideas can be found elsewhere (Olson, 1976).

RESEARCHERS' CONTRIBUTION TO THERAPISTS

(1) Researchers could assist therapists in operationalizing their terms.

(2) Researchers can also help therapists clarify the relevant dimensions and specific goals of treatment.

(3) Researchers can help therapists develop and use a greater variety of research methods, both for initial diagnosis and as measures of change during treatment.

(4) Researchers can aid therapists in formulating researchable questions.

(5) Researchers can also provide normative data of relevance to practitioners, not only on their client populations, but on comparable nonclinic families.

(6) Reseachers can assist the therapist in carrying out studies of the effectiveness of various therapeutic strategies.

THERAPISTS' CONTRIBUTION TO RESEARCHERS

Cooperation between a researcher and a therapist is a two-way street, and researchers can also benefit from the interchange. The following are some of the advantages which accrue to family researchers.

(1) If family researchers would observe actual families in treatment, this would not only stimulate their interest in therapy but it would broaden their perspective on the complexity of family dynamics.

(2) Clinical data from families can be useful in both generating and testing hypotheses.

(3) Clinical observation might also encourage researchers to develop new methods which would focus more on the entire family system and would rely on observation technique, both in the laboratory and field, rather than emphasize only self-report procedures.

(4) Working in clinical settings will also enable the researchers to test the validity of various research methods.

(5) In addition to providing researchers with another research population, which is no small consideration, clinical settings provide a useful place to test and validate theoretical ideas.

(6) A very significant and yet untapped advantage of a clinical setting to a researcher is the possibility, under proper therapeutic conditions, to legitimately control some independent variables.

THE IDEAL RELATIONSHIP

The bridging of research, theory, and application has been lacking in the field of marriage and the family. Although some headway has been made in bridging this gap in some marital and family therapy projects, it has been primarily because one individual had all three perspectives, and not because of cooperative efforts by professionals specializing in these three domains. Some of these more integrative projects by Alexander, Guerney, and Patterson are described in greater detail elsewhere (Olson, 1976).

Ideally, theoretical formulations should be derived from real-life situations and then research should evaluate the validity of these ideas when they are later applied in these situations. A similar proposal was made regarding the field of social psychology by McGuire (1969), who suggested that the best of all worlds would be to do theory-oriented research in natural settings. He stated: "My best-of-both-worlds solution of testing basic theoretical derivations in natural settings would hopefully show the relevance to the real concerns of man of our seemingly trivial and jargon-laden theorizing. A more profound possible effect of such natural testing would be the development of theories in a somewhat more reality-oriented direction" (McGuire, 1969, p. 30).

First, let us consider the ideal benefits that an integration of research, theory, and practice can provide. The wise utilization of theory has greatly facilitated rapid advances in many fields of science. Ideally, theory aids in summarizing present knowledge by reducing phenomena to basic underlying and interrelated principles or propositions. In so doing, it enhances our explanatory power. As stated elsewhere (Olson, 1970), theory can also offer significant contributions to research and practice by directing one to yet unobserved principles or relationships which are derived deductively from theory.

If research, in addition to being theoretically grounded, would also focus on applied problems, there would be numerous advantages. First of all, an integrative approach would greatly increase the relevance of the research and theory so that they might be used by those who are in pressing need of practical solutions to their problems. Second, it could increase the validity of the findings by testing them out in real, rather than contrived and artificial, situations. Third, if the research is theoretically based, it could yield a more adequate test of the theory and would enable it to have consequences in practice. Fourth, it could increase the probability that researchers would include a greater variety of significant variables, rather than rely on the same few variables repeatedly utilized by others. And finally, it could increase the extent to which the results could be generalized and would encourage people to apply such findings, instead of the research simply remaining in the journals for colleagues to read.

In conclusion, research cannot be properly conducted without the guidance of theory, nor can theory be adequately developed or substantiated without empirical verification. If, in addition, theory-oriented research investigated real-life problems, the coordinated approach would facilitate a complementary cycle of development in each area.

INSIDERS' AND OUTSIDERS' VIEWS

A critical part of bridging research, theory, and practice is the choice of research methods. One significant question that must be answered is whose definition of reality is most important, those who are directly involved in the relationship (the insiders), or those who externally observe those individuals (the outsiders). This choice not only determines to a great extent the type of research method that is used, but greatly effects what is found empirically. Table 5.1 illustrates the four types of research methods that can be used.

Most marriage and family research has relied exclusively on self-report methods and has often asked the wife to describe how she perceives the family. In the last decade, about 10% of family research has utilized behavioral methods in which the interaction of family members is observed and coded. Very few studies have relied on both self-report and behavioral methods.

Research in the last decade which has used multimethod assessments has clearly demonstrated that different methods will usually produce conflicting findings (Olson & Cromwell, 1975; Olson, 1977). This might lead one to conclude that one method is more valid than the other and encourage an investigator to choose the most valid method. But both observational (outsiders) and self-report data from questionnaires or interviews (insiders) are interrelated parts of the same system. Riley (1964) stated in this regard:

> Observation and questioning often give quite different results; but this occurs not because one method is necessarily more valid than the other, but because the two focus directly on different, though interrelated, sets of social system properties.

Using only one research method *conceals* rather than *reveals* the true complexity of marital and family systems that so often has eluded investigators. Both the insider and outsider methods provide valid, but different, perspectives on a system. It is this difference in perspectives that can be used to generate new hypotheses and increase our understanding of family dynamics.

TABLE 5.1   Four Types of Research Methods

Reporter's Frame of Reference	Types of Data	
	Subjective	*Objective*
Insider	Self-report methods	Behavioral self-report methods
Outsider	Observer subjective reports	Behavioral methods

Although there are many conceptual and methodological advantages of a multimethod approach, a few of the major points will be highlighted. First, it enables an investigator to more adequately assess a range of theoretical concepts. Second, it permits testing of hypotheses that relate to the insider and outsider perspectives. Third, using a multimethod multitrait approach (MM-MT) enables the investigator to increase the scientific rigor of the project and also assess validity issues. Four, it provides a more comprehensive, but often perplexing and conflicting, view of a marriage and family system. Finally, it helps to illuminate rather than eliminate the complexity of these systems. A more comprehensive discussion of the value of a multimethod assessment using the insider's and outsider's perspective is contained elsewhere (Olson, 1977).

TYPOLOGIES OF
MARITAL AND FAMILY SYSTEMS

Typologies of couples and families are a major breakthrough for the field because they help to bridge the gaps between research, theorizing, and practice. Typologies, whether developed empirically or intuitively (theoretically and clinically), offer numerous conceptual and methodological advantages over traditional variable analysis. Conceptually, they bridge research and practice because the focus is on couples and families rather than on variables. Methodologically, they pool the variance across variables and relate them to an actual couple or family type. The result is that typological studies are easier to translate directly and apply to couples and families.

Conceptually, the goals of typologies are to: (1) classify and describe couples and families rather than variables; (2) summarize numerous characteristics of all the cases within a particular type; (3) establish criteria which determines whether a couple or family fits within a particular type; and (4) distinguish and describe differences between types.

Methodologically, typologies enable an investigator to: (1) pool statistical variance, since a number of variables are uniquely related to each type; (2) empirically discover more stable and meaningful relationships between variables and types; and (3) translate the findings directly to couples and families rather than to variables.

Although typologies provide conceptual and methodological advantages to the family field, statistically the results are equivalent to those that would be obtained from traditional multivariate analysis. In a sense, typological and variable analyses are opposite sides of the same coin. The difference is whether the goal is to describe types of couples or families or to describe variables. One of the first psychologists to clearly demonstrate the value of the focus on the person rather than on variables was William Stephenson (1953), who developed the Q-sort technique. He clearly demonstrated the value of the "Q" analysis versus the traditional "R" factor analysis. Using couple data, Ryder (1964) also clearly demonstrated that profile factor analysis describing couples was statistically equivalent to the traditional factor analysis of variables.

Most of the past research and theorizing about families has focused on single variables or dimensions, such as power or marital satisfaction. This traditional approach of variable analysis is, first of all, conceptually limiting because it usually deals with individual scores rather than couple or family scores. Second, the analysis is limiting conceptually because the results are analyzed and reported in terms of variables rather than in terms of couples. Methodologically, the traditional single variable analysis usually does not utilize multivariate statistics which would pool sufficient variance. The result is that the findings may be statistically significant, but practically meaningless. If multivariate statistics were used, it would be possible to increase the value of the results, but it would still be more difficult to apply the results directly to couples and families.

Typologies and taxonomies have been used for decades in other scientific fields. In the life sciences, plants and animals are classified into families, genera, and species. The medical field has classified diseases by their unique combinations of symptoms. Geologists have described rocks, meteorologists have identified clouds, and astronomers have classified types of planets. In the more related field of psychology, personality types have been empirically identified by the MMPI.

In the last few years, there has been increasing interest among family scholars to identify types of marital and family systems. The major typologies have been developed intuitively and have suffered from one or more of the following problems: (1) criteria for classifying are not clearly specified; (2) procedures for assigning couples to types are subjective and ambiguous, with unknown reliability; (3) types are not exhaustive or mutually exclusive (Miller & Olson, Note 2).

Cuber and Haroff (1955) developed one of the first intuitively derived typologies of marriages based on interviews with higher status couples. Ryder (1970) developed a typography of husbands and wives regarding personality traits that emerged from condensed interview reports with 200 couples.

Kantor and Lehr (1975) developed a typology of families based on the concepts of open, closed, and random systems. Constantine (Note 3) has extended their four-player model into a more comprehensive and unified typology. Lewis et al. (1976) developed a descriptive analysis of dysfunctional, midrange, and healthy families.

Wertheim (1973) developed a typology based on three aspects of the morphogenesis-morphostatis dimension. She described eight types of family systems and these were related to the empirical types of families described by Reiss (1971).

The empirical approach to developing typologies of marital and family systems is becoming more popular because of recent developments in computer programs that do cluster analysis and small space analysis. Some of the first attempts to develop couples types empirically were done by Goodrich et al. (1968) and Ryder (1970), in which profile analysis was used to describe newly-wed couples. Shostrum and Kavanaugh (1971) used a self-report instrument to develop types of couples based on their scores on the dimensions of anger-love and strength-weakness. Moos and Moos (1976) developed a typology of families based on their Family Environment Scale. Using the Ravich Interpersonal Game-Test, Ravich and Wyden (1974) described eight types of marital interaction patterns.

Olson and his colleagues have been working for the past five years developing two different approaches to couple and family typologies, one empirical and the other theoretical. The empirical approach has focused on typologies of couples and families based on their verbal interaction patterns (Miller & Olson, Note 2). The interaction was generated by the Inventory of Marital Conflicts (Olson & Ryder, 1970) for couples. The theoretical typology is based on the Circumplex Model of Marital and Family Systems developed by Olson et al. (1979). Both of these typological approaches will be described in greater detail later in this chapter.

TYPOLOGIES OF
MARITAL AND FAMILY INTERACTION

Developing typologies of marital and family interaction is one way of building bridges between research and therapy. For the last decade, Olson and his colleagues have been developing marital and family interaction tasks that can be used to develop typologies. Historically, the first instrument developed was the Inventory of Marital Conflicts (IMC) developed by Olson and Ryder (1970). Since then, similar inventories have been developed for premarital couples, parent-child relationships, and parent-adolescent relationships.

The inventories were designed to generate dialogue among family members so that their styles of decision making and conflict resolution could be systematically investigated. In developing these inventories, the goal was to have situations that were *relevant* for different stages of the family life cycle. All the instruments follow the same "revealed difference format" (RDT) developed by Strodtbeck (1954). Therefore, the inventories could be used in longitudinal studies of marital and family development. The following inventories have been used in one or more studies:

Inventory of Premarital Conflict

Inventory of Marital Conflict

Inventory of Parent-Child Conflict

Inventory of Parent-Adolescent Conflict

A couple or family taking one of the inventories first completes a self-report portion individually. After they have completed this portion, they are given some items that they have disagreed on and are asked to discuss them and resolve their differences. They are usually given either 15 or 30 minutes to discuss these issues, and the interaction is either tape-recorded or video-taped so that it can later be coded.

Both self-report and interaction data can be obtained from the inventories. The self-report data provides information on the following variables: *relevance* of the items, *perceived conflict, authority patterns, predicted outcomes,* and *empathy.* The interaction data can be coded using a variety of coding systems. However, a Marital and Family Interaction Coding System (MFICS) was specifically developed by Olson and Ryder (Note 4) and has been most frequently used with these inventories. The three dimensions that consistently emerge from these codes are: Task Leadership, Conflict, and Affect.

Typologies of couples and families have been developed over the past five years from interaction data generated by these inventories. In the first project, 396 couples took the IMC as part of a marriage study directed by Ryder and Olson. Miller (Note 5) used cluster analysis to analyze this data and found nine distinct types of marital interaction patterns. Since that study, about ten related projects have been completed by Olson and his colleagues. A book is currently in progress that describes these projects in greater detail.

The process of developing typologies from these inventories has now been rather clearly established. First, the interaction data is coded using the MFICS coding system. Second, the interaction data is scored using a Computer Analysis Program (CAP; Olson et al., Note 6) which provides frequency and percentage data interrater and split-half reliability for every code. Third, the most reliable and frequent codes are factor analyzed, and the three consistent factors that emerge are Task Leadership, Conflict, and Affect. Cluster analysis is then used to determine the number of types that most adequately describes the data, and the types are described as they relate to each of the three dimensions and are given descriptive labels. The types are then related to the self-report variables from the IMC and other research scales used in the study. The final result is a description of the specific couple types and the unique characteristics of each of these types.

In order to illustrate these steps more clearly, the cluster analysis of 396 couples who took the IMC will be presented. A more detailed presentation of this research can be found elsewhere (Miller & Olson, Note 2). Table 5.2 illustrates the 13 most frequent and reliable codes from the MFICS coding system. The table also indicates the frequency, percentage, and interrater and

TABLE 5.2   IMC Factors, Frequency, Percentage, and Reliabilities: Abbreviated
Marital and Family Interaction Coding System (MFICS)

	H	Average Frequency W	Total	Average Percentage	Interrater Reliability	Split-Half Reliability
Task Leadership						
01 Initiation	12	6	18	8	.98	.90
11 Outcome Question	9	6	15	7	.85	.89
21 Reading	31	16	47	20	.97	.91
Conflict						
31 Self Disclosure	17	17	34	14	.96	.70
51 Outcome Agreement	13	15	28	12	.92	.64
61 Outcome Disagreement	3	3	6	3	.84	.55
62 Process Disagreement	1	1	2	1	.84	.42
34 Partisan Opinion	19	20	39	17	.89	.61
44 Reiteration	2	2	4	2	.68	.45
26 Relevant Information & Opinion	9	11	20	8	.95	.75
Affect						
04 Laughter	6	11	17	7	.94	.82
63 Disapproval of Spouse	1	1	2	1	.69	.74
64 Disapproval of Self	1	2	3	1	.90	.44
Total/Averages	124	111	235	100	.88	.68

NOTE: N = 396 couples who took the complete IMC and discussed all 18 items.

split-half reliabilities of these codes. The factor analysis revealed three primary factors and Table 5.2 indicates the variables that loaded in each factor.

In order to do the factor and cluster analysis, the Tryon and Bailey (1970) cluster analysis program (BC-TRY) was used. Although we have found that this program is very efficient and relatively easy to use, a variety of other cluster and small space analysis programs are currently available. The analysis indicated that nine groups or types of couples adequately described 97% of the sample. Only about 3%-4% of the couples were unique enough that they did not fit into any of the nine types.

Table 5.3 indicates the three dimensions and the nine types of couples discovered in this project. The three dimensions (factors) of Task Leadership, Conflict, and Affect are indicated, and three levels were assigned for each of these factors. A descriptive term was also developed to label the Conflict-Affect dimensions. A final typological name was then assigned to each of the nine types based on their scores on the three dimensions. The frequency and percentage of each of the nine marital interaction types are also listed, along with the z-score for each of the three dimensions.

TABLE 5.3 IMC Dimensions and Types

THREE DIMENSIONS (Factors)			
Cluster Scores	*I. TASK LEADERSHIP*	*II. CONFLICT*	*III. AFFECT*
High	Husband Leadership	High Conflict	High Affect
Medium	Shared Leadership	Moderate Conflict	Moderate Affect
Low	Wife Leadership	Low Conflict	Low Affect

COMBINED CONFLICT-AFFECT DIMENSIONS		
DESCRIPTION	*CONFLICT*	*AFFECT*
DISENGAGED	Low	Low
CONGENIAL	Low	Moderate
EXPRESSIVE	Low	High
RATIONAL	Moderate	Low
COOPERATIVE	Moderate	Moderate
ENGAGING	Moderate	High
COMPETITIVE	High	Low
CONFRONTIVE	High	Moderate
CONFLICTED	High	High

NINE IMC TYPES

Name	n	%
WIFE LED DISENGAGED Wife Leadership (34)*; Low Conflict (40); Low Affect (42)	43	10.8
WIFE LED CONGENIAL Wife Leadership (41); Low Conflict (43); Mod. Affect (53)	40	10.1
WIFE LED CONFRONTIVE Wife Leadership (34); High Conflict (63); Mod. Affect (53)	22	5.5
HUSBAND LED DISENGAGED Husband Leadership (55); Low Conflict (42); Low Affect (43)	75	18.9
SHARED LEADERSHIP COOPERATIVE Shared Leadership (50); Mod. Conflict (52); Mod. Affect (47)	47	11.8
HUSBAND LED ENGAGING Husband Leadership (55); Mod. Conflict (46); High Affect (61)	37	9.3
HUSBAND LED CONFRONTIVE Husband Leadership (57); High Conflict (65); Mod. Affect (47)	25	6.3
HUSBAND LED CONFLICTED Husband Leadership (56); High Conflict (65); High Affect (66)	20	5.5
HUSBAND LED COOPERATIVE Husband Leadership (59); Mod. Conflict (48); Mod. Affect (49)	72	18.1
UNIQUE COUPLES	15	3.7
TOTAL Couples	396	100.0

*Z-scores have a mean of 50 and standard deviation of 10 for each dimension.

This is an example of how typological analysis can be obtained from marital or family interaction data. The couple and family types can then be used related to other variables in order to form a more comprehensive and global picture of each couple/family type. A counselor's manual has also been developed (Bell & Olson, Note 7), which demonstrates how the inventories can be used in counseling situations.

In conclusion, developing typologies of marital and family interaction patterns facilitates the usefulness of the data for theory development and clinical work. But it also helps overcome some of the major research problems in dealing with interaction data. Most interaction studies end up with so much data that the investigator almost "gets buried" in the mass of information. Also, many interaction studies focus on the variables or on individuals and fail to develop a system for describing couples or families. The typological analysis provides an effective way for integrating self-report information and relating it to specific types of couples.

CIRCUMPLEX MODEL OF
MARITAL AND FAMILY SYSTEMS

A theoretically based typological approach specifically developed to bridge research, theory, and practice is the Circumplex Model of Marital and Family Systems (Olson et al., 1979). The Circumplex Model contains two central dimensions of *family adaptability* and *family cohesion* which emerged from a conceptual (rather than empirical) clustering of numerous concepts from family therapy and other social science fields. These two dimensions are placed at right angles to each other into a circumplex model. The model identifies 16 types of marital and family systems. A variety of diagnostic and research scales have been developed so that the model can be used in clinical and research settings.

Figure 5.1 illustrates the 16 types of marital and family systems, derived from the 4 levels of cohesion and adaptability. The Circumplex Model proposed that a *balanced level* (two central areas) of cohesion and adaptability are most functional to marital and family development. Marital and family systems that are extreme on *one* or *both* of the dimensions are hypothesized to have more individual and family problems.

To date, there are a number of studies completed and under way that are testing and further developing the Circumplex Model. A recent paper (Olson et al., 1980) reviews the empirical studies that demonstrate the importance of the two dimensions and validate the hypotheses derived from the model. Three empirical studies that demonstrate the construct validity of the model with

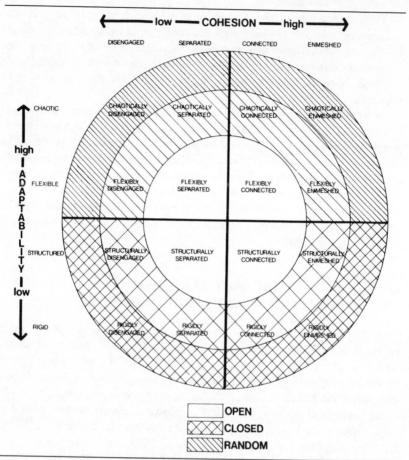

Figure 5.1   Sixteen Possible Types of Marital and Family Systems Derived
from the Circumplex Model

couples (Sprenkle & Olson, 1978), with family triads with an adolescent female
(Russell, 1979), and with families with a female status offender (Druckman,
1979) have been completed. Two other empirical studies investigated family
triads with an adolescent who had run away (Bell, Note 8) and family triads
with an adolescent in family treatment (Portner, Note 9), as compared with
control family triads. The clinical utility of the Circumplex Model with marital
and family systems with an alcoholic member is described in another paper
(Killorin & Olson, Note 10).

Clinical and research indicators have also been developed for each of the two
dimensions. The indicators for family cohesion are: emotional bonding, inde-

pendence, family boundaries, coalitions, time, space, friends, decision making, interest, and recreation. The indicators for family adaptability are: assertiveness, control, discipline, negotiations, roles, and rules.

In order to diagnose a couple or family on one of the 16 types, a variety of instruments have been developed. A self-report scale called FACES (Family Adaptability and Cohesion Evaluation Scales) was recently developed by Olson et al. (Note 11). FACES can be given either to couples (Couple Form) or to family members above the age of 12. For families with children below the age of 12, a Family Wellness Kit was developed (Olson, Note 12) with abbreviated 5-item scales for cohesion (togetherness) and adaptability (change). Also, a Clinical Rating Scale (Olson & Killorin, Note 13) has been developed which a counselor or researcher can use in conjunction with a family interview.

Since the primary purpose of the Circumplex Model is to integrate research, theory, and practice, a variety of clinical and research projects are under way to demonstrate the empirical and clinical utility of the hypotheses derived from the model. A recent paper (Olson et al., 1980) indicates in greater detail the current state of the model and the new hypotheses being investigated. It also reviews how the model applies to different stages of the family life cycle and to other social systems (departments, agencies, communes).

In conclusion, the Circumplex Model provides a theoretical typology of marital and family systems. This enables clinicians, researchers, and theorists to have a *common system* for *describing* couples and families. Applying the model to clinical settings facilitates the application of research and theory to real situations and facilitates the development of all three domains. It is hoped that the development of the Circumplex Model and other typologies will help advance the family profession by bridging research, theory, and practice, and improve our ability to serve couples and families.

REFERENCE NOTES

1. MEAD, M. Address to Orthopsychiatry Association, 1975.

2. MILLER, B., & OLSON, D. H. *Typology of marital interaction and contextual characteristics: Cluster analysis of the IMC.* Unpublished manuscript, University of Minnesota, 1978.

3. CONSTANTINE, L. *A unified system theory of human process.* Paper presented at Family Social Science, University of Minnesota, 1977.

4. OLSON, D. H., & RYDER, R. G. *Marital and Family Interacting Coding System (MFICS).* Unpublished manuscript, Family Social Science, University of Minnesota, 1972.

5. MILLER, B. C. *Types of marital interaction and their relation to contextual characteristics in the sample of young married couples.* Unpublished doctoral dissertation, University of Minnesota, 1975.

6. OLSON, D. H., WILSON, L., & MANGEN, D. *Computer Analysis Package (CAP) for the MFICS.* Unpublished manuscript, Family Social Science, University of Minnesota, 1978.

7. BELL, R. Q., & OLSON, D. H. *Clinical use of inventories of conflict.* Unpublished manuscript, Family Social Science, University of Minnesota, 1978.

8. BELL, R. Q. *Families with runaways: Interaction styles and test of the circumplex model.* Unpublished doctoral dissertation, University of Minnesota—St. Paul, 1981.

9. PORTNER, J. *Families in counseling: Interaction styles and test of the circumplex model.* Unpublished doctoral dissertation, University of Minnesota—St. Paul, 1980.

10. KILLORIN, E., & OLSON, D. H. *Clinical application of the circumplex model to chemically dependent families.* Unpublished manuscript, Family Social Science, University of Minnesota, 1980.

11. OLSON, D. H., BELL, R. Q., & PORTNER, J. *Family Adaptability and Cohesion Evaluation Scales* (FACES). Clinical and research instrument, Family Social Science, University of Minnesota, 1978.

12. OLSON, D. H. *Family Wellness Kit. Family Enrichment Tool.* Aid Association for Lutherans. Appleton, Wisconsin, 1979.

13. OLSON, D. H., & KILLORIN, E. *Clinical rating scales for circumplex model.* Family Social Science, University of Minnesota, 1980.

REFERENCES

CUBER, J. F., & HAROFF, P. B. *The significant Americans: A study of sexual behavior among the affluent.* Englewood Cliffs, NJ: Prentice-Hall, 1955.

DRUCKMAN, J. A family-oriented policy and treatment program for female juvenile status offenders. *Journal of Marriage and the Family,* 1979, *41,* 627-636.

GOODRICH, D. W., RYDER, R. G., & RAUSCH, H. L. Patterns of newlywed marriage. *Journal of Marriage and the Family,* 1968, *30,* 383-389.

KANTOR, D., & LEHR, W. *Inside the family.* San Francisco: Jossey-Bass, 1975.

LEWIS, J. M., BEAVERS, W. R., GOSSERT, J. T., & PHILLIPS, V. A. *No single thread: Psychological health in family systems.* New York: Brunner/Mazel, 1976.

MCGUIRE, W. J. Theory-oriented research in natural settings: The best of both worlds for social psychology. In M. Sherif & C. Sherif (Eds.), *Interdisciplinary relationships in the social sciences.* Chicago: Aldine, 1969.

MOOS, R., & MOOS, B. A typology of family social environments. *Family Process,* 1976, *15,* 357-371.

OLSON, D. H. Marital and family therapy: Integrative review and family critique. *Journal of Marriage and the Family,* 1970, *32,* 501-538.

OLSON, D. H. (Ed.). *Treating relationships.* Lake Mills, IA: Graphic Publishing, 1976.

OLSON, D. H. Insiders and outsiders view of relationships: Research studies. In G. Levinger & H. Rausch (Eds.), *Close relationships.* Amherst: University of Massachusetts Press, 1977.

OLSON, D. H., & CROMWELL, R. E. Methodological issues in family power. In R. E. Cromwell & D. H. Olson (Eds.), *Power in families.* New York: Halsted, 1975.

OLSON, D. H., & RABUNSKY, C. Validity of four measures of family power. *Journal of Marriage and the Family,* 1972, *34,* 224-234.

OLSON, D. H., RUSSELL, C. S., & SPRENKLE, D. H. Circumplex model of marital and family systems II: Empirical studies and clinical intervention. In J. P. Vincent (Ed.), *Advances in family intervention, assessment and theory* (Vol. 1). New York: 1980.

OLSON, D. H., & RYDER, R. G. Inventory of marital conflicts: An experimental interaction procedure. *Journal of Marriage and the Family,* 1970, *32,* 443-448.

OLSON, D. H., SPRENKLE, D. H., & RUSSELL, C. S. Circumplex model of marital and family systems I: Cohesion and adaptability dimensions, family types and clinical applications. *Family Process,* 1979, *18,* 3-28.

RAVICH, R., & WYDEN, B. *Predictable pairing.* New York: Wyden, 1974.

REISS, D. Varieties of consensual experience I: A theory for relating family interaction to individual thinking. *Family Process*, 1971, *10*, 1-27.

RILEY, M. W. Sources and types of sociological data. In R. E. L. Farris (Ed.), *Handbook of modern sociology*. Skokie, IL: Rand McNally, 1964.

RUSSELL, C. S. Circumplex model of marital and family systems III: Empirical evaluation with families. *Family Process*, 1979, *18*, 29-45.

RYDER, R. G. Profile factor analysis and variable factor analysis. *Psychological Reports*, 1964, *15*, 119-127.

RYDER, R. G. Dimensions of early marriage. *Family Process*, 1970, *9*, 51-68.

SHOSTRUM, E., & KAVANAUGH, J. *Between man and woman*. Los Angeles: Nash, 1971.

SPRENKLE, D. H., & OLSON, D. H. Circumplex model of marital systems: An empirical study of clinical and non-clinic couples. *Journal of Marriage and Family Counseling*, 1978, *4*, 59-74.

STEPHENSON, W. *The study of behavior*. Chicago: University of Chicago Press, 1953.

STRODTBECK, F. The family as a three person group. *American Sociological Review*, 1954, *19*, 23-29.

TRYON, R. C., & BAILEY, D. E. *Cluster analysis*. New York: McGraw-Hill, 1970.

WERTHEIM, E. Family unit therapy and the science and typology of family systems. *Family Process*, 1973, *12*, 361-376.

6

PRACTICAL APPLICATIONS OF
BEHAVIORAL MARITAL ASSESSMENT

Gayla Margolin

Behavioral marital therapy, with its foundation in experimental psychology, has promoted the use of standardized assessment procedures to understand intimate relationships. For the most part, assessment procedures have been used to identify processes that differentiate couples with satisfying relationships from those with dissatisfying relationships. Certain instruments also have been used as treatment outcome measures. Some procedures, while highly informative, have developed with seemingly little attention being paid to their clinical applicability. On the one hand, it is appropriate that the newer instruments not be subjected to widespread clinical application when evidence of their psychometric utility is still lacking. On the other hand, despite the demonstrated reliability and discriminative validity of certain instruments, they have remained within the purview of the researcher rather than the clinician.

This chapter considers the clinician's standpoint in the behavioral assessment of couples and describes assessment procedures that have been used primarily for research purposes but that show potential for clinical application as well. Attention also is paid to procedures that are highly familiar to the

AUTHOR'S NOTE: Preparation of this chapter was partially supported by Grant 1RO1 MH32616, awarded to the author by the National Institute of Mental Health. The author wishes to thank Andrew Christensen and Robert L. Weiss for their helpful comments on an earlier draft of this work.

clinician and are not behavioral in origin, but that can be used to foster the objectives of behavioral assessment. The organization of this chapter reflects two recent directions in the conceptualization of behavioral marital therapy, that is, the inclusion of principles from general systems theory and cognitive psychology (Birchler & Spinks, 1980; Jacobson, in press; Jacobson & Margolin, 1979; Margolin & Jacobson, in press; Weiss, 1978, 1980). Emphasis is placed on assessing relationships as systems, assessing spouses' cognitions about the relationship, and assessing the relationship between cognitions and behavior. After a brief consideration of issues surrounding the assessment of relationships from this framework, the impact of these conceptual advances for the practice of behavioral marital assessment will be explored.

One of the greatest challenges facing the marital therapist is that of translating the concept of a relationship *as a system* into a target for assessment. As articulated by Lederer and Jackson (1968, p. 188): "Marriage is a complex unity made of at least three different but interdependent systems; the system of the male, the system of the female and the marital system . . . [which] springs into being spontaneously when the systems of male and female join. It is a good example of the whole being *more* than the sum of its parts, of one plus one equaling three." To add to this already complex picture, the marital system exists in relation to other systems, such as the nuclear family, the extended family, and the community at large. The marital system also exists in relation to time; it evolves a learning history that is shared by both partners, and yet is also influenced by the experiences unique to each individual and other relationship systems of which each spouse has been a part.

Because of this concept of relationships as systems, it is difficult to employ standard ways for thinking about the functional analysis of behavior, that is, identifying the relationship between a specific behavior and environmental conditions that control the behavior. The partners in a marital relationship are constantly influencing and controlling one another in a continuous flow of interaction. Thus, it is both theoretically misleading and clinically inadvisable to attempt to understand the behavior of one member independently of the other, or to attribute singular causation to one person's behavior vis-à-vis the other (Jacobson & Margolin, 1979; Peterson, 1977).

Including the role of cognitions in behavioral assessment also poses challenges to the behavioral marital assessor. Since "relationship satisfaction" has long been recognized as a fundamental goal of behavioral marital assessment, it has been crucial to assess spouses' personal impressions of the marriage. Equally important to assess are the attitudes and expectations that spouses hold regarding marriage that serve as a reference point for judging satisfaction. Yet the difficulty arises in discerning how to assess cognitive processes without being vulnerable to the same criticisms that behaviorists are fond of raising in regard to traditional global self-report data.

A second important cognitive variable concerns spouses' ongoing processing of relationship information. A notable contribution of behavioral marital assessment in this regard has been the focus on the relationship between behavior and cognition. There has been increasing recognition that spouses' ongoing behavioral responses are not simply a mechanical or reflexive response. They reflect the manner in which spouses receive and input data from one another (Gottman et al., 1976; Weiss, 1978, 1980). This conceptualization leads to an expansion of the model of reciprocal behavioral influences between spouses to include how cognitions about oneself and one's partner mediate the ongoing, observable interaction.

Presented below is an overview of marital assessment measures that address these conceptual priorities and also are relevant to the clinician. Some of these instruments are well-established in the behavioral marital literature, while others represent more recent developments. Speculations presented on the clinical utility of these instruments are to be interpreted cautiously; in no instance is there adequate evidence of a demonstrated empirical relationship between assessment data and accurate predictions regarding clinical decision making. For a more comprehensive review of the psychometric properties of behavioral marital assessment procedures, the reader is referred to the following sources: Jacob (1975); Jacobson et al. (in press); Margolin and Jacobson (in press); Weiss and Margolin (1977).

THE COUPLE AS A SYSTEM

From the social learning perspective of marital interaction, it is much more important to identify characteristics of the relationship system per se than to analyze individual processes. Adopting a stance compatible with systems theory, the social learning approach is focused on the identification of recurrent interaction patterns that characterize the relationship (Margolin & Wampold, Note 1; Weiss, 1980). For the most part, these relationship transactions describe ways that partners exert either positive or negative behavioral control; that is, they represent transactions in which a variation in one partner's behavior reduces uncertainty about the other partner's behavior. The social learning perspective of marriage, based largely on social exchange theory, suggests that the relationship patterns develop because spouses strive toward parity between inputs and outputs of relationship benefits (or costs; Carson, 1969; Thibaut & Kelley, 1959). The more spouses tend toward an immediate response-contingent parity in their interaction, the more they demonstrate the predictability or "structural rigidity" that systems theorists associate with marital disturbance (Haley, 1964; Waxler & Mishler, 1970).

The assessment of the relationship as a system through the identification of recurrent transactions has evolved primarily through direct observation by the therapist during structured problem-solving tasks or during an interview. More recently developed procedures rely on the couple to provide information about relationship patterns that occur during their day-to-day interaction.

PROBLEM-SOLVING DISCUSSIONS

Based on the assumption that marital distress is largely of function of how couples interact rather than what content issues are particularly troublesome, social learning theorists have devoted a great deal of effort to developing procedures to describe couples' communication. The specific emphasis in social learning theory on how couples negotiate relationship change (Patterson et al., 1976; Weiss et al., 1973) has resulted in the application of observational procedures to time-limited problem-solving discussions. While the couple attempts to solve a problem that is troubling to their relationship, the discussion is videotaped for detailed coding at a later time. Specific instructions for these discussions range from the vague injunction, "Discuss this topic," to the more deliberate, "Discuss this topic as you would at home," or, "Attempt to resolve this problem to the best of your abilities." The two predominant systems which have evolved for coding couples' problem-solving discussions are the Marital Interaction Coding System (MICS; Hops et al., Note 2) and the Couples Interaction Scoring System (CISS; Gottman, 1979), which are discussed in Chapters 2 and 7 of this volume.

Although observational procedures were developed to explore couple interactions, simply examining behaviors exhibited by each individual in the company of the other does not fully capture this dimension (Gottman, 1979). The principal value of these coding systems for understanding relationship patterns comes from their representation of the ongoing sequential patterning of behavior. The application of sequential analyses to these data examines the degree of predictability in couples' interactions. The extent to which each spouse's behavior is affected by the other partner can be determined by examining shifts in the probability that a response will occur given that a particular stimulus has occurred (Gottman & Bakeman, 1979; Gottman & Notarius, 1978). With behavioral sequences as the primary unit of analysis, specific patterns of interaction, such as reciprocity, can be tested empirically. Sequential analysis of MICS and CISS data, for example, reveals that distressed couples are more likely than nondistressed couples to be characterized by the immediate reciprocity of negative behavior. Response-contingent positive reciprocity appears to characterize both distressed and nondistressed couples, but in a somewhat different temporal patterning (Gottman, 1979; Gottman et al., 1977; Margolin & Wampold, Note 1).

The clinical potential of sequential analysis is virtually untapped. The application of sequential analysis to pretreatment negotiation tapes could be used to identify idiosyncratic interactional patterns that demand attention during the course of therapy. Comparisons between pretherapy and posttherapy negotiation sessions could be used to evaluate whether treatment has successfully altered the patterning of communication, instead of the more prevalently examined question of whether the frequency of certain behaviors has changed. Yet, because observational coding systems such as the MICS and the CISS require substantial resources, including laboratory assistants and videotape equipment, they come under attack as impractical data collection procedures for most clinicians. To train and maintain a dedicated corps of observers is an arduous and time-consuming task, even under the best of circumstances. Gottman (1979), for example, estimates that it takes approximately 28 hours to transcribe and code each hour of videotape. Furthermore, sequential analyses of the data require access to and familiarty with a computer facility as well as resources to input the data into the computer. It is inconceivable for most clinicians to undertake these procedures.

Careful inspection reveals the difficulty with this type of assessment is not a function of the data collection aspects of the task but of the coding and the data analysis procedures. Engineering some facsimile of the problem-solving task with the intention of conducting a less systematized observation can be accomplished without any special equipment or facility. There is no evidence, for example, that the discussion would be hampered if the therapist simply were to remain in the room (as opposed to behind a one-way mirror) and directly observe (rather than videotape) the couple's interaction. Simultaneous audiotaping of the interaction would provide a means for playback to the couple or for comparisons across time. Furthermore, for therapists who do have access to videotape equipment, there now are services available to which tapes can be sent for coding and analysis, for example, through Weiss's Marital Studies Center.

Working from the assumption that obtaining samples of communication is more valuable than having the couple describe their interaction, the clinician has a variety of options available. Although infrequently reported in the clinical literature, research data indicate that audiotapes from home interaction promise to be a rich source of clinical material (Christensen, 1979; Gottman, 1979). The couple can be instructed to audiotape a time-limited negotiation session at home that can be listened to by the therapist alone or by the therapist and couple together in the next session. An alternative instruction is for the couple to audiotape any arguments that they have. This instruction tends to produce exceedingly realistic examples of how the couple express marital tensions. Or, as clinicians well know, it sometimes produces the paradoxical and clinically advantageous effect of the couple returning to the next therapy session and "apologizing" for not having any arguments.

Without the assistance of formal coding systems, the therapist is left to his or her own devices for identifying recurrent communication patterns. Seasoned clinicians from a variety of persuasions train themselves to identify patterns in couples' interaction, and listen to a couple's discussion with the following sorts of questions in mind: How does a constructive discussion turn into a destructive one, or vice versa? What determines whether a proposed solution is accepted or rejected? What happens when one partner starts lecturing? What provokes a pattern of one person talking incessantly while the other withdraws? How do the partners get sidetracked from the main topic? As these questions illustrate, it is not sufficient to know whether a certain behavior, such as withdrawal, occurs. The more important information comes from understanding the conditions that elicit the withdrawal, the effect produced by the withdrawal, and ways that the withdrawn person becomes reintegrated into the discussion.

THE CONJOINT INTERVIEW

An alternative and readily accessible way for the therapist to obtain observations of the couple as a system is during the conjoint interview. The types of observations available during the interview depend upon the extent to which the therapist structures the session as a time for information gathering versus active intervention. At the minimal level of direct intervention, the couple is allowed relatively free rein to describe why they have sought therapy while the therapist obtains a firsthand view of how the partners interact with one another, and how they present themselves to a third party. Who takes the lead? Do the spouses elaborate upon or refute one another's positions? What is the reaction when one partner becomes upset in the session? What does the silent partner do while the other speaks?

Even when the primary objective is that of observing, it is recommended that the therapist direct the process enough that the interview proceeds in an orderly fashion (Haley, 1976). For example, if one partner repeatedly interrupts the other, the therapist should let the interruption happen to observe it briefly. However, rather than let this continue unchecked, the therapist then should intervene, returning to the person first speaking, while also communicating that both partners will have ample time to express themselves. Similarly, if one person is reluctant to talk, the therapist may want to observe that pattern long enough to understand what it means for the marital system. However, by letting that pattern get too well established, the therapist communicates that she or he is interested only in one partner's point of view. To discover what intervention works best to increase the participation level of the quiet partner, the therapist might monitor the effects of several different attempted strategies, such as addressing questions directly to that person, asking him or her to comment upon what the other person has said, and reinforcing that person for speaking by expressing interest in what she or he has said. At this stage, there generally is no reason to comment upon or interpret these sorts of process observations as long as the therapist's actions convey interest and respect for each partner.

The intake interview situation also may be used to actively probe the couple's interaction with the objective of assessing the range and flexibility of the couple's response repertoire. Once the therapist has observed the couple's initial style of presentation, she or he may wish to test how readily the spouses can get beyond what is often a well-rehearsed, and typically unconstructive, interaction. The following probe, for example, might be used with the couple who quickly and repeatedly finds themselves in rapid-fire exchanges of accusations and criticisms:

> I've noticed that as soon as one of you starts making accusations, the other does the same. In fact, both of you appear quite expert at getting each other to retaliate. Regardless of who has the last word, I get the sense that you both end up feeling generally upset. Since this process doesn't seem to be getting anywhere, I'm going to ask you to try something that I imagine will be extremely difficult. I want you to continue to express your individual points of view, but to do so in a way that does not elicit a counterattack.

Since the therapist has already observed these partners' capabilities for provoking each other into verbal attacks, this intervention permits the assessment of the couple's capability for alternative transactions. While the therapist has indicated a desired outcome, that is, refraining from repetitive arguments, there has been no instruction as to how this might be accomplished. Thus, compliance with this respect would indicate the spouses' abilities to state concerns in a more constructive manner and their awareness of how they contribute to this pattern of accusations and counteraccusations.

Some direct probes, even at the stage of the initial evaluation, have direct implications for the couple's responsiveness to later therapeutic interventions. In the previous example, the couple's cooperation with the directive to interact in a less hurtful manner is indicative of their willingness to cooperate with the therapist as well as to interact with one another in a more understanding and/or collaborative fashion. While cooperation and collaboration certainly are not expected at this beginning stage of therapy (Jacobson & Margolin, 1979; Weiss, 1980), it is important for the therapist to assess the extent to which these issues need to be dealt with in therapy.

Additionally, some intake interviews also provide the opportunity to observe a couple's reaction to a cognitive reframe, that is, a reinterpretation of an undesirable behavior that offers a more affirmative perspective on the relationship, even though the behavior itself still is objectionable. The couple's acceptance or rejection of these reframes may be indicative of their willingness to entertain alternative, more positive ways of viewing the relationship. As suggested by Weiss (1980, p. 42), "If a couple fails to respond to such probes—that is, the spouses are unable to give up their cassette long enough to consider these possibilities—one must question whether the point of contact has more to do with blame assignment than a mutually focused outcome."

While interviews provide an excellent opportunity to observe the couple, impressions formulated from this data base must be viewed as highly specific to the situation. The couple's presentation is, of course, influenced by their expectations of what occurs in therapy and their perceptions of the demand characteristics of the situation. More importantly, the couple's interaction as a system is influenced by the therapist's presence. As systems therapists accurately note, the therapist is an acting and reacting member of the therapeutic system (Haley, 1976; Minuchin, 1974). What occurs in the therapeutic situation is actually a three-way interaction process, with each individual affecting the other two and with a reciprocal influence also occurring between the therapist and the marital system. Possible recurrent patterns shown by the couple vis-à-vis the therapist that would influence the intitial intervention include the following: (a) The spouses join together to effectively reject the therapist's directives, that is, just when one partner is ready to comply the other is not. By alternating roles in this process the spouses work together to keep the therapist at a distance. (b) An individual spouse attempts to establish a close relationship with the therapist to the exclusion of his/her partner ("Maybe if I could just tell you a few things alone . . ."). (c) The couple is willing to adopt the framework proposed by therapist, thereby forming a three-way working relationship.

It is equally important to note that the therapist is not immune from the process of mutual influence. The therapist's task as an observer in the interview is inherently difficult due to the demands of simultaneously being an active participant. Additionally, the therapist's objectivity in this situation may be influenced by personal reactions, including the degree to which she or he likes the couple, feels competent about the way the interview has gone, and detects a similarity between what the couple presents and what has occurred in the therapist's own relationships. Obviously the therapist considers these reciprocal influences between himself or herself and the couple in formulating any clinical impressions based on the interview.

SPOUSE TRACKING

The spouses themselves are an alternative resource for obtaining descriptions of couple transactions, particularly in view of the large number of interactions pertinent to intimate relationships that are unlikely to occur during the therapy session or in the presence of an observer. However, having spouses provide information regarding their relationship as a system may require training the couple to think in terms of transactions rather than in terms of individual behaviors. As Weiss (1980) noted, relationship transactions can occur quite independently of how they are cognitively perceived. Two relatively new procedures that have been designed to assist couples in the daily tracking of significant relationship transactions are described below.

Interaction Record (IR). Peterson (1979) has translated a sophisticated paradigm for viewing interpersonal behavior into the IR, an easily administered but comprehensive analysis of critical incidents. Spouses independently use the IR to identify the most important interaction that occurred that day. They are to describe: (a) the conditions under which the exchange took place, including setting and feelings; (b) how the interaction started; and (c) what happened from start to finish, including actions, emotions, cognitions, and outcomes. These records are then coded in terms of *affect* ("I hate you"), *construal* ("I think it was your fault that our bank account is overdrawn"), and *expectations* that each partner held in regard to the subsequent response of the other. To interpret these records, each interaction is broken down into major "acts," with any pair of adjoining acts called an interaction cycle; these cycles represent interaction patterns, such as enjoyment, support, conflict, retaliation, affection, cooperation, or conciliation. From Peterson's description, reliable coding of the records seems to occur with relatively little formal training. Peterson (1979) reports that the IR has been used clinically by himself and his students for several years. Although the details of how the IR can be used clinically are not provided, it appears that these records could be readily utilized to: (a) identify recurrent interaction patterns that constitute either relationship problems or strengths; (b) offer direction as to whether the target for treatment should be the actions, construals, affect, or some combination of these; and (c) provide a basis, albeit subjective, for evaluating the effects of therapy.

Daily Behavior Report (DBR). The DBR, designed by Christensen and Margolin (Note 3), examines two types of relationship transactions: occasions of tensions and central relationship problems. Since this instrument was designed to assess the entire family system, it conveys information about individual family members and family subsystems (Margolin, in press b). While the DBR could be used to record only couple information, it has the advantage of describing the couple relationship vis-à-vis other family transactions, such as parent-child or sibling interactions. The first part of the inventory is designed for the sequential recording of incidents of family tensions. Before beginning to record this information, the therapist and family identify the most common ways that tension is expressed between family members in this particular household. The following information then is obtained for each incident of tension: What family members were involved? Were these persons active participants or uninvolved observers? Was there an initiator? Events are coded to permit the examination of temporal patterning, for instance: During what times of the day are tensions likely to occur? Do marital tensions tend to precede or follow parent-child tensions?

The second part of the inventory is designed for tracking behaviors that, due to their occurrence or nonoccurrence, affect the quality of the relationship. While the specific behaviors chosen are idiosyncratic to a family, some common examples include having sex, sharing feelings, and refusing to answer a question. The format of the DBR allows for a great deal of flexibility in defining central relationship concerns as well as more structured and sequential analysis of family tensions. It requires some practice on the part of the family member who is primarily responsible for reporting. The reliability and validity of this instrument are as yet undetermined.

Behavioral tracking procedures typically are designed to collect information on one or more target behaviors through highly individualized data collection procedures. The IR and DBR, in contrast, elicit data through relatively standardized procedures on a *type* or *class* of couple transactions—"important interactions" for the IR and "occasions of tension" in the DBR. The format of each instrument permits sequential analysis of behavioral transactions and considers such transactions in a larger context. That is, the IR considers behavior in the context of construal, affect, and expectation, while the DBR considers the couple's tension events within the context of the entire family system.

As all marital therapists know, to intervene effectively with couples it is important to disrupt the destructive, repetitive patterns that are a product of long-term mutual shaping. As stated in greater detail elsewhere (Margolin & Jacobson, in press; Margolin & Wampold, Note 1), sequential analysis is one vehicle for exploring these patterns and for providing a truly interactive picture of how spouses respond to one another. Thus far, formal application of sequential analysis occurred on a microanalysis level, exploring couples' moment-by-moment communications during standardized problem-solving tasks (Gottman et al., 1976; Gottman et al., 1977; Margolin & Wampold, Note 1). While there is a tremendous amount to be gained by this approach, the level of analysis employed in these studies is limited by (a) its unavailability to the clinician, and (b) the undetermined ecological validity of these data, that is, whether they are representative of naturalistic data and whether or not they correspond to a couple's eventual handling of a conflictual issue are still in question (Margolin & Jacobson, in press). Perhaps as more is discovered about couples' interactions in general and about the validity of these systems and their individual code categories, recommendations will emerge for examining couples' interactions that are more responsive to the needs of the clinician.

In the meantime, it is of equal importance to examine sequential patterning in more extended relationship transactions, such as cycles of fighting-intimacy-fighting, and the like, that consitute chains of behavior that evolve over hours, days, or perhaps weeks. These make up the material that clinicians are most likely to embrace. The newer assessment procedures such as the IR and DBR, which rely on spouse tracking, have been designed for the evaluation of long-standing, perpetuating relationship cycles. The seeming advantages of these measurement procedures for the clinician are that they: (a) are inexpensive and easy to administer, (b) require minimal experience to interpret, (c) provide important data for planning and evaluating therapy, and (d) permit repeated measurements across the duration of therapy. Since these recording procedures involve subjectivity on the part of the reporter, there is the advantage of providing access to covert processes but a potential disadvantage in terms of obtaining accurate data. From a therapeutic standpoint, these procedures begin to train the couple to think in terms of dyadic transactions, which may be useful preparation for a therapeutic intervention designed to alter the marital system rather than the individuals.

THE RELATIONSHIP BETWEEN OVERT AND COVERT BEHAVIORS

Although behavioral marital assessment emphasizes the direct observation of behavior, it also attends to the mutual regulation between overt and covert events. Certainly there are times when the conclusions that spouses draw from the partner's behavior, rather than the behavior itself, constitute the primary problem. An exciting direction of behavioral marital assessment has been taken in the recent attempts to define the interface between overt and covert behavior. The following questions emerge from an assumption of circular causality between external and internal processes: (a) How do spouses' interpretations and attributions influence the way they process behavior? (Gottman et al., 1976; Jacobson & Margolin, 1979; Weiss, 1978.) (b) What behaviors increase or decrease marital satisfactions? (Weiss & Margolin, 1977.) Several procedures that address these questions are described below.

ONGOING SPOUSE RATINGS

The problem-solving discussions described previously have been rated by the spouses themselves to assess the attributions and personalized meanings that spouses assign to their interactions, and that are unavailable to outside observers. Having spouses code what they subjectively experience during a discussion provides a metacommunicative perspective on "how I see myself" and "how I see you in relation to me" (Knudson et al., 1980; Watzlawick et al., 1967). Since these personal interpretations reflect the way that spouses process behavior, they serve as important links in understanding the ongoing chain of observable behavior.

Gottman and his associates (Gottman et al., 1976) utilized a "talk table" which allowed spouses to code ongoing communication along a 5-point Likert scale from supernegative to superpositive. As each spouse finished speaking, the listener rated the *impact* of the message received while the speaker rated the *intent* of the message sent. Research findings on these measurement procedures have shown that impact, but not intent, ratings (a) differentiate distressed and nondistressed couples (Gottman et al., 1976), and (b) are predictive of relationship satisfaction at a 2½-year follow-up (Markman, 1979).

Margolin and Weiss (1978) describe a similar electromechanical system designed to help facilitate constructive communication and to evaluate the effectiveness of communication training. This system was constructed so that spouses can either record their perceptions of communication helpfulness during assessment stages, or signal one another on the occurrence of helpfulness during the intervention phase.

These sorts of cuing and recording procedures circumvent the tendency by behavioral marital therapists to make a priori assumptions about what behaviors are facilitative or destructive to a couple's communication. These procedures entail having spouses operationally define for themselves and one another what they find helpful in a problem-oriented discussion, helping spouses become careful observers of those behaviors, and structuring a way for them to give positive feedback to one another on the occurrence of these behaviors during the intervention phase. Even without electromechanical procedures, clinicians can utilize this general format for communication assessment and training by having spouses listen to and rate audio tapes of their problem-solving discussions, examining agreements and disagreements in the spouses' perceptions, and using this information to identify and train new communication behaviors.

SPOUSE OBSERVATION CHECKLIST

The question noted above, regarding the types of behaviors that increase or decrease marital satisfaction, has received substantial attention through the Spouse Observation Checklist (SOC; Patterson, 1976; Weiss & Perry, Note 4). The SOC, which is one of the most versatile instruments available to the marital therapist, was designed to provide a behavioral accounting of the types of activities that spouses engage in that have a positive or negative impact on the relationship. As such, the SOC is an extremely comprehensive listing, made up of 400 relationship events ranging across the following categories: Companionship, Affection, Consideration, Sex, Communication Process, Coupling Activities, Household Management, Financial Decision Making, Child Care and Parenting, Employment-Education, Personal Habits, and Self-and-Spouse Independence. Spouses are to complete the SOC before retiring each night, reading through the entire inventory and placing checkmarks to indicate what items occurred during the previous 24 hours. Spouses are also instructed to indicate their satisfaction with the relationship for that day by marking a 9-point scale which ranges from 1 (totally dissatisfied) to 9 (totally satisfied).

One of the most innovative uses of the SOC has been to examine the effects that specific behaviors have on overall marital satisfaction. This important question has been explored by measuring the degree of association between fluctuations in the daily satisfaction rating and the daily totals for each of the SOC categories. Three studies that have examined this relationship (Jacobson, et al., 1980; Margolin, in press a; Wills et al., 1974) suggest that there is some similarity across individuals regarding the association between types of behavior and general satisfaction: It has been found, for example, that the satisfaction ratings of distressed couples, compared with nondistressed couples, are more strongly influenced by the occurrence of displeases. Yet there also is substantial variation across individuals (Jacobson & Margolin, 1979). Through examination of these relationships for each spouse, the clinician and couple learn what types of behavior affect daily satisfaction. For example, while the wife's satisfaction may be highly dependent upon displays of physical affection, the husband's satisfaction may be associated with spending time in shared activities. These relationships may be circular in that the couple is more likely to engage in physical affection or shared activities during times that they feel relatively content with the relationship. Still, there is much to be gained by this knowledge in terms of planning a treatment that capitalizes on the types of behaviors that are likely to correspond with marital happiness.

Overall, the SOC is an invaluable tool for the clinician. It is unequaled by any other one instrument in terms of providing information that spans many domains of interaction and indicating how these dimensions differently affect satisfaction over time. Without any sophisticated interpretation, the therapist can readily perceive the absence of certain desirable behaviors and the presence of undesirable behaviors, which provide important information for launching and evaluating an intervention. Although time consuming for couples to complete, it introduces them to the behavioral approach and encourages them to operationalize vague relationship impressions. Yet, a note of caution is in order: Although originally designed as a behavioral observation measure, recent studies suggest that SOC data are subject to selective tracking (Christensen & Nies, 1980; Robinson & Price, 1980). Thus, it has been recommended that the therapist treat these data as a measurement of the subjective, rather than objective, reality of a couple's world (Jacobson et al., in press; Margolin & Jacobson, in press).

MARITAL SATISFACTION TIME LINE (MSTL)

The MSTL, developed by Williams (1979), has an objective similar to the SOC in terms of identifying what types of behaviors influence spouses' ratings of their time together. However, in contrast to the SOC, spouses using the MSTL rate quality of time for every 15-minute segment rather than an entire day, and then identify behaviors that they believe to have influenced their satisfaction, rather than indicate all behaviors that have occurred. To use the MSTL, spouses independently rate each quarter-hour segment as positive, neutral, or unpleasant. Spouses also indicate the most pleasant and least pleasant behaviors that occurred during the morning, afternoon, and evening, and that influenced their ratings for these time periods. Although the rating scale of the MSTL is interactional, the identification of behavior focuses on the partner rather than the couple as a system. Unfortunately, the equally pertinent questions, "What about your own behavior (or about your joint interaction) made the time more pleasant?" are absent. Although Williams primarily reports findings that compare happily and unhappily married couples' responses on this scale, it is clear that the MSTL produces qualitative data that could be of great value to the clinician. This instrument helps couples identify what behaviors have either been *committed* or *omitted* that influence quality ratings. For purposes of treatment planning, it differentiates between couples who are maritally distressed due to an excess of negative exchanges and those who are distressed due to a deficit of positive exchanges. It also differentiates between negative reactions that are related to specific behaviors and those that are responses to the very presence of the partner. Although not yet used as a therapy outcome measure, it might provide answers to a number of important questions: Does the number or length of negative interaction time segments decrease? Do partners attribute positive experiences to the occurrence of positive behavior or the nonoccurrence of negative behavior? What is the degree of reciprocity in spouses' positive and negative interactions?

ANGER CHECKLIST (AN)

The AN (Margolin et al., Note 5) was designed primarily as a clinical assessment aid to be used with couples whose relationships were deteriorating due to excessive expressions of physically and emotionally damaging anger. In contrast to the SOC and the MSTL, which examine behavior related to overall marital satisfaction, the AN was constructed to monitor overt and covert processes that are associated with the subjective experience of anger, particularly that which is directed towards one's partner. The checklist contains specific anger reactions, such as Somatic Cues (clenched jaw, rush of adrenalin), Feelings (hurt, numb), Actions (pacing, breaking objects), Thoughts ("You're wrong"), and Words (name calling, accusations). Spouses record each incident of anger by checking each reaction that they observed in themselves or their partners. They also describe the setting (location, time, and persons present). This inventory is still in a formative stage, but it appears to be useful in making spouses aware of the multiple components of their own anger and in helping them to become careful observers of how anger escalates between the two partners. This information can be used to help spouses develop ways to cope with anger that are constructive rather than destructive to the relationship (Margolin, 1979).

In sum, the importance of the instruments just reviewed is evidenced in criticism previously directed to behavioral marital therapy for paying insufficient attention to the mutual regulation of cognitions, affect, and behavior (Gurman & Knudson, 1978). One can assume too quickly that a behavior is dysfunctional instead of inquiring into the meaning of the behavior and the affective response it elicits. The laboratory-based spouse ratings of behavior sequences during problem-solving discussions provide one very promising procedure for identifying ongoing perceptions regarding one's own and one's partner's behavior. This type of procedure could also be expanded to have spouses comment upon their affective and cognitive reactions rather than just rate the behavior (Knudson et al., 1980; Peterson, 1977). The SOC, MSTL, and AN provide data on a more molar scale regarding behaviors at home that are associated with fluctuations in marital satisfaction or the more specific reaction of anger. These instruments tend to capture the clients' interest with their face validity and engage couples in the process of examining the relationship between overt and covert behaviors. Although the accuracy of these data is subject to the same problems that plague all self-report instruments, these procedures are designed for the repeated measurement of prospective, ongoing events, rather than global, retrospective impressions. Furthermore, each of these procedures can serve the dual functions of assessment and training. Their utility as outcome measures tends to be compromised by their potential for reactivity and by the fact that they often are employed as part of an intervention. Still, the data they provide on the impact and meaning of behavior is crucial for identifying appropriate targets for change and for increasing spouses' awareness of the complex interactions among thoughts, feelings, and behaviors.

OVERALL RELATIONSHIP IMPRESSIONS

Since the social learning model adopts a largely idiosyncratic stance toward a couple's attempt to form and maintain a satisfying relationship (Jacobson, in press), spouses' individualized impressions of the relationship have been valued both as an outcome criterion and for treatment planning. Rapport building between therapist and clients depends to a large extent on the therapist's ability to communicate his or her understanding of the partners' accumulated subjective experiences in the relationship. This understanding may also foster a clearer appreciation of the appropriateness of marital therapy versus separation counseling. The instruments described below offer ways to obtain information of the sort to complement what is gathered through a conjoint interview.

MARITAL ADJUSTMENT SCALE (MAS) AND DYADIC ADJUSTMENT SCALE (DAS)

The MAS (Locke & Wallace, 1959) and DAS (Spanier, 1976) are two widely used self-report questionnaires that have largely overlapping pools of items. They are primarily used to provide overall indices of satisfaction: The scores obtained on these measures tend to be stable over time and can be compared to well-established norms. The questionnaires also provide interesting subjective impressions, such as whether a spouse would remarry the same person if she or he had to make the choice again.

AREAS OF CHANGE QUESTIONNAIRE (AC)

The AC (Patterson, 1976; Weiss & Perry, Note 4) is a self-report questionnaire that focuses on the spouses' perceptions of current strengths and weaknesses in the relationship. The questionnaire contains 34 specific areas of interaction, such as decision making about finances, time spent with relatives, and frequency of sex. Each spouse first indicates whether she or he wants the partner to increase, decrease, or not change the rate of each behavior. Repeating the same set of items, the respondent then indicates his or her impressions of how much change the spouse wants in each area. The instrument has been hailed for its behavioral specificity, although its relationship to actual frequencies of specific behaviors is still to be determined (Margolin & Jacobson, in press). The summary score it provides appears to be a valid index of global marital satisfaction, similar to the DAS and MAS, and data on individual items can be used to speculate about possible behavioral targets.

MARITAL PRECOUNSELING INVENTORY (MPI)

Stuart and Stuart (1972) developed the exceptionally comprehensive MPI to assess a variety of specific dimensions and general impressions of a relationship. This instrument was designed to provide: (a) socialization into the therapy process by directing clients' observations to positive elements of their own and their spouses' behaviors; (b) information relevant to the setting of therapeutic goals; and (c) a vehicle for periodic evaluation. The 13 separate sections of the MPI focus spouses' attention on the operationalization of their objectives for therapy. As such it is particularly useful for the clients and therapist in preparing for the beginning of the counseling process. Features that set this inventory apart from instruments previously described include: its multidimensional view of relationships; the focus on personal goals and personal strengths, as well as the more typical focus on the partner's behavior; its attention to situation specificity and situation control; and its emphasis on positive relationship aspects.

In sum, while the self-report questionnaires reviewed above are susceptible to the same demand characteristics and social desirability factors as traditional modes of marital assessment, they serve an important role in the assessment of behavioral marital therapists. They are currently viewed as instruments of choice to evaluate the global construct of marital "satisfaction" or "adjustment." As such, they are also consistent choices for easily administered, inexpensive outcome measurements. While the secondary purpose of these instruments, particularly the AC and MPI, is to identify intervention targets, prudent clinical practice would be not to draw firm conclusions from these data but to use the information as a basis for formulating tentative hypotheses.

SUMMARY AND RECOMMENDATIONS

While not an exhaustive review of standardized procedures in behavioral marital assessment, this chapter presents a considerable array of options for

assessing marital relationships. As with psychological assessment more generally, there exists a large variety of possible assessment procedures with a few
guidelines for selecting among them. It is recommended that methodological,
practical, and conceptual considerations all be taken into account in deciding
upon an assessment strategy. Methodologically, it is important to obtain data
from multiple situations, settings, and observers. Aside from the obvious reasons for this recommendation, that relationships involve more than one person
and occur across a variety of situations, recent data suggest persons' concepts of
marital adjustment are multidimensional (Margolin, 1978).

Practical and conceptual considerations dictate that there must be an integration between what is to be gained from assessment procedures and the clinicians' framework for understanding and intervening with couples. Certainly the
manner in which a clinician conceptualizes relationship problems places
boundaries around the types of interventions that she or he is likely to engage in
with couples. An assessment procedure that produces data that are foreign to
the clinician's way of understanding couples, or that simply reiterates what the
clinician already knows about the case, does not enhance the clinician's
decision-making process. To be of value, the assessment data must fit well
enough within the clinician's general conceptual framework to alter the manner
in which she or he approaches the case.

The assessment procedures presented here stem from a framework that
views relationship problems as a function of faulty interactional patterns that
can develop between intimate partners, misinterpretations and misattributions
in the way spouses view behavior, and the mutual regulation between behavioral and cognitive processes. For many of the instruments, discriminant validity has been demonstrated by differentiating between satisfied and dissatisfied
couples along one or more of these dimensions. However, statements regarding
the clinical utility of the procedures must wait for empirical verification that
they can be used to make accurate predictions regarding the assignment of
couples to different intervention strategies. This criterion translates into the
following types of questions: What does information from a particular assessment procedure indicate for the therapist intervention? How does the clinician
combine information from different data collection modalities to determine the
essential treatment components as well as effective ordering of those components? In the absence of answers to questions such as these regarding the
interpretation and combination of data, even the most sophisticated assessment
procedures cannot be used successfully in clinical decision making. To obtain
answers to these questions requires more widespread use of the assessment
procedures, systematic collection of information on the relationship between
assessment data and clinical outcomes, and the application of that information
to develop an empirical basis for future clinical decision.

REFERENCE NOTES

1. MARGOLIN, G., & WAMPOLD, B. E. *A sequential analysis of conflict and accord in distressed and nondistressed marital partners.* Paper presented at the meetings of the Western Psychological Association, Honolulu, 1980.

2. HOPS, H., WILLS, T. A., PATTERSON, G. R., & WEISS, R. L. *Marital interaction coding system.* Unpublished manuscript, University of Oregon and Oregon Research Institute, 1972.

3. CHRISTENSEN, A., & MARGOLIN, G. *Investigation and treatment of multi-problem families.* Unpublished manuscript, University of California, Los Angeles and University of Southern California, 1979.

4. WEISS, R. L., & PERRY, B. A. *Assessment and treatment of marital dysfunction.* Unpublished manuscript, University of Oregon, 1979.

5. MARGOLIN, G., OLKIN, R., & BAUM, M. *The anger checklist.* Unpublished inventory, University of California, Santa Barbara, 1977.

REFERENCES

BIRCHLER, G. R., & SPINKS, S. H. Behavioral-systems marital and family therapy: Integration and clinical application. *American Journal of Family Therapy,* 1980, *8,* 6-28.

CARSON, R. C. *Interaction concepts of personality.* Chicago: Aldine, 1969.

CHRISTENSEN, A. Naturalistic observation of families: A system for random audio recordings in the home. *Behavior Therapy,* 1979, *10,* 418-422.

CHRISTENSEN, A., & NIES, D. C. The spouse observation checklist: Empirical analysis and critique. *American Journal of Family Therapy,* 1980, *8,* 69-79.

GOTTMAN, J. M. *Marital interaction: Experimental investigations.* New York: Academic, 1979.

GOTTMAN, J. M., & BAKEMAN, R. The sequential analysis of observational data. In M. E. Lamb, S. J. Suomi, & G. R. Stephenson (Eds.), *Social interaction methodology.* Madison: University of Wisconsin Press, 1979.

GOTTMAN, J., MARKMAN, H., & NOTARIUS, C. The topography of marital conflict: A sequential analysis of verbal and nonverbal behavior. *Journal of Marriage and the Family,* 1977, *39,* 461-477.

GOTTMAN, J. M., & NOTARIUS, C. Sequential analysis of observational data using Markov chains. In T. Kratochwill (Ed.), *Strategies to evaluate change in single subject research.* New York: Academic, 1978.

GOTTMAN, J., NOTARIUS, C., MARKMAN, H., BANK, S., YOPPI, B., & RUBIN, M. E. Behavior exchange theory and marital decision making. *Journal of Personality and Social Psychology,* 1976, *34,* 14-23.

GURMAN, A. S., & KNUDSON, R. M. Behavioral marriage therapy I: A psychodynamic-systems analysis and critique. *Family Process,* 1978, *17,* 121-138.

HALEY, J. Research on family patterns: An instrument measurement. *Family Process,* 1964, *3,* 41-65.

HALEY, J. *Problem solving therapy.* San Francisco: Jossey-Bass, 1976.

JACOB, T. Family interaction in disturbed and normal families: A methodological and substantive review. *Psychological Bulletin,* 1975, *82,* 33-65.

JACOBSON, N. S. Behavioral marital therapy. In A. S. GURMAN & D. P. KNISKERN (Eds.), *Handbook of family therapy.* New York: Brunner/Mazel, in press.

JACOBSON, N. S., ELLWOOD, R., & DALLAS, M. The behavioral assessment of marital dysfunction. In D. H. Barlow (Ed.), *Behavioral assessment of adult disorders*. New York: Gilford, in press.

JACOBSON, N. S., & MARGOLIN, G. *Marital therapy: Strategies based on social learning and behavior exchange principles*. New York: Brunner/Mazel, 1979.

JACOBSON, N. S., WALDRON, H., & MOORE, D. Toward a behavioral profile of marital distress. *Journal of Consulting and Clinical Psychology*, 1980, *48*, 696-703.

KNUDSON, R. M., SOMMERS, A. A., & GOLDING, S. L. Interpersonal perception and mode of resolution in marital conflict. *Journal of Personality and Social Psychology*, 1980, *38*, 751-763.

LEDERER, W. J., & JACKSON, D. D. *Mirages of marriage*. New York: Norton, 1968.

LOCKE, H. J., & WALLACE, K. M. Short-term marital adjustment and prediction tests: Their reliability and validity. *Journal of Marriage and Family Living*, 1959, *21*, 251-255.

MARGOLIN, G. The relationship among marital assessment procedures: A correlational study. *Journal of Counseling and Clinical Psychology*, 1978, *46*, 1556-1558.

MARGOLIN, G. Conjoint marital therapy to enhance anger management and reduce spouse abuse. *American Journal of Family Therapy*, 1979, *7*, 13-23.

MARGOLIN, G. Behavior exchange in distressed and nondistressed marriages: A family cycle perspective. *Behavior Therapy*, in press. (a)

MARGOLIN, G. The reciprocal relationship between marital and child problems. In J. P. Vincent (Ed.), *Advances in family intervention, assessment and theory: An annual compilation of research* (Vol. 2). Greenwich, CT: Jai, in press. (b)

MARGOLIN, G., & JACOBSON, N. S. The assessment of marital dysfunction. In M. Hersen & A. S. Bellack (Eds.), *Behavioral assessment: A practical handbook*. New York: Pergamon, in press.

MARGOLIN, G., & WEISS, R. L. Communication training and assessment: A case of behavioral marital enrichment. *Behavior Therapy*, 1978, *9*, 508-520.

MARKMAN, H. J. Application of a behavioral model of marriage in predicting relationship satisfaction of couples planning marriage. *Journal of Consulting and Clinical Psychology*, 1979, *47*, 743-749.

MINUCHIN, S. *Families and family therapy*. Cambridge, MA: Harvard University Press, 1974.

PATTERSON, G. R. Some procedures for assessing changes in marital interaction patterns. *Oregon Research Institute Bulletin*, 1976, *16*(7).

PATTERSON, G. R., WEISS, R. L., & HOPS, H. Training of marital skills: Some problems and concepts. In H. Leitenberg (Ed.), *Handbook of behavior modification*. Englewood Cliffs, NJ: Prentice-Hall, 1976.

PETERSON, D. R. A functional approach to the study of person-person interactions. In D. Magnusson & N. S. Endler (Eds.), *Personality at the crossroads: Current issues in interactional psychology*. Hillsdale, NJ: Lawrence-Erlbaum, 1977.

PETERSON, D. R. Assessing interpersonal relationships by means of interaction records. *Behavioral Assessment*, 1979, *1*, 221-236.

ROBINSON, E. A., & PRICE, M. G. Pleasurable behavior in marital interaction: An observational study. *Journal of Consulting and Clinical Psychology*, 1980, *48*, 117-118.

SPANIER, G. B. Measuring dyadic adjustment: New scales for assessing the quality of marriage and similar dyads. *Journal of Marriage and the Family*, 1976, *38*, 15-28.

STUART, R. B., & STUART, F. *Marital pre-counseling inventory*. Champaign, IL: Research Press, 1972.

THIBAUT, J. W., & KELLEY, H. H. *The social psychology of groups*. New York: John Wiley, 1959.

WATZLAWICK, P., BEAVIN, J. H., & JACKSON, D. D. *Pragmatics of human communication*. New York: Norton, 1967.

WAXLER, N. E., & MISHLER, E. G. Sequential patterning in family interaction: A methodological note. *Family Process,* 1970, *9,* 211-220.

WEISS, R. L. The conceptualization of marriage from a behavioral perspective. In T. J. Paolino & B. S. McCrady (Eds.), *Marriage and marital therapy: Psychoanalytic, behavioral, and systems theory perspectives.* New York: Brunner/Mazel, 1978.

WEISS, R. L. Strategic behavioral marital therapy: Toward a model for assessment and intervention. IN J. P. Vincent (Ed.), *Advances in family intervention, assessment, and theory: An annual compilation of research* (Vol. 1). Greenwich, CT: Jai, 1980.

WEISS, R. L., HOPS, H., & PATTERSON, G. R. A framework for conceptualizing marital conflict: A technology for altering it, some data for evaluating it. In L. A. Hamerlynck, L. C. Handy, & E. J. Mash (Eds.), *Behavior change: Methodology, concepts and practice.* Champaign, IL: Research Press, 1973.

WEISS, R. L., & MARGOLIN, G. Marital conflict and accord. In A. R. Ciminero, K. S. Calhoun, & H. E. Adams (Eds.), *Handbook for behavioral assessment.* New York: John Wiley, 1977.

WILLIAMS, A. M. The quantity and quality of marital interaction related to marital satisfaction: A behavioral analysis. *Journal of Applied Behavior Analysis,* 1979, *12,* 665-678.

WILLS, T. A., WEISS, R. L., & PATTERSON, G. R. A behavioral analysis of the determinants of marital satisfaction. *Journal of Consulting and Clinical Psychology,* 1974, *42,* 802-811.

PART II

INNOVATIONS IN DATA COLLECTION

7

THE COUPLES
INTERACTION SCORING SYSTEM

Clifford I. Notarius
Howard J. Markman

The scientific study of human behavior requires a language system that enables a description of behavioral events. This necessary step, of detailed description, is a prerequisite to the construction of models and theories that provide explanations for the recorded observations. The greater the complexity of the behaviors under study, the greater is the need for an objective descriptive tool.

The marital relationship is an extremely complex system, and early in our work with marital and premarital couples we decided that we needed a means for describing the interaction patterns of couples. The Couples Interaction Scoring System (CISS; pronounced "kiss") provides an objective, descriptive assessment of marital and premarital interaction. The objective of CISS is to provide a detailed observational record of communication between partners. The utility of CISS should be judged by the contribution it makes to our ability to: (1) describe interaction differences in distressed and nondistressed couples; (2) clarify the processes involved in marital interaction; (3) assess change following an intervention program; and (4) target problematic interactional styles as a basis for clinical intervention.

AUTHORS' NOTE: The authors would like to thank Lowell Krokoff and John Gottman for their comments on an earlier draft of this chapter.

BACKGROUND

Several systems have been developed to describe couples' interaction. Some of these have been based on coding systems developed for groups, such as the Interpersonal Behavior Rating System (Leary, 1957) and Bales Interaction Process Analysis (Bales, 1950), while others were developed specifically for marital interaction, such as Olson and Ryder's (Note 1) Marital and Family Interaction Coding System, Raush et al.'s (1974) Coding Scheme for Interpersonal Conflict, and the Marital Interaction Coding System (Hops et al., Note 2). The latter three were influential in the development of some of the CISS codes. These coding systems are described in Chapter 15 of this volume.

Given the availability of several behavioral observation systems for couples interaction, it is reasonable to wonder, "Why add another to the list with CISS?" This question has most meaning when one considers the difficulty of generalizing results across studies that have used different coding systems. The rationale for CISS was our evaluation that the other systems were lacking in one or more respects. The coding systems developed for groups did not capture one or more aspects of marital interaction that we believed to be important. The major difference between CISS and other behavioral observation systems is that CISS recognizes the importance of the *nonverbal* aspects of message delivery and message reception in human interaction. The nonverbal aspects of communication are essential in the transmission of feelings (Mehrabian, 1972; Harper et al., 1978) and these feelings provide a context for understanding the meaning of a verbal message. For example, the same content can take on different meanings if facial expression, voice tone, or both, communicate anger, sarcasm, humor, or affection.

OVERVIEW OF CISS

The development of CISS began in the spring of 1973, as part of a large project studying distressed and nondistressed marriages. We had interviewed and videotaped 30 couples as they interacted on both high and low conflict and on personal and impersonal topics (see Gottman, Notarius, Markman, et al., 1976; Gottman et al., 1977; Gottman, 1979). The CISS was developed in order to compare the conflict resolution behavior of the two groups of couples and assess whether specific behaviors, representing positive communication skills, would discriminate the two groups of couples (Markman, Note 3; Notarius, Note 4).

The CISS is essentially two different coding systems: a content analysis system representing the coding of verbal behaviors, and an affect analysis system representing the coding of nonverbal behaviors. Each codable unit of interaction receives a content code and a nonverbal behavior code. In addition, the listener's nonverbal behavior, which provides the context for a given message, can also be coded (see Gottman et al., 1977; Gottman, 1979). The coding unit will be discussed in greater detail later in this chapter. The content codes went through several iterations as we learned from experience with coders working with the system. The guiding principles were to produce a system that had the capability to (a) exhaustively code marital interaction, (b) capture the richness of intimate dialogue, and (c) be taught to others also interested in coding couples' conversation. Over an 18-month period we arrived at the current system of 8 summary codes based on 28 content codes.

The three nonverbal behavior codes proved to be somewhat easier to develop. The literature on nonverbal behavior suggested a set of face, voice, and body cues that could be used to code the speaker's and listener's nonverbal behavior as positive, negative, or neutral. Combining the content and speaker nonverbal behavior codes, the CISS assigns one of 24 (8 content × 3 nonverbal) unique codes to each coding unit.

CISS CONTENT CODES

This section describes the 8 summary content codes of CISS along with the components of each summary code. Since each of the 28 original content codes are contained in the 8 summary codes, the usefulness of each CISS subcode can be evaluated.

In reviewing the components of each of the 8 summary codes, the reader may be curious about the criteria used to establish the summary categories. While it is tempting to believe that the more precise the coding system, the better it is, in practice there is a point of diminishing returns as the number of codes grows large. This is due to such factors as the low frequency of rare codes, the ambiguity inherent in speech that makes fine discrimination difficult or impossible, the lack of utility in separating functionally similar statements, and the need for data reduction for the purposes of analysis and interpretation. With these reasons in mind, the summary codes were formed. Gottman (1979) has described the process we used to establish the current 8 summary codes. The two primary criteria for combining content codes were semantic similarity and functional similarity. Similar function between codes was determined by examining the strength of the sequential connections between the codes. Thus, within each summary category, the independent codes are semantically similar and/or they are sequentially related to each other, suggesting that they serve as functional equivalents.

The 8 summary codes are presented in Table 7.1. Each of the summary codes and the associated individual content codes are described below with examples.

TABLE 7.1   CISS Summary Content Codes

Code	Definition	Examples
PF	Problem information or feelings about problem	The problem is that we don't have enough money.
		That makes me sad.
MR	Mind reading; attributing thoughts, feelings, motives, attitudes, or actions to spouse	You always get mad in those situations.
PS	Proposing a solution	Let's take out a loan.
CT	Communication talk	We're getting off the issue.
AG	Agreement	Yeah, you're right.
		I am sorry for last night.
DG	Disagreement	No, because it's too late.
		Yes, but . . .
SO	Summarizing other	What you're saying is I drink too much.
		We're both suggesting a vacation.
SS	Summarizing self	I told you, I'm not going.

A more detailed discussion of the codes is available in several versions of the CISS training manuals.[1]

EXPRESSING FEELINGS OR ATTITUDES ABOUT A PROBLEM (PF)

There are four content codes which make up the PF summary code.

Generalized problem talk (GT) is a statement directly concerning the relationship but phrased in abstract or depersonalized terms, or which generalizes to a whole population or subgroup. Example: "Most people are selfish about how they want to spend their free time."

Relationship issue problem talk (PT) is a statement concerning a relationship problem that the couple is discussing. The statement may deal with the existence, nature, cause, effect, and/or implication of the problem. Examples: "We have a problem with the kids" (existence of problem); "Our financial situation is pretty bad because of your doctor bills" (nature of problem); "Maybe we have a problem with the children because I tell them to do one thing and you tell them to do another" (cause of problem); "If you continue to deny me attention it is bound to destroy our relationship" (implication or prediction about problem). A speaker's opinion, attitude, evaluation, or thought process directly related to the problem would also be included in this type of PF statement; for example, "The way I see it, we should have made it clear to your parents how long we could stay with them before we went."

Feeling (F) is a statement which directly reveals the immediate affective experience of the speaker occurring in the past, present, or future. F statements are coded when the speaker describes the feeling being communicated, the situation in which the feeling occurs, or the problem to which the feeling refers. Examples: "I am very happy right now"; "I've gone to those parties with you before and I've been miserable."

MINDREADING (MR)

There are two content codes that make up the MR summary code.

Mind reading feeling, attitude, or opinion (MR$_1$) is a statement which makes an inference about feelings, attitudes, opinions, and/or motives of the spouse or the couple. The mind-reading statement does not have to be an accusation, nor does it have to have a negative voice tone. It can seem like a factual statement. Examples: "You hate to go to my mother's"; "You love to go to parties."

Mind reading behaviors (MR$_2$) is a statement which makes an assumption about and/or attributes past, present, or future behaviors or facts *solely* to the other person. Examples: "You didn't work at all last weekend," "You won't go to the library to study." "We" behaviors, such as, "We haven't eaten for a long time," are coded as problem solving and information exchange (PS), which is described below.

AGREEMENT (AG)

There are five content codes which make up the AG summary code.

Direct agreement (A) is a statement of direct acknowledgment of agreement with the other person's views. Direct agreement requires some preceding point of view to be expressed, with which the speaker agrees. Examples: "You're right"; "OK."

Accepts responsibility (AR) is a statement in which the speaker acknowledges and accepts responsibility for a past or present problem, accepts criticism of behavior, or makes an apologetic statement. Examples: "You're right, I have been putting wet towels in the hamper"; "I am sorry for the way I acted." Statements in which the speaker recognizes that he or she *should* or *ought* to accept more responsibility for behavior necessary to solve a defined problem (such as, "I ought to do more to help you around the house") are called PF, since they represent an attitude or opinion about a problem.

Accepting modification (AM) is a statement in which the speaker changes his or her opinion as a result of influence from the other person. The speaker must have previously stated an opinion and then changed as a function of his or her spouse's opinions and/or arguments. Examples: "OK, you're right and I'm wrong"; "I never saw it that way before, Bill; the kids can take care of themselves while we're at the movies."

Compliance (C) is a statement that complies with a request or command. Examples: Husband: "Put out your cigarette" (command). Wife: "OK" (C); Wife: "Pick up some bread when you go to the store" (command). Husband: "I will" (C).

Assent (A) is a brief verbal response, such as "yeah," or "mm hmm," while the other person is talking; it usually acknowledges listening or attention. Repetition of a spouse's statement in a neutral tone of voice is also coded as an A statement.

DISAGREEMENT (DG)

The DG summary code comprises five types of content codes.

Direct disagreement (D) is a statement that expresses a simple disagreement with a spouse's viewpoint or denies responsibility for a problem. Examples: "No, it's never been twice a week"; "No, I don't think we agreed to do that"; "I don't really think that would be a good idea"; Husband: "You never pick up my clothes at the cleaner." Wife: "Yes, I do" (D).

Yes, but (YB) is a statement of qualified agreement or apology which can be explicit or implicit. Examples: "I'm sorry I made you mad, but I really felt that I had to make my point"; "Ok, you're right; however, that situation will never arise."

Disagreement with rationale supplied (RA) is a statement in which the speaker provides a rationale, justification, reason, or explanation for his or her disagreement. Example: "You're wrong; it's important to save money in case of an emergency."

Command (CM) is a statement telling or ordering the partner to do something or not to do something. Example: "Listen to me"; "Let me do that"; "Shut up."

Noncompliance (NC) is a failure to fulfill demands of an immediately preceding command or clarification request. Example: Husband: "Say that again" (C). Wife: "You're not listening to me. Every night you come home and sit down in front of the TV" (NC).

PROBLEM SOLVING AND INFORMATION EXCHANGE (PS)

There are five content codes which make up the PS summary code.

Plan (PL) is a specific plan or method for how to arrive at a solution to a problem or a specific solution to a specific problem. The plan must speak to the issue at hand. Examples: "You had your way last time, so it's my turn"; "Let's write down all possible solutions and then discuss each one separately."

Nonspecific plan (NP) is a statement which suggests a solution to a problem, expressed in nonspecific terms. The nonspecific plan is more one of problem recognition than of a specific solution to a problem; it is more a final outcome rather than an actual method for arriving at such an outcome. Examples: "I think you should never be late again"; "Let's be happy."

Relationship information (RI) is a statement which presents information or behavioral facts related to couple or speaker issues, stated in past, present, or future tense. Sensory reports are also included in this category. Examples: "We're taking the kids to the park this Sunday"; "We have a 2 p.m. appointment in the clinic today"; "I saw you speaking to Stella."

Nonrelationship information (NR_1) is statement which presents facts of information not directly associated with the relationship. These statements never involve self-disclosure. Examples: "My pencil lead broke"; "It's 3:15."

Nonrelationship opinion, feeling, or attitude (NR_2) is a subjective expression about the speaker's preference or evaluations concerning issues totally unrelated to the couple's relationship. Examples: "I think God is a woman"; "This chair is uncomfortable."

COMMUNICATION TALK (CT)

The CT category comprises four content codes.

Back on beam type 1 (BM_1) is a statement which directs the conversation back to a topic from which the couple has strayed. This includes a restatement of a problem or a redescription of a problem. Examples: "John, that's getting away from the issue"; "That's all fine and good, but getting back to the issue of the budget book . . . "

Back on beam type 2 (BM_2) is a statement directing the couple's communication toward the resolution of a problem. This kind of statement serves the function of "beaming" the couple toward a solution by recognizing that some action must be taken toward resolution. Examples: "We have to reach a decision on this issue"; "Let's talk for only five more minutes."

Metacommunication (MC) is a statement about a discussion or communication about communication. These statements often involve a "stop" in the action of a conversation to comment on it. Also included are statements that communicate understanding or lack of understanding on the part of the speaker concerning previous statements of the partner. Examples: "I don't think we are getting anywhere with the discussion"; "We are just going around in circles and getting ourselves confused"; "Hold it, I'm not sure what you are saying."

Clarification request (CL) is a question or statement requesting clarification, repetition, or rephrasing of a previous statement when the speaker does not hear or understand partner's statement. Examples: "I didn't get that"; "Would you say that again"; "I'm sorry, I didn't hear your first point."

SUMMARIZES OTHER (SO)

There are two content codes which make up the SO category.

Summarizes other (S) is any statement or set of statements by the speaker which summarizes the previous statements of the other person. Examples: "It seems to me that what you are saying is . . . "; "To put it simply, you're tired of the way things are . . . "

Summarizes both (SB) is any statement or set of statements which present a review or summary of the couple's conversation. Examples: "What we talked about yesterday was the kids"; "Thus far we have discussed . . . "

SUMMARIZES SELF (SS)

SS is coded when the speaker reviews or presents a summary of his or her previous statements. SS statements tend to occur at the end of a long message. Word-for-word repetition of the speaker's previous statement is also included. Examples: "What I have said so far is . . . "; "So all I'm saying, Ted, is that I don't want to take the responsibility for the housework."

Any statement which cannot be coded because it is unaudible for unintelligible, such as "Well, I . . . er . . . I'm not . . . why don't . . . uh, well, I just . . . " is coded as a Blurp (BL).

CISS NONVERBAL BEHAVIOR

CISS uses three codes, positive ($+$), neutral (0), and negative ($-$), to assess the nonverbal behaviors of the speaker and the listener. These codes are not intended to measure the "inner state" of a spouse, rather, they are intended to identify the effects of a person's nonverbal behavior upon the "emotional interpersonal climate" that exists between the partners.

In assigning a $+$, 0, or $-$ nonverbal behavior code, the coder first scans the facial expression, then voice tone, and finally body movement. Using this hierarchy, if facial expression is $+$ or $-$, this is the code assigned; if facial expression is 0, voice tone is scanned for $+$ or $-$, and if identified, it is coded; if voice tone is 0, body position is scanned. This hierarchy is based on Mehrabian's (1972) studies of nonverbal behavior, in which he reports that total affect is the product of an additive model in which facial expression is weighted .55, voice tone is weighted .38, and verbal content is weighted .07. Although body position is not entered in the equation, body position is a component of Mehrabian's immediacy dimension, which contributes to the communication of positiveness.

The nonverbal cues used to code the face, voice, and body are summarized in Table 7.2. Coders are instructed that these cues need not occur in an exaggerated form in order to be coded. In addition, coders are coached to avoid questioning the *intention* of a spouse when coding the nonverbal behavior; if a spouse speaks with an accusing tone of voice, this is taken as a negative cue, whether or not the spouse "intended" it to be negative. Finally, coders are instructed to avoid attributing any significance to positive and negative nonver-

TABLE 7.2   Nonverbal Cues Used to Code Affect in the CISS

Channel	Cues for CISS Affect Code			
	Positive		Negative	
Face	smile empathetic expression head nod		frown sneer fearful expression cry smirk angry expression disgust glare	
Voice	caring warm soft tender relieved empathetic concerned loving affectionate	satisfied buoyant bubbly cheerful chuckling happy joyful laughter	cold tense scared impatient hard clipped staccato whining blaming	sarcastic angry furious blaring hurt depressed accusing mocking laughter
Body	touching distance open arms attention relaxation forward lean		arms akimbo neck and hand tension rude gestures hands thrown up in disgust pointing, jabbing, slicing inattention	

bal ratings. For example, the coders are told that high rates of negative behaviors may be a sign of expressiveness (that is, a "good" sign) rather than a "bad" sign associated with a troubled marriage.

It is possible to code nonverbal behaviors with far greater precision than is attempted by CISS. For example, Ekman and Friesen's (1975) coding system of the face enables considerable detail about specific patterning of the facial musculature. Whether or not the cost of such coding justifies its use remains unanswered. However, to understand the precise, and perhaps idiosyncratic, cues that each partner uses to arrive at an affective evaluation does require detailed coding beyond that provided by the current CISS affect codes.[2]

CODING UNIT

Riskin and Faunce (1972), in their review of family interaction research, describe coding units varying from the smallest, the "act," which consists of a simple grammatical sentence, to the "speech," which is defined as everything spoken until there is a floor switch, to the very global "theme." In CISS our coding unit is the "thought unit." The thought unit is most often a grammatical phrase, separated by pauses, commas, ands, buts, or periods. However, the thought unit is not fixed; sometimes it will be a sentence, sometimes a phrase, and sometimes a speech fragment. We arrived at the thought unit after attempting to code interaction first according to 6-second and then according to 30-second intervals. Because couples speak with vastly differing paces, it proved impossible to code according to a fixed time interval. Instead, we found that research assistants had no difficulty placing slashes on a transcript after each "thought" was uttered and that individuals were extremely reliable in independently "slashing" a transcript into thought units. The thought unit thus became the basic coding unit, each thought unit receiving one content code, one speaker nonverbal behavior code, and one listener nonverbal behavior.

The thought unit is the unit of analysis both for estimating reliability and for data analysis. However, for the purpose of data analysis, consecutive thought units that are identical as to content and nonverbal behavior are merged into behavioral units.

TRAINING CODERS

We have trained undergraduates, graduate students, and nonprofessionals to use CISS. It takes about 30-40 hours of training before a coder masters the content codes, and somewhat less time for the nonverbal behavior codes.

Mastery of the content codes of CISS begins with memorizing the code book. Although only the 8 summary codes are used in data analysis, coders learn all 28 individual content codes. After memorization of the codebook is demonstrated via written "quizzes," coders practice assigning codes to specific examples taken from the code book. Coders are next presented with new statements taken from couple's transcripts. Working with a group, the trainer reviews the coder's codes and discusses difficulties in applying the coding rules. It is important for the trainer to have a firm grasp on the CISS codes and to serve as an authoritative resource for the group. Coders are then presented with a transcript of a couple's interaction for coding and then discussion. If the coders appear to be coding with little error, they are presented with a videotape and transcript for coding. If there are many problems with responses to the transcript, additional practice coding transcripts are scheduled prior to coding the videotape.

Training of nonverbal behavior coders proceeds in the same general manner as that of the content coders. The major difference is that, after memorizing the system, coders start coding video sequences rather than transcripts. The reason for this is the need for nonverbal cues only available on video for use of the nonverbal behavior codes.

ACHIEVING INTEROBSERVER AGREEMENT

The most difficult task in training coders is achieving interobserver agreement. After practice with one or more videotapes, the trainer compares the individual codes of each coder on each thought unit. This information enables an assessment of specific codes that are not being used correctly and helps to identify individual coders who are not using code categories correctly, are making systematic errors in coding, or who are generally inconsistent in applying codes. After assessing observer agreement on a 30- to 60-minute interaction, the trainer can determine the above coding outcomes. If interobserver agreement is sufficiently high, the coding of the data set can begin. If not, the group continues training until adequate coding performance is achieved.

A useful method for computing an observer agreement estimate is to prepare a table similar to Table 7.3. Since interobserver agreement coefficients do not account for the probability of agreement due to chance, Cohen (1960) has proposed a measure "kappa" which reflects observer agreement beyond that which would be expected by chance alone. Table 7.3 presents an agreement matrix between two coders using four codes from which kappa is calculated. Hollenbeck (1978, pp. 91-92) discussed the advantages of organizing coding data as in Table 7.3. He writes:

> Organizing new data in this fashion is valuable when training observers. Differences in agreement are easy to detect [they appear as off-diagonal elements] and confusion among codes can be pinpointed by identifying the types of errors that are made.

TABLE 7.3   An Agreement Matrix for Calculation of Kappa

CISS Codes		Observer 1				Proportion of Total for Observer 1 (P_1)
		PF	MR	AG	DG	
Observer 2	PF	27	3	1	2	33/59 = .559
	MR	4	9	0	1	14/59 = .237
	AG	1	0	6	0	7/59 = .119
	DG	0	0	0	0	5/59 = .085
Proportion of Total for Observer 2 (P_2)		32/59 = .542	12/59 = .203	7/59 = .119	8/59 = .136	

NOTE: P_o = observed agreement = Sum of diagonal entries/total of all entries = 47/59 = .797.
P_c = chance agreement = $\Sigma(P_1 \times P_2)$ = (.559 × .542) + (.237 × .203) + (.119 × .119) + (.085 × .136) = .377.
Kappa = $P_o - P_c/1 - P_c$ = (.797 − .377)/(1 − .377) = .67.

From Table 7.3, we would be concerned about the confusion between MR and PF made by our two observers. Inspection of a table constructed like Table 7.3 can also help identify a "popular" coding category that becomes a "dump" for coders' uncertainties. The outcome of this process is high agreement with trivial meaningfulness.

Haynes (1978) has summarized several factors that affect the accuracy of observers. These factors include the training procedure, observer drift, observer bias, observer decay, and the methods used to assess reliability. To reach and maintain a high level of reliability in our coders, we have found the following procedures most helpful: (1) proceed through a graded training program on using CISS as discussed above; (2) continue weekly meetings of coders to discuss coding progress and resolve confusions; (3) inform coders that frequent and random reliability checks will be conducted throughout the coding project; (4) change pairs of observers for estimating interobserver agreement to minimize the opportunity for pairs of coders to agree with each other but not with the coding manual (this has been called "consensual observer drift" by Johnson & Bolstad, 1973); and (6) have an "expert" occasionally code the interaction as a reliability criterion to assess observer drift (Johnson & Bolstad, 1973; Lipinski & Nelson, 1974).

A MESSAGE TO NEW USERS OF CISS

We have found it helpful to "innoculate" new coders against the initial frustration most experience during the early stages of training. A statement such as the following seems to normalize the experience and to reduce the frustration of learning a coding system:

> Learning to code is a grueling and frustrating experience for most coders. The human mind rebels against breaking down the rich fabric of experience and interaction into a small set of categories, so most of you will go through a process of hating the coding system and thinking that it is ambiguous. But if you stick with it, you will find that you can start using the coding system more easily.

In approaching each coding assignment, coders are instructed to watch the entire interaction on video tape before beginning to code. This allows familiarization with the couple, an appreciation of individual style, a context for the couple's discussion, and a frame of reference for each coding decision.

RELIABILITY OF THE CISS

When we address the reliability of a coding system, we are asking a question about the quality of the data that is generated by our observational methods. There are at least three different strategies available to assess the reliability or quality of observational data. The most common way of thinking of reliability with observational data is the extent to which two (or more) observers, coding alone, agree on what behaviors are occurring. A second way is to consider observational measurement as a psychometric test that should be evaluated via classical test theory, that is, the "test" should demonstrate several forms of reliability, including test-retest, internal-consistency, alternate-forms, and so on. A final way to evaluate the quality of observational data is to assess the representativeness of the data by assessing the contributing sources of variation in the observational coding process. This third strategy has been developed by Cronbach et al. (1972) and is called generalizability theory. Mitchell (1979) reviews each of these approaches and presents a cogent set of recommendations for establishing the quality of observational data.

Reliability of an observational system should be assessed with a strategy that is able to determine the adequacy of that system for the task for which it was designed. Different tasks suggest different reliability procedures and estimates. We will summarize the strategies we have used for our purposes.

First, a reliability estimate should be computed on the same units of analysis that are used to test the hypotheses under study. This means that when performing a sequential analysis (see Chapter 13, this volume), reliability must be estimated for specific codes occurring in specific thought units. It is not sufficient to gauge reliability on the overall frequencies of each code for sequence analysis. This latter strategy might be appropriate if one were interested only in the overall frequency of specific codes.

Second, reliability should always be estimated on the data set that is part of the study being reported, using coders who will code that data set. It is not appropriate to train coders on "practice" material, assess reliability on these practice materials, and suspend reliability evaluation when beginning to code the "real" data. Likewise, it is not acceptable to train a group of coders to acceptable criteria of reliability, and then replace them midway through the study without reassessing reliability.

Finally, both an interobserver agreement index and generalizability coefficients should be reported, as each gives important information. Interobserver agreement is best estimated with Cohen's kappa (see Table 7.3). This index should be reported because it gives information about chance agreements and information about a major source of error in observational coding studies, that is, observer agreement. Generalizability coefficients, derived from a generalizability study, have the advantage of accounting for the variance from sources other than subjects and measurement error. An advantage of carrying out a small generalizability study as part of an observational project is that it necessarily demands that the researcher specify the conditions (facets) over which the coding results are expected to generalize.

The written CISS manual, as presented in this chapter, has been used with many groups of coders in different laboratories and has been found to yield reliable results. Of course, new users must establish reliability for their own purposes with their own coders. In reliability studies reported by Gottman (1979), Cohen's kappas for content codes averaged .909 (standard deviation = .404) and for the nonverbal behavior codes kappas averaged .715 (standard deviation = .169). In a series of generalizability studies, both content and nonverbal behavior codes were found to have high Cronbach alpha generalizability coefficients. In an interesting generalizability study designed to test for reliability of CISS to decay over time, Gottman (1979) found no evidence for decay and some tendency for reliability to increase over time.

USING CISS OBSERVATIONAL DATA

CISS has been used to assess two types of hypotheses about marital satisfaction and marital distress. Each hypothesis assumes that communication variables account for a major source of the variance in marital distress. The first hypothesis concerns differences in the proportions of communication categories (for example, social skills) in maritally nondistressed and distressed couples. An example of a prediction stemming from this type of hypothesis would be: "Clinic couples will show a larger ratio of agreements to agreements plus disagreements." This, in fact, was found to be true (Gottman et al., 1977).

A second type of hypothesis concerns the sequential patterning of CISS content and nonverbal behavior codes over time. Here the interest is in the interactional dependencies that exist between husbands and wives in distressed and nondistressed couples. CISS has been used to identify and describe these sequential patterns and to test predictions that specific sequences of interaction will discriminate between distressed and nondistressed couples. An example of a sequential hypothesis that has been tested with CISS codes is that interaction in nondistressed couples is characterized by positive reciprocity.

We might also mention that a graphical portrayal of the emotional flow between spouses over a conversation is possible with "point-graphs" constructed from CISS codes (Gottman et al., 1977). The shapes of these pointgraphs may provide a basis for classifying couples into types representing different interactional styles (Gottman, 1979). These point-graphs also provide a basis for detailed *within*-couple analyses.

A CLOSING COMMENT

We would like to close our presentation of CISS by briefly mentioning some of its potential uses. First, a CISS coded interaction can be reconstructed and examined to determine the flow of conversation over time. This reconstruction provides a powerful summary of where problems in interaction occur, the type of intervention necessary to aid the couple, and, if desired, a convenient communications assessment summary to share with the couple. For example, it is one thing to point out that spouse A often disagrees with spouse B; it is another to present evidence that when spouse B proposes a solution to a problem, spouse A disagrees while displaying negative nonverbal behaviors with a frequency of X. Second, the CISS codes provide an objective measure of the couple's interaction patterns. The couple's subjective evaluation of the same behaviors can be compared with the "objective reality" obtained by CISS analysis in order to provide preliminary assessment of cognitive sets or perceptual screens (Floyd, Note 5), which may interfere with progress in therapy. Third, the CISS assessment provides a pretherapy base line, which can be used as a pretest measure to assess therapeutic change if similar posttherapy and follow-up data are obtained. Fourth, CISS coding can be an important training aid for young therapists. Our experience suggests that it is a difficult task to shift therapy trainees away from the content of a marital disagreement and toward the process of interaction. When therapists are trained to use CISS, they are provided with a language system to describe the communication process.

Finally, as it is no doubt apparent, CISS has been developed and is used within a behavioral and a communications framework. It is within this framework that its utility has been assessed. While it may also be useful to therapists and researchers within another perspective, this would depend on the extent to which concepts could be operationalized in terms of CISS categories. If the concepts cannot be described with behavioral referents, than no observational system will be useful. Establishing the validity of such "unobservable" concepts would then be the task of the researcher/therapist.

NOTES

1. Coding manuals are available from the authors at the following addresses: C. Notarius, Department of Psychology, Catholic University of America, Washington, DC 20064; and J. Gottman, Department of Psychology, University of Illinois, Champaign, IL 61820.

2. Gottman has developed a coding system for evaluating voice tone. The coding manual for the voice tone codes is available from him at the Department of Psychology, University of Illinois, Champaign, IL 61820. Detailed information on Ekman and Friesen's FACT, for coding the face, is available from Consulting Psychologists Press, Inc., Palo Alto, CA 94306.

REFERENCE NOTES

1. OLSON, D. H., & RYDER, R. G. *IMC coding system.* Unpublished manuscript, Section on Family Development, Child Research Branch, National Institute of Mental Health, 1973.

2. HOPS, H., WILLS, T. A., PATTERSON, G. R., & WEISS, R. L. *The Marital Interaction Coding System (MICS).* Unpublished manuscript, University of Oregon, 1972.

3. MARKMAN, H. J. *A description of verbal and nonverbal communication in distressed and nondistressed marital dyads.* Unpublished master's thesis, Indiana University—Bloomington, 1976.

4. NOTARIUS, C. I. *A behavioral competency assessment of communication in distressed and nondistressed marital dyads.* Unpublished master's thesis, Indiana University—Bloomington, 1976.

5. FLOYD, F. *Insiders' and outsiders' perspectives of the communication of distressed and nondistressed married couples.* Unpublished master's thesis, Bowling Green State University, 1980.

REFERENCES

BALES, R. F. *Interaction process analysis.* Reading, MA: Addison-Wesley, 1950.

COHEN, J. A. A coefficent of agreement for nominal scales. *Educational and Psychological Measurement,* 1960, *20,* 37-46.

CRONBACH, L. J., GLESER, G. C., NANDA, H., & RAJARATNAM, N. *The dependability of behavioral measurements: Theory of generalizability for scores and profiles.* New York: John Wiley, 1972.

EKMAN, P., & FRIESEN, W. V. *Unmasking the face.* Englewood Cliffs, NJ: Prentice-Hall, 1975.

GOTTMAN, J. M. *Marital interaction.* New York: Academic, 1979.

GOTTMAN, J. M., MARKMAN, H., & NOTARIUS, C. The topography of marital conflict: A study of verbal and nonverbal behavior. *Journal of Marriage and the Family,* 1977, *39,* 461-477.

GOTTMAN, J. M., NOTARIUS, C., GONSO, J., & MARKMAN, H. *A couples guide to communication.* Champaign, IL: Research Press, 1976.

GOTTMAN, J. M., NOTARIUS, C., MARKMAN, H., BANK, S., YOPPI, B., & RUBIN, M. E. Behavior exchange theory and marital decision making. *Journal of Personality and Social Psychology,* 1976, *34,* 14-23.

HARPER, R.G., WIENS, A. N., & MATARAZZO, J. D. *Nonverbal communication: The state of the art.* New York: John Wiley, 1978.

HAYNES, S. N. *Principles of behavioral assessment.* New York: Gardner, 1978.

HOLLENBECK, A. R. Problems of reliability in observational research. In G. P. Sackett (Ed.), *Observing behavior* (Vol. 2): *Data collection and analysis methods.* Baltimore, MD: University Park Press, 1978.

JOHNSON, S. M. & BOLSTAD, O. D. Methodological issues in naturalistic observation: Some problems and solutions for field research. In L. A. Hamerlynck, L. C. Handy, & E. J. Mash (Eds.), *Behavior change: Methodology, concepts and practice. The fourth international conference on behavior modification.* Champaign, IL: Research Press, 1973.

JONES, R. R., REID, J. B., & PATTERSON, G. R. Naturalistic observation in clinical assessment. In P. McReynolds (Ed.), *Advances in psychological assessment.* San Francisco: Jossey-Bass, 1975.

LEARY, T. *Interpersonal diagnosis of personality.* New York: Ronald Press, 1957.

LIPINSKI, D., & NELSON, R. Problems in the use of naturalistic observation as a means of behavior assessment. *Behavior Therapy,* 1974, *5,* 341-351.

MEHRABIAN, A. *Nonverbal communication.* New York: Adline-Atherton, 1972.

MITCHELL, S. K. Interobservor agreement, reliability, and generalizability of data collected in observational studies. *Psychological Bulletin,* 1979, *86,* 376-390.

RAUSH, H. L., BARRY, W. A., HERTEL, R. K., & SWAIN, M. A. *Communication, conflict, and marriage.* San Francisco: Jossey-Bass, 1974.

RISKIN, J., & FAUNCE, E. E. An evaluative review of family interaction research. *Family Process,* 1972, *11,* 365-455.

WIGGINS, J. S. *Personality and prediction.* Reading, MA: Addison-Wesley, 1973.

8

THE HOME OBSERVATION
ASSESSMENT METHOD

Peter Steinglass
Lydia Tislenko

The vast bulk of psychosocial research data about the family is derived from two basic sources: self-report, retrospective data obtained by questionnaires or interviews, and direct observations of behavior occurring in a laboratory or treatment setting. Despite an emerging enthusiasm for the notion of studying behavior in its natural environment (spurred on particularly by the developing fields of ethology and ecological psychology), remarkably little research has been done utilizing in-home observations of American families. One possible reason for the discrepancy between rhetoric and action has been the difficulty in operationalizing the collection of data from the in-home setting and utilizing such data for systematic hypothesis testing.

The Home Observation Assessment Method (HOAM) is an observational system specifically designed to collect accurate data of interactional behavior in the home as it unfolds in a real-time framework. The method was originally developed in conjunction with a major study of alcoholic families, but it was designed for wide applicability. A follow-up study of these families utilized a

AUTHORS' NOTE: This work was supported by Grant 5 R01 AA 01441-05 from the National Institute on Alcohol Abuse and Alcoholism. An earlier version of this chapter was published in *Family Process* 18: 337-354, 1979. Reprinted by permission.

second version of the HOAM that incorporated an improved coding system. It is this revised version that will be described in this chapter.

Three considerations were paramount in our thinking about the design of a home observation method: first, the method should minimize intrusiveness of the observers; second, the coding system should be composed of nonjudgmental, objective categories and be amenable to on-line coding; and third, because a session was expected to last up to four hours, occurring nine times over a six-month period, the design of the study demanded a method that would avoid fatigue in both observers and family members.

Our reading of the research literature indicated that the home environment had been explored from three different perspectives (a) the home had been used as a setting for administering formal interaction procedures to families—the notion being that home behavior may be more representative than laboratory behavior (Kent & Foster, 1977); (b) parenting behavior in the home had been of particular interest to child development researchers (Bradley & Caldwell, 1976; Clark-Stewart, 1973; Lytton, 1971); and (c) the relationship of home behavior to psychopathology had been of interest to a small number of family researchers (Henry, 1965; Kantor & Lehr, 1975). None of the methods employed in these studies, however, was able to satisfy the three design considerations listed above as critical for our own study. Therefore, it was necessary to undertake the design of a new instrument.

DESCRIPTION OF THE HOAM

DESIGN BIASES

Three research biases strongly influenced the design of the HOAM instrument. The first was a bias toward data obtained from the direct observation of behavior. This bias not only led us to avoid the use of questionnaires or interview data, it also argued against the use of technology that might inadvertently come between observer and subject (such as video and audio recording equipment). The second bias was a predilection for an ecological approach to naturalistic research (Barker, 1968). Because of our conviction that behavior is profoundly influenced by the context or setting within which it occurs (Raush et al., 1974), we felt that care must be taken to accurately preserve the naturalistic setting in the design of an observation instrument. The third bias was a preference toward measurable data as contrasted with narrative data. This bias was based on an assumption that interactional behavior can be studied profitably by breaking it down into a series of structural components capable of objective measurement, components that are in effect significant descriptors of interactional behavior. Prior examples illustrating the success of this approach can be found in studies by Flanders (1970), Minuchin et al. (1969), and Rebelsky and Hanks (1971).

Reflecting these three clinical and research biases, our in-home observation method was developed with the following major characteristics and features:

(1) It was designed to collect data in a real-time framework; that is, timed observations are carried out over extended periods.

(2) An attempt was made to preserve the natural relation between behavioral events and meaningful contextual variables for these events.

(3) Coding categories emphasized objective-structural variables rather than subjective-process variables.

(4) The coding system was capable of generating sequential data regarding selected variables.

(5) Content coding of verbal interaction was kept to a minimum. Where included, it is specifically theory-related and relatively objectified.

HOW DOES THE CODING OCCUR?

Coding is performed by a two-person team of "behavioral observers." In its current design, the method is intended for use in coding traditional nuclear families; each observer is assigned to one spouse/parent in the family under observation. For the duration of the coding session, it is the responsibility of the behavioral observer to record accurately the behavior of the spouse/parent to whom he or she is assigned.

All coding is done on-line. Observers bring to the coding session a supply of coding sheets, clipboard, and an electrical timer that allows them to record accurately time samples of behavior (to be described below). The behavioral observer is conceptualized as a "participant-observer" who will be "living with" a particular family for the time period of the observation (usually two to four hours). The "participant-observer" model seems an appropriate one to employ because it must be assumed that the coder, once he or she enters the family's home, has a specific, although undetermined, influence in shaping the behavior that subsequently occurs. The behavioral observer is trained to assume a passive and quiet role in the interactional field, allowing the family to mold him or her into the family's interactional pattern, rather than imposing his or her own set on the family.

To further facilitate the smooth integration of coders into the home, it is made clear to subject families that it is they who are "in charge" of the observation session. It is their prerogative, for example, to define certain locations in the house as off limits to the behavioral observers. Issues related to privacy are handled in like fashion. Spouse/parents inform coders when they want the observers to back off for reasons of privacy, and all such requests are automatically honored.

The critical, "mechanical" design issue of the HOAM is the decision to have observers follow selected members of the family around their home environments, rather than preselect a particular area of the house where either a relatively stationary observer or a camera could be placed to record any interactional behavior that happens to occur in the particular field. The assumption is that what little advantage the stationary observer or the camera might have in minimizing interference with natural patterns of interaction is far outweighed by the mobile observer's ability to record accurately the natural unfolding of the behavior of the member of the family being coded.

The family under observation therefore accepts a two-person team into the home, for periods of up to four hours, and agrees to carry out, as much as is possible, its usual interactional behavior while these two "outsiders" follow two members of the household around the physical plant with clipboards in hand and electrical timers periodically emitting low, but definitely audible, buzzes. Although the coders have become well known to the family over the course of multiple observations, they never reach the status of membership within the family, often described as a feature of participant observation in anthropological studies.

One might reasonably argue that the coding method we are describing cannot help but be so disruptive of family life as to make the information collected meaningless. Obviously, it is impossible to refute such a contention with total conviction. We can report, however, that families being observed did not themselves experience disruption in their usual routines or in the flavor of their interactional behavior. By and large, families, although reporting a general sense of strangeness during the first two observation sessions, found themselves consciously ignoring the coders by the third or fourth session.

STRUCTURE OF OBSERVATION SESSIONS

The coding session is structured in the following fashion: The overall time block is subdivided into active coding periods and rest periods. The two behavioral observers synchronously code up to four 40-minute time blocks, followed by 15-minute breaks. Each 40-minute coding session is further subdivided into 20 two-minute segments. The start of each new two-minute coding period is indicated by an audible signal from electronic timers that both observers carry.

During each two-minute block, two types of coding decisions are carried out. The first verbal interaction that occurs between the observer's subject and any other person currently in the household is labeled the Initial Interactional Sequence, and the coder is asked to render a series of coding decisions about this interaction (including some decisions about the content of the interaction). These interactions, because of the manner in which they are defined (to be discussed below), usually do not occupy an entire two-minute time segment. For the rest of the two-minute time segment, a series of objective coding decisions are made and recorded by the observer in the precise sequential order in which they occur. All coding decisions are recorded on a coding sheet that reflects the above segmental arrangment of time during the coding session.

Within each two-minute time block, four basic types of coding decisions are carried out: context codes (location, persons in the field, interactional dis-

tance); behavioral characteristics codes; who-to-whom speech codes; and interaction codes (subjective judgments about the task orientation, affective level,
and outcome of the Initial Interactional Sequence).

Contextual codes represent a series of objective, descriptive statements that
can be thought of as establishing the physical context within which interaction
occurs. They are the scene setters; facts that "set the stage" upon which a series
of interactions are played. They include the two fundamental questions that can
be asked about any interaction, namely, where it is occurring (location) and
who is present (persons in the field). In addition, for those time-sampled verbal
interactions that are coded (Initial Interactional Sequences), the physical distance between interactants is also coded. The vast literature in social psychology about personal space and territoriality points to this particular descriptor as
a critical contextual variable of interaction.

Who-to-whom speech codes (speech initiations and speech receptions) provide an accurate record of the speech activity and patterns for the subject being
coded.

Behavioral characteristics codes provide a running description of the behavior engaged in by subjects during the observation sessions. The codes are
purely descriptive, requiring little subjective interpretation by the coder, and
are intended to identify major blocks of time devoted to specific activities by the
subject being coded. In addition, several behavioral characteristics codes, such
as physical contact, are included for empirical interest.

Interaction codes, as previously explained, apply only to the first verbal
exchange between the subject and other members of the household during each
two-minute time segment. Coders are asked to make three content-related
decisions about this verbal interaction: first, the type of interaction formulated
in terms of "task orientation"; second, the affective level associated with the
interaction; and third, the outcome of the interaction from the subject's perspective.

All codes are specific enough to allow representation by number or letter,
and symbolic notation on the coding sheet is adequate to represent all coding
decisions. The coding sheet is also organized to correspond to the logical
sequence of decisions that have to be made during the coding process. Com-
puter-card keypunching can therefore be performed directly from the coding
sheets with no further data reduction or translation necessary. A manual providing detailed description of the various codes and the mechanics of scoring is
available from the author by request.

To date, 7 teams of behavioral observers have been trained and have used the
HOAM for approximately 350 coding sessions of 31 separate families. Observers are trained using a practicum method and are able to achieve acceptable
reliability levels with ease. Interrater reliability is assessed using both observer
percentage of agreement and the Kappa statistic (Bartko & Carpenter, 1976) as

the measurement criteria.[1] Special coding sessions are designed for reliability checks in which both observers code the same spouse, and their coding sheets are compared.

REPRESENTATIVE DATA

As has already been mentioned, the HOAM was developed in conjunction with a longitudinal study of alcoholism and the family. As part of the data collection procedures for this project, 31 families have been studied for approximately 350 coding sessions. Data from this project provide a picture of the potential usefulness of the HOAM and some of the options available because of its on-line capacity to reduce data to a form that is computer compatible. We will review the alcoholic family data first, then present some illustrations of graphics that can be produced from this type of data.

ALCOHOLIC FAMILY DATA

The HOAM coding system produces raw data that are, in essence, a series of frequency counts of selected aspects of interactional behavior. Although several coding categories have proven useful measures of important dimensions of family interaction exactly as they are recorded, most of the coding categories have been conceptualized as structural building blocks out of which more complex and theoretically meaningful indices of interactional behavior could be developed.

In our study of alcoholic families, 25 such indices were calculated for each family. The indices were intended to reflect a series of dimensions or tracks for interactional behavior and to describe the family's behavior within each track from two points of view: an activity or engagement level, and a variability level. For a particular dimension, the activity level was defined as the mean rate of that behavior over all observation sessions; the variability level was defined as the coefficient of variance (V) for the session means. All indices were calculated as couple level means.

The indices and their distributional characteristics are summarized in Table 8.1. As can be seen, there was considerable variability in the behavior exhibited by the 31 families along all 25 indices, evidence that the HOAM system is identifying aspects of interactional behavior that can be used to distinguish families one from another. Figure 8.1 and Table 8.2 outline the results of a principal axis factor analysis (using Varimax rotation) of these 25 indices. The most satisfactory factor structure yielded 5 factors, accounting for 67.4% of the variance. They are briefly described as follows:

Intrafamily Engagement. Families scoring high on this factor interact frequently with each other while at the same time tending to ignore the presence of the behavioral observers.

TABLE 8.1   HOAM Variables: Means and Ranges

Variable	Scale	Range	Mean	Standard Deviation
PHYSICAL LOCATION IN HOME				
Location Shifts/Hour	No. Shifts/Hr	11.1-54.10	28.55	10.55
Location Shifts/Hour (corrected for room size)	No. Shifts/Hr × Avg. Rm. Size	1463-6994	3516.44	1350.50
Location Shifts/Hour (percent to kitchen)	0-1.0	.10-.36	.21	.06
Location Shifts/Hour (variability)	V^a	.12-.71	.41	.12
PEOPLE IN ROOM WITH SUBJECT				
Percent Time Alone	0-1.0	.09-.66	.32	.16
Percent Time with Family and/ or Extrafamily Members	0-1.0	.00-.44	.07	.10
INTERACTIONAL DISTANCE				
Mean Distance (all interactions)	Actual Feet	4.30-9.27	6.83	1.99
Mean Distance (interactions when alcohol not visible)	Actual Feet	4.10-12.00	7.15	1.46
Mean Distance (variability across sessions)	V	.07-.44	.23	.08
Mean Distance (variability within sessions)	V	.50-1.14	.81	.17
INTERACTION RATIOS				
Percent Interaction with Coder	0-1.0	.02-.51	.16	.11
Percent Interactions with Coder: Husband and Wife Skew	-1.0-+1.0	-.88-+.75	-.16	.40
Physical: Potential Interaction Ratios	0-1.0	.22-.77	.45	.11
Verbal: Potential Interaction Ratios	0-1.0	.19-.60	.36	.10
Verbal: Physical Interaction Ratios	0-1.0	.57-1.23	.81	.14
Physical: Potential Contacts (variability)	V	.15-.74	.31	.13
Verbal: Potential Contacts (variability)	V	.16-.61	.32	.11
Verbal: Physical Contacts (variability)	V	.07-.39	.18	.08
TYPE OF VERBAL EXCHANGE				
Percent Decision-Making Exchanges	0-1.0	.01-.17	.07	.04
Percent Decision-Making Exchanges (when alcohol not visible)	0-1.0	.01-.19	.07	.04
Percent Decision-Making Exchanges (variability)	V	.29-2.06	.84	.41
AFFECTIVE LEVEL OF VERBAL EXCHANGE				
Mean Affect	-3.0-+3.0	.45-1.21	.86	.20
Mean Affect (variability)	V	.07-.47	.25	.13

TABLE 8.1 (continued)

Variable	Scale	Range	Mean	Standard Deviation
OUTCOME OF VERBAL EXCHANGES				
Percent Negative & Uncertain	0-1.0	.01-.15	.05	.04
Percent Negative & Uncertain (variability)	V	.44-2.00	.97	.43

a. V=Coefficient of variation (standard deviation divided by the mean).

Distance Regulation. A complex factor reflecting a particular style of family interaction. Families scoring high on this factor exhibit behavior in which people come together in the same location only if they intend to talk with one another for some purposeful reason. Although interaction occurs, it is done at a considerable distance and family members do not appear to be comfortable with one another in the same location at home. Families scoring low on this factor tend to "huddle" together in the home, rarely leaving each other for independent projects.

Extrafamily Engagement. Families scoring high on this factor are open to the presence of extrafamily members in the home, and more tolerant of individual-level differences in interactions with strangers.

Structural Variability. Families scoring high on this factor demonstrate considerable variability of interactional behavior and physical movement from one coding session to another. Families scoring low on this factor most likely have a highly patterned and fixed style of interaction.

Content Variability. Families scoring high on this factor manifest both higher rates of decision-making behavior and variability of affect associated with verbal interaction. The direction of this variability indicates that such families have a relative tolerance for ambiguity, a tolerance which allows unsettled issues to be raised and discussed at length, rather than be quickly resolved or decided separately by individual family members and not discussed within the family.

The results of this analysis demonstrate that by paying attention to the routines of daily living, and by measuring concrete aspects of these behaviors, more complex factors representing dimensions of interactional behavior associated with the family's regulation of its internal environment can be developed. While the small sample size invites replication, it must be noted that the measures on each family came from multiple observation sessions, and the results produced by the HOAM are striking in their clarity. The five HOAM factors identified demonstrate strong similarities to previously described dimensions of family behavior as they have appeared in the clinical and research literature. Olson et al. (1979), in a recent article reviewing this literature, suggest that

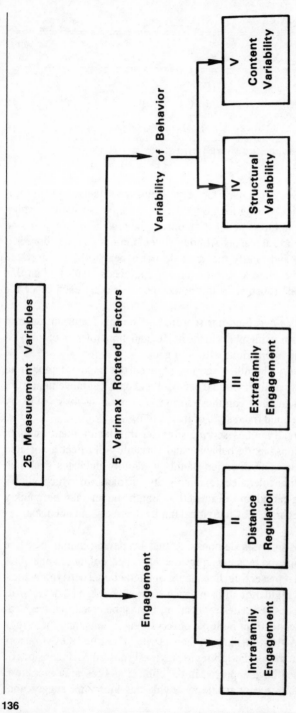

Figure 8.1 HOAM Factor Analysis

TABLE 8.2 Varimax Rotated Factor Matrix with HOAM Variables

Variables	Intrafamily Engagement	Distance Regulation	Extrafamily Engagement	Structural Variability	Content Variability
Location Shifts/Hour	.296	.653	−.068	−.271	−.215
Location Shifts/Hour (corrected for room size)	.232	.756	−.304	−.307	−.177
Location Shifts/Hour (percent to kitchen)	.236	−.676	−.357	.006	.134
Location Shifts/Hour (variability)	.175	−.161	.125	.634	.415
Percent Time Alone	−.400	.530	.163	.481	−.391
Percent Time with Family and/or Extra-family Members	−.058	.036	−.695	−.268	.119
Mean Distance (all interactions)	−.382	.664	.053	.074	.261
Mean Distance (interactions when alcohol not visible)	−.105	.646	.062	.114	.388
Mean Distance (variability across sessions)	.504	.049	−.138	.309	.213
Mean Distance (variability within sessions)	.560	.061	.143	−.331	−.027
Percent Interaction with Coder	−.635	.252	.025	.426	−.342
Percent Interactions with Coder: Husband and Wife Skew	.059	−.302	.303	−.293	−.259
Physical: Potential Interaction Ratios	.830	−.292	−.023	−.063	.033
Verbal: Potential Interaction Ratios	.853	.232	.165	.014	−.039
Verbal: Physical Interaction Ratios	.148	.722	.218	.322	−.139
Physical: Potential Contacts (variability)	−.146	.385	−.107	.780	−.323

(Continued)

TABLE 8.2 (continued)

Variables	Intrafamily Engagement	Distance Regulation	Extrafamily Engagement	Structural Variability	Content Variability
Verbal: Potential Contacts (variability)	-.111	.145	-.126	.795	-.276
Verbal: Physical Contacts (variability)	-.130	-.149	.055	.753	-.054
Percent Decision-Making Exchanges	.133	.010	-.001	-.133	.931
Percent Decision-Making Exchanges (when alcohol not visible)	.200	-.014	-.087	-.135	.884
Percent Decision-Making Exchanges (variability)	.092	.012	.246	.082	-.734
Mean Affect	.079	.165	-.234	.002	-.797
Mean Affect (variability)	.152	.142	.464	.081	.600
Percent Negative & Uncertain Outcomes	.056	.176	.737	-.167	.253
Percent Negative & Uncertain Outcomes (variability)	.048	-.104	-.618	.467	.082

many of these dimensions center around two fundamental properties of family behavior, one which they call "cohesion" and the second which they call "adaptability." The cohesion dimension includes not only notions of togetherness-separateness, but also such issues as the quality of family boundaries and the family view of time, space, and friends. The adaptability dimension incorporates notions of rigidity versus flexibility and patterned versus chaotic qualities in family life.

Were we to speculate about our HOAM dimensions, using the Olson et al. classification scheme, there would appear to be strong similarities between the HOAM factors, Intrafamily Engagement and Distance Regulation (at the level of the family's regulation of time and space in the home), and the dimension Olson et al. labeled "cohesion." The HOAM factors, Structural Variability and Content Variability, reflect the extent to which behavior in the home is patterned or regimented. If one considers such a patterning to be an indication of rigidity-flexibility of regulation of internal life, then these factors might be thought of as a component part of the family's "adaptability." The HOAM factor, Extrafamily Engagement, appears to reflect the quality of boundaries the family maintains vis-à-vis non-family members in the home. In this sense, it is a measure of the permeability of family boundaries, a quality Olson et al. argue is a component of their cohesion dimension, but conceptually seems more profitably identified as a separate dimension of family behavior. (We are currently administering the FACES instrument, purported by Olson et al. to measure "cohesion" and "adaptability," to the families also observed via the HOAM, and will be examining correlational patterns between these two instruments.)

Of equal interest, both conceptually and methodologically, is the work of Kantor and Lehr (1975). They also emphasize the value of focusing on the commonplace to gain a better understanding of the important processes that govern family life. Based on their work, which included observation of families in their homes, they have proposed a model of family functioning which they term a "Distance-Regulation Model." This model also emphasizes concepts of internal and external family environments, as well as the use of time and space as dimensions for delineating these environments.

While the similarities between the HOAM factor structure and the conceptualizations of family process as delineated by Kantor and Lehr are evident, the great advantage of the HOAM is its capacity to produce objective data concerning the family's regulation of its internal environment by systematically counting behaviors that relate to the family's use of time and space in the home, rather than relying on clinical asessment and empirical judgments. These measures are then amenable to both statistical analysis and graphical representations.

A wide range of analytical procedures have been carried out with the five HOAM factors as dependent variables. These include correlational analyses,

analyses of variance, and discriminant function analyses. Questions explored
thus far have included analyses of differential patterns of home behavior related
to family developmental variables (Steinglass, 1980b), the relationship between HOAM factors and traditional measures of psychopathology, such as
psychiatric symptomatology (Steinglass, 1980a), and specific hypotheses related to alcoholism and the family (Steinglass, in press; Tislenko & Steinglass,
Note 1), including the effect of the sex of the identified alcoholic on patterns of
interactional behavior in the home. This particular question was effectively
analyzed from both a family- and an individual-level analysis, on option that is
afforded due to the design of the HOAM.

An interesting picture is beginning to emerge from the analyses. Briefly
summarized, most of the independent variables mentioned above are associated
with predictable patterns of home behavior, but along selected dimensions. We
have yet to examine an independent variable that seems to exercise an "across-
the-board" effect on the pattern of family behavior at home. Instead, it appears
that each of the HOAM factors is "sensitive" to different influences. To take the
analyses relating the HOAM dimensions to traditional clinical measures, the
results indicate that each measure is responsive to a different set of factors.
Distance Regulation, for example, appears to be exquisitely sensitive to the
magnitude of alcoholism in one member of the family, whereas other aspects of
behavior appear hardly affected at all. We would argue that these findings are
actually more interesting than their alternative. In this case, if all aspects of
behavior were varying in relation to magnitude of psychopathology, it might
suggest that family life at home is merely being overwhelmed by the presence of
a pathological individual in the family. The more selective findings are con-

TABLE 8.3   ANOVA Summary Table: Two Family Developmental Schemes

Groups	Group Means for HOAM Factors				
	Intrafamily Engagement	Distance Regulation	Extrafamily Engagement	Structural Variability	Content Variability
Years Married					
0-6	1.19	−.02	−.07	.01	−.49
7-20	.02	−.16	.18	−.12	.28
21 or more	−.82	.31	−.27	.20	−.17
F Ratios[a]	12.09**	.62	.59	.27	1.51
Number of Children					
0	.24	.58	.10	.74	−.59
1	.12	−.07	−.45	−.10	.13
2 or more	−.16	−.29	.08	−.36	.28
F Ratios[a]	.49	2.46	.60	4.35*	2.51

* F value significant at p less than .05; ** F value significant at p less than .01.
a. Univariate F ratio with 2 and 28 degrees of freedom.

sistent instead with a hypothesis that regulatory mechanisms for controlling the family's internal environment tend to be finely tuned and selectively adjusted to meet certain contingencies the family must face.

An equally valuable application of the HOAM is the study of family interaction patterns over time. How stable are the mechanisms families use for regulating their internal environments? How sensitive are these behaviors to developmental changes within the family or to superimposed crises? Analyses of HOAM data already collected suggest that Intrafamily Engagement and Structural Variability are sensitive to such developmental variables as years of marriage and family composition (Table 8.3). However, the actual time frame and critical transition points around which these changes occur still remain to be elucidated. We are currently analyzing follow-up data collected three years after our original observations of our sample of alcoholic families. These data will provide an initial glimpse into the long-term stability of the HOAM dimensions.

GRAPHICS FROM HOAM DATA

Data generated by the HOAM may be graphically presented preserving the sequential order in which it was collected or it may be organized around particular behaviors and summarized at different levels. The subject's physical location in the home will be used to illustrate a temporal display of data. The use of the alcohol codes to organize the data will demonstrate another available option.

As the subject moves through the house during an observation session, each location shift is recorded in the order in which it occurs. It is therefore possible to produce a graph from the raw data recorded by the observers which shows in a real-time framework both the use of space in the home and the relative rate of movement. Combining the husband and wife on the same graph provides an indication of their relative synchrony of movement as well as their pattern of interaction. The addition of the floor plan of the house to the graph gives added information concerning the utilization of space in the home.

Figures 8.2 through 8.4 illustrate representative observation sessions for three very different couples. The "midrange" couple (Figure 8.2) shows a pattern of interaction in which blocks of time with consistent physical and verbal contact are interspersed with periods of singular activity. In contrast, the "huddling" couple (Figure 8.3) rarely venture from each other's sight, preferring to remain in one small room of the house over the course of the four hours of observation. The members of the "distant" couple (Figure 8.4) infrequently come together in the same location. These patterns of interaction were consistent for each couple throughout all their observation sessions.

Displays of data from the HOAM may also be arranged based on specific areas of interest to the researcher. Since ours was a study of alcoholic families,

(text continues on page 146)

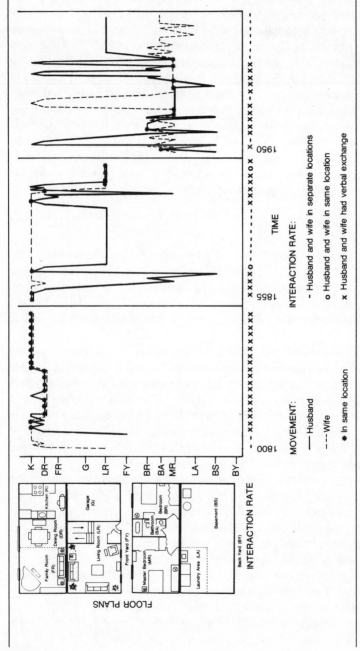

Figure 8.2 Movement of Husband and Wife During a Week Night In-Home Observation Session—Midrange Couple

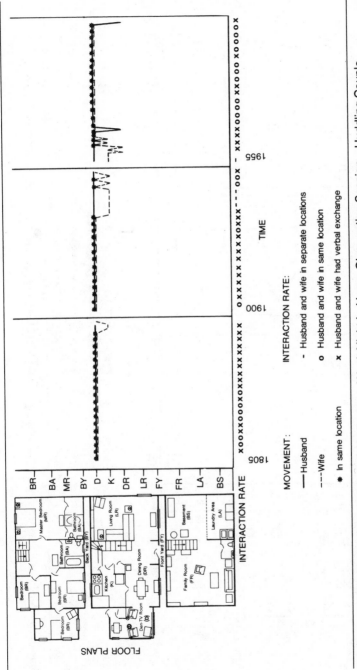

Figure 8.3 Movement of Husband and Wife During a Week Night In-Home Observation Session—Huddling Couple

143

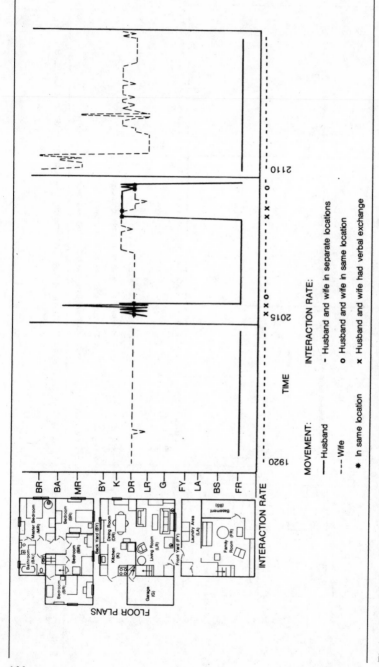

Figure 8.4   Movement of Husband and Wife During a Week Night In-Home   Observation Session—Distant Couple

FLOOR PLANS

BR — Bedroom (BR)
BA — Bathroom (BA)
MR — Master Bedroom (MR)
BY — Back Yard (BY)
K — Kitchen (K)
DR — Dining Room (DR)
LR — Living Room (LR)
G — Garage (G)
FY — Front Yard (FY)
LA — Laundry Area (LA)
BS — Basement (BS)
FR — Family Room (FR)

INTERACTION RATE

TIME
1920   2015   2110

MOVEMENT:

—— Husband
--- Wife
* In same location

INTERACTION RATE:

- Husband and wife in separate locations
o Husband and wife in same location
x Husband and wife had verbal exchange

144

IN-HOME OBSERVATION FAMILY SUMMARY TABLE.
ALC. CODES AS INDEPENDENT VARIABLE. FREQUENCIES AND MEANS

FAMILY 32

ALC CODE CODES	TOTAL ALC. CODES	PEOPLE IN FIELD(PERC.)(NOT 9.99) NONE	SPOUSE ONLY	CHILD ONLY	SPOUSE +CHILD	FAM + EX FAM	INTER DIS (MEAN)	TASK CODES (PERCENT) PI	PF	PQ	WT	IE	NC	AFFECT (MEAN)	OUTCOME(PER) +	0	-
CS 1	163	0.23	0.64	0.04	0.09	0.01	5.4	0.03	0.01	0.01	0.09	0.86	0.0	0.75	0.97	0.01	0.02
2	253	0.75	0.56	0.03	0.06	0.00											
CM 1	32	0.0	1.00	0.0	0.0	0.0	3.9	0.0	0.0	0.0	0.06	0.94	0.0	1.00	1.00	0.0	0.0
2	40	0.0	1.00	0.0	0.0	0.0											
CC 1	122	0.02	0.94	0.12	0.12	0.0	3.8	0.03	0.01	0.02	0.08	0.86	0.0	0.81	0.96	0.02	0.02
2	150	0.01	0.95	0.03	0.13	0.01											
V 1	52	0.77	0.40	0.12	0.10	0.02	7.3	0.0	0.0	0.0	0.19	0.81	0.0	0.81	0.98	0.02	0.0
2	63	0.45	0.37	0.03	0.10	0.0											
NV 1	431	0.25	0.59	0.08	0.08	0.00	6.2	0.01	0.0	0.0	0.15	0.85	0.0	0.93	1.00	0.00	0.0
2	566	0.35	0.51	0.06	0.07	0.00											
TOT 1	830	0.20	0.65	0.06	0.09	0.00	5.6	0.01	0.00	0.00	0.12	0.85	0.0	0.87	0.98	0.01	0.01
TOT 2	1082	0.30	0.53	0.04	0.08	0.00											
TOTAL	1912	0.26	0.61	0.05	0.09	0.00	5.6	0.01	0.00	0.00	0.12	0.85	0.0	0.87	0.98	0.01	0.01

Figure 8.5   Computer Printout of Summary of Interactional Behavior Arranged by Alcohol Codes

145

selected summary tables were developed around five alcohol consumption codes developed specifically for the study, as seen in Figure 8.5. Other behaviorally focused studies (for example, marital interaction and obesity) could easily substitute other relevant behaviors for the alcohol-related behaviors tracked in our study (for example, behaviors related to food consumption). Different levels of data may be utilized in this type of display as well, ranging from ten-minute segments to the totality of the observation sessions for each family, which is the case in the table presented here. Another organizational possibility is the use of the behavioral characteristics codes to differentiate blocks of time when certain types of activity are occurring and then to examine the contextual patterns associated with these behaviors. A family's handling of meal activity, for example, might provide insight into the extent to which the family is structurally organized or relatively chaotic.

SUMMARY

The Home Observation Assessment Method was developed to focus primarily on the marital couple and to collect accurate data regarding interactional behavior in the home as it occurs over an extended period of time. Major design decisions, reflecting both clinical and research biases, included preserving the context in which behavior occurred, the use of a real-time framework for observation, and a concentration on objective/structural aspects of interactional behavior rather than subjective/process variables.

The data generated from the HOAM to date support the notion that a close examination of the manner in which the family carries out its routines of daily living provides a valuable window into the family's regulation of its internal environment. Principal axis factor analysis of the variables developed from the HOAM produces five factors, each hypothesized as representing a different dimension of interactional behavior. Analyses relating to different questions using these HOAM factors as both dependent and independent variables have shown significant and meaningful results.

NOTE

1. Detailed data regarding observer reliability was included in the earlier version of this report published in *Family Process,* which should be consulted if the reader is intending to use the HOAM.

REFERENCE NOTE

1. TISLENKO, L., & STEINGLASS, P. *The relationship between sex of the alcoholic and patterns of interaction in the home.* Manuscript submitted for publication, 1980.

REFERENCES

BARKER, R. B. *Ecological psychology.* Stanford, CA: Stanford University Press, 1968.

BARTKO, J. J. & CARPENTER, W. T. On the methods of reliability. *Journal of Nervous and Mental Disorders,* 1976, *163,* 307-317.

BRADLEY, R. H., & CALDWELL, B. M. Early home environment and changes in mental test performance in children from six to thirty-six months. *Developmental Psychology,* 1976, *12,* 93-97.

BRANDT, R. M. *Studying behavior in natural settings.* New York: Holt, Rinehart & Winston, 1972.

CLARK-STEWART, K. A. Interactions between mothers and their young children: Characteristics and consequences. *Monograph Social Research and Child Development,* 1973, *38,* 1-109.

FLANDERS, N. A. *Analyzing teacher behavior.* Reading, MA: Addison-Wesley, 1970.

HENRY, J. *Pathways to madness.* New York: Random House, 1965.

KANTOR, D., & LEHR, W. *Inside the family.* San Francisco: Jossey-Bass, 1975.

KENT, R. N., & FOSTER, S. L. Direct observational procedures: Methodological issues in naturalistic settings. In A. Ciminero, K. Calhoun, & H. Adams (Eds.), *Handbook of behavioral assessment.* New York: John Wiley, 1977.

LYTTON, H. Observation studies of parent-child interaction: A methodological review. *Child Development,* 1971, *42,* 651-684.

MINUCHIN, P., BIBER, R., SHAPIRO, E., & ZIMILES, H. *The psychological impact of school experience.* New York: Basic Books, 1969.

OLSON, D. H., SPRENDLE, D. H., & RUSSELL, C. Circumplex model of marital and family systems I: Cohesion and adaptability dimensions, family types, and clinical applications. *Family Process,* 1979, *18,* 3-28.

RAUSH, H. C., BARRY, W. A., HERTEL, R. K., & SWAIN, M. A. *Communication, conflict and marriage.* San Francisco: Jossey-Bass, 1974.

REBELSKY, R., & HANKS, C. Fathers' verbal interaction with infants in the first three months of life. *Child Development,* 1971, *42,* 63-68.

STEINGLASS, P. A life history model of the alcoholic family. *Family Process,* 1980, *19,* 211-226.(a)

STEINGLASS, P. Assessing families in their own homes. *American Journal of Psychiatry,* 1980, *137,* 1523-1529.(b)

STEINGLASS, P. The alcoholic family at home: Patterns of interaction in dry, wet, and transitional stages of alcoholism. *Archives of General Psychiatry,* in press.

9

THE DYADIC INTERACTION
SCORING CODE

Erik E. Filsinger

A number of factors need to be weighed when choosing a data collection strategy for observing marital interaction. These factors include the purpose of the research, the concepts to be measured, the sophistication of the observers, the resources available to the investigator, and the quality of the data desired. Many of the existing data collection strategies differ in large part because of those issues. For example, the Couple Interaction Scoring System (Notarius & Markman, Chapter 7, this volume) is one of the most sophisticated and elaborate coding systems. However, it requires that research personnel spend a great deal of time coding the data. As a result, the CISS is particularly well suited to the academic researcher with research assistants who wishes to produce data of the highest quality.

Other investigators may meaningfully select among the alternative data collection packages. For those researchers who desire flexibility of setting, transportability of research team, and ease of data collection and data processing, the Dyadic Interaction Scoring Code (DISC) may be of interest. The DISC is a machine-aided method of collecting observational data on the interaction

AUTHOR'S NOTE: Phil McAvoy provided a provocative critique of an earlier draft of this chapter. My thanks must be extended to him. The research was supported in part by Grant 1 ROL DA02286-01 from the National Institute on Drug Abuse.

between two people. It is a complete coding system in that it involves not only the coding of behaviors, but also data interface with the computer.

The target behaviors in the DISC and their definitions are closely related to those in the Marital Interaction Coding System (MICS; Hops et al., 1972), the Marital and Family Interaction Coding System (MFICS; Olson & Ryder, 1978), and the Couple Interaction Scoring System (CISS; Notarius & Markman, Chapter 7, this volume). In addition, development of the DISC was influenced by the work of Duncan and Fiske (1977) and Hersen et al. (1974).

The first three coding systems, the MICS, MFICS, and the CISS, tend to emphasize positive, negative, and task-oriented behaviors, although each does so in slightly different ways. The Marital and Family Interaction Coding System is specifically tied to the situations and tasks incorporated in the Inventory of Marital Conflict (Olson & Ryder, 1970). Gottman (1979) has suggested a structural model of marital interaction incorporating positiveness, reciprocity, and dominance behaviors. Those three dimensions presumably lie behind the CISS.

In contrast, the conceptualization behind the DISC is that of social competence. Positiveness, negativeness, and task orientation are taken as behaviors which fit under that construct. Essentially this is an individual social competence conceptualization of adequate functioning in marital relationships (Filsinger, Note 1). Competence is conceived as the ability to emit behaviors in marital interaction which are positively reinforced, and not to emit behaviors which are punished. This definition is consistent with many of the current definitions of social skills and social competence (Filsinger, Note 2). Gottman (1979, ch. 12) has provided evidence that supports the notion of individual social competence in marital relationships, but he notes that it is most likely peculiar to the marital situation and not an individual trait which holds across all interpersonal situations.

This chapter is intended to provide the reader with a working knowledge of the DISC by: (1) overviewing and defining target behaviors; (2) giving instructions on the use of the DISC on the Datamyte 900 Data Collector; (3) suggesting training procedures and ways to measure interrater reliability; and (4) discussing data output and analysis possibilities via a research example.

THE DISC—FORM A CODES

The DISC-A measures the structure and content of each spouse's behavior. The data is collected by having one coder focus on the husband and the other coder focus on the wife. This gives an exact record of what each partner is doing at any given time. Structure is assessed through duration measures. These are coded behaviors that have beginning and ending markers so that duration can be calculated. The duration measures are speaking turn and gazing, though gazing is measured as a back-channel phenomenon only (Duncan & Fiske, 1977).

The other aspect of couple interaction is the occurrence of specific content behaviors. These include behaviors that reflect agreement, disagreement, positive and negative affect to self and partner, and so on. The codes have been structured with the second digit of 1 referencing positive types of things and with the second digit of 2 referencing negative types of things. This facilitated memorization.

DURATION MEASURES

11—Begin speaking; 12—stop speaking. These two codes define the beginning and ending of each speaking turn. The time elapsed between each pair of 11 and 12 is the duration of the speaking turn. When neither partner is speaking an 11 is recorded at the beginning of any spoken sentence. At the end of the speaking turn, a 12 is recorded. If there is a question of the speaker pausing and restarting, the coder may wait three seconds to see if the speaker continues. If after three seconds the speaker does not restart, a 12 is recorded. If the speaker does restart, it is considered the same speaking turn and no code is recorded. However, a clear floor switch, such as partner speaking, can be coded immediately.

When the partner is speaking, any attempt to gain speaking turn is first recorded as an interruption (code 17); however, if more than four words are spoken when interrupting, the speech is considered a speaking turn and a 12 is entered at its completion. The start code for that speaking turn can be entered during editing the data file on the computer.

61—Start gazing; 62—stop gazing. The second duration measure concerns directed looking at the partner while the partner is speaking. It is recorded as a back-channel behavior; that is, gazing is recorded only when the partner has the speaking turn, making it a measure of listening. Coding gazing for speaking turns proved too complex.

The same general rules regarding the starting and stopping of speaking turn apply to gazing. If the individual looks at the partner while the partner is speaking, a 61 is recorded. If the individual looks away, a 62 is recorded. If there is a question or a pause, the coder waits three seconds. If the gaze returns it is considered a continuous gaze. If the gaze does not return within three seconds, the 62 is recorded.

CONTENT CODES

15—Back-channel attending. Remarks, head-nodding, and other behaviors made while the partner has the speaking turn are coded as back-channel attending. These indicate attending to the conversation; they are not considered interruptions (17). (For example: "Uh huh"; "Yeah.") If continuous, they are coded every three seconds.

17—Interruption. An attempt to gain the speaking turn, successful or not, is coded an interruption. It has to occur while the partner actually has the turn. If four or more words are used, it can also be coded a speaking turn (11-12). (For example: "I don't . . . "; "Wait a minute.")

18—References to drugs. Any reference to drugs is coded an 18. These references would include any of the current slang phrases and code words for illicit drugs. This particular code could vary with the subject population. "Drugs" was the reference because the current population of subjects had an opiate-involved lifestyle.

20—Problem description. Statements that describe a problem in the relationship which the couple should face or which is relevant to their functioning in either the immediate or broader context are coded as problem descriptions. Opinions about other topics and nonrelationship information are not coded. When used with the Inventory of Marital Conflict, the problem description refers to the couples in the story. (For example: "We need to be more consistent in disciplining the children."; "The issue here is whether John should have done that.")

21—Agreement. Agreement is coded when the partner offers an opinion and the speaker agrees with that viewpoint. If the partner has not voiced an opinion, for example, "It was raining earlier," neither agreement nor disagreement is coded. (For example: Partner: "We probably spend too much money on drugs." Speaker: "Yes."; Partner: "The kids were a pain in the butt yesterday." Speaker: "That's right."; Partner: "I don't like the current president." Speaker: "Nor do I.")

22—Disagreement. This is coded when the partner offers an opinion and the speaker disagrees with that viewpoint. If the partner has not voiced an opinion, for example, "It was raining earlier," neither agreement nor disagreement is coded. (For example: Partner: "We should try to eat better." Speaker: "I think we eat O.K."; Partner: "I didn't like that song." Speaker: "But I did.")

30—Requests for change in partner. This code refers to behaviors aimed at changing either the immediate or long-term behaviors of the partner. These range from commands to requests for changes in the relationship. The key is that the speaker wants the partner to change behaviors in some specified way. (For example: "Pick up that pencil"; or, Partner: "What can I do to make you happy?" Speaker: "Tell me about how things go at work each day.")

31—Compliance. When a requested action is carried out within 10 seconds of the end of the partner's speaking turn, compliance is coded. Requests for future action, such as, "Will you take the garbage out after supper?" can be followed by verbal compliance, "I will."

32—Noncompliance. Noncompliance is coded when a requested behavior is not carried out within 10 seconds of the end of the partner's speaking turn, or no acknowledgment of the intention to comply is evident in 10 seconds.

36—Introducing a compromise. The speaker makes an attempt at a solution to some issue of concern by suggesting how each person can give a little to reach agreement. The trade-off is explicit. (For example: "If you'll do this, I'll do that."; "I'll make a deal with you."; "You get your way this time, but next time I get mine.")

41—Positive self-statements. The speaker refers to himself or his feelings in a favorable light. The statements are positive in that they show a fundamental confidence and enthusiasm. (For example: "I liked that."; "I could do that again!"; "I had an interesting experience today.")

42—Negative self-statements. The speaker refers to himself or his feelings in a negative light, such as self-deprecation, guilt, insecurity, indecision. (For example: "I feel like such a kid."; "I don't know what to do.")

43—Goal orientation. The speaker directs the interaction by changing its direction or by directing the conversation back to its original topic. (For example: "Let's go on to the next topic."; "We should make a decision.")

45—Requesting information or clarification. The speaker asks a question or makes a statement referring to obtaining some piece of information. (For example: "I'm sorry, I didn't catch that."; "What's the meaning of X?"; "Would you repeat that?"; "What did Sally tell you?")

51—Positive affect toward partner. The speaker expresses approval of or concern for partner. (For example: "I like the way you handled that."; "That's a good idea!"; "Can I do something to make you feel better?") This code supercedes other codes, such as the first statement 41 (positive self-statement) or in the third statement 45 (question).

52—Negative affect toward partner. These are personal attacks or statements designed to make the partner feel bad. (For example: "Here I am slaving away and you're out playing around."; "You can really ruin a good day!"; "That's a stupid thing to say!")

79—Laugh. An audible laugh by the individual, done in good faith, is coded here. If the laugh might be one of ridicule it is not coded as a laugh. In other words, this laugh code is meant to capture the good-hearted laugh of camaraderie.

91—Positive physical contact on partner. This is a touch that conveys some degree of friendship or affection. A break of three seconds is required for it to be coded again.

92—Negative physical contact on partner. This is a physical contact that expresses hostility or seeks to constrain the partner against his or her will. A break of three seconds is required for it to be coded again.

Based on the way similar behaviors have been grouped in the MICS and the CISS, two larger combinations of codes can be used as combined scores in some analyses. Codes 15, 21, 31, 36, 41, 43, 51, 61, 79, and 91 are thought to be Facilitative behaviors, while codes 17, 22, 30, 32, 42, 45, 52, and 92 are thought to be Dysfunctional behaviors. Facilitative behaviors are those which help the flow of communication; Dysfunctional behaviors are those judged to hinder it.

The justification for this distinction is twofold. In part, the behaviors are grouped on the basis of the researcher's judgment that these behaviors are similar and serve the stated purpose. Moreover, to the extent to which the groups are based on the categories of the CISS, they have an empirical basis for functional similarity. Gottman (1979) grouped his codes on the basis of those behaviors which elicited the same behaviors from the spouse. The behaviors in each group tended to function in a similar way in the interaction. Because of that influence, the DISC codes are not grouped entirely on an a priori basis.

Several other comments on the coding are necessary. In contrast to some of the coding systems, not all of the behaviors emitted by a focal subject are coded. The coders are instructed to code only the unambiguous occurrences of target behaviors. This decision is due in part to the rapid coding of ongoing behaviors. The time required for coding ambiguous responses is problematic for a single pass by the coder through an observational session, such as is required in naturalistic observation. In addition, it should be noted that DISC coders are asked to rely on their own social perception ability and override the content of a message if it is delivered, for example, in a particularly negative manner. Finally, while some coding systems provide for a double coding of behaviors which communicate more than one thing, the DISC uses hierarchical rule: Dysfunctional behaviors are coded over Facilitative behaviors.

USING THE DISC

The DISC-A was developed for use with the Datamyte 900 Data Collector. When engaged in input-mode 3, the Datamyte automatically enters the two-digit code upon depression of the second key. While that arrangement was well suited for recording behavior, another convention was adapted to enter session information. To identify the session, twelve digits of information were required, for example, *00112091879. The "*" was used as a delimiter. The next three digits, 001, referred to the couple number, in this case Couple 001. The fifth digit was the coder and the sixth, the session—in this case, Coder 1 and Session 2. The last six digits were the date, September 18, 1979. Because of input-mode 3, however, those twelve digits were entered two digits at a time— *0, 01, 12, 09, 18, and 79.

The need to have the timers on the session synchronized was handled by having a universal start code, 98. The synchronization was accomplished by having the second digit, 8, pressed simultaneously on the two Datamytes, thereby assuring exactly where the timer on each Datamyte was at the start of the session (pressing the second digit automatically entered the time). A computer program later corrected the respective timer readings for any discrepancy.[1] Similarly, the end of a session was recorded by a 99, also followed by an end-of-record (EOR) key depression on the Datamyte keyboard.

After the Datamyte has been used in a session, it can be returned to a computer terminal and the data it contains can be dumped into computer storage. These files usually have to be edited on the computer to clean up miscodes and so on.

TRAINING CODERS

Because of the usage of the Datamyte and its computer entry features, the coders must be trained with regard to the DISC coding scheme, the Datamyte, and the computer. Training sessions have interwoven the three components. Usually, however, the best procedure is to begin with an entirely cognitive approach stressing memorization of the codes, including complete recall of both the numeric codes and the definitions. Videotapes of husband-wife interaction prove excellent sources for examples of the target behaviors. Initially, these videotapes can be the basis for discussion and learning. Later, videotapes and live practice can provide testing of the coders' progress.

Precoded videotapes ensure learning and can help avoid observer drift (O'Leary & Kent, 1973). It is good practice to use precoded videotapes to track the coders' progress throughout data collection in order to keep both reliability and validity high.

After the first several training sessions, in which memorization of the codes is stressed, the coders are introduced to the Datamyte 900. This introduction includes having them read the manual and having the Datamyte demonstrated to them, followed by their own practice on it as a machine. After their cognitive understanding of the codes is brought to the level of their quick recognition of natural occurrences of the target behaviors, the coders begin practicing recording the behaviors on the Datamyte.

The coders need a working knowledge of the computer, particularly the editing functions, as soon as they are ready to begin checking reliability. This checking is to be encouraged as soon as possible, so that examination of the output can indicate which codes are giving the coders particular problems. If these behaviors are identified, the coders and the investigator can expend the time necessary to clean up definitions and ensure the proper intercoder agreement.

ASSESSING INTERCODER RELIABILITY

Reliability can be checked by videotaping sessions and having the coders switch focal subjects the second time through. The comparison can be, for instance, Coder A watching the husband the first time through, and Coder B watching him the second time through. Because sequential analyses are a major concern, reliability has been checked at the level of the specific occurrences of the behavior, rather than as correlations between session rates across a number of couples.

The measure of intercoder reliability used with the DISC is the Efficient Percentage Agreement (Jensen, 1959). Calculation of this coefficient does not require the use of mutual nonobservations of a behavior. It is the ratio of mutual observations to the sum of mutual observations and nonmutual observations. The reliability level chosen as a criterion to be reached on three consecutive videotapes prior to beginning data collection is .70. This is taken as a session figure, but it is important to examine the reliability of the individual codes to make sure that they are stabilized. Periodic coding checks (every three or four couples) are useful to ensure high reliability (Hartmann & Gardner, Chapter 12, this volume).

It is given that the coders are aware that they are recoding a data tape; a solution has not yet been found to the somewhat elevated reliability figures encountered when it is known that reliability is being checked (Reid, 1970).

The average session reliability found on the Efficient Percentage Agreement for 12 couples was .77. A more detailed investigation of the psychometric properties of the individual codes is available, as well as evidence for the stability of the codes across two different situations (Filsinger, Note 3). The internal consistency of the Facilitative and Dysfunctional groups have also been checked, alpha = .65 and .59, respectively.

Results have also been reported on the validity of the DISC. Lewis and his colleagues (Chapter 16, this volume) found that the Facilitative and Dysfunctional DISC codes were significantly related to measures of more traditional self-report measures of marital quality. They did a principal component analysis and found that the DISC codes loaded on the principal component along with their measures of marital quality. Lewis and his colleagues (Note 4) have also found that the DISC Facilitative and Dysfunctional behaviors significantly differentiated among three levels of opiate-involved lifestyles: current addicts, methadone-maintained addicts, and former users. They found that current addicts were in relationships characterized by more Dysfunctional and by less Facilitative behaviors than were methadone or former user groups. This finding confirmed the hypothesis of the study.

The finding of the first study, which employed correlational and principal component analysis, suggests the construct validity of the DISC, while the second study, in which hypotheses concerning group differences were supported, suggests the predictive validity of the DISC. It would appear, then, that the basic validity of the DISC's predecessors, such as the MICS and the CISS, has been retained in its machine-operable form.

A RESEARCH EXAMPLE

Opiate-involved husband-wife dyads were observed in a laboratory setting. The couples were asked to complete the Inventory of Marital Conflict (IMC; Olson & Ryder, 1970). The discussion section of the task was videotaped. In the IMC mild conflict was achieved by having the spouses read slightly different versions of similar episodes and then having them attempt to resolve the differences created by the stimuli.

As an illustration of the DISC, the data for one couple are presented in Tables 9.1 and 9.2. The couple met in college. She completed her degree and now works in a clerical position for a social agency. He did not complete his degree and works as a salesman. They live together in an apartment, but are not married. Both of their ages are in the early 20s. They do not have any children.

TABLE 9.1   Rates for Husband and Wife Behaviors

Behavior	Code	Husband		Wife	
		Number	Rate	Number	Rate
Back-channel attending	15	1	.05	9	.41
Interruption	17	13	.59	16	.73
References to drugs	18	—	—	—	—
Problem description	20	11	.50	14	.64
Agreement	21	1	.05	4	.18
Disagreement	22	3	.14	17	.78
Requests for change in partner	30	1	.05	2	.09
Compliance	31	—	—	3	.14
Noncompliance	32	—	—	—	—
Introducing a compromise	36	—	—	—	—
Positive self-statement	41	12	.55	1	.05
Negative self-statement	42	—	—	1	.05
Goal orientation	43	6	.27	3	.14
Requesting information or clarification	45	19	.87	11	.50
Positive affect toward partner	51	2	.09	1	.05
Negative affect toward partner	52	1	.05	—	—
Laugh	79	4	.18	18	.82
Positive physical contact on partner	91	—	—	—	—
Negative physical contact on partner	92	—	—	—	—
Mean speaking		80	.11	62	.12
Mean gazing		2	.17	9	.27

Their combined annual salary is about $25,000. She realizes that she is too dependent on him and feels that he spends too much money, especially on drugs. He feels she is childish at times and that she lectures him too much. He wants to have better control of money and desires to be more aware of others' needs.

Table 9.1 contains the rates for the coded behaviors. These rates are behaviors emitted per minute. It can easily be seen that the woman engages in more back-channel comments (15), laughing (79), and disagreeing (22). The man talks more and is more likely to make positive self-statements (41).

The data for this couple were also analyzed by a sequential analysis. In this procedure, the sequencing of the behaviors is taken into account. Event lags were used. Table 9.2 contains some of these analyses. Only the husband-to-wife lags are presented. Given that the husband stops talking, there is a greater likelihood than chance that the wife will start talking (.35) and that she will stop talking after he starts (.32). The statistical test is the Z-statistic suggested in Gottman and Notarius (1978), with Z-scores 2.00 or higher indicating a probable relationship. The p-value is approximate.

Similarly, the likelihood of behaviors occurring can be pulled out of the second and third lags. The question answered is that given that the husband does something, how likely it is that the wife will respond in such and such a way two behaviors forward, for example, his stopping will be followed two behaviors forward by her stopping, probably an indication of floor switches.

TABLE 9.2   Sequential Analysis of Couple's Interaction

| | | Wife Responses | | | |
Husband Stimuli	Lag	W starts (N = 62)	W stops (N = 62)	W facilitative (N = 48)	W dysfunctional (N = 47)
H starts	1	.15	.32*	.45*	.07*
(N = 80)	2	.30	.20	.37*	.12
	3	.21	.11	.37*	.30
H stops	1	.35*	.15	.28	.21
(N = 80)	2	.11	.37*	.28	.22
	3	.23	.22	.41*	.12
H facilitative	1	.32	.14	.46*	.07
(N = 28)	2	.25	.14	.35	.25
	3	.14	.35	.28	.21
H dysfunctional	1	.18	.24	.51*	.05*
(N = 37)	2	.35	.18	.32	.13
	3	.13	.21	.37*	.27
Unconditional probabilities		.28	.28	.22	.21

*p less than .01

What is interesting about this couple's interaction is the unique tendency for the wife to respond in a positive way following any behavior of the husband. If he starts speaking, her next three behaviors are more likely than chance to be positive. Similarly, there are higher rates when he stops talking. Not only does she emit more positive behaviors when he does so, but she also emits positive behaviors following his negative ones. It should be kept in mind that back-channel comments and laughing, as well as initiating gazing, are grouped as positive behaviors.

This way of looking at the data is consistent with the conceptualization of social competence mentioned in the introduction. The husband obtains high positives from the wife to any of his behaviors and obtains low negative behaviors. In fact, in two cases, his speaking and his negatives, her negatives occur at a degree lower than one would expect by chance, .07 and .05, respectively. Ideologies aside, he seems to have pretty firm control of the relationship.

SUMMARY

The various alternative coding schemes possess different features. The Dyadic Interaction Scoring Code offers researchers a machine-aided coding system specifically designed for use with the Datamyte 900 Data Collector, a hand-held digital data acquisition system with features for data collection, storage, and computer interface. The DISC has quite a bit of flexibility in its usage because of the portability of the Datamyte. The DISC captures elements of couples' positive and negative behaviors. The codes are defined in ways basically consistent with other existing coding systems. An overview of general instructions for its usage was provided, and a research example illustrating its usage was presented.

It may also be useful to speculate as to other uses of the DISC. The coding system appears capable of capturing theoretically relevant positive and negative behaviors. Moreover, it appears useful in discovering recurrent patterns of those positive and negative behaviors. It may be, for example, that the DISC would have a positive value in the training of therapists and counselors, especially where videotaping is already used to assess their skills. The DISC could be used to identify facilitative and dysfunctional aspects of their interactions with clients.

NOTE

1. Computer programs have been written for the DISC by Craig Roberts, computer programmer on the NIDA project.

REFERENCE NOTES

1. FILSINGER, E. E. *Social competence in long- and short-term relationships*. Paper presented at the Theory Construction and Methods Workshop, National Council on Family Relations, Portland, Oregon, October 1980.
2. FILSINGER, E. E. *Conceptualizations of social competence: An integrative review*. Unpublished manuscript, Arizona State University, 1980.
3. FILSINGER, E. E. *A machine-aided behavioral coding scheme: The Dyadic Interaction Scoring Code*. Paper presented at the annual meetings of the National Council on Family Relations, Portland, Oregon, October 1980.
4. LEWIS, R. A., FILSINGER, E. E., CONGER, R. D., & McAVOY, P. *The quality of couple relationships among heroin users: Self-report and behavioral differences*. Paper presented at the First World Congress of Victimology, Washington, D.C., September 1980.

REFERENCES

DUNCAN, S., Jr., & FISKE, D. W. *Face to face interaction: Research, methods, and theory*. Hillsdale, NJ: Lawrence Erlbaum, 1977.

GOTTMAN, J. M. *Marital interaction: Experimental investigations*. New York: Academic, 1979.

GOTTMAN, J. M., & NOTARIUS, C. Sequential analysis of observational data using Markov chains. In T. R. Kratochwill (Ed.), *Single subject research*. New York: Academic, 1978.

HERSEN, M., EISLER, R. M., & MILLER, P. M. An experimental analysis of generalization in assertive training. *Behavior Research and Theory*, 1974, *12*, 295-310.

HOPS, H., WILLS, T. A., PATTERSON, G. R., & WEISS, R. L. *Marital Interaction Coding System*. Eugene: University of Oregon and Oregon Research Institute, 1972. (Order from ASIS/NAPS, c/o Microfiche Publications, 305 E. 46th Street, New York, NY 10017)

JENSEN, A. R. The reliability of projective techniques: Methodology. *Acta Psychologica*, 1959, *16*, 108-136.

O'LEARY, K. D., & KENT, R. N. Behavior modification for social action: Research tactics and problems. In L. Hamerlynck, L. C. Handy, & E. J. Mash (Eds.), *Behavior change: Methodology, concepts, and practice*. Champaign, IL: Research Press, 1973.

OLSON, D. H., & RYDER, R. G. Inventory of Marital Conflicts (IMC): An experimental interaction procedure. *Journal of Marriage and the Family*, 1970, *32*, 443-448.

OLSON, D. H., & RYDER, R. G. *Marital and Family Interaction Coding System* (MFICS): *Abbreviated coding manual*. St. Paul: Family Social Science, University of Minnesota, 1978.

REID, J. B. Reliability assessment of observation data: A possible methodological problem. *Child Development*, 1970, *41*, 1143-1150.

10

EXPANDING THE FRONTIERS
OF INTERACTION RESEARCH

G. Hugh Allred
James M. Harper
Rex A. Wadham
Bruce H. Woolley

This chapter is a preliminary report of a project designed to provide in-depth analyses of couples' multichannel (verbal, nonverbal, physiological, and covert) interactional response patterns. We hope that this project can help meet the needs in marriage and family therapy identified by Beck (1976) for improved diagnostic and evaluation measures and for procedures that will tap new dimensions for analyzing change in interaction. Also, we hope that our multidimensional in-depth approach can help answer the call by Cromwell et al. (1976) for gathering information that will be more useful than that which is presently available.

In this report, we describe (1) the advanced computer technology we use to record simultaneously the multichannel responses of the couples and (2) the instruments we employ to identify the verbal, nonverbal, physiological, and covert responses. We also discuss the procedures we utilize to determine significant characteristic patterns of synchrony or asynchrony among subjects' multichannel responses.

DESCRIBING THE COMPUTER TECHNOLOGY

The computer system we are using in the project is known as the "timed interval, categorical observation recorder" coupled to a data analysis computer (TICOR-DAC; Wadham, Note 1). The TICOR unit of the system is a patented special-purpose portable battery-powered computer based on the Z80 microprocesser chip (McMullen & Wadham, Note 2). It is designed to automate collection of large amounts of data representing multiple channels of time sequential events simultaneously recorded on a digital microcassette tape for later or concurrent analysis by a table-top computer known as the DAC unit. The version of the TICOR computer console being used in the current research consists of a 64-key keyboard system providing 14 programmable function keys and 50 multiple event keys. Add-ons include a 5-key subject-response pad unit with rheostat control. Up to 60 of these units can be daisy-chained into the TICOR console. When our research applications overload the computational and data storage capacity of the DAC, data is processed through the TICOR-DAC onto a DEC 10 system.

The 50 multiple event keys on the main console have two general modes of operation called "label mode" and "duration mode." In the label mode, the operator uses the keys to label data sets, to write annotated comments before or after a data set, and to provide mnemonic codes for sorting the data into biographical classifications, such as the dyadic relation or birth order of subjects (Bishop et al., Note 3). Under the duration mode, the keys provide both a primary *identification* for the event and a related *modifying* function. Primary keys record the onset of an event, such as talk undefined, followed by one or more modifying keys used to define the nature of and/or the purpose of the talk. Since these keys are also under programmable control, the flexibility of the process is limited only by the user's ability to be inventive. For instance, a modifying key can define not only the nature of the talk, but also its intensity, such as harshness or softness within the normal speech range.

The versatility of the subject-response pads is similar to that of the main console. When the pads are used as recorders of covert responses, subjects can simultaneously insert their feelings (such as "I feel sad" or "I feel happy") into the recorded flow of the observed interaction. Additional observers can also use these in tandem with the main console to record nonverbal interaction. All of these procedures can be accomplished simultaneously.

TICOR, in addition to the above features, has a 16-channel analog/digital converter built into the main console, which is designed to input physiological devices such as a monitor for heart rate, body temperature, or other similar measures. Analog input to the console is obtained either through an FM transmission or direct wire. It is through these features that the system offers the family-oriented researcher a powerful observational procedure designed to capture multiple dimensions of complex dyadic and higher-order event patterns of family or other types of interactions. Our present procedures are based on the premise that interaction is a fluid process of interdependent and interconnected events. For example, we believe that a single verbal bossing behavior from a husband to a wife is not random, but part of a complex flow of verbal, nonverbal, and physiological responses occurring simultaneously between the two partners. To achieve our goal of obtaining a more complete profile of dyadic interactions, we, acting as the design team, kept foremost in mind that each event is a slice of a larger and more complex multichannel event process (Dell, 1980).

In addition to using reliable coding instruments, it was equally important to us to maintain a high level of fidelity for each of the multichannel input signals. Fidelity controls were therefore built into the hardware and software support systems. Fidelity of the input data is under the control of a microprocessor. Through a series of alerts consisting of audio beeps or alpha-numeric codes, the coder can identify such things as incorrect keyboard operation, dyads that require entry of additional information, and incorrect sequencing of modifiers. The total computer package is flexible enough to allow for the collection and analysis of a wide range of data recorded in many different settings (such as home, school, work and so on).

IDENTIFYING VERBAL INTERACTION

The Allred Interaction Analysis (AIA; Allred, 1976) is the instrument we have selected for use with TICOR-DAC to analyze couples' verbal communication. Adlerian vertical and level (horizontal) models of relationships (Sicher, 1954, Dreikurs, Note 4; Allred, 1976) provide the basic framework for the AIA. Vertical relationships are exemplified by competitive struggles, beliefs that one must appear superior to others to have a place with them, and feelings of insecurity. By contrast, level relationships are represented by cooperative efforts that influence the self and others is constructive ways, beliefs that one need not strive to appear superior to belong, and feelings of security (Allred, 1976). (Selecting an instrument that is grounded in theory is consistent with the advice of Cromwell et al., 1976, that researchers should investigate theoretical constructs that are relevant to treatment.)

The strength of the vertical and level models is indicated by the convergent thinking of Benedict, in her descriptions of high and low synergy (Maslow, 1971), Horney (1945), in her concepts of moving against, away from, and toward others, and the system theorists' models of symmetrical, complementary, and parallel relationships (Watzlawick et al., 1967). Also, in a recent book analyzing family relationships and child-rearing models, the authors, who are not Adlerians, identify the Adlerian level (horizontal) relationship as the primary condition for fostering moral maturity (Boyce & Jensen, 1978). Additional support for the value of these models is indicated by their widespread use in Adlerian therapy and prevention programs. The first author of this chapter, G. Hugh Allred, has also found these models useful for communicating ideas concerning ineffective and effective relationships to lay and professional audiences. He believes that the imagery evoked by the vertical and level concepts enables people to focus on and to retain the ideas being taught.

There are twelve categories which make up the AIA as it is used with the TICOR-DAC to collect and analyze the incoming data. Of these, six codify the level model of constructive interpersonal relationships: (1) Disclosing Thoughts, (2) Seeking to Understand, (3) Negotiating, (4) Committing, (5) Encouraging, and (6) Disclosing Feelings. Communication must be voiced with warmth, sincerity, empathy, and respect to be classified in one of the six level categories. Five categories codify the vertical model of destructive verbal behavior: (7) Soliciting Attention, (8) Bossing, (9) Punishing, (10) Distancing, and (11) Surrendering. The twelfth category is identified as Confusion. It is not classified as either level or vertical. (See Allred, 1976, or Allred & Graff, 1979, for additional information on each of the AIA categories.)

RELIABILITY

To test the reliability of the present version of the AIA, two trained observers, following rules for observers developed by Amidon and Flanders (1963) and revised by the instrument's designer, analyzed the interaction between the partners in each of twenty married couples. Reliability was computed using methods developed by Bijou et al. (1969). Reliability coefficients were found to range from .82 to .96, with a mean of .90. These results were consistent with those instruments upon which it was modeled (Amidon & Flanders, 1963; Allred & Kersey, 1977). In a more recent test of reliability, two trained observers maintained their reliability coefficients at .85 or higher when they analyzed two interaction episodes for each of 61 dyads (Allred & Graff, 1979).

VALIDITY

Evidence for the concurrent validity of the AIA was found by Graff (Allred & Graff, 1979). Subjects' AIA scores derived from observers' ratings were consistent with subjects' scores on the Interpersonal Communication Inventory (ICI) developed by Bienvenu (1970) to differentiate good and bad communication patterns, and on the Jones-Mohr Listening Test, developed by Jones and Mohr (Pfeiffer et al., 1976) to test a subject's understanding of a message from emotional verbalizations. The results on all three measures showed significant positive changes for the experimental group. An analysis of the means on all three tests at the end of the eight-week follow-up indicated that subjects maintained their gains.

ANALYSIS

Combining the AIA with the TICOR-DAC enables us to compute unit-by-unit verbal behavior more efficiently for any given point in time and to determine the amount of time an individual or couple spends in talking in the level or vertical interaction style. The TICOR-DAC also computes the time subjects spend in each of the AIA categories as recorded by the AIA observers. The AIA observers' ratings are combined with the nonverbal, physiological, and covert response measurements to provide us with an in-depth analysis of subjects' simultaneous multichannel responses.

IDENTIFYING NONVERBAL BEHAVIOR

Verbal and nonverbal behavior interlock, creating precise social meanings in interpersonal relationships. Although the AIA provides a mental map to describe verbal interaction, it does not allow for observation of crucial areas such as kinesics and proxemics. Thus a scheme had to be developed to classify nonverbal behavior occurring in conjunction with the verbal interaction coded with the AIA.

Preliminary studies have suggested that some nonverbal behavior parallels a linguistic system built on formal rules of language (Birdwhistle, 1970; Scheflen, 1974). Kendon (1969) discovered that in dyadic interaction the flow of movement in the listener may be rhythmically coordinated with the flow of the speaker. Characterizing the flow of nonverbal interaction as a series of contrasting waves of movement, he describes complex sequences within which the smaller waves may be contained in the larger waves. This rhythmic coordination is called *interactional synchrony*. Kendon further concludes that the ways in which individuals may be in synchrony with one another vary, and these variations are related to their respective roles in interaction.

DESIGNING THE NONVERBAL CODING SYSTEM

To assess the nonverbal part of this interactional synchrony, we have developed several categories of nonverbal behaviors based on earlier notation systems for facial posture and body position developed by Birdwhistle (1970) and Kendon (1969). Birdwhistle's notation system for body movement is undoubtedly the most comprehensive coding scheme available. Kendon condenses many of Birdwhistle's categories for more practical use. Since initial use of these categories proved that modification was necessary for our project, we added new categories and refined others. The present coding scheme is shown in Table 10.1.

TABLE 10.1   Nonverbal Observation Scheme

HEAD:	1. Turned to left 2. Erect, face pointing forward 3. Turned to right 4. Nodding	
FACE:	A. Brows:	1. Raised 2. Normal position 3. Frowning
	B. Eyes:	1. Looking at other 2. No eye contact
	C. Mouth:	1. Smiling, mouth not open 2. Laugh or smile with mouth open 3. Inexpressive mouth 4. Pursed or pouting lips
TRUNK:	1. Leaning forward 2. Erect 3. Leaning backward	
ARMS:	1. Crossed 2. Open 3. One or both raised, covering face 4. One or both raised, not covering face	
HANDS:	1. Clenched 2. Open 3. Touching other person 4. Pointing, jabbing, slicing	
LEGS/FEET:	1. Crossed right 2. Crossed left 3. Open, both touching floor 4. Nervous jiggling of one or both feet	

SELECTING WHAT TO OBSERVE

Total head. Most kinesic analysis schemes include several observations of the head, including head nods (which way and how many), head sweeps, whether the head is cocked, and direction of turn. In our project, direction of head turn and nodding are the crucial units. Only these two basic elements are used because Ekman et al. (1969) suggest that head orientations may communicate gross affective states, but usually not specific emotions. Head nodding has been frequently used in interactional observation, and seems to indicate approval-seeking behaviors as well as marking the rhythm of verbal behavior. Direction of the head turn factor is based on Mehrabian's (1972) work on interpersonal attraction.

Face. Nonverbal observers have recorded in this category such things as brow movements, direction of gaze, wide eyes, squints, closed eyes, nostril flare, several kinds of smiles, tightened temples, scalp movement, and muscle tension. Because many of these units are difficult to observe, they were eliminated from our present scheme. Ekman and Friesen (1975) identified three basic areas of the face as most crucial to the observer: eyebrow area, eye area, and lower face. They discovered that a combination of different expressions in these three parts conveyed emotional expression. For example, in trying to appear reasonable, an angry husband may display a pained grin which is the combination of a frowning brow and a slight smile (mouth not open). These three basic areas (eyebrows, eyes, and mouth) were therefore selected for our observations.

Body. The study of body movement has investigated the relationships among kinesics and attitudes, status, emotion, approval seeking, quasicourtship behavior, inclusiveness, deception, warmth, and interaction markers (Knapp, 1974). In a review of studies in the above areas, we have discovered that most nonverbal researchers concern themselves with four major parts of the body: (1) trunk position, (2) openness of arms, (3) tension in hands, and (4) frequency of movement and openness of legs/feet. Mehrabian (1972) has identified all of these as important indicators of attitude, status, and interpersonal attraction. We have chosen to include them in our observations, as seen above.

ANALYSIS

The TICOR system allows us to determine the time required for a rater to make each entire body sweep from head to legs/feet. A limit of fifteen seconds of sweep time has been established. The machine is started at exactly the same time as the verbal coding machine so that the verbal and nonverbal sequences of data correlate in time. This yields unit-by-unit multichannel behavior for any given point in time as well as frequency per minute, latency, duration of events in .10-second intervals, and Markovian probabilities.

MEASURING PHYSIOLOGICAL RESPONSES

It is becoming more and more evident that a major correlation exists between the physiological and the psychological aspects of behavior (Krupp & Chatton, 1978). Proper management and treatment of couples' interaction thus depends on a holistic understanding of the disrupted behavioral patterns (Krupp & Chatton, 1978; Boedeker, 1974). The therapist must understand the altered physiological patterns in association with the more readily observable patterns of verbal and nonverbal behavior. However, the research that will lead to the establishment of a comprehensive assessment of such patterns has not been fully explored (Malasanos et al., 1977).

A basic understanding of assessment parameters, laboratory values, and diagnostic tests, as well as the potential variables in pathological behavioral changes, is a necessity for the clinical or research-oriented social scientist (Woolley, 1978). This understanding, correlated with observable behavior and interaction patterns, enables the therapist to more accurately monitor and assess the psychopathology. When the reported lab value or physiological function does not appear to coincide with the expected result, the therapist should be aware that drugs, food, and herbs can alter physiologic function and laboratory values (Sandford-Todd, 1974).

The full significance of these physiological parameters for interaction and behavior is not yet known, and much research must be undertaken (Malasanos et al., 1977). Such projects as the correlation of these parameters with verbal and nonverbal observable behaviors have the potential of establishing a new horizon in behavioral and interactional clinical assessment.

The determination of specific contributing factors and outcomes of behavior and interaction utilizing both physiological and psychological parameters will initially include pulse, body temperature, respiration, blood pressure, and perspiration. However, we will first incorporate pulse measures into our analyses and then add the other four physiological measures as we gain experience.

Measurement will utilize physiographical techniques with a time correlation to the observations recorded into the TICOR system. Each set of data will include the observed verbal and nonverbal behavior and subjects' covert responses, and the physiological measurements made with physiographical instrumentation. The following discussion is guided by Guyton (1971).

Pulse. Alterations in the pulse can be caused by changes in the stroke volume of the heart or in the capacitance of the arteries. Abnormal measurements of these two variables may or may not indicate a pathologic state and, depending on magnitude or duration, may either elicit or cause behavioral changes that may be transitory or permanent. The changes that occur in various observable behavioral changes will be measured and the significance of the data will be determined.

Body temperature. Subtle variations in body temperature occur daily due to diurnal variation. However, changes beyond the normal variations may be indicators of a pathological state. It has been reported that stress factors may also alter the ability for maintenance of homeostatic function. The significance of body temperature in interactional behavior has not been clearly elucidated and may not prove to be significant. However, this variable must be considered as a potential indicator of mood and/or overt behavioral change.

Respiration. Stress, as well as many other psychological behavioral patterns, can alter respiration rate, exertion, edema, and wheezing. As interactional patterns emerge from the development of the research data, a correlation will be made with variations in the respiratory pattern.

Blood pressure. Blood pressure fluctuates widely in response to emotional stress, especially anger, resentment, and frustration. The repeated measurement of blood pressure, in association with behavioral pattern assessment, is required for a thorough search for specific causes of pathophysiological features and may be of significant value in dealing with interactional communication problems.

Perspiration. Nervousness, anxiety, stress, mood variations, and other behavioral factors can change the intensity and volume of perspiration. Measurement of the perspiration on the palm of the hand will ascertain if this physiological response can be utilized in a correlated interactional measurement of problems that may not be verbalized by clients.

The physiological parameters listed above are but a few of the many potential indicators of interactional psychopathology. It should be clearly understood that none of these parameters taken in isolation is a clear indicator, but we expect that the significance of various correlations may become clear in the ongoing project. The determinations of how they may be utilized in combination with clinical expertise and judgment, demographic data (including food, drug, or herb ingestion), and the presenting signs and symptoms will be investigated in this project.

SUMMARY

In this chapter, we have described a holistic approach to observing and analyzing couples' interaction. We have also described the TICOR-DAC, a new patented computer system designed specifically for researching interaction in human subjects. The verbal, nonverbal, and physiological measurements used in our observations were presented. Combining verbal, nonverbal, covert, and physiological responses into observations synchronized in time provides the potential for typifying dyads based on a holistic view of interaction. It is our hope not only to identify diagnostic types of dyads, but also to discover the complex rules of synchrony and ways of intervening to produce more loving, nurturing, and satisfying relationships.

REFERENCE NOTES

1. WADHAM, R. A. *Microcomputer applications in interaction analysis.* Paper presented at the meeting of the American Educational Research Association, San Francisco, April 1979.

2. McMULLEN, J. W. G., & WADHAM, R. A. United States Patent #4197651. April 8, 1980.

3. BISHOP, R. H., GALE, L., RENCHER, A. C., WADHAM, R. A., WILCOX, R., & YOUNG, J. R. *Assessing bilingual instruction practices and outcomes: A precision approach to an old dilemma.* Paper presented at the meeting of the American Educational Research Association, San Francisco, April 1979.

4. DREIKURS, R. *The courage to be imperfect.* Paper presented at a meeting of the School of Education, University of Oregon, Eugene, July 1957.

REFERENCES

ALLRED, G. H. *How to strengthen your marriage and family.* Provo, UT: Brigham Young University Press, 1976.

ALLRED, G. H., & GRAFF, T. T. The AIA, a mental map for communicators: A preliminary report. *Journal of Marital and Family Therapy,* 1979, *5,* 33-42.

ALLRED, G. H., & KERSEY, F. L. The AIAC, a design for systematically analyzing marriage and family counseling: A progress report. *Journal of Marriage and Family Counseling,* 1977, *3,* 17-25.

AMIDON, E. J., & FLANDERS, N. A. *The role of the teacher in the classroom: A manual for understanding and improving teachers' classroom behavior.* Minneapolis, MN: Paul S. Amidon and Associates, 1963.

BECK, D. F. Research findings on the outcomes of marital counseling. In D. H. L. Olson (Ed.), *Treating relationships.* Lake Mills, IA: Graphic Publication, 1976.

BIENVENU, M. J. Measurement of marital communication. *Family Coordinator,* 1970, *19,* 26-31.

BIJOU, S. W., PETERSON, R. F., HARRIS, F. R., ALLEN, K. E., & JOHNSTON, M. S. Methodology for experimental studies of your children in natural settings. *Psychological Record,* 1969, *19,* 177-210.

BIRDWHISTLE, R. L. *Kinesics and context.* Philadelphia: University of Pennsylvania Press, 1970.

BOEDEKER, E. C. *Manual of medical therapeutics* (21st ed.). Boston: Little, Brown, 1974.

BOYCE, W. D., & JENSEN, L. C. *Moral reasoning: A psychological-philosophical integration.* Lincoln: University of Nebraska Press, 1978.

CROMWELL, R. E., OLSON, D. H. L., & FOURNIER, D. G. Diagnosis and evaluation in marital and family counseling. In D. H. L. Olson (Ed.), *Treating relationships.* Lake Mills, IA: Graphic Publication, 1976.

DELL, P. F. The Hopi family therapist and the Aristotelian parents. *Journal of Marital and Family Therapy,* 1980, *6,* 123-130.

EKMAN, P. & FRIESEN, W. V., *Unmasking the face: A guide to recognizing emotions from facial cues.* Englewood Cliffs, NJ: Prentice-Hall, 1975.

EKMAN P., FRIESEN, W. V., & TAUSSIG, T. VID-R and SCAN: Tools and methods in the analysis of facial expression and body movement. In G. Gebner, O. Holst, K. Krippendroff, W. Paisley, & P. Stone (Eds.), *Content analysis.* New York: John Wiley, 1969.

EKMAN, P., FRIESEN, W. V., & TOMKINS, S. S. Facial affect scoring technique: A first validity study. *Semiotica,* 1971, 37-58.

GUYTON, A. *Textbook of medical physiology* (4th ed.). Philadelphia: W. B. Saunders, 1971.

HORNEY, K. *Our inner conflicts: A constructive theory of neurosis.* New York: Norton, 1945.

KENDON, A. J. Progress report of an investigation into aspects of the structure and function of the social performance in two-person encounters. In M. Argyle (Ed.), *Social interaction.* New York: Atherton, 1969.

KNAPP, M. L. *Nonverbal communication in human interaction.* New York: Holt, Rinehart & Winston, 1974.

KRUPP, M. A., & CHATTON, M. J. *Current medical diagnosis and treatment.* Los Altos, CA: Lange Medical Publications, 1978.

MALASANOS, M. L., BARKANSKAS, V., MOSS, M., & STOLTENBERG-ALLEN, K. *Health assessment.* St. Louis: Mosby, 1977.

MASLOW, A. H. *The farther reaches of human nature.* New York: Viking, 1971.

MEHRABIAN, A. Nonverbal communication. In J. K. Cole (Ed.), *Nebraska symposium on motivation.* Lincoln: University of Nebraska Press, 1972.

PFEIFFER, J. W., HESLIN, R., & JONES, J. E. *Instrumentation in human relations training* (2nd ed.). La Jolla, CA: University Associates, 1976.

SACKETT, G. P. The lag sequential analysis of contingency and cyclicity in behavioral interaction research. In J. Osofsky (Ed.), *Handbook of infant development.* New York: John Wiley, 1978.

SANDFORD-TODD. *Clinical diagnosis by laboratory methods* (15th ed.). Philadelphia: W. B. Saunders, 1974.

SCHEFLEN, A. E. *How behavior means.* New York: Gordon & Breach, 1974.

SICHER, L. Education for freedom. *Journal of Individual Psychology,* 1954, *11*(2).

WATZLAWICK, P., BEAVIN, J. H., & JACKSON D. D. *Pragmatics of human communication.* New York: Norton, 1967.

WOOLLEY, B. H., & OPPENHEIMER, P. R. *Clinical pharmacy in ambulatory care.* Miami: Symposia Specialists Medical Books, 1978.

11

USING DATA LOGGING EQUIPMENT

Richard A. Holm

Direct observation and systematic recording of behavior have played major roles in the development of the behavioral sciences. In the early phases observations were largely descriptive, thus each field has a long tradition of some form of case reports, specimen records, or field notes. There is now a growing shift in the nature of direct observation from general description to a more analytical approach characterized by the generation of specific questions or hypotheses, gathering quantitative data, and using statistical methods in determining the viability of the hypotheses. The quality and quantity of data required by the new orientation, coupled with technological advances in electronics, have led to a rapid evolution of data collection equipment and methodologies.

MODERN DATA LOGGING EQUIPMENT

Modern data logging equipment allows the coder merely to press keys representing the behaviors of interest as those behaviors occur. The equipment automatically clocks and adds time or duration information to each event code and stores the events in sequence. The stored codes can be directly transferred to a larger computer for subsequent analyses. Alternative recording techniques, described by Hutt and Hutt (1970) and Holm (1978), make use of paper-and-pencil checklists, clocks and counters, transcriptions from voice recordings,

TABLE 11.1   Sample Data as Stored on Host Computer

T	CS	CL SC	OB	MMDDYY	SET	SUBJ	GR	S	AGE
3	EC	03 05	24	090180	243	1532	50	1	1423
		124	11	0					
		255	8	7					
		252	30	15					
		235	8	45					
		301	0	60					
		234	20	52					
		.							
		.							
		.							
		124	145	120					
		252	35	265					
	−1			300					

and stripchart event recorders. Three portable data loggers are commercially available (Datamyte, Electro General Corp., 14960 Industrial Rd., Minnetonka, MN 55343; MORE, Observational Systems, Inc., 1103 Grand Ave., Seattle, WA 98122; SSR System 7, Semeiotic Systems Corporation, 105 Marinette Trail, Madison, WI 53705) and several articles describe custom-made devices (Fitzpatrick, 1977; Gass, 1977; Sackett et al., 1973; Sanson-Fisher et al., 1979; White, 1971). The author is most familiar with the MORE data logger and its associated software package for data manipulation, ODAP. Specific details in this chapter will relate to the MORE/ODAP system, but the principles illustrated are general to all data logging equipment and data manipulation programs.

Table 11.1 presents a general format for observational data as output by the MORE/ODAP system. The first two lines contain header or identification information. The data are presented in three columns. The first column lists the events in the order they occurred. In this sample, three digits were used to describe each event. The number of digits in each event code and the meaning of the code are defined by the coding scheme. The first code (124) in one scheme might represent wife (1)—neutral affect (2)—agrees with husband (4); in another scheme, the same digits could represent low level (1)—disharmony (24). The second column provides the durations of the codes in column one and the third column provides the time from the start of the observation period to the start of each event. The first two lines in the sample sequence indicate that event 124 lasted for 11 seconds starting at time 0 and was followed by event 255, which lasted for 8 seconds starting at time 7. The first 4 seconds of the second event were concurrent with the last 4 seconds of the first event. The event coded on line five (301) is a momentary event which occurred 60 seconds into the trial and 8 seconds after the start of the durational event 234. All information regarding frequency, duration, sequence, and simultaneity is retrievable from data in this format.

The potential importance of data loggers to marital research and clinical practice is indicated by the substantial time savings they offer and by the feasibility of collecting durational and sequential information. Detailed observational information, which is central to most questions about social interaction, is costly to collect. Recovery of such data without the aid of data logging equipment requires video or audio taping of the session, with subsequent transcription and timing of the recordings, or it requires collecting the data on a multichannel stripchart event recorder and measuring the lengths of various line segments to recover the durations (Holm, 1978). These processes typically take 10 to 30 times as long as the actual observation. Gottman et al. (1977), in a study of marital conflict using the Couples Interaction Scoring System (Notarius & Markman, Chapter 7, this volume), report that "the total time for verbatim transcribing, content and affect coding was approximately 28 hours per hour of videotape." In a study coding each communicative act between deaf preschoolers and their mothers (Greenberg, 1980), the coding time was 10 to 20 times the observation time (Greenberg, personal communication). The use of data logging equipment and a somewhat simplified coding scheme can virtually eliminate this data recovery time, as indicated by Filsinger (Chapter 9, this volume). Data logging equipment can also substantially reduce the time required to code audio or videotape in cases where the study question requires information too detailed to code in real time. Coding from video or audiotape is discussed in a separate section below.

An apparent disadvantage of the data loggers is their high initial cost; however, this is quickly recovered in savings of coder time that would have to be expended in data recovery and entry if other recording techniques were used. There is a relatively long initial start-up time required to get familiar with the data logging equipment, the host computer, and to develop computer programs. The quantity of data typically collected in studies using data loggers requires extensive use of a digital computer for data storage, management, manipulation, and analysis. Depending upon the investigators' familiarity with available computers and the feasibility of using program packages already developed, the computer portion of the start-up time could range from a week to months. The start-up time drops dramatically on subsequent studies. Few investigators realize that software development typically costs more than the equipment. Appropriate use of existing software packages can greatly reduce these costs. The MORE and SSR System 7 both offer the support of sophisticated software packages. The packages are interesting to compare because each approaches the data collection and manipulation tasks quite differently. It is easy to put off the development of computer programs and begin collecting data as soon as the coding scheme is developed. However, as indicated below, coding schemes and analysis programs can affect each other considerably, thus it is undesirable to develop one without knowledge of the other.

DEVELOPING CODING SCHEMES
FOR DATA LOGGERS

Successful use of data loggers lies in developing a coding scheme which is in balance with the level of detail required by the study question. The coding scheme includes the list and definitions of events to be coded (taxonomy) and the methods for sampling, entering, and timing the events. Developing behavioral taxonomies is discussed in other articles (Rosenblum, 1978; Blurton-Jones & Woodson, 1979). A difficult step in developing coding schemes is discarding the approach of coding "everything" with the hope of discovering the important variables in subsequent analyses. The more specific the initial question or hypothesis, the easier the entire process of coding scheme development, coder training, data collection, summarization, and analysis becomes. It would be difficult to overemphasize this point.

SAMPLING METHODS

Obtaining data similar to those presented in Table 11.1 requires recording every frequency or duration of codable behavior occurring in the observation session. For some questions gathering a complete record may not be practical or necessary. In such cases, coding selected samples of the ongoing behaviors using one of the methods discussed by Altmann (1974) or Sackett (1978) could greatly simplify data collection. For example, Steinglass and Tislenko (Chapter 8, this volume) sampled verbal interactions by coding the subject's first verbal interaction in each 2-minute block of the observation period. Some data loggers can be set to cue the observer each time a sample is to be taken. Care must be taken to assure that the samples can be considered random. Two commonly used sampling methods, zero-one and *Ad Libitum* sampling, produce data which, unfortunately, are of questionable value (Altmann, 1974).

ENTERING DATA

There are a variety of ways of entering any taxonomy into a data logger. For example, an investigator decides to code each marital partner's affect using three levels (positive = 3, neutral = 2, negative = 1). A two-digit coding scheme could be used in which the first digit indicates the person being described (wife = 1, husband = 2) and the second digit indicates the affect; thus, a 13 would indicate wife-positive. When either the husband or the wife changes affect the code for both is entered. A second method is to use a two-digit code in which the first digit is the wife's affect and the second digit is the husband's; thus, a 13 would indicate wife-negative and husband-positive. A third method uses a one-digit scheme in which the digits 1-9 represent the nine possible combinations of affect (wife-positive, husband-positive=1; wife-positive, husband-neutral=2, and so on).

Several general points can be made in comparing these three methods. The third method, while using fewer key strokes, is more difficult to memorize and use. Building a syntax into the code can greatly simplify data entry and analysis. The second method has produced a mutually exclusive coding scheme from two nonexclusive categories. Each line represents the complete description of dyadic state at that point in time, whereas when using the first method, several lines may have to be searched to determine the dyadic state at any point in time. Mutually exclusive coding schemes have some useful properties when an analysis of the data is considered. Using the second method, the frequency, duration, and sequence of dyadic states are directly available and the information for individuals is recoverable by analyzing each column separately and combining the durations of equal consecutive codes.

However, all three methods carry the same amount of information. Data collected using one method can be transferred to the format of the other methods. Data can therefore be collected by the method easiest for the observer to use and transformed via a computer program to the format best suited for analysis.

Some coding schemes take advantage of the spatial configuration of the keyboard. On a standard 10-key numeric pad, the first column of keys (7, 4, 1) could be used for the husband's affect and the second column (keys 8, 5, 2) for the wife's. The top keys (7, 8) would represent positive affect, the middle (4, 5) neutral, and the bottom (1, 2) negative. The observer would code by position

TABLE 11.2   Code-Time Pairs for Sample Data

Event Code	Start Time
124	0
255	7
024	11
252	15
235	45
234	52
301	60
243	72
.	.
.	.
.	.

with no need to learn the numeric values. Using this scheme, the dyadic state husband-neutral, wife-positive would be represented by 48 (middle-top). The redundancy built into the coding scheme (person being defined by both digit position and value) would provide a nice error check while placing little or no added burden on the observer.

COMPUTER PROGRAM AND
CODING SCHEME INTERACTION

Much of the flexibility associated with data loggers is actually built into the programs which aid in processing the data on the host computer. The MORE's task while collecting the data displayed in Table 11.1 was simply to store the time at which the first digit of each event code was pressed, along with the event code. The first eight of these code-time pairs are presented in Table 11.2. The code-time pairs were transmitted from the data logger to a larger computer. The host computer program which received the code-time pairs calculated the durations displayed in Table 11.1 according to the following rules.

(1) A code that starts with a 1 continues clocking time until it is explicitly turned off by a code which starts with a 0 and has the same last two digits as the starting code. Thus the duration of 124 was calculated by subtracting its start time (0) from the start time of the next 024 (11).

(2) A code starting with a 2 is terminated by the next code that also starts with a 2. Thus the duration of 225 is 8 (15 minus 7).

(3) Any code starting with a 3 is considered a momentary event. These codes are all given dummy durations of 0.

The important point is that during the development of the coding scheme subsets of the event codes can be defined. The host computer can be programmed to recognize these subsets and handle them differently based on the needs of the study question.

DATA TYPES

FREQUENCIES

Taxonomies consisting of momentary events or events with little variation in their durations are analyzed using scores based on the frequencies of each category. Some taxonomies with substantial variability in event durations can be conceptualized in ways that make frequency and sequential summaries the measures of choice. For example, the CISS (Notarius & Markman, Chapter 7, this volume) is based on classifying each "thought unit" in a couples interaction. The analysis of their frequencies and sequences provides sufficient information for the questions asked. Event frequencies are the easiest data to collect. The coder keys in the event description for each occurrence and the data logger store the data in chronological order.

DURATIONS

The diversity of coding strategies in use today is largely due to the variety of approaches used in recovering event durations. When the taxonomy includes categories that have considerable variability in their durations, the extra effort required to recover the durational information appears well worthwhile. In studies of monkey social behavior we have found that analyses based on duration scores are considerably more powerful and more consistent across studies than similar analyses based on frequency scores of the same behavioral categories. This has been true across a variety of measures and studies.[1] Presented below are four strategies for recovering durational information.

Onset-offset coding. In order to recover the duration of an event, both the onset and the offset must be indicated. These can be explicitly keyed into the data logger as done for two of the categories in the DISC (Filsinger, Chapter 9, this volume), where an 11 indicates the beginning of speaking and a 12 the end of speaking and a 61 marks the onset and a 62 the offset of gazing. This method works nicely when the number of categories is small and the categories are rarely contiguous.

Mutually exclusive and exhaustive schemes. An alternative to onset-offset coding is to massage the taxonomy into a mutually exclusive (only one event category can occur at any given time) and exhaustive (all time in the observation session can be classified) coding scheme. Then only the onsets of events need be entered, because the offsets are implied by the onset of the succeeding event. The levels of affect as defined in the CISS could be coded in this manner if durations were to be recovered. This is the method of choice when: (1) the number of categories for which durations are desired is large; or (2) the duration categories are frequently contiguous in time. When the events are contiguous, onset-offset coding doubles the entry task. There is a widely held but apparently untested belief that the onsets of events are easier for a coder to recognize and code than are the offsets. If true, this suggests that mutually exclusive and exhaustive schemes may be easier for coders to learn than onset-offset coding of the same complexity.

Zero-one coding. This method is used to generate frequency scores that are sensitive to duration. The observation session is considered as a series of consecutive sample periods (usually 5-15 seconds each) and a summary score is derived for each code category by cumulating the number of sample periods in which the category occurred. The DISC uses a variation of this strategy in coding back-channel attending, in which the code 15 is entered to mark events such as head-nodding, or remarks such as "uh huh" or "yeah," which, if continuous, are recoded every three seconds (Filsinger, Chapter 9, this volume). The score derived from such coding is neither a frequency nor duration and does not consistently reflect one or the other. For example, using the DISC, a score of 10 back-channel comments would result from either a single head-nod during each of 10 interactions or a 30-second bout of head-nodding during a single interaction. As indicated above, other methods of sampling are usually preferable (Altmann, 1974).

Point sampling. A series of sample periods are clocked out during the observation. The data logger cues the coder at the end of each sample period and the events occurring at that instant are coded. This is an efficient way of estimating the distribution of times spent in various categories, but it provides no information on the durations of events. Sequential and frequency information are not recoverable using this method.

SIMULTANEOUS EVENTS

Entering the onset and offset of each event allows the coding of categories that overlap in time. If the number of categories is above seven or eight, coding using this strategy becomes difficult. The following strategies help minimize this difficulty.

Multiple coders. The nonexclusive taxonomy can be divided into simpler mutually exclusive taxonomies. For live coding, separate observers code the behaviors simultaneously, each using one of the mutually exclusive taxonomies. When coding from tape, a separate pass can be made for each simpler taxonomy. The codes from the simpler schemes are aligned and combined on the host computer to construct the complete sequence.

Forming a mutually exclusive taxonomy. This is a variation of the multiple coder strategy designed for one observer. An example of this technique is the second method of coding dyadic affect described in the "Entering Data" section above. Each code entered is the concatenation of the current states of all subtaxonomies. Whenever the value of one subtaxonomy changes, the entire code is reentered. This strategy is only practical with a small number of subtaxonomies, each of which has a limited range of values.

Point sampling. As discussed above, this is a simple and efficient way of estimating the amount of time various categories overlap.

RECORDING FROM VIDEOTAPES OR AUDIOTAPES

The advantage of coding from tapes is that segments can be reviewed several times to recover detailed information which could not be coded in direct real-time observations. Taking advantage of this capability typically requires 10 to 30 hours of coding time per hour of observation, which is the principal disadvantage of this technique. If coders are allowed to replay portions of tape until they are confident that they have made the correct classification and timing judgments, coding time can easily become longer than justified by the increased precision in measurement. One method to bring coding time back under the researcher's control is to divide a complex coding scheme into several simpler schemes, each of which can be coded in a nonstop pass through the tape and then merged together to form the complex description. Another method makes multiple nonstop passes using the complex scheme. The coding errors introduced by this method can be reduced by aligning the multiple passes on a computer, generating a new summary record based on averaging the multiple passes, and referring back to the tape to resolve discrepancies that are not handled by the averaging algorithm. All of these procedures require timing information to be stored with each event.

Timing tapes. Streamlining data collection from tapes is based on an efficient and accurate method of recovering time information. This is obvious for analyses based on event durations. For frequency and sequential-based analyses, the timing information is needed in order to align the multiple passes correctly and to facilitate cross referencing event codes and tape for resolving discrepancies.

The MORE data logger has a unique feature designed for these applications. The MORE can write a time base on an audio track of the tape while the session is being recorded (or this can be dubbed on tapes that have already been recorded). The time base consists of the cumulative time from the start of the trial. It is updated and written on the audio track every tenth of a second. During coding the MORE is connected to the time base track. It will then automatically recover and store the time whenever an event is keyed in by the coder. The time base is an integral part of the tape. This allows the tape to be repositioned whenever needed during coding, and the event times will still be correct. Multiple passes can be made through the tape with confidence that the times will mesh exactly.

Several devices used for editing videotapes also provide this capability. They use a format specified by the Society for Motion Picture and Television Engineers and are referred to as SMPTE coders and SMPTE readers. SMPTE readers are more flexible in their time recovery than the MORE. They can read the time base with the tape going at various speeds, backward or forward. Their principal disadvantage is that the output of the time base is on a visual display which the observer would have to enter along with the event codes. Some SMPTE readers can pass the time to external devices via a connecter. However, to take advantage of this feature a custom interface would have to be constructed. Contact a local audio-visual department or supplier for information on SMPTE coders and readers.

OTHER POSSIBILITIES FOR STREAMLINING THE CODING PROCESS

There are several important decisions to be made in developing the coding scheme for which explicit use of a cost-benefit approach is helpful. The costs are not only monetary. The large amount of time required has resulted in observational studies typically having small sample sizes and therefore producing results that are not very powerful in a statistical sense. Savings in observer time can often be invested in observations on additional subjects, with a concomitant increase in statistical power.

One of the largest costs is coder training. This is heavily influenced by the complexity of the taxonomy, the level of reliability used to signify successful training, and observer turnover rate. On many projects, especially those using students as observers, the average observer can be expected to stay on the project for about six months. In this situation, two months of training seems excessive. The training period can be reduced by simplifying the taxonomy. Many researchers are hesitant to do this because they wish to capture as much of the richness of the interaction as possible. This concern can be softened somewhat by considering that most of the articles reporting direct observation data use less than 20 event categories. The apparent scenario is to collect data with a detailed taxonomy, then collapse the data into a few grosser categories using somewhat arbitrary criteria, and finally do statistical analysis on the grosser categories. Choosing the grosser categories ahead of time and coding at that level can save considerable time. A specific hypothesis or orientation is invaluable here.

Another way of shortening coder training is to use a less stringent criterion of trainee to experienced observer reliability. Given that the study design is sound (that is, observers are counterbalanced across comparison groups), the main function of reliability measures is to provide an estimate of measurement error and to serve as a tool in attempts to reduce that error. Reducing measurement error increases statistical power, but it must be remembered that increasing the number of subjects also increases the statistical power. Time spent on an extra month in coder training to achieve a modest increase in reliability may be better spent observing additional subjects at the lower level of reliability. A reasonable approach is to continue training until the reliability estimates reach some sort of asymptote.

SUMMARY

Analysis of marital interactions using systematic observational techniques has great research and clinical potential. The use of observational methodologies has been restricted by the amount of time required to obtain summary scores. Modern data logging equipment can greatly reduce and sometimes eliminate this summary time while improving the quality of data by making it practical to collect frequency, durational, and sequential data.

NOTE

1. See Sackett and Ruppenthal (1973) for a description of the types of measures.

REFERENCES

ALTMANN, J. Observational study of behavior: Sampling methods. *Behaviour*, 1974, *49*, 227-267.

BLURTON-JONES, N. G., & WOODSON, R. H. Describing behavior: The ethologists' perspective. In M. E. Lamb, S. J. Suomi, & G. R. Stephenson (Eds.), *Social interaction analysis.* Madison: University of Wisconsin Press, 1979.

FITZPATRICK, L. J. Automated data collection for observed events. *Behavior Research Methods and Instrumentation*, 1977, *9*, 447-451.

GASS, C. L. A digital encoder for field recording of behavioral, temporal, and spatial information in directly computer-accessible form. *Behavior Research Methods and Instrumentation*, 1977, *9*, 5-11.

GOTTMAN, J., MARKMAN, H., & NOTARIUS, C. The topography of marital conflict: A study of verbal and nonverbal behavior. *Journal of Marriage and the Family*, 1977, *39*, 461-477.

GREENBERG, M. T. Social interaction between deaf preschoolers and their mothers: The effects of communication method and communication competence. *Developmental Psychology*, 1980, *16*, 465-474.

HOLM, R. A. Techniques of recording observational data. In G. P. Sackett (Ed.), *Observing behavior* (Vol. 2): *Data collection and analysis methods.* Baltimore: University Park Press, 1978.

HUTT, S. J., & HUTT, C. *Direct observation and measurement of behavior.* Springfield, IL: Charles C Thomas, 1970.

ROSENBLUM, L. A. The creation of a behavioral taxonomy. In G. P. Sackett (Ed.), *Observing behavior* (Vol. 2): *Data collection and analysis methods.* Baltimore: University Park Press, 1978.

SACKETT, G. P. Measurement in observational research. In G. P. Sackett (Ed.), *Observing behavior* (Vol. 2): *Data collection and analysis methods.* Baltimore: University Park Press, 1978.

SACKETT, G. P., HOLM, R. A., & RUPPENTHAL, G. C. Social isolation rearing: Species differences in behavior of macaque monkeys. *Developmental Psychology*, 1976, *12*, 283-288.

SACKETT, G. P. & RUPPENTHAL, G. C. Development of monkeys after varied experiences during infancy. In S. A. Barnett (Ed.), *Ethology and development.* London: Spastics International Medical Publications, 1973.

SACKETT, G. P., STEPHENSON, E., & RUPPENTHAL, G. C. Digital acquisition systems for observing behavior in laboratory and field settings. *Behavior Research Methods and Instrumentation*, 1973, *5*, 344-348.

SANSON-FISHER, R. W., POOLE, A. D., SMALL, G. A., & FLEMING, I. R. Data acquisition in real time: An improved system for naturalistic observations. *Behavior Therapy*, 1979, *10*, 543-554.

WHITE, R. E. C. WRATS: A computer compatible system for automatically recording and transcribing behavioral data. *Behavior*, 1971, *40*, 135-161.

PART III

INNOVATIONS IN DATA ANALYSIS

12

CONSIDERATIONS IN ASSESSING
THE RELIABILITY OF OBSERVATIONS

Donald P. Hartmann
William Gardner

Before considering the more technical aspects of the design of reliability assessments, it will be helpful to review the concerns which prompt the assessment of reliability. The object of the assessment of reliability can be given a straightforward and succinct expression: "Are two (or more) scores obtained for the same subject identical, or are they not?" But this question can often be given an even more succinct answer: "No." As usual, the natural usage of a word is richer and far more informative than its social scientific definition. In English, reliability means trustworthiness, safety, and security. Many productive questions now arise. "Trustworthy in what circumstances?" "Secure against which perils?" Answers to these questions will touch upon the fundamental assumptions guiding an investigator's research.

Unreliable measurements betray us by degrading the quality of our research. Reliability assessment attempts to measure and hence to contain the vagueness and uncertainty inherent in relations between observation terms and their referents in the real world. We want our measurements to be:

(1) Accurate. The measurements should correspond to the events being observed. Accurate data share two characteristics: they are *unbiased* and *precise*.

Unbiased observations match, in the long run, the actual frequencies or durations of the behaviors observed. The circumstances of observation should produce neither an underestimate nor an overestimate of the behaviors observed. Bias can result from reactivity, observer expectations or cheating, or other measurement artifacts (see Haynes, 1978; Kazdin, 1977). Reliability as unbiasedness affects the outcome of hypothesis testing by its effects on internal validity. With reliable (in the sense of unbiased) observations we are less likely to arrive at false decisions concerning statistical hypotheses.

Precise observations have little random error or noise. Inattention of observers, uncontrolled factors in the observation setting, and other chance factors should produce no worse than minor disturbances in the data. Reliability as precision affects the outcome of hypothesis testing by its effects on statistical power. With reliable observations we are more likely to reject a false null hypothesis. Conversely, we are more likely to interpret acceptance of the null hypothesis as an indication of the true state of affairs, rather than as evidence of poor experimental technique (Cook & Campbell, 1979; Greenwald, 1975).

(2) Generalizable. Generalizable observations are representative of the observations that would have been obtained by other observers, at other times, and across other dimensions or facts of the observations, such as settings. Reliability as generalizability allows the investigator to extend the conclusions of a study beyond the unique circumstances in which the data were obtained. The generalizability conception of reliability was proposed by Cronbach and his associates (see Cronbach et al., 1972). Their generalizability theory encompasses unbiasedness, precision, and generalizability *per se*. In addition, it offers a detailed conceptual analysis of the components of an observation, methods for conducting and statistics for summarizing the analysis, and an interpretative framework for evaluating the limits of generalizability of the observation.

GENERALIZABILITY FACETS

The facets (or dimension) of generalizability an investigator intends to assess may include time, settings (for example, laboratory versus home), conditions (observer presence versus observer absence), observers, sources of data (observations versus self-ratings), items, or some combination of these facets. Each facet or set of facets answers a different reliability question and requires the collection of different data. If a single facet is being assessed and a traditional reliability approach is adopted, the investigator must choose among a variety of alternative statistical techniques. If a generalizability theory approach is adopted, and one or more facets are being assessed, all questions of reliability can be accommodated by a single conceptualization and a single set of statistical procedures.

In any reliability analysis, scores are compared across two, and sometimes more, levels of a facet, such as observers or settings; for example, across two or more observers. After selecting relevant facets and levels of these facets, the investigator must decide upon the level(s) of data at which the reliability analysis will be conducted (Johnson & Bolstad, 1973). Ordinarily, reliability and substantive analyses of the dependent variables are conducted at the same level of data. The investigator must then choose the statistics to be used in summarizing each reliability analysis.

We discuss these and related issues in two sections. The first considers *observer reliability,* or the generalizability of data across observers. Observer reliability is a necessary but *not* sufficient facet of reliability for any observation system. The second considers the *adequacy of the data sample* upon which experimental decisions will be based. This may involve a number of dimension of observations systems, including observers.

OBSERVER RELIABILITY

Observer reliability has traditionally encompassed two related but conceptually distinct paradigms: comparison of an observer's ratings with criterion ratings, sometimes referred to as *observer accuracy;* and comparison between two or more observers' ratings, variously referred to as *interobserver agreement, reliability,* or *consistency* (Hartmann & Wood, in press). Both procedures assess the adequacy of code development, recording procedures, and observer training. Observer accuracy, however, should typically exceed interobserver reliability when both are assessed on the same set of data using the same statistical procedures (Hartmann, 1979). This difference is due to the nature of the data compared in the two paradigms: Accuracy paradigms compare a flawed source of data with a presumably errorless source (the criterion), whereas interobserver reliability paradigms compare two flawed sources of data. Exceptions occur when observers develop idiosyncratic but shared definitions of the target behaviors over the course of a study—called consensual observer drift (Johnson & Bolstad, 1973). Consensual observer drift may produce substantial interobserver reliability but low observer accuracy (see De-Master et al., 1977). Methods of avoiding drift are discussed by Hartmann and Wood (in press); Nay (1979) describes methods for constructing criterion ratings for accuracy assessments.

BEHAVIOR UNITS

Before an observer reliability analysis can be conducted, the investigator must determine the appropriate behavior units (or levels of data) upon which to conduct the analysis. Two issues involving behavior units will be discussed

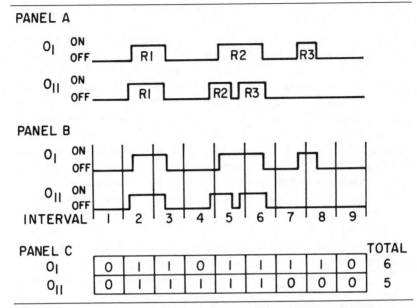

Figure 12.1   Panel A illustrates the frequency and duration of responses as
               might be recorded on event recorders by two observers (O_I and
               O_{II}). The numbers under the raised portion of the recording line
               identify the responses. Panel B shows the same data with
               10-second intervals superimposed upon the recording line. Panel
               C shows how these data might be scored using a whole interval
               scoring procedure (Powell et al., 1975).

here: identifying molecular units and developing composites of molecular
units.

The problem of identifying molecular units can be illustrated with the data
shown in Panel A of Figure 12.1. This panel shows the frequency and duration
of a behavior over a brief observation period, as that data might be recorded on
an event recorder by each of two observers.

In analyzing reliability at this molecular level, the problem is how to match
the observers' recordings so that they can be compared. Examination of Panel A
indicates that no problem occurs in matching the first response, R_1, for the two
observers. Problems do occur, however, in finding matches for responses R_2
and R_3.

This matching problem is frequently solved by dividing the recorded stream
of behavior into brief intervals of, say, 10 seconds' duration, as illustrated in
Panel B of Figure 12.1. Each interval would then be scored according to a rule;
for example, score "1" if the behavior occurs anywhere in the interval and score

"0" if the behavior does not occur anywhere in the interval. Scores resulting from this procedure (sometimes referred to as interval recording) are displayed in Panel C of Figure 12.1. This procedure resolves the problem of identifying matching units by changing the unit of analysis from an individual response to an individual interval. The solution comes at some expense, as the resulting unit corresponds neither to frequency nor to duration of responding (see Altmann, 1974; also see Hartmann & Wood, in press). If an investigator's interest is in events, a related method that preserves the frequency property of the data is to score each interval only if a response has been initiated in the interval (Sackett, 1978). If the investigator's interest is in behavioral states, a related method that preserves the duration property of the data is to score the interval only if the behavior occurs at some fixed point in the interval, such as at the very end of the interval. This latter technique is referred to as scan or momentary time-sampling (Altmann, 1974).

Observer reliability assessed at this molecular level of analysis is particularly useful for identifying specific disagreements that indicate the need for more observer training, for revising the observer code, or for modifying the recording procedures. Often, however, major analyses are conducted on a more molar unit, such as a session score. Session scores formed by summing the molecular scores, such as interval scores within a session, are illustrated on the right margin of Panel C in Figure 12.1. In assessing the reliability of these composite scores an observer-by-session data array would be generated, as in Part A of Table 12.1. In general, session scores will be more reliable than the interval scores of which they are composed (see Hartmann, 1976).

Scores other than simple frequency or duration scores may be of interest to an experimenter. For example, in some studies the focus may be sequential events, such as wife-assert at time t_i and husband-respond at t_{i+1}. Suppose the intended experimental comparison concerns the difference between the unconditional probability of husband-respond and the conditional probability of husband-respond at t_{i+1} given wife-assert at t_i. If the test of a difference between these probabilities is conducted from data obtained from one couple, then reliability would be assessed on the interval or similar scores for the two variables produced by that couple. If, on the other hand, data are obtained from many distressed and nondistressed couples, and the difference between conditional and unconditional probabilities for each couple contributes to the analysis, then reliability must be assessed directly on this difference obtained from session scores.[1]

SUMMARY STATISTICS

Once the data are placed in an observer-by-unit of analysis matrix (see Panel C of Figure 12.1 or Part A of Table 12.1), the investigator is ready to summarize the data with one of the twenty or more reliability statistics described in the

TABLE 12.1   Fictitious Reliability Data (Part A), Analysis of Variance of These Data (Part B), and Estimates of Variance Components Resulting from this Analysis (Part C)

Part A

Units (e.g., Ss)	Observers	
	I	II
1	10	8
2	7	5
3	9	8
4	8	6
5	11	10
6	7	7

Part B

ANOVA Summary

Sources	Mean Squares (MS)
Subjects (S)	5.40
Observers (0)	5.33
S × 0	.33

Part C

Variance Components

$$\sigma^2_e + \sigma^2_{s \times o} = MS_{s \times o} = .33$$

$$\sigma^2_o = (MS_o - MS_{s \times o})/n = (5.33 - .33)/6 = .83$$

$$\sigma^2_s = (MS_s - MS_{s \times o})/k = (5.40 - .33)/2 = 2.59$$

literature (Berk, 1979; Tinsley & Weiss, 1975; Frick & Semmel, 1978). While some of these summary statistics provide identical results under some conditions (Fleiss, 1975), many of the statistics will produce different, and in some cases dramatically different, values when applied to the same data (Frick & Semmel, 1978; Hartmann, 1977). Selecting a statistic will depend upon the specific question the reliability assessment is intended to answer and upon the form of the data (see Hartmann, 1977). Our discussion will emphasize the form of the data as a determinant in selecting a summary statistic.

Observational data are typically obtained in one or both of two forms: categorical data such as the 0/1 interval scores presented in Panel C of Figure 12.1, and quantitative data such as the response frequency, rate, or duration scores presented in Part A of Table 12.1.

Categorical data. The percent agreement statistic is the most common index for summarizing the interobserver reliability of categorical scores (Kelly, 1977). Percent agreement is the ratio of the number of agreements on both occurrences and nonoccurrences to the total number of observations (agreements plus disagreements) multiplied by 100. This agreement statistic has been repeatedly criticized, since inflated reliability estimates may result when the target behavior occurs at extreme rates (Johnson & Bolstad, 1973; Hartmann, 1977). A variety of techniques have been suggested to remedy this problem.

Some procedures preserve the form of the percent agreement statistic, but exclude high base-rate agreements (either occurrence or nonoccurrence agreements) before calculating the agreement statistic (for example, see Hawkins & Dotson, 1975). Other procedures, such as the "kappa-like" statistics, provide formal corrections for chance agreements (Hartmann, 1977; Hollenbeck, 1978). Kappa (Cohen, 1960), the forerunner and most popular of these statistics, is particularly useful. In addition to correcting for chance agreements, kappa can be used for summarizing observer accuracy data, for assessing agreement among many observers, or for evaluating scaled (partial) agreement among observers (see Fleiss, 1975). Intraclass correlation coefficients may also be used to summarize the reliability of categorical data (see next section); Fleiss (1975) and Winer (1971, pp. 293-296) discuss this application of intraclass correlations.

Quantitative data. Marginal agreement (Frick & Semmel, 1978), a percentage agreement statistic for quantitative data, is occasionally reported in the behavioral literature. Marginal agreement is calculated by taking the ratio of two observers' scores (smaller divided by larger) times 100. For the observer totals in Panel C of Figure 12.1, the marginal agreement statistic equals 83% ($100 \times 5/6$). This agreement statistic has also been criticized for inflating reliability estimates (Hartmann, 1977). Flanders (1967) offers a chance corrected formula.

Correlational statistics traditionally have been used for summarizing quantitative interobserver reliability data. More recently, the intraclass correlation has become increasingly popular for summarizing the results of interobserver reliability analyses whether they are conducted on categorical or on quantitative data (Berk, 1979). The intraclass correlation expresses reliability as a ratio of the universe (subject or true score) variance to all sources of obtained variance. In an investigation in which n subjects are observed by each of k observers, an intraclass correlation (ρ) for estimating the reliability of the data in which each subject is observed by a different judge is equal to $\sigma_s^2/(\sigma_s^2 + \sigma_0^2 + \sigma_{s \times o}^2 + \sigma_e^2)$. In this formula, σ_s^2 is the variance due to subjects, σ_0^2 is the variance due to observers, $\sigma_{s \times o}^2$ is the variance due to the interaction of subjects and observers, and σ_e^2 is the variance due to error. Estimates of these variance components are obtained through analysis of variance procedures. For the data given in Table 12.1, the value of the intraclass correlations equals $2.59/(2.59 + .83 + .33) = .69$. (See Parts B and C of Table 12.1.) Illustrations of the use of intraclass correlations are given in Jones et al. (1975), in Shrout and Fleiss (1979), in Wiggins (1973), and in Winer (1971, Section 4.5). The advantages of intraclass correlations and the generalizability theory approach to reliability are described by Berk (1979), Mitchell (1979), and Cronbach et al. (1972).

Potential limitations are discussed by Winer (1971, p. 296) and Jones (1977). Solutions for these problems for single-subject research are presented by Strossen et al. (1979).[2]

ADEQUACY OF THE BEHAVIOR SAMPLE

Whether they are conducting correlational or experimental studies, investigators must be concerned about the adequacy of the sample of data that enters into their analyses. In traditional assessment, judgments of the adequacy of a data sample are often based on the number of items included in the measurement instrument. In observation studies of families or of married couples, one would be concerned with the duration of the observation session or the number of sessions from which scores are obtained. However, other aspects of an observation system might be equally relevant to the assessment of the adequacy of the data sample, such as the number of observers whose scores are averaged, or the number of settings from which data are collected. To determine the adequacy of a sample, reliability must be assessed across all the dimensions or facets relevant to the calculation and interpretation of the scores.

To illustrate an assessment of the adequacy of a behavioral sample, consider an investigation in which the length of the observation session is at issue. Data have been obtained on 15 dyads over a 40-minute observation session. To determine whether 40 minutes of observation provide sufficient data, the investigator divides the session into 20-minute sections and calculates two scores, each based on 20 minutes of observation data, for each dyad. If the appropriate intraclass correlation calculated on these data were low (for example, $\rho = .40$), the investigator would probably conclude that the data sample was inadequate. In such a case, three options are available. First, the investigator can proceed to analyze the scores obtained from the 40-minute observation period, but limit any conclusion based upon these data to that specific observation period. Second, the observational setting may be modified to improve consistency, for example, by removing distracting stimuli or by adding a brief habituation period to each observation session. This approach is sometimes referred to as gaining experimental control over sources of variability (see Sidman, 1960). A third alternative is to increase the length of the observation period until a session duration is discovered which will provide consistent data.

Similar alternatives could be generated for any other facet, such as settings or observers. For example, if consistency across observers were inadequate, the investigator might: (a) use a single observer's data with the realization that the same results might not be obtained if a different observer had collected the data; (b) train observers more extensively, improve observation and recording conditions, and clarify definitions; (c) use more than one observer to gather data and analyze the average of the observers' scores; or (d) combine choices b and c.

Which of these options is selected will depend upon the purpose of the study and practical considerations, such as the investigator's ability to identify and control undesirable sources of variability or the feasibility of increasing the number of sessions or their duration. For variability due to settings, restricting conclusions to a particular observational setting might be the preferred alternative; for variability due to observers, experimental control might be the solution to unwanted sources of variability; for variability due to sessions, increasing the number of sessions may be the solution of choice.

For assessing consistency across those dimensions that are relevant for assessing the adequacy of the behavioral sample, investigators must also identify the appropriate unit for analysis and select an appropriate statistical index.

SELECTING THE APPROPRIATE UNIT

The adequacy of a behavior sample, as in the case of interobserver reliability, should be assessed at the level of data at which the experimental analysis will be conducted. There are two related errors involving composite scores that investigators may make in selecting a unit of analysis for assessing the adequacy of the data sample. First, the reliability analysis may be conducted on a composite score when the primary analyses are performed on the components which are summed to form the composite. If a composite score is composed of positively correlated components, composite score reliability will overestimate the reliability of its separate components (Nunnally, 1978). For example, the reliability of the composite "physical affectionate behaviors" may seriously misrepresent the reliability of "hugs," "kisses," "pats," and other behaviors summed to form this composite. If analyses were to be conducted on "hugs," "kisses," and the other component scores, then the adequacy (reliability) of each component score must be assessed separately.

A slightly different situation occurs when the composite is a difference score, such as the difference between husband's positives delivered to wife and wife's positives delivered to husband. If the two scores composing this difference score are positively correlated, the difference score will be less reliable— sometimes substantially less reliable—than the average of the reliabilities of the two component scores (McNemar, 1969). If analyses are conducted on difference scores, then the adequacy of the difference score itself must be assessed.

Once a suitable unit of analysis has been chosen, and data have been gathered over the levels of one or more relevant facets, the investigator must select a statistic summarizing the adequacy of the behavioral sample.

SUMMARY STATISTICS

Information concerning the adequacy of the data sample is usually summarized with a correlational statistic. Intraclass correlations are particularly well-suited statistics for this purpose (Cronbach et al., 1972) as they have the advantage of summarizing consistency information across the levels of a single facet, such as session duration, or across combined facets. Moreover, intraclass correlations can be interpreted using generalizability theory to provide estimates of how much the data sample would be improved under changed circumstances; for example, if the duration of the sessions were lengthened or the number of observations were increased (see Cronbach et al., 1972). Using the data in Table 12.1, reliability would be improved if two different observers, rather than just one, collected data for each subject. In this latter case, $\rho = \sigma_s^2$ / $\left[\sigma_s^2 + .5(\sigma_o^2 + \sigma_{s \times o}^2 + \sigma_e^2) \right]$ = 2.59/2.59 + .5(.83 + .33) = .82. It would be improved still further if the same observer collected data for each subject; $\rho = \sigma_s^2 / (\sigma_s^2 + \sigma_e^2)$ = 2.59/(2.59 + .33) = .89. Clearly, the estimation function served by this approach could save investigators substantial time and effort.

FURTHER CONSIDERATIONS

Our discussion of the reliability of observation data has, of necessity, been brief and selective. Readers who require additional information may find the following references useful. General discussions of reliability issues are given by Berk (1979), Frick and Semmel (1978), Hollenbeck (1978), Mitchell (1979), and Tinsley and Weiss (1975). Arrington's (1943) summary of methodological issues in early child observation research provides an enlightening baseline for comparing current practices. Two recent issues of the *Journal of Applied Behavior Analysis* (1977, 1979) include sometimes lively discussions of a variety of issues involved in assessing the reliability of observation data, including chance agreements, significance tests, graphic displays, and correlational versus agreement summary statistics. Sources of systematic errors in observations, such as observer biases, expectancies, and cheating are reviewed by Kazdin (1977), Kent and Foster (1977), Nay (1979), and Wildman and Erickson (1977). Weick (1968) discusses the few attempts made to apply a coherent conceptual model to systematic observer errors. Johnson and Bolstad (1973) critically evaluate the quality of observation data published in the behavioral literature, and provide a useful discussion of issues involved in selecting a unit of analysis. Kazdin reviews recent work on the reactivity of observations (1979b) and on the limiting effects of settings on the generalizability of observation data (1979a), while Cone (1977) discusses the generalizability of data across assessment sources. Haynes (1978), Nay (1979), and Paul and Lentz (1977) present useful suggestions for observer training. Finally, Hartmann and Wood (in press) discuss the problems of establishing an "acceptable" level of reliability, and summarize recommendations advanced for reporting reliability information.

NOTES

1. Gottman (1980) has proposed a radically different approach to the assessment of reliability for analyses of sequential connections. He argues that point-for-point (or interval-by-interval) agreement is an excessively stringent procedure for assessing the reliability of sequential data. Instead, Gottman recommends assessing the reliability of sequential data by calculating the relevant sequential statistics (for example, the Z-statistics) separately from the data of each of two observers. If the two observers' data produce the same statistical decision—both result in either acceptance or rejection of the null hypothesis—then adequate reliability has been demonstrated. This approach is clearly problematic.

The first and lesser problem is a consequence of the nature of the data used to conduct the analysis. The data from all dyads would be concatenated to form one continuous stream (as if all the data came from one dyad). This procedure may be a consequence of the sample size requirements of the statistic Gottman proposes to use. Its effect, however, will be to underestimate the reliability with which each individual dyad could be observed, since between-dyad differences in sequential structure now appear as within-dyad error variance. The second and more serious problem stems from the ambiguity of the results of the analysis. Suppose that the results of the sequential analysis of both observers' data indicate a nonsignificant difference. Does this result mean that both observers are accurately reporting the independence of wife-assert and husband-respond? Or does it mean that the measures are so flawed that a real difference is obscured by observer error? Furthermore, any evaluation of observers' ratings based on their collectively exceeding (or not exceeding) a criterion of statistical significance is certain to be arbitrary. Suppose we use the p less than or equal to .05 level of statistical significance. Then a Z-value for the difference between a conditional and an unconditional probability of 1.96 for one observer's data would be significant, but so would a Z-value of 10.96 obtained for the second observer's data. By Gottman's method, the conclusion drawn in this case would be that adequate reliability had been shown, since each observer obtained the same statistical decision. However, have the observers detected the same sequential structure? Suppose the second observer obtained a nonsignificant Z of 1.94. Have the observers found different sequential structures? It is our belief that the vagueness and imprecision of Gottman's (1980) procedure makes it unsuitable for reliability assessment.

2. Investigators who apply statistical procedures to individual-subject data must exercise unusual caution. Most common applications of *inferential* statistics to these data will yield highly misleading probability values if the data are serially dependent (see Hartmann et al., 1980). For example, ordinary χ^2 procedures applied to a two-by-two summary table of individual-subject data such as those shown in Figure 12.1, Panel C, may yield highly inaccurate probability values (Gardner et al., in press). Thus, Birkimer and Brown (1979) may be incorrect in suggesting that a significant probability value obtained in this manner indicates the lower boundary of acceptable interobserver reliability.

REFERENCES

ALTMANN, J. Observational study of behavior: Sampling methods. *Behaviour,* 1974, *49,* 227-267.

ARRINGTON, R. E. Time sampling in studies of social behavior: A critical review of techniques and results with research suggestions. *Psychological Bulletin,* 1943, *40,* 81-124.

BERK, R. A. Generalizability of behavioral observations: A clarification of interobserver agreement and interobserver reliability. *American Journal of Mental Deficiency,* 1979, *83,* 460-472.

BIRKIMER, J. C., & BROWN, J. H. Back to basics: Percentage agreement measures are adequate, but there are easier ways. *Journal of Applied Behavior Analysis,* 1979, *12,* 535-543.

COHEN, J. A coefficient of agreement for nominal scales. *Educational and Psychological Measurement*, 1960, *20*, 37-46.

CONE, J. D. The relevance of reliability and validity for behavior assessment. *Behavior Therapy*, 1977, *8*, 411-426.

COOK, T. D., & CAMPBELL, D. T. *Quasi-experimentation: Design and analysis issues for field settings*. Skokie, IL: Rand McNally, 1979.

CRONBACH, L. J., GLESER, G. C., NANDA, H., & RAJARATNAM, N. *The dependability of behavioral measurements*. New York: John Wiley, 1972.

DeMASTER, B., REID, J., & TWENTYMAN, C. The effects of different amounts of feedback on observer's reliability. *Behavior Therapy*, 1977, *8*, 317-329.

FLANDERS, N. A. Estimating reliability. In E. J. Amidon & J. B. Hough (Eds.), *Interaction analysis: Theory, research, and application*. Reading, MA: Addison-Wesley, 1967.

FLEISS, J. L. Measuring agreement between two judges on the presence or absence of a trait. *Biometrics*, 1975, *31*, 651-659.

FRICK, T., & SEMMEL, M. I. Observer agreement and reliabilities of classroom observational measures. *Review of Educational Research*, 1978, *48*, 157-184.

GARDNER, W., HARTMANN, D. P., & MITCHELL, C. The effects of serial dependency on the use of χ^2 for analyzing sequential data. *Behavioral Assessment*, in press.

GOTTMAN, J. M. Analyzing for sequential connection and assessing interobserver reliability for the sequential analysis of observational data. *Behavioral Assessment*, 1980, *2*, 361-368.

GREENWALD, A. G. Consequences of prejudice against the null hypothesis. *Psychological Bulletin*, 1975, *82*, 1-20.

HARTMANN, D. P. Some restrictions in the application of the Spearman-Brown prophesy formula to observational data. *Educational and Psychological Measurement*, 1976, *36*, 843-845.

HARTMANN, D. P. Considerations in the choice of interobserver reliability estimates. *Journal of Applied Behavior Analysis*, 1977, *10*, 103-116.

HARTMANN, D. P. Inter- and intra-observer agreement as a function of explicit behavior definitions in direct observation: A critique. *Behaviour Analysis and Modification*, 1979, *3*, 229-233.

HARTMANN, D. P., GOTTMAN, J. M., JONES, R. R., GARDNER, W., KAZDIN, A. E., & VAUGHT, R. S. Interrupted time-series analysis and its application to behavioral data. *Journal of Applied Behavior Analysis*, 1980, *13*, 543-559.

HARTMANN, D. P., & WOOD, D. D. Observation methods. In A. S. Bellack, M. Hersen, & A. E. Kazdin (Eds.), *International handbook of behavior modification and therapy*. New York: Plenum, in press.

HAWKINS, R. P., & DOTSON, V. A. Reliability scores that delude: An Alice in Wonderland trip through the misleading characteristics of interobserver agreement scores in interval recording. In E. Ramp & G. Semb (Eds.), *Behavior analysis: Areas of research and application*. Englewood Cliffs, NJ: Prentice-Hall, 1975.

HAYNES, S. N. *Principles of behavioral assessment*. New York: Gardner, 1978.

HOLLENBECK, A. R. Problems of reliability in observational research. In G. P. Sackett (Ed.), *Observing behavior* (Vol. 2): *Data collection and analysis methods*. Baltimore: University Park Press, 1978.

JOHNSON, S. M., & BOLSTAD, O. D. Methodological issues in naturalistic observation: Some problems and solutions for field research. In L. A. Hamerlynck, L. C. Handy, & E. J. Mash (Eds.), *Behavior change: Methodology, concepts, and practice*. Champaign, IL: Research Press, 1973.

JONES, R. R. Conceptual vs. analytic uses of generalizability theory in behavioral assessment. In J. D. Cone & R. P. Hawkins (Eds.), *Behavioral assessment: New directions in clinical psychology*. New York: Brunner/Mazel, 1977.

JONES, R. R., REID, J. B., & PATTERSON, G. R. Naturalistic observation in clinical assessment. In P. McReynolds (Ed.), *Advances in psychological assessment* (Vol. 3). San Francisco: Jossey-Bass, 1975.

Journal of Applied Behavior Analysis, 1977, *10*(1).

Journal of Applied Behavior Analysis, 1979, *12*(4).

KAZDIN, A. E. Artifact, bias, and complexity of assessment: The ABCs of reliability. *Journal of Applied Behavior Analysis*, 1977, *10*, 141-150.

KAZDIN, A. E. Situational specificity: The two-edged sword of behavioral assessment. *Behavioral Assessment*, 1979, *1*, 57-75. (a)

KAZDIN, A. E. Unobtrusive measures in behavioral assessment. *Journal of Applied Behavior Analysis*, 1979, *12*, 713-724. (b)

KELLY, M. B. A review of the observational data-collection and reliability procedures reported in *The Journal of Applied Behavior Analysis*. *Journal of Applied Behavior Analysis*, 1977, *10*, 97-101.

KENT, R. N., & FOSTER, S. L. Direct observational procedures: Methodological issues in naturalistic settings. In A. R. Ciminero, K. S. Calhoun, & H. E. Adams (Eds.), *Handbook of behavioral assessment*. New York: John Wiley, 1977.

McNEMAR, Q. *Psychological statistics* (4th ed.). New York: John Wiley, 1969.

MITCHELL, S. K. Interobserver agreement, reliability, and generalizability of data collected in observational studies. *Psychological Bulletin*, 1979, *86*, 376-390.

NAY, W. R. *Multimethod clinical assessment*. New York: Gardner, 1979.

NUNNALLY, J. *Psychometric theory* (2nd ed.). New York: McGraw-Hill, 1978.

PAUL, G. L., & LENTZ, R. J. *Psychological treatment of chronic mental patients: Milieu versus social-learning programs*. Cambridge, MA: Harvard University Press, 1977.

POWELL, J., MARTINDALE, A., & KULP, S. An evaluation of time-sample measures of behavior. *Journal of Applied Behavior Analysis*, 1975, *8*, 463-469.

SACKETT, G. P. Measurement in observational research. In G. P. Sackett (Ed.), *Observing behavior* (Vol. 2): *Data collection and analysis methods*. Baltimore: University Park Press, 1978.

SHROUT, P. E., & FLEISS, J. L. Intraclass correlations: Uses in assessing rater reliability. *Psychological Bulletin*, 1979, *86*, 420-428.

SIDMAN, M. *Tactics of scientific research*. New York: Basic Books, 1960.

STROSSEN, E. J., COATES, T. J., & THORESEN, C. E. Extending generalizability theory to single-subject designs. *Behavior Therapy*, 1979, *10*, 606-614.

TINSLEY, H. E. A., & WEISS, D. J. Interrater reliability and agreement of subjective judgments. *Journal of Counseling Psychology*, 1975, *22*, 358-376.

WEICK, K. E. Systematic observational methods. In G. Lindzey & E. Aronson (Eds.), *The handbook of social psychology* (Vol. 2; 2nd ed.). Reading, MA: Addison-Wesley, 1968.

WIGGINS, J. S. *Personality and prediction: Principles of personality assessment*. Reading, MA: Addison-Wesley, 1973.

WILDMAN, B. G., & ERICKSON, M. T. Methodological problems in behavioral observation. In J. D. Cone & R. P. Hawkins (Eds.), *Behavioral assessment: New directions in clinical psychology*. New York: Brunner/Mazel, 1977.

WINER, B. J. *Statistical principles in experimental design* (2nd ed.). New York: McGraw-Hill, 1971.

13

ANALYSIS OF
OBSERVATIONAL DATA

Clifford I. Notarius
Lowell J. Krokoff
Howard J. Markman

This chapter is intended as a guide to the analysis of observational data for researchers and clinicians interested in understanding couples interaction. Although there are many data analysis strategies, we will describe the most widely used procedures. It is important to remember that the decision to employ a particular analytic method should be closely guided by the theoretical objectives of a research project. It is equally important that no statistical procedure can take unreliable data generated by weak research designs and produce valid conclusions about the phenomena under study.

The data analysis techniques that we will describe are best suited for analyzing event-based sequential data. This data type results when an exhaustive behavioral observation coding system is used to assign a unique code to every behavioral event or unit of analysis (see Chapter 15, this volume). Each observational system may define an event somewhat differently; in the Couples

AUTHORS' NOTE: The authors would like to thank John Gottman, Randy Smith, and Nelly Vanzetti for their comments on a draft of this chapter.

Interaction Scoring System (CISS; see Chapter 7, this volume) an event resembles a simple grammatical phrase.

We will present three analytic strategies that have been used to understand couples interaction. First, we will describe the application of *nonsequential analyses* to test the idea that nondistressed couples produce differential frequencies, rates, or proportions of interactional events compared to distressed couples. Second, we will describe the application of *sequential analyses* to assess the interactional patterns that describe and/or discriminate between distressed and nondistressed couples. And third, we will present the application of some recent developments in the *spectral analysis of time-series data.*

NONSEQUENTIAL ANALYSIS

Nonsequential analysis methods may be used to assess the significance of observed differences in distressed and nondistressed couples. These methods allow one to address the basic question: "What, if anything, is different about the way partners in satisfying and unsatisfying marriages interact?" The "what" in this question is most likely to refer to rates (see Birchler et al., 1975) or proportions (see Gottman et al., 1977) of specific behavioral observation codes. Differences in these dependent variables are commonly tested by analysis of variance techniques, including multiple t-tests (for example, see Birchler et al., 1975) and multivariate analysis of variance (Gottman et al., 1977). Since data for husbands and wives are correlated, sex is considered as a repeated measure in ANOVA and MANOVA designs.

We will illustrate nonsequential analysis by describing how to evaluate the behavior exchange or social learning theory hypothesis that nondistressed spouses will be more positive to each other than distressed spouses (see Birchler et al., 1975). One way to operationalize verbal positiveness is to use the ratio of agreement to disagreement statements. Agreement and disagreement behavioral codes are provided by CISS, MICS, and other marital interaction coding systems (see Chapter 15, this volume). The data for the following example were obtained from an investigation of marital interaction that has been described in detail in Gottman et al. (1976, 1977) and Gottman (1979). In this study, couples were first videotaped as they attempted to resolve a troublesome marital problem, and then the videotapes were transcribed and coded with CISS. Differences between distressed and nondistressed couples in the proportion of agreements to agreements plus disagreements were assessed with a t-test. Our findings indicated that the above measure of positiveness successfully differentiated distressed from nondistressed couples. For husbands, $t(8) = 2.07$, p less than .05, with distressed husbands averaging .46 and nondistressed husbands averaging .66. For wives, t(8) = 7.78, p less than .0001, with distressed wives averaging .39 and nondistressed wives averaging .76.

In addition to t-tests, multivariate and univariate analyses of variance can be performed to assess differences between distressed and nondistressed couples in the proportions or rates of particular behaviors. To illustrate the application of these latter methods for analyzing observational data, let us continue to evaluate the hypothesis concerning positiveness in marriage. In the above example, we focused on verbal behavior; now we will assess differences in nonverbal positiveness. The videotapes from the study described above were coded for positive, neutral, and negative nonverbal behaviors using the CISS nonverbal codes (see Chapter 7, this volume). Data analysis consisted of four steps. First, for each couple the proportions of positive, neutral, and negative nonverbal behavior summed over all content codes were calculated. Second, because this analysis was performed on proportional data, the proportions were transformed using an arcsine square root transformation (Myers, 1966). Third, using a 2 × 2 design with distressed-nondistressed as between-subjects factor and husband-wife as a within-subjects factor, a multivariate analysis of variance was performed on the proportion of the three CISS nonverbal behavior codes. A multivariate analysis controls for the inflated type-I error rates that can result when t-test procedures are carried out on more than one dependent measure. This analysis revealed a significant distress main effect ($F(3,14) = 12.44$, p less than .0001), a nonsignificant husband-wife main effect, and no interaction effect of the husband-wife by the distress factor. Fourth, to assess the factors contributing to the distress main effect, separate univariate analyses of variance were performed on differences between distressed and nondistressed couples in the proportions of negative, positive, and neutral nonverbal behaviors. These analyses revealed that the proportion of negative and neutral nonverbal behavior, but not the proportion of positive nonverbal behavior, discriminated between the interactions of distressed and nondistressed couples.

In summary, this section has illustrated how analysis of variance procedures can be used to assess particular questions about social interaction. As we indicated at the beginning of this chapter, a primary objective of recent studies on marriage was to determine what, if anything, has been found to discriminate between the interactions of distressed and nondistressed couples. (For a more detailed discussion of these interactional differences, see Chapter 15.) Using t-tests and analysis of variance statistics, we were able to demonstrate that these two groups can be discriminated by looking at their respective levels (proportions) of positive and negative verbal and nonverbal behaviors. These same methods could be applied to test for differences in any behavior of interest as part of an exploratory, descriptive study (for example, see Gottman et al., 1977) or to test specific hypotheses derived from a particular theoretical model of marital distress (see Birchler et al., 1975).

Some words of caution concerning the independence of husband and wife behaviors are in order when considering analysis of variance techniques. In couples interaction there is a dependency in the partners' behavior that must be considered. If husband's and wife's scores are treated as independent observations, then the assumption of independence in analysis of variance is violated. This violation results in an inappropriate increase in the allowable degrees of freedom and a potential to incorrectly estimate the error variance. Thus husband and wife must be treated as a repeated measures factor, with the dyad as the unit of analysis. If husband and wife effects are not of interest, the dependency between their scores can be eliminated by using only couple scores in the analysis of variance. Kraemer and Jacklin (1979) have recently discussed the independence issue and have presented a general procedure for testing the effects of any dichotomous variable (such as sex) from the dependent responses observed in interacting dyads. These authors' suggestions can be applied to designs in which a spouse is first observed interacting with his or her marital partner and then with an opposite-sexed stranger partner. This useful design yields data that is particularly challenging to analyze, thus Kraemer and Jacklin's paper is most welcome.

Since the procedures for analyzing observational data described in this section can only be used to assess questions about the overall level of particular behaviors, and not questions about the sequential or contingent character of marital interactions, we refer to these methods as nonsequential analysis. However, in addition to determining the overall levels of positive and negative behaviors that characterize a couple's interactions, we can also look at how a husband is likely to respond to his wife's behaviors and vice versa. To assess these latter types of questions about social interaction requires *sequential analysis,* a form of which will be described in the next section.

SEQUENTIAL ANALYSIS

Let us imagine that we are watching a videotape of a couple's interactions and observe the husband complain about a relationship problem in an angry tone of voice. To understand this couple's marriage, it may be very helpful to know something about how the wife is likely to respond in this type of situation. For instance, does she reciprocate with a negative comment of her own, and, if so, does she do so immediately following the husband's statement or some time later? Or, instead, does the wife circumvent a possible argument by inquiring in a caring tone of voice about the reasons for his negative feelings? In addition to helping us understand a particular couple's relationship, the answers to the above types of questions may also shed some light on the communication patterns that distinguish the interactions of distressed couples from nondistressed couples. For example, differences in positive and negative reciprocity have been hypothesized to discriminate distressed from nondistressed couples. A test of this hypothesis requires an observational record that preserves the order in which a stream of behavior occurs and statistical procedures that, unlike those described in the preceding section, can assess sequences of observed behaviors. In the remainder of this section we will describe one such method, that is, sequential analysis.

The statistical procedures described here are based on *information theory,* the basic premise of which is that a behavior of one organism has communicative value in a social sense if it reduces uncertainty in our ability to predict the behavior of another organism (Miller, 1953; Attneave, 1959; Altmann, 1965; Raush et al., 1974; Gottman & Notarius, 1978; and Gottman, 1979). We can gain information from a sequence of events only in situations in which we have some degree of uncertainty. For example, a biased coin that always lands on "tails" will provide no information from a flip of the coin since the outcome is already completely determined—there is no uncertainty. This concept can also be illustrated by considering an extended example from the marital interaction domain. Let's suppose that we have videotaped a couple as they attempted to resolve a troublesome marital problem. In viewing the videotape, we note several shifts in the couple's nonverbal behavior over the course of the conversation. That is, one moment the husband may be speaking in a negative tone of voice, while at another point in the discussion his tone of voice may be positive. We observe similar nonverbal affective changes in the wife. We can record these changes in nonverbal behavior by coding the couple's interactions using the speaker nonverbal behavior codes of the CISS. These codes reveal whether or not the husband's and wife's speech is accompanied by negative, neutral, or positive nonverbal behaviors over the course of their conversation.

The resulting observational record might look, in part, as follows: H0 W0 H0 W0 H− W0 H− W− H− W+ H+ W+, and so on, where H0 = husband speech accompanied by neutral nonverbal behavior; W0 = wife speech accompanied by neutral nonverbal behavior; H+ = husband speaking with positive nonverbal behavior; W+ = wife speaking with positive nonverbal behavior; H− = husband speaking with negative nonverbal behavior; and W− = wife speaking with negative nonverbal behavior.

From the limited segment provided above, we can infer that the nonverbal affective tone does indeed shift, thus supporting our initial impressions. Although the above representation preserves the flow of the couple's interactions, it would be rather difficult to determine the precise significance of such information given the large number of behavioral codes generated by observational procedures such as CISS. In particular, we would like to know whether or not the husband's nonverbal behavior is somewhat related to his wife's, and vice versa. Unfortunately, these relationships are not readily apparent from our inspection of the observational record.

According to the information theory of communication, we can begin to unravel the contingent or sequential nature of an observed sequence by describing the participant's behaviors using the language of probability theory. That is, we need to ask the following types of probabilistic questions about the sequences contained in the observational record: "Given that a wife's nonverbal behavior has been coded as negative, what is the likelihood that the husband's consequent nonverbal behavior will also be negative? What is the likelihood that his consequent nonverbal behavior will be coded as neutral, or as positive?" We can ask similar questions about the husband's likely responses to his wife's neutral and positive behaviors, as well as questions about the wife's nonverbal behaviors that follow her husband's positive, neutral, and negative nonverbal behaviors.

To answer the above types of questions, we can record the number of times each of the three husband nonverbal behavior codes (positive, neutral, and negative) immediately follows each of the three wife nonverbal behavior codes (positive, neutral, and negative), and vice versa. Table 13.1 shows how this might look for the couple in our previous example. For the sake of brevity, we have only included this information for the wife's antecedent nonverbal behaviors and the husband's consequent nonverbal behaviors, although the corresponding table for the husband's antecedent nonverbal behaviors and the wife's consequent nonverbal behaviors is normally required to yield a complete picture of the contingent nature of a couple's interactions. Table 13.1 reveals, for example, that the husband immediately followed his wife's negative behavior 30 times with negative, 48 times with neutral, and 59 times with positive nonverbal behavior.

By converting the above figures to conditional probabilities, we can describe the couple's interactions in probabilistic terms. A conditional probability tells us the probability (P) that behavior A is observed given that behavior B has previously occurred. This statement is symbolized by the notation, $P(A/B)$. For

TABLE 13.1   Frequencies of Wife Antecedent → Husband Consequent Affect Codes

| | | Husband Consequent Code (N = 376) | | |
		Negative (n = 56)	Neutral (n = 144)	Positive (n = 176)
Wife Antecedent Code (N = 376)	Negative (n = 137)	30	48	59
	Neutral (n = 123)	11	55	57
	Positive (n = 116)	15	41	60

instance, the conditional probability that the husband's nonverbal behavior was coded negative, $P(H-/W-)$, is determined by dividing the number of occasions the husband's nonverbal behavior was coded negative following his wife's negative nonverbal behavior (30) by the number of occasions the wife's antecedent nonverbal behavior was coded negative (137). Thus, $P(H-/W-) = 30 \div 137 = .22$. The remaining conditional probabilities for each of the three husband nonverbal codes (positive, neutral, and negative) given the immediate prior occurrence of each of the three wife nonverbal codes (positive, neutral, and negative) are computed in a similar manner, and are presented in Table 13.2 for the couple in our previous example.

What does the information contained in Table 13.2 tell us about the contingent nature of the couple's interaction? The highest conditional probability found in Table 13.2 is for the conditional probability that the husband's nonverbal behavior was coded positive given his wife's antecedent positive nonverbal behavior, that is, $P(H+/W+) = .52$. Does this finding imply that these two behaviors are sequentially connected, that is, is the husband's positive nonverbal behavior somehow dependent on the previous occurrence of his wife's positive nonverbal behavior? From Table 13.2, we also note that one of the lowest conditional probabilities is found for the husband's negative response given that his wife's previous nonverbal behavior was coded negative, $P(H-/W-) = .22$. Does this finding imply that these behaviors are not sequentially linked, or that a statement made by the wife in a negative tone of voice has little bearing on the husband's consequent negativity? To respond in the affirmative to the above questions may be erroneous, considering the information we have at hand. For instance, the husband's nonverbal behavior may have frequently been coded positive following his wife's positive behavior, not because she somehow caused it, but rather because this may be his typical mode of expression. Perhaps he's just a happy-go-lucky guy! In a related manner, the much lower conditional probability, $P(H-/W-) = .22$, might mask a very important dynamic of the relationship, if the husband otherwise seldom expresses negative behavior. Thus we must in some way take account of the base rate (or the unconditional probability of occurrence) of the behaviors of interest.

TABLE 13.2   Conditional Probabilities of Wife Antecedent → Husband Consequent Affect Codes

| | | Husband Consequent Code | | |
		Negative	Neutral	Positive
Wife Antecedent Code	Negative	.22	.35	.43
	Neutral	.09	.45	.46
	Positive	.13	.35	.52

How then can we determine the communicative value of the wife's anteced-ent nonverbal behavior? To answer this question, recall the information theory definition of communication presented at the start of this section. That is, the behavior of one person, for example, the wife, has communicative value in a social sense if it reduces uncertainty in our ability to predict the behavior of another person, for example, the husband. We can assess the reduction of uncertainty by comparing the difference between a behavior's conditional prob-ability, for example, $P(H-/W-)$, and its simple or unconditional probability, for example, $P(H-)$ of occurring at any point in the sequence of interaction. The finding that the conditional probability is greater than the unconditional probability would provide support for the idea that the behaviors in question are sequentially connected. Using information theory terms, a sequential connec-tion exists if knowledge of an antecedent event contributes to a reduction in uncertainty of a consequent event above and beyond the knowledge of the consequent event's simple base rate of occurrence.

Let us return to our previous example and use the above framework to assess whether or not the knowledge that the wife's nonverbal behavior was coded negative reduces our uncertainty in predicting that the husband immediately follows with negative nonverbal behavior. This requires that we compare the conditional probability, $P(H-/W-)$, against the unconditional probability, $P(H-)$. Table 13.2 shows that $P(H-/W-) = .22$, thus we only need to compute the unconditional probability that the husband's nonverbal behavior was coded negative anywhere in the sequence of interaction. To compute $P(H-)$, we divide the number of times the husband's nonverbal behavior was coded negative independent of his wife's antecedent nonverbal behavior, which Table 13.1 reveals equals 56, by the total number of husband consequent codes, which Table 13.1 reveals equals a sum of 376. Thus, $P(H-/W-) = 56 \div 376 = .15$.

A statistical procedure proposed by Sackett (1978) can be used to assess whether or not the difference between $P(H-) = .15$ and $P(H-/W-) = .22$ is a reduction in uncertainty greater than would be predicted from chance alone. Sackett's test consists of calculating the Z-statistic using the following formula:

$$Z = \frac{X - NP}{\sqrt{NPQ}}$$

where X = the observed joint frequency of the antecedent-consequent pair = in our example, the observed joint frequency of wife's negative nonverbal behav-ior and husband's negative nonverbal behavior = 30, N = the frequency of the antecedent event = in our example, the frequency of the wife's negative nonver-bal behavior = 137, P = the unconditional probability of the consequent event = in our example, the unconditional probability of the husband's negative nonverbal behavior = .15, and $Q = 1 - P$ = in our example, $1 - .15 = .85$.

Thus, in the above example,

$$Z = \frac{30 - 137(.15)}{\sqrt{137(.15)(.85)}} = \frac{9.45}{4.18} = 2.26$$

Sackett (1978, p. 7) proposed the following guidelines for interpreting the Z statistic:

> If the Z equals or exceeds ±1.96, the difference between observed and expected probabilities has reached the .05 level of significance. If Z is positive, the matching behavior occurred more than expected by chance [an excitatory or positive dependency]. If Z is negative, the observed probability occurs less than expected by chance [an inhibitory or negative dependency].

Gottman (1979, p. 33) added the following interpretational criteria:

> The normal approximation to the binomial distribution states that the ... Z statistic approximates a standardized normal distribution, an approximation that is good only when N is larger than 25 (see for example, Siegel, 1956, p.50), but the convergence of the binomial to the normal distribution is more rapid when P is close to .50 and slower when P is near 0 or 1. Siegel (1956) suggests that "when P is near 0 or 1, a rule of thumb is that NPQ must be at least 9 before the statistical test based on the normal approximation is applicable (p.40)."

As revealed by the calculations in the above example, the Z-statistic (Z = 2.26) comparing the unconditional probability that the husband's nonverbal behavior was coded negative against the conditional probability that the husband's nonverbal behavior was coded negative given his wife's antecedent negative nonverbal behavior was greater than 1.96, and hence, significantly different from chance expectancy. Therefore, the above finding indicates that the occurrence of the wife's negative behavior reduces our uncertainty in predicting that the husband will immediately follow with negative nonverbal behavior as well.

We can also use Sackett's (1978) Z-statistic to assess the other sequence of interest in our previous example, that is, that the wife's positive nonverbal behavior (W+ → H+), which involves comparing the difference between P(H+) and P(H+/W+). Substituting into the above formula yields:

$$Z = \frac{60 - 116(.47)}{\sqrt{116(.47).53}} = \frac{5.48}{5.38} = 1.02$$

The Z-statistic, Z = 1.02, comparing the difference P(H+) and P(H+/W+) is less than 1.96, and therefore is not significant. Consequently, we cannot conclude that the wife's positive nonverbal behavior reduces uncertainty in predicting the husband's positive nonverbal behaviors, even though P(H+/W+) was relatively high. On the other hand, we earlier found some support for the idea that the wife's negative behavior influences the husband's negative nonverbal behavior, even though in this latter case the conditional probability of interest, $P(H-/W-)$, was relatively small. Viewed together, the above two findings reveal the utility of conceptualizing marital interactions in terms of the information theory definition of communication.

SACKETT'S LAG ANALYSIS

In the preceding section we defined the communicative value of a spouse's behavior in terms of its ability to reduce uncertainty in predicting his or her partner's consequent behavior. By operationalizing uncertainty reduction as the difference between a behavior's conditional and unconditional probability, and assessing this difference with Sackett's (1978) Z-statistic, we were able to identify a likely and unlikely wife-husband sequence in a hypothetical marital interaction. In particular, we found some support for the sequence, $W- \rightarrow$ $H-$, that is, knowing that the wife's nonverbal behavior was negative reduced our uncertainty in predicting that the husband's immediate consequent behavior would also be negative. On the other hand, the occurrence of the wife's positive nonverbal behavior did not reduce our uncertainty in predicting that the husband would immediately follow with positive nonverbal behavior, thus not supporting the idea of a sequence $W+ \rightarrow H+$.

However, the task of fully describing the flow of marital interaction involves more than simply identifying sequences which show only a spouse's *immediate* response to his or her partner's preceding behavior in *only one code* (for example, $H+ \rightarrow W+$; $H- \rightarrow W-$; $W0 \rightarrow H0$), but additionally, requires a consideration of longer sequences that reveal the patterning of spousal responses over time and in several codes (for example, $W- \rightarrow H- \rightarrow W+ \rightarrow H0 \rightarrow W+ \rightarrow$ $H+$). That is, when we observe a wife express a complaint about the marriage in a negative tone of voice, in addition to asking the question, "Does ths reduce our uncertainty in predicting that the husband will immediately follow with negative nonverbal behavior?" we need to ask other questions, such as: Does knowing that the husband immediately reciprocates his wife's negative behavior help us predict the wife's next response? Does she again respond with negative behavior? And if so, how long does this pattern of husband and wife negative nonverbal behavior reciprocation persist? Does this pattern lead to a major argument? Or does one spouse express a behavior in the verbal or nonverbal dimension that circumvents a conflict? And how about the unlikely $H+ \rightarrow$ $W+$ sequence in our previous example; does the failure to find support for the idea that the husband *immediately* follows his wife's positive nonverbal behavior with positive behavior completely rule out a connection between occurrences of positiveness in the husband and wife? Perhaps it takes some time for the wife's positiveness to influence the husband's behavior, in which case her antecedent positive behavior may be more predictive of his positive nonverbal behavior later in the interactional sequence.

To evaluate the above types of questions requires an analytic procedure that can assess sequential connections across several behavioral codes in time, an analysis which would be extremely unwieldy using the procedure described earlier. Fortunately, a procedure that meets the above specifications, called lag analysis, was proposed by Sackett (Note 1).

In particular, lag analysis can be used to assess two types of questions about interactional sequences. First, lag analysis can be used to identify the sequence of behavioral codes that is likely to follow the occurrence of a selected behavioral code. For example, given that we are coding husband's and wife's interactions with the CISS content and nonverbal behavior and we observe the husband expressing his feelings (that is, complaining) about a relationship problem in a neutral tone of voice, what is the sequence of interaction that is likely to occur? Furthermore, we may ask, "Can the maritally satisfied be discriminated from the maritally dissatisfied by the interactional sequences that are likely to occur?" Answers to these questions can provide important behavioral descriptions of communication patterns in distressed and nondistressed couples as a prerequisite to building an empirical theory of marital satisfaction.

Whereas the above type of question involves the identification of sequences with unknown elements, lag analysis can be used in a second way to assess the probability of a sequence with known elements. In this case, we restrict our analysis to a predetermined, or known, sequence. For example, given that a wife's initial nonverbal behavior is coded negative, what is the likelihood that she and her husband will subsequently engage in a sequence of interaction characterized by the reciprocation of negative behavior? Do the maritally satisfied and dissatisfied differ in the reciprocation of negative behavior over time? Answers to these questions can be used to test specific interactional hypotheses about marital satisfaction and marital distress. Since the same logic and procedure are followed when lag analysis is used to answer both types of questions, we will present a discussion only of the steps used to identify sequences.

IDENTIFYING SEQUENCES

The application of lag analysis for identifying unknown sequences has been described in detail in Sackett (Note 1), Bakeman and Dabbs (1976), Gottman et al. (1977), and Gottman (1979). This procedure consists of several steps which we will describe in detail below:

Select a criterion code. The first step in lag analysis is to designate one behavior as the criterion. The criterion represents the behavior that precedes the sequence we would like to identify. For example, let us select the husband's expression of feelings about a relationship issue delivered with neutral nonverbal behavior (HPFO) as the criterion code.

TABLE 13.3   Example of Lag Sequential Analysis

Criterion: HPFO[a], Husbands feeling or information about a problem delivered with neutral affect.	Lag					
	1	2	3	4	5	6
Nonclinic Couples						
WPFO	.24	.13	.18	.16	.17	.18
WAGO	.30	.05	.19	.09	.15	.11
HPFO	.00	.38	.14	.26	.17	.22
HAGO	.02	.11	.08	.07	.08	.07
Z-score	9.77	10.31	5.11	3.57	2.38	<1.96
Clinic Couples						
WPFO	.23	.11	.17	.14	.16	.12
WAGO	.16	.03	.08	.05	.06	.09
HPFO	.00	.33	.15	.25	.17	.20
HAGO	.01	.07	.05	.06	.06	.07
Z-score	3.90	9.11	2.50	5.02	<1.96	2.10

NOTE: Broken lines indicate sequence.
a. Similar patterns emerged when WPFO was made the criterion.

Computation of lagged conditional probabilities. After selecting the criterion code, the next step in lag analysis is to calculate the conditional probability that each of the behavioral codes will immediately follow the criterion (lag 1), follow as the second behavior (lag 2), follow as the third behavior (lag 3), and so on, up to the nth behavior (lag n). These probabilities are called lag conditional probabilities. Table 13.3 contains the lagged conditional probabilities for the wife expressing feelings about a problem with neutral nonverbal behavior (WPFO), the wife expressing agreement with neutral nonverbal behavior (WAGO), the husband expressing agreement with neutral nonverbal behavior (HAGO), given the criterion code HPFO, for a group of clinic and nonclinic couples. The information contained in Table 13.3 was reported in Gottman et al. (1977) for couples engaged in the empirically derived "agenda building" phase of conflict resolution discussions, that is, the beginning phase of problem solving when feelings about problems were first aired and explored. Although the lagged conditional probabilities for all CISS codes were calculated in the above study (a computation that is required to identify sequences), Table 13.3 contains these figures only for the four behavioral codes that were involved in significant sequential connections.

Identifying the most probable sequence. The most likely sequence is suggested by selecting the behavior code at each lag that has the highest conditional probability with respect to the criterion code. For example, the sequence A → B → C → D → E is suggested if behavior code B has the highest conditional probability with respect to the criterion behavior code A at lag 1, if C has the highest conditional probability with respect to A at lag 2, if D has the highest conditional probability with respect to A at lag 3, and finally, if E has the highest conditional probability with respect to A at lag 4.

As table 13.3 reveals, different sequences were suggested for clinic versus nonclinic couples following the criterion code HPFO. Thus, for clinic couples the sequence HPFO → WPFO → HPFO → WPFO → HPFO was suggested. This sequence, called "cross-complaining," consists of the husband and wife exchanging complaints about a relationship problem over 4 lags. For nonclinic couples a different sequence was suggested, that is, HPFO → WAGO → HPFO → WAGO → HPFO. In this latter sequence, called "validation," the wife agrees with or acknowledges the husband's statements about a relationship problem over 4 lags. That clinic couples may be characterized by cross-complaining sequences and nonclinic couples by validation sequences makes sense conceptually, given the differences in the two groups' levels of marital satisfaction.

Testing suggested sequences. Gottman (1979) described a two-step procedure for assessing the most probable sequence. In the third step, we identified the most likely sequence by selecting the behavioral code with the highest conditional probability with respect to the criterion at each lag. According to the information theory definition of communication, the evaluaton of the suggested sequence must demonstrate that the criterion behavior code does indeed reduce uncertainty in predicting the code with the highest conditional probability at each lag. For this evaluation, we can use Sackett's Z-statistic. Thus, the first step in confirming the suggested sequence, A → B → C → D → E, requires that Z-scores comparing the following unconditional probabilities against lagged conditional probabilities should all be greater than 1.96: the conditional probability of B with respect to the criterion A at lag 1 (P[B/A, lag 1]) against the unconditional probability of B (P[B]), the conditional probability of C with respect to A at lag 2 (P[C/A, lag 2]) against the unconditional probability of C (P[C]), the conditional probability of D with respect to A at lag 3 (P[D/A, lag 3]) against the unconditional probability of D (P[D]), and the conditional probability of E with respect to A at lag 4 (P[E/A, lag 4]) against the unconditional probability of E (P[E]).

Table 13.3 presents the Z-scores testing the sequences suggested in our previous example for clinic and nonclinic couples. The Z-score listed at each lag in Table 13.3 is for the behavioral code with the highest conditional probability at that lag. As revealed by Table 13.3, the Z-scores for the identified sequence HPFP → WPFO → HPFO → WPFO → HPFO in clinic couples were also greater than 1.96.

The first step in assessing the most probable sequence consisted of evaluating the connectedness of the criterion behavior code to the other codes in the sequence at various lags. Once we've demonstrated that the criterion behavioral code A reduces uncertainty in predicting the occurrence of B at lag 1, C at lag 2, D at lag 3, and E at lag 4, in order to confirm the sequence A → B → C → D → E, we now need to demonstrate the connectedness of the intermediate sequences B → C, C → D, and D → E. These intermediate connections can be assessed with Sackett's (Note 1) "lag-one connection rule."

Thus, to test the sequence A → B → C → D → E, using the lag-one connection rule, Gottman (1979) recommended the following procedure: make B the criterion behavior and determine if the conditional probability of C with respect to B at lag 1 from B is higher than the conditional probabilities of the other codes; then make C the criterion behavior and determine if the conditional probability of D with respect to C at lag 1 from C is higher than the conditional probabilities of the other codes; and finally, make D the criterion behavior and determine if the conditional probability of E with respect to D at lag 1 from D is higher than the conditional probabilities of the other codes. If all of the above conditional probabilities have in fact been confirmed, then each of the lag 1 connections involving the intermediate codes are tested with Sackett's Z-statistic. Thus, Z-scores comparing P(C/B, lag 1) against P(C), P(D/C, lag 1) against P(D), and P(E/D, lag 1) against P(E) should be greater than 1.96 to demonstrate the connectedness of B → C, C → D, and D → E, respectively. The sequence A → B → C → D → E is identified if and only if the above comparisons suggest that the intermediate codes B and C, C and D, and D and E are connected.

Using Sackett's lag-one connection rule, we found support for the idea that clinic couples are more likely to engage in cross-complaining sequences and less likely to engage in validation sequences than nonclinic couples in the early stages of problem-solving discussions. For the sake of brevity, we will not present the data involved in this analysis here. For a description of other sequences that have been identified with the procedures discussed in this section and that also differentiate between the interactions of clinic and nonclinic couples, the reader is referred to Gottman et al. (1977) and Gottman (1979).

In summary, the preceding section described a strategy based on information theory to assess the communicative value of a spouse's behavior in terms of its ability to reduce uncertainty in predicting his or her partner's consequent behavior. Uncertainty reduction was operationalized as the difference between conditional and unconditional probabilities and a method for testing uncertainty reduction, Sackett's Z-statistic, was described. We concluded this section with a discussion of Sackett's (Note 1) lag analysis, which represents a helpful method for identifying and assessing interactional sequences over time.

COMMENTS ON SEQUENTIAL ANALYSIS

In using sequential analysis strategies there are several issues the researcher needs to consider. First is the assumption of a stable or constant probability structure in the interactional events under study. Thus we expect the probability structure between events at the beginning of the interaction will be approximately the same probability structure at the end of the interaction. Of course, it is possible to subdivide a long interactional exchange into separate and distinct sections with each section characterized by its own probability structure. This should be done, for example, if there is reason to believe that the interactional process changes during the course of a conversation. Gottman (1979), for example, reported the characteristics of three distinct phases of a problem-solving discussion in clinic and nonclinic couples. The phases of the discussion were based on partitioning the couples' discussion into equal thirds based on the total number of CISS interactional units produced by each couple.

A second issue concerns the homogeneity of observed patterns across couples. When the researcher is interested in going beyond first-order sequential dependencies, the data from many couples may have to be pooled to yield adequate estimates of conditional probabilities. To the extent that individual couples contribute markedly different probability structures to the group data, our assumption of homogeneity may be called into question. To assess whether or not the simple conditional probabilities of each couple's behavioral sequences can be considered as samples from the same population (that is, characterized by the same probability structure), Castellan (1979) describes a test statistic which is asymptotically distributed as chi-square.

A third issue concerns the independence of observations during social interaction. Since the interactional data is likely to be highly correlated, there is a potential lack of independence in the observational data submitted to sequence analysis. Attention to this problem is most important when the investigator collapses data across subjects, time, settings, or partners. Just how serious potential violations of the independence assumption are is largely unknown in sequence analysis. There is a long history of statistical investigation of contingency tables in which observations are not independent. This literature supports the use of the usual test statistics which have been shown to be asymptotically chi-square random variable (see Anderson & Goodman, 1957). As a matter of practice, the researcher who follows the guidelines for Sackett's lag analyses described by Gottman (1979) and summarized in this chapter can confidently report her or his findings. To review, the normal approximation to the binomial distribution is good when sample sizes are over 30 and expected values are not skewed beyond .1 or .9. Thus Gottman (1979) has suggested using the Z-statistic only when N is greater than 30, and that when P is near 0 or 1, NPO must be at least 9 before using the normal approximation to the binomial distribution. An alternative way to state the limit for sequence analysis is to calculate the minimum number of times the criterion should occur given the probability (P) of the consequent. For example, if the consequent unconditional probability = .17 and we seek NPO equal to at least 9 (Siegel, 1956), then solving for N we have $N = 9/(.17)(.83)$ approximately equals 64. Given this probability, then, we would examine sequences only if they are based on 64 occurrences of the criterion.

A final issue concerns the large number of tests that are typically produced when completing a sequence analysis among all codes. The problem here is the familiar one of Type I error. Given the large number of tests performed, we expect on the basis of chance alone a number of significant findings. Thus the experimenter should at least demonstrate that a greater number of tests are significant than would be expected on the basis of chance alone with a .05 level of significance and that the identified sequences are conceptually meaningful.

THE SPECTRAL ANALYSIS
OF TIME-SERIES DATA

Time-series measures retain information about patterning over time whereas rate measures of relative proportions of a code collapse information across the time dimension. A time-series is thus a set of observations ordered in time, such as weekly ratings of presidential popularity before an election. The following discussion applying time-series analysis to detect affective patterning between husband and wife interaction is taken from Gottman (1979). The objective of this analysis is to assess the extent to which affective behaviors of one spouse affect the affective behaviors of the partner over time.

Since we are interested in the relationship between two time series (wife's affect and husband's affect), we are dealing with bivariate time-series analysis. In univariate time-series analysis we are interested in assessing fluctuations of a single variable over time. Although there are several types of questions that can be asked about the relationship between two time series (see Glass et al., 1975, on the interrupted time series; Box & Jenkins, 1970, on transfer functions), the study of "lead-lag" relationships, as described in Gottman (1979), is ideally suited for assessing sequential patterning in marriage. For instance, one way of studying the bivariate time series x_t and y_t, where x_t = observations of the wife's affect over time and y_t = observations of the husband's affect over time, is to assess whether or not changes in x_t follow changes in y_t at some fixed lag (in which case we would say the husband's behavior leads and the wife's behavior lags—hence, the term lead-lag relationship), and vice versa. Thus, the analysis of lead-lag relationships in bivariate time series represents an effective strategy for assessing affective shifts within an observational record of a husband and wife's coded interaction.

An application of the analysis of lead-lag relationships in bivariate time series can be found in Gottman's (1979) innovative study of dominance in marital interaction. The study of dominance in family and marital interaction has a long history and has consistently been examined as a source of difference between distressed and nondistressed samples (Jacob, 1975; Riskin & Faunce, 1972). Equivocal results concerning dominance may be traced to inadequate operationalizations of the concepts and relatively unpowerful statistical tests. If we apply the analysis of lead-lag relationships to couples interaction, we might find, for example, that changes in a wife's behavior tended to follow her husband's behavior at some fixed lag, while the converse might not be found. This finding would then suggest that the wife's behavior is more predictable from the husband's past behavior than is the husband's behavior from his wife's past behavior. Thus, we would suggest that the husband is dominant in this interactional system. By conceptualizing dominance in terms of sequential patterning and, in particular, defining dominance as an asymmetry in the predictability of behavior between a husband and a wife, it might be hypothesized that the interaction of distressed married couples would be characterized by more asymmetry in predictability than the interactional behavior of nondistressed couples.

To perform a time-series analysis requires a large number of observational points; for example, Gottman (1979) worked only with time series with a minimum of 65 points. However, particular CISS content codes are not amenable to time-series analysis because such coding does not yield the necessary number of observational points. The univariate scaling of CISS content and affect codes, which was used in the construction of the point graphs described in Gottman et al. (1977) and Gottman (1979), provides a solution to this problem, as such scaling yields a sufficient observational series. Gottman (1979, P. 171) summarized the univariate scaling procedure as follows:

> Summing across all behavior units within one floor switch, each spouse's codes were scaled according to the following system: (a) Each positive listener or speaker nonverbal behavior = +1; (b) Each negative listener or speaker nonverbal behavior = −1; (c) Negative mindreading (MR-) = −2; (d) Problem solving = +1 if it is followed by an agreement within the floor switch; and (e) Agreement = +1 and Disagreement = −1.

Thus, the floor switches (the point at which one person stops talking and gives up "the floor" and the other person begins talking) represented a series of observational points in time, and the resulting tally for the husband and the tally for the wife were plotted cumulatively for each point on a graph. In addition to providing the sufficient number of observational points for time-series analysis, the cumulative recording of husband and wife scores also provided a conceptually meaningful indicator of fluctuation in each spouse's affect.

Gottman (1979) used a spectral analysis of a time-series model recommended by Granger and Hatanaka (1964) to assess sequential patterns for a set of point graphs of clinic and nonclinic couples. The point graphs were constructed for the data obtained in a study reported in Rubin (Note 2). The Granger and Hatanaka (1964) time-series model not only assesses lead-lag relationships between fluctuation in husband's and wife's affect, but reveals these relationships for specific components of the bivariate time series. To explain this point a brief discussion of some time-series concepts and terminology is required.

There are two procedures for the analysis of univariate time series: time-domain analysis and frequency-domain analysis. Time domain analysis seeks to answer the question, "How predictable is the series from its past?" In frequency-domain analysis, the basic question is, "What are the component oscillations in the series?" Our interest is in frequency-domain analysis. Each time series generates a function called the *spectral density function*, which provides information about the frequency components contributing to an observed series. These univariate time-series relationships can be generalized to the bivariate case.

Gottman (1979) has described the procedure that can be used, in the bivariate case, to reveal the lead-lag relationships between a frequency component in one series and a frequency component in another series. Using the Granger and Hatanaka (1964) model, the frequency range is divided into two parts; a slow frequency component and a fast frequency component. Applying this model to the point-graph data to uncover affective patterning, we may view the slow component as slow variations in affect, as in a mood state, and the fast component may be viewed as rapid variations in affect, as in emotional expressions. Gottman (1979) calls the former mood fluctuations and the latter expression fluctuations.

Recall that the primary objective of this analysis is to uncover lead-lag relationships between frequency components in one series (such as husband's affective points) and frequency components in another series (such as wife's affective points). Since a two-component model is used, lead-lag relationships are assessed for each component in the husband's and the wife's series. The specific relationships are revealed by examining the slope of the phase spectrum in each of the two component halves of the frequency range. For example, the model assesses the lead-lag relationship between the slow frequency component in the husband's series and the slow frequency component in the wife's series (mood fluctuations). Also assessed are the fast components in each spouse's series (expression fluctuations) and the slow components of one spouse's series and the fast components of the partner's series. In all, nine specific lead-lag relationships are possible when assessing three states in husband's and wife's series (zero, positive, and negative slope, and two frequency components—slow-mood and fast-expression).

Using the point-graph data from couples interacting on a number of improvisation tasks (Rubin, Note 2), Gottman (1979) performed the above bivariate time-series analysis. He found that nondistressed couples were characterized by equalitarian dominance patterns represented by no lead-lag relationships or a pattern in which sometimes the wife lags and sometimes the husband lags. In contrast, distressed couples were characterized by a dominant husband represented by a wife who lags her husband's rapid changes in affect expression. This pattern of results was obtained only for couples interacting on a high-conflict task; on low-conflict tasks both clinic and nonclinic couples were characterized by an equalitarian dominance pattern.

SUMMARY

We have reviewed three data analytic strategies for observational data: nonsequential analysis, sequential analysis, and spectral analysis of time-series data. The dependent variables for the various analyses are behavioral observation codes (or some combination of codes) that result when marital interaction is systematically coded by trained observers using one of several marital observation coding systems. The analyses are most frequently used either to describe interaction in distressed and nondistressed couples or to test specific interactional hypotheses related to marital satisfaction and marital distress.

REFERENCE NOTES

1. SACKETT, G. P. *A nonparametric lag sequential analysis for studying dependency among responses in observational coding systems.* Unpublished manuscript, University of Washington, 1974.
2. RUBIN, M. D. *Differences between distressed and nondistressed couples in verbal and nonverbal communication codes.* Unpublished doctoral dissertation, Indiana University—Bloomington, 1977.

REFERENCES

ALTMANN, S. Sociobiology of rhesus monkeys: II. Stochastics of social communication. *Journal of Theoretical Biology,* 1965, *8,* 490-522.
ANDERSON, T. W., & GOODMAN, L. A. Statistical inference about Markov chains. *Annals of Mathematical Statistics,* 1957, *28,* 89-110.
ATTNEAVE, F. *Applications of information theory to psychology: A summary of basic concepts, methods, and results.* New York: Holt, Rinehart & Winston, 1959.
BAKEMAN, R., & DABBS, J. M., Jr. Social interaction observed: Some approaches to the analysis of behavior streams. *Personality and Social Psychology Bulletin,* 1976, *2,* 335-345.
BIRCHLER, G. R., WEISS, R. L., and VINCENT, J. P. A multi-method analysis of social reinforcement exchange between maritally distressed and nondistressed spouse and stranger dyads. *Journal of Personality and Social Psychology,* 1975, *31,* 349-360.
BISHOP, Y. M. M., FIENBERG, S. E., & HOLLAND, P. W. *Discrete multivariate analysis.* Cambridge, MA: MIT Press, 1975.
BOX, G. E. P., & JENKINS, G. M. *Time-series analysis: Forecasting and control.* San Francisco: Holden-Day, 1970.

CASTELLAN, N. J. The analysis of behavior sequences. In R. B. Cairns (Ed.), *The analysis of social interactions: Methods, issues, and illustrations*. Hinsdale, NJ: Erlbaum, 1979.

GLASS, G. V., WILLSON, V. L., & GOTTMAN, J. M. *Design and analysis of time-series experiments*. Boulder: Colorado University Associated Press, 1975.

GOTTMAN, J. M. *Marital interaction*. New York: Academic, 1979.

GOTTMAN, J. M., MARKMAN, H., & NOTARIUS, C. The topography of marital conflict: A study of verbal and nonverbal behavior. *Journal of Marriage and the Family*, 1977, *39*, 461-477.

GOTTMAN, J. M., & NOTARIUS, C. Sequential analysis of observational data using Markov chains. In T. Kratochwill (Ed.), *Strategies to evaluate change in single-subject research*. New York: Academic, 1978.

GOTTMAN, J. M., NOTARIUS, C., MARKMAN, H., BANK, S., YOPPI, B., & RUBIN, M. E. Behavior exchange theory and marital decision making. *Journal of Personality and Social Psychology*, 1976, *34*, 14-23.

GRANGER, C. W. J., & HATANAKA, M. *Spectral analysis of economic time-series*. Princeton, NJ: Princeton University Press, 1964.

JACOB, T. Family interaction in disturbed and normal families: A methodological and substantive review. *Psychological Bulletin*, 1975, *82*, 33-65.

KRAEMER, H. C., & JACKLIN, C. N. Statistical analysis of dyadic social behavior. *Psychological Bulletin*, 1979, *86*, 217-224.

MILLER, G. A. What is information measurement? *American Psychologist*, 1953, *8*, 31-41.

MYERS, J. L. *Fundamentals of experimental design*. Boston: Allyn & Bacon, 1966.

RAUSH, H. L., BARRY, W. A., HERTEL, R. K., & SWAIN, M. A. *Communication, conflict, and marriage*. San Francisco: Jossey-Bass, 1974.

RISKIN, J., & FAUNCE, E. E. An evaluative review of family interaction research. *Family Process*, 1972, *11*, 365-455.

SACKETT, G. P. The lag sequential analysis of contingency and cyclicity in behavioral interaction research. In J. Osofsky (Ed.), *Handbook of infant development*. New York: John Wiley, 1978.

SEIGEL, S. *Nonparametric statistics for the behavioral sciences*. New York: McGraw-Hill, 1956.

14

EQUITY IN DYADIC
AND FAMILY INTERACTION:
IS THERE ANY JUSTICE?

Rand D. Conger
Stevens S. Smith

The notion of equity in social relationships concerns the degree to which social interaction can be described as adhering to some rule or rules of justice.[1] Traditionally, studies of equity have used a paradigm wherein experimental subjects interact indirectly through some third party. For example, actors A and B may work together on a task for which they are both evaluated and compensated by some other person (for example, the experimenter). More recent studies, however, have investigated direct social exchange between individuals within specific dyads, including those with and those without previous histories of interaction (Burgess & Nielson, 1974; Cook & Emerson, 1978; Gottman, 1979; Walster et al., 1978). Of interest is not only the degree to which such relationships are equitable but also the problems that arise when equity fails. According to Walster and her associates (1978), when an intimate relationship becomes inequitable both partners will be distressed—although it is likely that the partner receiving fewer benefits will be the more anguished of the pair (Homans, 1974).

AUTHORS' NOTE: This study was supported in part by grants from the National Institute of Mental Health (MH-32143) and the National Institute on Drug Abuse (DA-02286).

Thus, the implications of equity theory go beyond simply describing whether or not fair rules of exchange, however defined, exist in social interaction. Perhaps the most important hypothesis of the paradigm is one that suggests that when a relationship is not equitable, both partners will be dissatisfied. This dissatisfaction, in turn, produces attempts to restore equity. In intimate dyads, some possible reactions to inequity include withdrawing from the relationship, devaluing the worth of the partner, or seeking other, more satisfactory unions. To determine whether inequitable behavior exchange actually has these or other consequences, methodological techniques must be developed for estimating the degree of equity actually existing in a dyad or larger group.

The primary task of this chapter is to describe certain analytic procedures that may prove useful for assessing equity when directly observed behavior between individuals is available. In addition, possible relationships predictable from equity theory between the outcomes of such analyses and other events are discussed and examples provided.

EQUITY IN THE DYAD

In order for equity to exist in a relationship, each individual's outcomes, relative to his or her behavioral investments, must equal the partner's outcomes. This conception of equity was described by Adams (1965) in the following equation:

$$O_p/I_p = O_a/I_a \qquad [1]$$

This equation simply states that if the ratio of outcomes to inputs is equal for person and other in an exchange, then equity exists. Importantly, the subscripts p and a may refer to two separate individuals or to two groups of individuals.

Adams's formula has been revised by several writers because of a crucial flaw—under certain circumstances a person with negative inputs may achieve positive outcomes, and vice versa, and yet equity may obtain according to the formula (see Moschetti, 1979). Developments in the equity equation since Adams's original conception of it have dealt primarily with this problem of negative inputs and outcomes (Harris, 1976; Moschetti, 1979; Walster et al., 1978). However, when the units of analysis are rates or frequencies of observed behavior, inputs and outcomes have positive values obviating the problem of negative signs. Therefore, the simple equation proposed by Adams appears to be adequate for the description of equity in behavioral interaction within a dyad, and can be rewritten:

$$O_A/I_A = O_B/I_B \qquad [2]$$

This equation states that when the behavioral outcomes for actor A, relative to his or her behavioral inputs, equals the same ratio for actor B, equity exists.[2]

In the case of direct behavior exchange, however, matters can be simplified even further. If inputs and outcomes involve the same behavioral dimension, for example, expressions of positive emotional affect, and if we assume that such verbalizations by one party in the exchange are roughly equivalent to those by the other, then A's outcomes are equal to B's inputs, and vice versa.[3] Substituting these identities in the equation leads to:

$$I_B/I_A = I_A/I_B \qquad [3]$$

which, after a little algebra, produces:

$$I_A = I_B \qquad [4]$$

This is a formula quite different than the usual proportional approach to describing equity. Indeed, in the dyadic case involving direct behavioral exchange, equity appears to reduce to a formula for reciprocity, the exchange of equivalents (see Cook & Emerson, 1978, who reach a similar conclusion).

For analyzing dyads alone, then, equity reduces to a question of reciprocity. That is, do partners in an intimate relationship tend to respond to one another in a like manner over time? After initial consideration, the interpretation of equation 4 appears straightforward. If particular behaviors by person A toward partner B equal those of B to A, then equity can be said to exist. Reciprocity, however, implies obligation such that B's rate of compliments, for example, should in some sense be elicited by A's behavior (Adams, 1965; Gouldner, 1960). As Gottman (1979) notes, any analytic technique designed to assess reciprocity must deal with this notion of *contingent interaction*. Moreover, simple correlations between rates of behavior across the same time period will not produce coefficients indicative of reciprocity because they do not establish whether one partner's behavior prompts the other's.

In addition to being contingent, reciprocal behaviors should be analyzed within a framework that allows for the *consideration of time*. For example, a pleasing gesture by one partner may lead to a similar response by the second, for example, a hug or kiss, but the reaction by the partner may not occur immediately. The fact that a reciprocal peck on the cheek occurs thirty seconds, one minute, or five minutes later may make it no less contingent on the initial behavior by one's mate.

Gottman (1979) suggests that the use of conditional and unconditional probabilities for the assessment of lagged behavioral events satisfies the contingency criterion for evaluating reciprocity in behavioral interaction. Using this technique, he has demonstrated that couples seeking assistance for marital problems are more reciprocal than nondistressed dyads in terms of aversive interactions; however, both groups are about equally reciprocal in their supportive or positive behaviors. Briefly, lag sequential analysis begins by determining each person's base-rate (unconditional) probability of behaving in a particular manner. For example, out of a total of 400 behaviors emitted by a wife, 20 may be aversive, yielding an unconditional probability of negative behavior by the wife, or $p(W-)$, of .05. However, the probability of a negative response by the wife can be computed contingent upon the occurrence of an aversive act by the husband, or $p(W-|H-)$, which reads "the probability of a wife negative given a previous husband negative." For example, if the husband behaves aversively 20 times and the wife reacts in kind on 5 of these occasions, then $p(W-|H-) = 5/20 = .25$. The two events considered together, that is, the husband negative behavior followed by a wife negative response, would be a lag 1 sequence.

The wife's increased likelihood of behaving negatively whenever her husband's immediately preceding response is irritating may be thought of as an indication of reciprocity. The degree of difference (in the above example) between the wife's unconditional negative responding (.05) and her conditional responding lag 1 (.25) can be assessed using the normal approximation to the binomial distribution or Z-score (Bakeman, 1978; Gottman, 1979; Sackett, 1978). If this test indicates that the conditional probability is substantially greater than the unconditional, one may conclude that the wife is responding reciprocally.[4] And, of course, the same procedure may be used to assess the husband's behavior. In addition, the analyses may be pursued beyond one lag; for example, does the probability that the wife will respond negatively to an aversive behavior by the husband increase at two, three, or any number of behaviors beyond the husband's initial provocation?

Although we agree with Gottman that the lag sequential approach meets the contingency criterion in the definition of reciprocity, it does seem that analyses using lagged behavioral events in the above fashion may place an emphasis on immediacy of response that is not apparent in the usual definition of the concept. As usually conceived, reciprocity simply means that specific behaviors by person A will tend to prompt similar responses by person B at a later point in time. As noted earlier, one may respond in kind to the actions of another in seconds, minutes, hours, or days, and yet the reaction still may be contingent. In the study of face-to-face interaction, it would seem that the most appropriate time interval for assessing reciprocity must be determined empirically and that this time dimension should be added to the procedures already developed for analyses of changing probabilities in behavioral events.

In order to assess the effect of adding a time component to lag sequential techniques for analyzing reciprocity, we first coded behavioral interaction between a husband and wife as they played some simple games together in their home. Interactions were scored using a Datamyte 900 event recorder, which allows observers to code and store individual behaviors and their times of occurrence.[5] Positive verbal responses, such as compliments, expressions of endearment, and supportive verbalizations, as well as negative behaviors, such as criticism and expressions of dislike, were analyzed. Table 14.1 contains the findings for the analyses of lagged behavioral events using the methods described earlier (Gottman, 1979).

TABLE 14.1   Lag Sequential Analysis of One Couple's Interactions

	Lag 1	Lag 2	Lag 3
Positive Interactions			
P(H+|W+)[a]	.034	.034	.000
P(W+|H+)[b]	.250 (2.65)	.200	.150
Negative Interactions			
P(H−|W−)[c]	.130	.109	.087
P(W−|H−)[d]	.189	.089	.081

NOTE: Z-scores greater than 2.00 are considered an index of reciprocity (in parentheses).
a. The unconditional probability of a positive behavior by the husband, p(H+), was .058.
b. The unconditional probability of a positive behavior by the wife, p(W+), was .085.
c. The unconditional probability of a negative behavior by the husband, p(H−), was .107.
d. The unconditional probability of a negative behavior by the wife, p(W−), was .134.

The unconditional probability of a positive behavior by the husband, p(H+), was .058 compared to .085, p(W+), for the wife. The figures in Table 14.1 show that the husband's probability of responding in a positive fashion after his wife engaged in such behavior, that is, p(H+|W+), actually decreased compared to the unconditional level. The probability that the very next behavior following a wife positive would be an equivalent response by the husband (lag 1) was only .034, and the probability of a husband positive two behaviors after the criterion behavior by the wife (lag 2) was the same. At lag 3, that is, the third behavior following a positive action by the wife, the husband never responded in kind.

When the husband's behavior was used as the criterion event, the data show that the wife apparently increased her positive behaviors in response to supportive acts by her husband—p(W+|H+). At lag 1, the Z-score (2.65) suggested that the conditional probability (.250) was substantially greater than the unconditional figure of .085.[6] The conditional probabilities at lags 2 and 3 were suggestive of similar reciprocation in that they were greater than the unconditional probability. However, they were not of sufficient magnitude to produce a Z greater than two, the criterion suggested by Bakeman (1978) and the standard used here as an index of contingency between behavioral events.

Turning to negative interactions, the unconditional probability of an aversive behavior by the husband was .107 compared to .134 for the wife. Although both lag 1 figures were suggestive of negative reciprocity, that is, p(H−|W−) = .130 and p(W−|H−) = .189, neither of them produced a Z-score greater than two. From the results presented in Table 14.1, then, one would conclude that, except for immediate positive responses by the wife to her husband's supportive behaviors, there is little reason to believe that these spouses were reciprocal in their affective behaviors. The next question was whether adding a time parameter to the lag sequential approach would improve our ability to uncover patterns of reciprocity that may actually exist.

TABLE 14.2   Lag-Time Sequential Analysis of One Couple's Interactions

	.10 min. (6 sec.)	.30 min. (18 sec.)	.50 min. (30 sec.)	.70 min. (42 sec.)	.90 min. (54 sec.)
Positive Interactions					
P(H+|W+)[a]	.000	.034	.034	.103	.103
P(W+|H+)[b]	.300 (3.45)	.100	.200	.150	.150
Negative Interactions					
P(H−|W−)[c]	.130	.196	.217 (2.42)	.217 (2.42)	.196
P(W−|H−)[d]	.216	.270 (2.43)	.342 (3.40)	.378 (4.36)	.216

NOTE: Z-scores greater than 2.00 are considered an index of reciprocity (in parentheses).
a. The unconditional probability of a positive behavior by the husband, p(H+), was .058.
b. The unconditional probability of a positive behavior by the wife, p(W+), was .085.
c. The unconditional probability of a negative behavior by the husband, p(H−), was .107.
d. The unconditional probability of a negative behavior by the wife, p(W−), was .134.

The basic argument is that, if a period of time after a criterion behavior (such as spouse positive or negative) were substituted for a series of discrete behavioral lags, a pattern of contingent response might emerge more clearly. For example, in Table 14.1, event lags 1, 2, and 3 might all occur within a few seconds after the criterion. Analyzing behaviors that occur within that period as separate lagged events may produce no significant findings, whereas results suggestive of reciprocity may be produced if the time period were treated as just one lag in time (see Bakeman, 1978, for a similar treatment of state transition probabilities). The data for our experimental couple were reanalyzed following this approach; the findings are presented in Table 14.2.

To construct the lag-time sequential analyses, each criterion behavior of interest (H+, W+, H−, W−) was inspected in relation to a specific time interval that followed it. In Table 14.2 the row p(H+ | W+) indicates that the criterion behavior was a positive behavior by the wife and that we searched various time intervals ranging from .10 minutes (6 seconds) to .90 minutes (54 seconds) for a similar response by the husband. The data in Table 14.2 indicate that, regardless of the interval employed, the conditional probability of a husband positive following a wife positive was not different from the husband's relative frequency (.058) of positive responding according to the Z-score criterion. The figures in the row labeled p(W+ | H+) indicate that the wife was likely to reciprocate a husband positive only in the shortest time interval (.10 minutes), thus, the results are quite similar to the lag 1 analysis in Table 14.1.[7]

However, there were dramatic changes in the findings concerning negative reciprocity. Apparently there was some latency in the husband's response to his wife's aversive actions, that is, p(H− | W−). At 6 seconds after a noxious act by his spouse, the husband's conditional response (.130) was not great enough to produce a Z-score of two or more. However, when the lagged time period increased to .30 minutes (18 seconds), p(H− | W−) = .196 compared to the unconditional probability of .107. At one-half minute the husband's aversive reactions to his wife's negative behavior exceeded the Z-score criterion (Z = 2.42) and remained at that level until it began to decline at .90 minutes. A similar pattern occurred for the wife's reactions to husband negatives, that is, p(W− | H−).

For this couple, then, the lag-time analysis described a pattern of negative reciprocity that was not apparent in the lag analyses of discrete behavioral events. Moreover, the results demonstrated that the conditional probabilities were likely to peak at between .50 and .70 minutes and then decline in magnitude (see Bakeman, 1978, for a similar conclusion regarding mother-infant interaction). The time interval for negative reactions, then, was psychologically meaningful and not simply an indicator of an "explosive" growth in responses that would lead to conditional probabilities of 1.00 if the intervals were increased repeatedly. Indeed, the conditional probabilities for negative interactions continued to decrease steadily out to 1.50 minutes—$p(H- \mid W-)$ = .130 and $p(W- \mid H-)$ = .162—the maximum interval used for these analyses.

If one were interested in the effects of equity on dyadic relationships, this lag-time approach to assessing reciprocity might be used as an indicator of the concept. For example, a researcher might predict that married couples who produced low scores on a measure of marital satisfaction would demonstrate less evidence of positive reciprocity than partners more content with their spouses. That is, the failure to reciprocate positively valenced behaviors during face-to-face interaction might lead to feelings of anger and resentment by one or both partners in a marriage. Differences in reciprocity between the two groups would be determined by using a one-way ANOVA on the Z-scores for each couple in the two samples. Contrary to some investigators (for example, Williams, 1979), Gottman (1979) found no differences in positive reciprocity between satisfied and unhappy couples; however, his analyses involved lagging discrete behaviors rather than behavioral lags in time. The procedures we have discussed may produce different results than Gottman's—findings that would be more consistent with equity notions.

To recapitulate, our earlier discussion demonstrated that, for dyads, equity reduces to a question of reciprocity. We then turned our attention to reciprocity per se and concluded that an operational definition of the concept should include parameters of both time and contingency. One of these requirements, behavioral contingency, is met by a lag sequential approach using discrete behavioral events. However, event lags do not take into account the fact that a reciprocal response does not need to be immediate to be contingent. Our analyses of interaction data for a single married couple suggest that a more satisfactory method for operationalizing reciprocity can be found using a lagged-time approach which allows for the incorporation of some latency in time between the behavior of one actor and the response of the second. A procedure for extending the lag-time technique to groups of dyads who differ on theoretically relevant dimensions was discussed.

The question to be addressed at this point is whether the behavioral study of equity can be pursued separately from the issue of reciprocity. In the section that follows, we answer this question in the affirmative and present a method for operationalizing equity in groups larger than a dyad.

EQUITY BEYOND THE DYAD

Once marital partners are embedded within a larger group, such as the family, it becomes possible to investigate the degree of equity in a system as a whole. In addition, each spouse can be located on a scale of benefits received relative to investments made. For example, it can be determined whether the wife engages in a greater number of supportive behaviors with other family members than she receives from them and whether the husband shares about the same position on the continuum.

Returning to Adams's (1965) original formulation (equation 1), equity exists in a group when each person's ratio of outcomes to inputs is equal, that is, O_i/I_i = r_i, and equity exists when r_i is the same for each member of the group. Again, we may use Adams's formula because behavioral data will not produce negative signs. Also, since the total inputs for the group will equal total outcomes, r_i will equal one for each individual when all interaction is equitable. Importantly, equity may exist in a group larger than a dyad even if inputs and outcomes are not equivalent for each pair of actors in the group. That is, as long as a family member receives about what he or she gives behaviorally, the inputs may be distributed differently than the outcomes. For example, a mother may emit most of her supportive behaviors to a young infant, who cannot reciprocate in kind. However, her spouse may offer her extra support such that her total input of positive behaviors to the system is matched by the positive outcomes she receives.[8]

In order to illustrate this approach to studying equity with actual families, positive verbalizations for two families were analyzed. These families differed in terms of characteristics that may be related to patterns of equity. One was known to have parents who were physically abusive toward their children, whereas the second family was a matched control. In terms of equity theory, abuse may be one means of imposing costs on children, that is, decreasing their interactional benefits when parents feel they are being treated inequitably in their role as parents (see Adams, 1965). Both families had two parents and three children and each group was observed for approximately 4 hours at home while playing simple games together. Details regarding the behavioral code and the procedures employed can be found elsewhere (see note 5).

As noted earlier, the behaviors included within the response class of verbal positives range from compliments or expressions of affection to remarks supportive of the other person's ongoing actions. Table 14.3 contains the results of the analyses. The figures in the column labeled inputs are the rates per minute of verbal positives by each family member. The outcome column contains the rates per minute of all verbal positives received by each family member.

In the abusive family, the mother is clearly the least benefited person in the group. The percentage columns indicate that she emitted 70.2% of all positive verbalizations in the family, yet was the recipient of only 17% of these behaviors. The r_i column (O_i/I_i) also demonstrates this inequity. In the ideal case, as noted above, each r_i would equal one. In the abusive family the r_i's varied from .24 for the mother to 6.25 for the youngest child. For the control family, the range in r_i's was from .47 for the father to 1.56 for the oldest child. A cursory

TABLE 14.3 Equity Analyses for Positive Verbalizations in Two Families

Persons	Inputs (rates)	%	Outcomes (rates)	%	r_i
Abuse Family					
Mother	.33	70.2	.08	17.0	.24
Father	.01	2.1	.04	8.5	4.00
Oldest child	.01	2.1	.01	2.1	1.00
Middle child	.08	17.0	.09	19.1	1.13
Youngest child	.04	8.5	.25	53.2	6.25
Control Family					
Mother	.26	28.8	.26	28.6	1.00
Father	.30	33.3	.14	15.4	.47
Oldest child	.09	10.0	.14	15.4	1.56
Middle child	.10	11.1	.15	16.5	1.50
Youngest child	.15	16.7	.22	24.2	1.47

inspection of the data suggests that neither family is closely matched to the ideal distribution of r_i's, but that the abuse group varies to a greater extent from the ideal case than do the control subjects.

However, when equity is perfect, that is, all r_i's $= 1$, the variance is zero and no test can be made between the ideal case and what is actually observed in a group. In addition, even if behavioral exchange were quite equitable in a family, the r_i's would never equal unity since sampling and measurement error will always create some distortion in the estimates of behavior rates by family members. It also seems reasonable to assume that as the variation in rates of behavior by individuals increases, the greater will be the variation in the r_i's. That is, a one-to-one match between inputs and outcomes would be harder to obtain if the activity level of individual family members varied a great deal.

For the above reasons, we suggest that rather than using a variance that approximates the ideal, that is, one that is very small, a *within-family test of equity* should involve the variance in the r_i's compared with the obtained variance for behavioral inputs. An appropriate test for homogeneity between variances (the Levene Test) has been suggested by Keppel (1973). This test is particularly well-suited to the present analysis because it does not require the assumption of normality in the distributions of scores to be compared.

In order to perform the Levene test, the scores from each distribution are standardized by obtaining the absolute difference of each score from the mean of the distribution. Table 14.4 contains the original set of figures for inputs and r_i's for both families, and their transformed values. The standardized scores are then submitted to a one-way analysis of variance in the usual fashion (Keppel, 1973). As shown in Table 14.4, the variance in r_i's for the abuse family is significantly greater than the variance in behavioral inputs ($F_{1,8} = 20.01$, p

TABLE 14.4   Within-Family Test for Equity

Inputs	$|Inputs-\bar{x}|$	r_i	$|r_i-\bar{x}|$
	Abuse Family		
.33	.236	.24	2.28
.01	.084	4.00	1.48
.01	.084	1.00	1.52
.08	.014	1.13	1.39
.04	.054	6.25	3.73
Variance: .018		6.380	
Mean: .094		2.520	

$F_{1,8} = 20.01$, p less than .01

Inputs	$|Inputs-\bar{x}|$	r_i	$|r_i-\bar{x}|$
	Control Family		
.26	.08	1.00	.20
.30	.12	.47	.73
.09	.09	1.56	.36
.10	.08	1.50	.30
.15	.03	1.47	.27
Variance: .009		.216	
Mean: .180		1.200	

$F_{1,8} = 9.59$, p less than .05

less than .01). Thus, we conclude that behavior in this family departs significantly from an equitable pattern of interaction. This result is intuitively appealing given the wide disparity in the outcome/input ratios.

For the control family, a statistically significant difference is also obtained between variation in inputs and the variation in the r_i's ($F_{1,8} = 9.59$, p less than .05). However, the degree of difference is statistically less stable than that for the abuse family, a finding that is also intuitively appealing. A number of simulations have shown that as divergences from ideal equity decrease, that is, when the r_i's depart from 1.0 by only .10 to .20 units, the resultant F will not be significant and the null hypothesis that the family does not diverge appreciably from equitable exchange will not be rejected.[9]

A *between-groups or between-families test of equity* is one that will determine whether two families, or two groups of families, differ in the degree to which they may be described as equitable in their interactions. In a straight forward extension of the Levene Test, we can determine, for example, whether the variance in the distribution of r_i's in the abuse family is greater than that for the control family. We simply take the absolute differences from the mean shown in Table 14.4 for each of the r_i distributions and calculate a one-way analysis of variance as before. The results of that analysis produce a significant F ratio ($F_{1, 8} = 14.28$, p less than .01), which leads to the conclusion that the variance in r_i's in the abuse family ($s^2 = 6.38$) is significantly larger than the same variance for the control family ($s^2 = .216$). The greater the variance in r_i's, of course, the more the distribution differs from the ideal case, in which the variance in r_i's would equal zero. The results of this single comparison, then, appear to be consistent with the equity theory prediction noted earlier.

If one wished to compare groups of families, one would calculate a mean r_i for each family in each group. Standardized scores could be determined by finding the differences between these family means and the average r_i for the group as a whole. Using these standardized scores, the Levene Test would be performed in the usual fashion in order to determine whether either group departed further from equitable behavior exchange than the other. The degrees of freedom in such a test would be determined by the number of families in each group, since individual families would be the independent units in such a sampling procedure. Drawing on equity theory, again, it would be expected that families experiencing some distress, such as disturbances in parent-child relations, would be less equitable in their interactions than nondistressed families. Although the example of the two families just presented is consistent with that hypothesis, it was provided only to describe the procedures of analysis, and not as a test of the theory.

DISCUSSION AND CONCLUSIONS

The preceding discussion suggests that there are reasonable ways in which to measure the degree of equity in behavioral exchange either at the dyadic or group level. The existence of such methods makes it possible to examine empirically some of the implications of equity theory at the level of social interaction. For example, theorists have often linked low levels of reciprocity or equity in groups, including dyads, to the emergence of possible problems in interpersonal relationships (Blau, 1964; Gouldner, 1960; Walster et al., 1978). Emerson (1972) has suggested that the victimized party in a dyad, who suffers from an inequitable rate of exchange, may choose to withdraw from or devalue the relationship. Certainly, these are likely responses for marital partners who no longer feel that they are reasonably benefited by continued interaction.

Beyond the dyad, Walster and her associates (1978) note that inequity leads to distress which may be experienced by many group members. The actions of the mother in the abuse family discussed earlier were probably influenced by the fact that her investment of positive/supportive behaviors in the family led to very little support of her in return. Her situation contrasts markedly with the extremely equitable position of the control mother. Moreover, it is likely that parents with very young children, in general, will suffer conditions of extremely inequitable social exchange within the family. This situation may partially account for the relative lack of satisfaction with family life often reported for that point in the life cycle (Clayton, 1978).

In substantive terms, then, assessments of behavioral equity and reciprocity in intimate and family relationships may tell us whether earlier theoretical reasoning is correct, that is, do failures in equity produce distress and concomitant problems in interpersonal functioning? Two procedures were presented for assessing equity in groups—one at the dyadic level of analysis, and the other for social systems with three or more members. Each of these techniques was elaborated in a fashion that suggests their usefulness in comparisons between samples of individuals who differ on some theoretically relevant dimension, such as the presence or absence of family violence. The ultimate test of their value, of course, will occur when they are used to describe interactional differences between populations predicted to vary in terms of equitable behavior exchange.

NOTES

1. The existence of rules of exchange or equity may or may not involve conscious cognitive processes. People may tend to follow well-accepted patterns of social interaction, for example, the use of "good manners," without considering in every instance the norm to which they are adhering.

2. Under some conditions a variable might be computed using behavioral rates or frequencies that would produce negative inputs or outcomes. For example, one might subtract negative outcomes from positive outcomes in order to assess *net gain* in payoffs. However, we would suggest, instead, the use of proportions, such as the proportion of all affective outcomes that are positive or negative, in order to avoid the problem of dissimilar signs.

3. In many circumstances, of course, this assumption may not be true. When it is not, then some weighting of inputs would need to be employed in order for our argument to hold. The question of how to derive such weights is beyond the scope of the present discussion.

4. As Bakeman (1978) has noted, the Z-score used in this fashion should be treated as a descriptive index rather than as an estimate of the probability that a particular event occurred by chance. This is so because the behaviors of individuals interacting with one another are serially dependent. Thus, the Z-score may be regarded as an objective criterion for assessing contingencies between behavioral events, but it cannot be interpreted as a test of statistically significant differences between them. Bakeman suggests that a Z of two or more be regarded as evidence that the conditional probability of a particular behavior is different than its unconditional probability of occurrence.

5. A complete description of the behavioral code and procedures of analysis can be obtained from the authors and from earlier papers (Burgess & Conger, 1978; Conger & McLeod, 1977).

6. Details concerning the computation and interpretation of the Z-score can be found in Bakeman (1978), Gottman (1979), and Gottman & Bakeman (1979).

7. It may seem unusual to get an immediate decrease in conditional probabilities as the time interval increases. However, if, for example, both the husband and wife emitted positive behaviors within the chosen time interval after a husband positive, the result was scored as both positive. In

these analyses only a reciprocal behavior by the spouse alone could be scored as such. This procedure maintains comparability between lag-time and lag-event analysis.

8. By their very nature, analyses of groups larger than n = 2 will be more molar, less microscopic, than the earlier reciprocity analyses of the dyad. Contingencies between behaviors, such as mother responses to child followed at a later time by the husband's attention to her, would be extremely difficult to track using the procedures discussed for assessing dyadic interaction. While the techniques presented in this section add information about the operation of a system larger than a dyad, specific pairs of actors in the group would need to be assessed using the methods described earlier to get information at the level of one person's specific actions and another's specific responses.

9. Conclusions regarding equity within families must be interpreted with caution, however, since the two variances being compared involve the same individuals. This problem is eliminated when comparisons are made between families.

REFERENCES

ADAMS, J. S. Inequity in social exchange. In L. Berkowitz (Ed.), *Advances in experimental social psychology* (Vol. 2). New York: Academic, 1965.

BAKEMAN, R. Untangling streams of behavior: Sequential analyses of observation data. In G. P. Sackett (Ed.), *Observing behavior* Vol. 2: *Data collection and analysis methods*. Baltimore, MD: University Park Press, 1978.

BLAU, P. *Exchange and power in social life*. New York: John Wiley, 1964.

BURGESS, R. L., & CONGER, R. D. Family interaction in abusive, neglectful and normal families. *Child Development*, 1978, *49*, 1163-1173.

BURGESS, R. L., & NIELSEN, J. M. An experimental analysis of some structural determinants of equitable and inequitable exchange relations. *American Sociological Review*, 1974, *39*, 427-443.

CLAYTON, R. R. *The family, marriage, and social change*. Lexington, MA: D. C. Heath, 1978.

CONGER, R. D., & McLEOD, D. Describing behavior in small groups with the datamyte event recorder. *Behavior Research Methods and Instrumentation*, 1977, *9*, 418-424.

COOK, K. S., & EMERSON, R. M. Power, equity and commitment in exchange networks. *American Sociological Review*, 1978, *43*, 721-739.

EMERSON, R. Exchange theory, part I: A psychological basis for social exchange. In J. Berger, M. Zelditch, Jr., and B. Anderson (Eds.), *Sociological theories in progress*. New York: Houghton-Mifflin, 1972.

GOTTMAN, J. M. *Marital interaction: Experimental investigations*. New York: Academic, 1979.

GOTTMAN, J. M., & BAKEMAN, R. The sequential analysis of observational data. In M. Lamb, S. Soumi, and G. Stephenson (Eds.), *Social interaction methodology*. Madison: University of Wisconsin Press, 1979.

GOULDNER, A. W. The norm of reciprocity. *American Sociological Review*, 1960, *25*, 161-178.

HARRIS, R. J. Handling negative inputs: On the plausible equity formulae. *Journal of Experimental Social Psychology*, 1976, *12*, 194-209.

HOMANS, G. C. *Social behavior: Its elementary forms* (Rev. ed.). New York: Harcourt Brace Jovanovich, 1974.

KEPPEL, G. *Design and analysis: A researcher's handbook*. Englewood Cliffs, N.J.: Prentice-Hall, 1973.

MOSCHETTI, G. Calculating equity: Ordinal and ratio criteria. *Social Psychology Quarterly*, 1979, *42*, 172-176.

SACKETT, G. P. The lag sequential analysis of contingency and cyclicity in behavioral interaction research. In J. Osofsky (Ed.), *Handbook of infant development.* New York: John Wiley, 1978.

WALSTER, E., WALSTER, G. W. & BERSCHEID, E. *Equity theory and research.* Boston: Allyn and Bacon, 1978.

WILLIAMS, A. M. The quantity and quality of marital interaction related to marital satisfaction: A behavioral analysis. *Journal of Applied Behavior Analysis,* 1979, *12,* 665-678.

PART IV

COMPARISON OF ASSESSMENT TECHNIQUES

15

BEHAVIORAL OBSERVATION SYSTEMS
FOR COUPLES: THE CURRENT STATUS

Howard J. Markman
Clifford I. Notarius
Timothy Stephen
Randell J. Smith

One of the pioneers of the terrain of marital relationships, Harold Raush, and his associates have stated that

> studying what people say about themselves is no substitute for studying how they behave. Self-reports, particularly those given in brief questionnaires, are subject to massive distortion. Questionnaires and scales of marital satisfaction and dissatisfaction have yielded very little. We need to look at what people do with one another [Raush et al., 1974, p. 5].

The beliefs expressed in this quotation and the hypothesis that communication patterns are related to marital satisfaction have led to the development of behavioral observation assessment strategies for couples. The empirical work that has refined these coding systems, and that has supported their utility in

AUTHORS' NOTE: The authors would like to thank Frank Floyd, for his helpful comments on this chapter, and Celeste Newman, for her help in preparing the chapter for publication. Further, we would like to thank our anonymous reviewer for his or her other useful comments.

assessing marital relationships, is an important contribution to our attempts to understand marriage. In the last decade, researchers have combined these detailed observational strategies with innovative data analytic techniques to develop and evaluate models of marital satisfaction and to assess the effectiveness of interventions for distressed couples.

In this chapter, we review the major coding systems that have been developed to assess marital interaction, summarize the contributions the coding systems have made to our knowledge of marital distress, and highlight the important conceptual and methodological issues which limit conclusions that can be drawn from the results of coding studies. By way of introduction, we first place the behavioral observation assessment strategies in the broad context of assessing a marriage and then present our rationale for use of behavioral observation strategies.

FRAMEWORKS FOR ASSESSING MARRIAGES

Assessment of marital interaction can occur from several different vantage points or sources, and in several different settings or situations. Olson and his colleagues (Cromwell, Chapter 3, this volume; Cromwell et al., 1976; Olson, 1978) have developed an assessment framework that considers two assessment dimensions, the observer's frame of reference, or vantage point, and the objectivity of the data. Observers may be either "insiders," relationship participants, or "outsiders," external observers, while assessed data may be classified as either subjective or objective. By crossing these two dimensions, a 2 × 2 matrix is formed (see Table 15.1). Inspection of Table 15.1 reveals that observational coding strategies belong in the "outsider-objective" cell of the matrix.

Weiss and Margolin (1977) and Jacobson and Margolin (1979) have expanded Olson's insider-outsider dimension (calling it "observer sources") to include self, spouse, trained other, and untrained other. In these expanded frameworks, observational coding strategies are located in any of the "trained

TABLE 15.1   Olson's Framework for Assessing Marriages

	Type of Data	
Observer's Perspective	Subjective	Objective
Insider (e.g., spouses)	Self-report methods	Behavioral self-report
Outsider (e.g., trained observers)	Observer reports	Behavioral observation

SOURCE: Adapted from Olson (1978).

other" cells, since coders typically receive extensive instruction prior to coding.

We now turn our attention to the "objective-outsider" cell of Table 15.1, as we provide a summary of the reasons for using behavioral observation coding techniques.

RATIONALE FOR BEHAVIORAL OBSERVATION

The assumptions underlying the assessment of behavior in general, and marital interaction in particular, often are left at an implicit level. We consider two fundamental questions to help clarify reasons for using behavioral observation strategies.

WHY FOCUS ON BEHAVIOR?

There are two major reasons for targeting behaviors for study. The first addresses the role of description in the evolution of scientific knowledge; the second addresses marked differences in assumptions which separate behavioral from traditional assessment.

Description. The important role of description in providing a sound data base for building and testing models and theories has not always been recognized in the behavioral sciences (Hutt & Hutt, 1970). This certainly holds true in the study of marriage, which until recently was characterized by an absence of careful descriptive research. As noted elsewhere, "without careful, detailed description, theorizing about marital interaction is likely to be premature and to generate controversies that produce more heat than light" (Gottman et al., 1977, p. 463).

We believe that a solid data base is a prerequisite to theory development and that the construction of such a data base can best be accomplished by descriptive studies which focus on observable behaviors. We focus on observable behavior to achieve the goals of description because we believe science can only advance knowledge if research results may be replicated by any observer. Further, cataloging observable behavior is the first step in becoming familiar with phenomena. Thus an interest in description of marital interaction leads to a focus on observing behavior.

In order to remain at a descriptive level, observables must be the target of measurement, as opposed to constructs, which can only be inferred and not directly measured. The goal of description of marital interaction is to catalog or map marital interaction, rather than to make inferences about the interactants and the interaction process. This distinction leads us into our next point.

Traditional versus behavioral assessment. The primary difference between behavioral and traditional assessment involves how we *interpret* the observed scores generated by our measurement procedures (Goldfried & Kent, 1972). In traditional assessment, test results are taken as signs of underlying or inferred constructs, such as personality traits or intrapsychic mechanisms. In contrast, in behavioral assessment, test results (observed patterns of behavior) are viewed as a sample of a person's performance capabilities or response tendencies in specific situations. It is apparent that when test results are considered as a sample of how spouses interact in similar, nonassessment situations, fewer inferences are required than when we view test results as reflecting hypothesized personality constructs. Despite the fact that *in practice* many observational researchers seem to interpret observational scores as reflecting constructs, the "raison d'être" of behavioral assessment is to assess what a person *does* rather than to infer what attributes a person *has* (Mischel, 1968).

Applying this to couples assessment, the focus is on what partners do in response to each other, rather than upon evaluating individual underlying traits. As noted by Bakeman (1978, p. 64):

A concern with interaction . . . is very likely to lead to an observational strategy. Individual characteristics can be gauged with simple probes or tests, but interaction . . . can hardly be measured by anything except observation.

WHY BEHAVIORAL OBSERVATION?

Below we will describe some of the advantages of marital observational strategies which highlight why Cone and Hawkins (1977, p. 390) refer to behavioral observation as the "sine qua non of behavioral assessment."

First, as expressed in the quotation at the beginning of this chapter, people are seldom accurate in their reports of their own and others' behavior. Weiss (1978) summarized evidence that spouses are poor trackers of each other's behavior. If we wish an accurate record of behavioral transactions, we must observe the behavioral stream with a formal observational system in the hands of reliable coders.

Second, behavioral observation allows us to describe the sequencing of behaviors as they occur over time. This record of transactions (that is, wife to husband to wife . . .) is uniquely suited to the study of the marriage as a system. This is an important contribution to the further development of interactional, social learning, behavior exchange, and other theories which view interactional deficits as important components of marital distress.

Third, behavioral observation data can be used in evaluating the outcomes of behavioral marital therapy (Jones et al., 1975), since achieving treatment goals involves changing communication patterns (Jacobson & Margolin, 1979).

Finally, behavioral observation strategies are uniquely suited for the study of marital relationships in naturalistic settings. Interaction samples, which provide the data base for observational systems, can be easily obtained in either home or lab settings, and coding can be accomplished "in vivo" (see Steinglass

& Tislenko, Chapter 8, this volume), via videotape (see Gottman et al., 1977), or audiotape (Wieder & Weiss, 1980).

DESCRIPTION OF BEHAVIORAL
OBSERVATION SYSTEMS

The application of behavioral observation methods to the study of marital interaction was a natural outgrowth of recent interest in applying behavior exchange, social learning, and systems principles and techniques to treating and understanding marital distress. Briefly, proponents of what Weiss (Chapter 2, this volume) refers to as the behavioral systems approach (for example, Birchler et al., 1975; Gottman et al., 1976; Jacobson & Margolin, 1979; Jacobson et al., 1980; Markman & Floyd, 1980; Stuart, 1969; Weiss, 1978) view marital distress as resulting from dysfunctional communication and conflict resolution. Thus, the couple's interaction is seen as the key determinant of marital distress.

This theory-based focus on couples' interaction has led investigators to search for methodological tools to assess couples' interaction patterns. The result has been the emergence of the use of behavioral observation systems for investigating the role of interaction patterns in marital distress for research and clinical purposes (see Margolin, Chapter 6, this volume; Markman & Notarius, Note 1). There are four major behavioral observation systems which have been used to provide a comprehensive record of couples' interaction: (1) the Couples Interaction Scoring System (CISS; Gottman et al., 1977; Markman, Note 2; Notarius, Note 3; Notarius & Markman, Chapter 7, this volume); (2) the Marital Interaction Coding System (MICS; Hops et al., 1972); (3) the Coding Scheme for Interpersonal Conflict (CSIC; Raush et al., 1974); and (4) the Marital and Family Interaction Coding System (MFICS; Olson & Ryder, Notes 4 and 5). We will briefly describe these four systems below. A critical review of some of the conceptual, methodological, and psychometric problems associated with the use of marital observation systems will be presented later.

There are several other coding systems which we will not review, either because they are reviewed in other chapters or because they are similar to the above systems. These include: (1) the Dyadic Interaction Scoring Code (DISC; Filsinger, Chapter 9, this volume); (2) the Home Observation Assessment Method (HOAM; Steinglass & Tislenko, Chapter 8, this volume); and (3) the Verbal Interaction Coding System (VICS; Margolin, Note 6). In addition, researchers have combined codes from several systems (for example, Billings, 1979) and/or developed their own codes (see Koren et al., 1980).

COUPLES INTERACTION SCORING SYSTEM

The CISS is the only coding system that provides for independent coding of verbal and nonverbal aspects of communication and therefore produces two codes for each unit of interaction. The purpose of the CISS is to describe couples' interaction in a variety of situations (Markman, Note 2; Notarius, Note 3). In addition, the CISS has codes designed to assess specific communication skills described by marital therapists as being important to marital satisfaction. The CISS is used to code videotaped sequences of couples' interaction. A more detailed description of the history of the CISS is presented by Notarius and Markman (Chapter 7, this volume) and Gottman (1979).

There are 28 verbal and 3 nonverbal codes (see Gottman, 1979, and Notarius & Markman, Chapter 7, for a detailed description of the CISS codes). The CISS uses the term *content* codes to refer to verbal codes and *affect* codes to refer to nonverbal codes. Since "content" and "affect" have theoretical connotations attached to them, the present review will use the more descriptive terms, verbal and nonverbal. The verbal codes were derived, in part, from codes used in the MICS and MFICS. For the purposes of data analysis, the 28 verbal codes have been reduced to eight summary codes (problem information, mind reading, proposing a solution, communication talk, agreement, disagreement, summarizing other, summarizing self). Each coding unit receives one summary code and one of the three nonverbal codes (positive, negative, neutral). Thus there are 24 possible codes (for example, agreement with positive nonverbal behaviors) that are typically used.

The basic coding unit is the thought unit, which is defined as a simple grammatical unit of speech. Transcripts are made from videotapes of the couples' interaction and thought units are identified by slashes made on the transcript. Thought units that receive identical verbal and nonverbal codes are combined to form behavior units.

The reliability of the CISS in terms of interobserver agreement has been documented in several studies (Gottman, 1979; Markman, Note 2; Notarius, Note 3). Further, Smith and Notarius (Note 7) and Gottman (1979) have provided evidence for the generalizability of CISS codes across several facets of observation, including coders and coding occasions.

The major advantage of the CISS is that it allows independent coding of verbal and nonverbal dimensions of communication. However, as noted by Jacobson et al. (in press), those coding nonverbal behaviors may not rely entirely on nonverbal cues, since the coders hear the content of the interaction. Similarly, those coding verbal behavior typically see the nonverbal behaviors of the couples. The reader is referred to Gottman (1979) for a more detailed discussion of this important problem and for some potential solutions. A second advantage of the CISS is that it provides a more comprehensive description of couples' interaction than other behavioral observation systems, because the CISS assigns one of 24 codes (8 verbal × 3 nonverbal) to each coding unit and other systems use fewer summary codes.

MARITAL INTERACTION CODING SYSTEM

The MICS is the most widely used coding system and has been frequently described and evaluated (see Jacobson et al., in press; Wieder & Weiss, 1980; Weiss et al., 1973; Weiss & Margolin, 1977). The MICS was developed by the "Oregon Group" (Hops et al., 1972) and is an outgrowth of the Family Interaction Coding System[1] (Patterson et al., Note 8). The original purpose of the MICS was to "objectively record verbal and nonverbal behaviors that occur as marriage partners attempt to negotiate, in a laboratory setting, resolutions of their marital problems" (Hops et al., 1972, p. 1). Like the CISS, the MICS was developed to code videotaped interaction sequences. However, recently Wieder and Weiss (1980) demonstrated that the MICS can be used to code audiotaped interaction as well.

The original MICS had 28 codes which provided an exhaustive record of the couples' interaction. In recent revisions, some codes have been dropped and others added from other coding systems (such as mind reading, from CISS; Wieder & Weiss, 1980). In actual use, these 28-30 codes are typically reduced to summary codes ranging from two codes (positive, negative; Jacobson, 1977) to six codes (problem solving, verbal positive, verbal negative, nonverbal positive, nonverbal negative, problem descriptions).[2] Despite the use of nonverbal codes, the MICS does not provide for independent coding of verbal and nonverbal behavior, as does the CISS. Therefore, distinctions between verbal and nonverbal behaviors are blurred.

The basic coding unit is a 30-second block of interaction. This contrasts with the CISS, which defines the basic coding unit in terms of units of speech. In the original version of the MICS code book, the speaker receives one of the 28 codes, while the listener receives a nonverbal code. However, to our knowledge, data on listener behaviors has never been presented in a MICS study.[3]

The reliability of the MICS in terms of interobserver agreement has been documented in numerous studies (for example, Birchler et al., 1975; Vincent et al., 1979; Wieder & Weiss, 1980). Further, several recent studies have provided evidence for the generalizability of the MICS across coders and coding occasions (Vincent et al., 1979; Wieder & Weiss, 1980).

The major advantage of the MICS is that it is the most widely used system and, hence, more comparison data is available than with other systems. A second advantage is that the MICS attempts to code both verbal and nonverbal behaviors, although, unlike the CISS, each unit typically receives either a verbal *or* a nonverbal code.

CODING SYSTEM FOR INTERPERSONAL CONFLICT

Although not published until 1974, the CSIC is probably the first exhaustive coding system developed exclusively for coding couples' interaction. The CSIC was developed by Raush and his associates (1974) as part of an ambitious developmental study of the early stages of marriage. This pioneering project was directed by Wells Goodrich and spawned many classic studies (for example, Goodrich & Boomer, 1963). The purpose of the CSIC was to "encompass the range and refinements in the events produced by our young couples faced with conflict-provoking issues" (Raush et al., 1974, p. 112). Notice the similarity in purpose to the CISS and MICS in terms of exhaustively describing problem-solving interactions.

The CSIC has 36 codes, which are intended to provide an exhaustive record of couples' interactions. These codes are reduced to six summary categories (cognitive, resolving, reconciling, appealing, rejecting, and coercive or personal attacks) for the purpose of data analysis and increased reliability (Raush et al., 1974).

The basic coding unit is called an act, which is a "statement or action of one person bounded by the statement or action of another" (Raush et al., 1974, p. 214). Whereas MICS provides a time-based unit of analysis, the CSIC, similar to the CISS, is statement-based. A more detailed review of the CSIC, in terms of coding coercion, is provided by Sullivan (Note 9). The reliability of the CSIC in terms of interrater agreement has been documented by Raush et al. (1974), Billings (1979), and Sullivan (Note 9).

The major advantage of the CSIC is that it provides a more conceptually rich analysis of couples interaction than other systems. For example, Sullivan (Note 9), after reviewing all available coding systems, concluded that the CSIC provides the best codes for capturing the element of coercion, which is one of the basic constructs of the social learning conceptualization of marriage (see Patterson & Hops, 1972). However, this conceptual richness reduces the objectivity of the system and increases the need for coder inference. On a theoretical level, this may worry some behaviorally oriented researchers. On a practical level, as noted by many writers (for example, Kent & Foster, 1977), as complexity of the system increases, reliability decreases.

MARITAL AND FAMILY INTERACTION CODING SYSTEM

The MFICS was developed by Olson and Ryder (Notes 4 and 5) to code data from an interaction task, the Inventory of Marital Conflict (IMC; Olson & Ryder, 1970). The MFICS has been extensively used by Olson and his associates at the University of Minnesota to code IMC data from numerous marital and premarital couples. According to the authors, the MFICS is "a descriptive non-theoretically based coding scheme that was developed for coding marital interaction" (Olson & Ryder, Note 4, p. 1). Unlike the CISS and MICS, the MFICS was originally used to code audiotaped, as opposed to videotaped, interaction. Thus nonverbal behaviors, with the exception of voice tone, are not coded.

There are 29 codes, which are intended to provide a comprehensive record of the content of couples' interaction. This number is reduced to 13 (initiation, outcome of question, reading, self-disclosure, outcome agreement, outcome disagreement, process disagreement, partisan opinion, reiteration, relevant information and opinion, laughter, disapproval of self, disapproval of spouse) for the purposes of reliability checking and data analysis (Miller & Olson, Note 10). The basic coding unit is the statement, which is defined as any "utterance bounded at the beginning and end by another person's utterance" (Miller & Olson, Note 10, p. 9). This is identical to the act used by the CSIC.

The major advantage of the MFICS is that it provides codes relevant to nonpersonal problem-solving situations, such as the IMC, which may be lost in other coding systems. However, this feature is a weakness when it comes to coding other commonly used problem-solving tasks, such as a discussion of a couple's top problem area.

Thus far, our review has indicated that the four behavioral observation systems have the following features in common: (1) exhaustive coding of couples' interaction; (2) intent to *describe* interaction; (3) intent to describe problem-solving situations; and (4) use of summary codes. The development of these coding systems has provided the technology to systematically describe and quantify marital interaction. In the following section, we will review the research which has used these four observational systems, as well as others, to increase our understanding of marital relationships.

INVESTIGATIONS OF MARITAL DISTRESS

To our knowledge, the first study using observational methods to investigate marital interaction was conducted by Ryder (1968), who employed what we now would consider a primitive coding system. Since this pioneering work, there have been numerous coding studies designed to accomplish one or more of three purposes: (1) describe marital interaction patterns (Gottman et al., 1977; Miller & Olson, Note 10; Winter et al., 1973); (2) test hypotheses concerning marital distress within a behavior exchange or social learning framework (Billings, 1979; Birchler et al., 1975; Fineberg & Lowman, 1975; Koren et al., 1980; Robinson & Price, 1980; Vincent et al., 1975; Wieder, Note 11); and (3) examine methodological problems associated with behavioral observation strategies (Cohen & Christensen, 1980; Gottman, 1979; Haynes et al., 1979; Margolin, 1978a, 1978b; Resick et al., Notes 12 and 13; Vincent et al., 1979; Wieder & Weiss, 1980).

The popularity and heuristic value of marital observation methods is evidenced by the adoption of interactional research strategies by marital researchers at the Max Planck Institute in West Germany (see Revenstorf et al., 1980; Wegener et al., 1979). Also, the use of behavioral observation systems to evaluate specific goals of marital therapy (for example, see Jacobson, 1977, 1978) and premarital intervention programs (Markman, Note 14) highlights the utility of these systems.

We have summarized the relevant aspects of the marital interaction studies noted above in Table 15.2, and we will refer to this information throughout the rest of the chapter.[5]

The design of these studies typically involves comparing the interaction patterns of distressed and nondistressed couples. These groups are defined on the basis of levels of marital satisfaction as measured by the Locke and Wallace (1959) or Locke and Williamson (1958) Marital Adjustment Test (MAT). Some studies use at least one other measure of marital satisfaction (such as seeking marital therapy) to provide a convergent criterion for assignment to distressed versus nondistressed groups of marital satisfaction. The almost universal usage of the MAT should not be taken to indicate that this is necessarily the most valid measure of the construct of marital satisfaction. As noted by several writers (Kimmel & van der Veen, 1974; Laws, 1971; Spanier, 1976; Snyder, 1979), much work needs to be done in improving our definitions of marital satisfaction and distress.

The interaction samples are typically generated by having the couples discuss one or more of several types of tasks (see Table 15.2). The three most popular tasks are the Inventory of Marital Conflicts (Olson & Ryder, 1970), a personal problem discussion of varying levels of conflict (Gottman et al., 1976), and a set of improvisation tasks developed by Raush et al. (1974). These tasks all involve problem-solving discussions which pull for couples to use communication and problem-solving skills. These skills are directly relevant to social exchange and social learning conceptions of marriage.

Although most of the tasks require couples to reach agreement, some researchers have also investigated "free conversation" situations (see Birchler et al., 1975) and problem discussions with no demand for resolution (Resick et al., Notes 12 and 13). The time provided for discussion and the amount of time coded by observers also varies from study to study (see Table 15.2).

The major goals of the observational studies are to describe how the interaction of distressed couples differs from that of nondistressed couples, and to test conceptualizations of marital distress from a behavior exchange and social learning perspective. The major findings from the marital interaction studies are summarized below.

(text continues on page 248)

TABLE 15.2 Observation Studies of Marital Interaction

Study	Subjects Average Age or N Age Range	Average Length of Marriage or Range	Behavioral Observation System	Name of Summary Codes	Constructs Employed	Major Purpose of Study	Interaction Task	Interaction Time	Setting	Sex Effects Analyzed	Comments
Ryder, 1968	120 young	5 mo.	developed own	choice initiation task discussion disapproval laughter own mode (irrational plan) disagreement number of statements	rationality affectivity	compare spouse and stranger interaction	color matching test	not stated	lab	no	codes related to tasks; reliability seems too high
Winter, Ferreira, & Bowers, 1973	40 19-29	?	developed own	spontaneous agreement decision time choice fulfillment silence interruption explicit information exchange politeness		compare spouse and stranger interaction	decision-making task	12-15 min.	lab	no	not an exhaustive coding system
Raush, Barry, Hertel, & Swain, 1974	48 23	newlyweds	CISC	coercion or personal attack cognitive resolving reconciliation appealing rejecting	coercion	study early stages of marriage	improvisation tasks	10 min.	lab	yes	longitudinal study
Birchler, Weiss, & Vincent, 1975	24 26	4 yrs.	MICS	positive negative problem solving	social reinforcement	test social reinforcement hypotheses marital distress	IMC free conversation	10 min. 4 min.	lab	no	same subjects as in Vincent et al.
Vincent, Weiss, & Birchler, 1975	24 26	4 yrs.	MICS	positive negative problem solving	problem solving	test social reinforcement hypotheses re marital distress	IMC free conversation	10 min. 4 min.	lab	no	same subjects as in Birchler et al.

Study	N	Age	Years married	Coding system	Individual codes	Summary codes	Purpose	Task	Time	Setting	Reliability	Notes
Fineberg & Lowman, 1975	20	20-30	1-5 yrs.	developed system based on O'Leary's Behavior Checklist	submission dominance love hate	submission dominance	compare distressed and nondistressed couples in terms of effect and status	discuss 7 questions	not stated	lab	no	
Gottman, Markman, & Notarius, 1977	28	25	4 yrs.	CISS	problem information mind reading proposing a solution communication talk agreement disagreement summarizing other summarizing self	communication skills problem	assess interactional differences between distressed and nondistressed couples	problem discussion	no limit	lab	no	
Wieder, 1978	24	28	5 yrs.	combination (including CISC)	approach avoidance	approach avoidance	test hypotheses re effects of approach and avoidance behaviors	problem discussion; desert survival task	5 min. coded	lab	no	
Margolin, 1978	27	?	11 yrs.	MICS	positive negative neutral	communication skills	assess convergent validity of behavioral marital assessment techniques	negotiation discussion (2)	10 min.	lab	no	
Resick, Welsh, Zitomer, Spiegel, Meidinger, & Long, 1978	19	25	4 yrs.	MICS	used all 28 individual codes		refinement of MICS system	problem discussion	7 min.	lab	yes	used multiple regression techniques to find predictive power of combination of individual codes
Resick, Welsh, & Zitomer, 1979	22	30	9 yrs	MICS	used all 28 individual codes		refinement of MICS system	problem discussion	7 min.	lab	yes	cross-validation of 1978 study
Billings, 1979	24	33	10 yrs.	Leary IBRS	friendly-dominant friendly-submissive hostile-dominant hostile-submissive	problem-solving coercion dominance submission	test reciprocity of positive and negative behaviors in distressed and nondistressed couples	improvisation tasks	not stated	lab	no	

(Continued)

TABLE 15.2 (continued)

Study	N	Average Age or Age Range	Average Length of Marriage or Range	Behavioral Observation System	Name of Summary Codes	Constructs Employed	Major Purpose of Study	Interaction Task	Interaction Time	Setting	Sex Effects Analyzed	Comments
				CISC	coercion or personal attack cognitive resolving reconciliation appealing rejecting							
Gottman, 1979	48	23	newlyweds	CISS	problem information mind reading proposing a solution communication talk agreement disagreement summarizing other summarizing self	communication skills problem solving	recode Raush et al., 1977 study with CISS codes	improvisation tasks		lab	no	recoding of Raush et al. data
Haynes, Follingstad, & Sullivan, 1979	13	?	9 yrs.	10 MICS codes	smile eye contact positive physical contact compliment agreement suggestion criticism interruption disagreement no response		assess discriminant and criterion validity of MICS and Locke-Wallace	free interaction after dinner	25 min., 3 separate evenings	home	no	found high correlation of indices
Vincent, Friedman, Nugent, & Messerly, 1979	40	30	9 yrs.	MICS	positive problem solving problem description	problem solving	assess sensitivity of MICS to demand characteristics	IMC	10 min.	lab	no	

Study	N	Age	Length	Coding system	Codes	Constructs	Purpose	Task	Time	Setting		Notes
Wegener, Revenstorf, Hahlweg, & Schindler, 1979	30	early 30s	5-9 yrs.	developed own	verbal negative verbal positive nonverbal negative nonverbal positive	empathy communication skills	develop coding system to reflect rogerian skills	IMC problem discussion	5 min. per task analyzed	lab	no	
Revenstorf, Vogel, Wegener, Hahlweg, & Schindler, 1980	20	20-40	less than 10 years	MICS	problem description problem solution positive negative listen neutral	reciprocity problem solving	describe differences between distressed and nondistressed couples	IMC problem discussion	?	lab	no	MICS translated in German for purposes of study
Wieder & Weiss, 1980	14	late 20s	4½ yrs.	MICS	positive verbal positive nonverbal total positive negative verbal negative nonverbal total negative	problem solving	assess generalizability of MICS	problem discussion	?	lab	no	
Koren, Carlton, & Shaw, 1980	60	early 30s	9 yrs.	developed own	solution proposal inquiry responsiveness criticism	responsiveness influence criticism	assess role of criticism and responsiveness in interaction	improvisation tasks	10 min.	lab	no	
Robinson & Price, 1980	8	20s	short	combination of systems	pleasurable behaviors	pleasurable behaviors	test reciprocity hypothesis	free conversation	1 hr. for coding session	home	no	
Cohen & Christensen, 1980	12	20s	short	VICS and own codes	positive response negative response	communication effectiveness	assess demand characteristics	problem discussion	7 min.	lab	no	
Miller & Olson, 1980	396	18-27	?	MFICS	used 13 individual codes (see text for names, p. 10)	leadership conflict affect	develop typology of couples interaction	IMC	not stated	lab	yes	

BEHAVIORS WHICH DISCRIMINATE
DISTRESSED FROM NONDISTRESSED COUPLES

Perhaps the most striking aspect of the results of the marital observation studies is the emergence of a set of behaviors which reliably discriminate distressed from nondistressed couples. Specifically, distressed couples, as compared to nondistressed couples: (1) use more negative behaviors and fewer positive behaviors (Birchler et al., 1975; Gottman et al., 1977), although positive behaviors have less discriminatory power (Gottman et al., 1977; Gottman, 1979); (2) tend to respond to negative behaviors with negative behaviors and thereby increase the chances of escalation into cycles of negative interaction (Billings, 1979; Gottman et al., 1977; Revenstorf et al., 1980); and (3) use fewer problem-solving statements (Vincent et al., 1975). Perhaps the most intriguing finding is that, contrary to expectations, there are few differences between groups in use of behaviors such as disagreement, expression of feeling, mind reading, and summarizing, which the marital therapy literature suggests are important in successful relationships. However, when the nonverbal concomitants of these behaviors are assessed, striking differences emerge. For example, distressed couples are more likely to disagree with negative affect than nondistressed couples (Gottman et al., 1977). These findings highlight the important role of nonverbal behaviors in communication.

DESCRIPTION OF MARITAL INTERACTION

The marital observation studies have provided fascinating descriptive information concerning interaction sequences in distressed and nondistressed marriages (Billings, 1979; Gottman, 1979; Gottman et al., 1977; Raush et al., 1974; Revenstorf et al., 1980). These studies have provided evidence for the patterning of marital interaction (Tharp, 1963) and have provided descriptions of typical patterns of interaction. For example, in an earlier paper we described patterns that resembled clinical phenomena, such as negative exchanges, contracts, validation, and cross-complaining. Gottman (1979) has extended our earlier work to identify four types of couples, differing primarily with regard to interaction patterns. Further, he provides preliminary evidence for differences in dominance patterns in distressed versus nondistressed couples based upon time-series analyses. In fact, one of the major contributions of marital observation studies has been the application and development of data analysis strategies, such as sequential analyses (Bakeman, 1978) and time-series analyses (Gottman, 1979), to enable a detailed description of marital interaction which makes sense empirically and clinically and to test complex hypotheses concerning marital distress (see Chapter 13, this volume).

CONCEPTUAL CONTRIBUTIONS

In addition to providing valuable descriptive data, the marital observation studies have provided tests of hypotheses about marital distress generated by behavior exchange (Gottman et al., 1975; Markman, 1979), social learning (Birchler et al., 1975), and communication (Gottman et al., 1977) theories. As noted above, these theories have in common the assertion that couples' interaction processes are a key determinant of marital distress or satisfaction. Although the assumptions underlying behavioral observation involve gathering samples rather than measuring underlying constructs, in practice investigators often make inferences or deductions based on constructs generated by social learning conceptions of marital distress (see Table 15.2 for example of these constructs).

From an exchange theory perspective, the differences in rates of positive and negative behaviors during interaction are seen as indicating that nondistressed couples have developed a mutually rewarding exchange system which enables them to maximize rewards or minimize costs (Markman, 1979).

From a social learning perspective, the positive and negative behaviors are viewed as social reinforcers. The results are seen as supporting the hypothesis that distressed couples rely on negative reinforcement strategies (such as coercion) to change their partners' behavior, whereas nondistressed couples rely on positive reinforcement strategies (Birchler et al., 1975).

Finally, from a communication skill perspective, the results are seen as providing evidence that distressed couples are deficient in communication and problem-solving skills necessary for effective marital functioning (Gottman et al., 1977).

In addition, the results have provided empirical foundations for the development of marital therapy programs aimed at improving communication and problem-solving skills (Gottman et al., 1976; Jacobson & Margolin, 1979; Weiss et al., 1973) as well as premarital intervention programs designed to prevent marital distress (Markman & Floyd, 1980).

CRITIQUE OF MARITAL OBSERVATION SYSTEMS AND STUDIES

Despite the impressive contributions of observation methods to the empirical study of marriage, there are several conceptual and methodological issues that need to be addressed. We limit our critique to issues pertaining to conclusions that can be drawn from the results of the marital interaction studies, rather than providing a detailed overview of methodological issues in behavioral observation and behavioral assessment in general. There are several excellent reviews of these issues (see Bernstein & Neitzel, 1980; Cone & Hawkins, 1977; Goldfried & Linehan, 1977; Goldfried & Sprafkin, 1974; Jacobson et al., in press; Jones et al., 1975; Kent & Foster, 1977); the interested reader is referred to these sources.

Noteworthy by its omission in the present chapter is discussion of observer agreement, reliability, and generalizability theory typically found in such reviews. These issues have been conceptualized adequately and reasonable solutions have been proposed in a number of excellent reviews (Cronbach et al., 1972; Jacobson et al., in press; Kent & Foster, 1977; Mitchell, 1979; Wiggins, 1973).

We consider issues concerning validity, research design, and data analysis below.

VALIDITY

When marital observation scores are viewed as a sample of behavior, the basic validity question concerns the representativeness of the obtained sample of couples' interaction in other situations and at other times. Generalizability theory (Cronbach et al., 1972) provides a set of procedures for assessing the extent to which sampled interaction represents a *valid sample*. Wieder and Weiss (1980) and Gottman (1979) provide excellent demonstrations of how generalizability theory can be applied to evaluating the *representativeness* of marital observation systems.

However, as noted earlier, many researchers implicitly or explicitly use marital observation scores as a basis for inferences about other aspects of marital relationships. In these situations the basic validity questions are the same as in evaluating any other psychological assessment instrument: "(a) What can be inferred about what is being measured by the test? (b) What can be inferred about other behavior?" (American Psychological Association, 1974, p. 25.)

As noted in previous reviews of observational methods (for example, Bernstein & Neitzel, 1980; Jacobson et al., in press), there has been relatively little attention paid to establishing the validity of marital observation systems. Further, previous discussions of validity suffer from lack of agreement in the labeling of what type of study establishes what type of validity. For example, the terms discriminative and concurrent validity are used to describe the same validity issues (Haynes et al., 1979; Jones et al., 1975). However, there is agreement that different validity questions are raised by different uses of marital observation systems.

We will describe each type of validity and how it is relevant to the objectives of marital interaction researchers. Cronbach and Meehl's (1955) discussion of four types of validity will be used to provide a framework for evaluating the evidence for validity of the marital interaction systems. Cronbach and Meehl (1955) distinguish among predictive validity, concurrent validity, content validity, and construct validity, although they consider predictive and concurrent validity as both representing criterion-oriented validity.

Criterion-oriented validity. Criterion-oriented validity is established when test scores are shown to correlate with a criterion of interest for the same sample of couples. Concurrent validity involves measures taken at the same point in time, while predictive validity involves using test scores to predict criteria measured later in time.

Criterion-oriented validity is most relevant, therefore, when the investigator's primary objective is relating marital observation data (such as test scores) to criteria of interest, such as MAT scores and distressed versus nondistressed groups. As noted above, the results of the marital interaction studies provide strong evidence that summary codes successfully discriminate between distressed and nondistressed couples. Thus, the marital observation studies provide strong support for the concurrent validity of the coding systems when distressed versus nondistressed is used as the criterion. However, Margolin (1978a) used self-reports of relationship satisfaction (MAT scores) and a spouse checklist as criteria and found no correlation between MICS codes and these criteria. This is surprising, since the distressed/nondistressed criterion relies heavily on MAT scores (see Birchler et al., 1975). One explanation is that marital observation data may be sensitive to differences between widely divergent groups (for example, distressed versus nondistressed) but not to differences between more similar couples. Since there is no "objective" criterion of marital distress against which to validate marital observation data, we need to assess the concurrent validity of marital observation systems against criteria suited to research and clinical purposes of the system. In other words, we need to ask and answer the question: Validity for what purpose?

To our knowledge, there is no evidence available on the predictive validity of marital observation data.[6] Longitudinal investigations of the development of marital distress are needed to assess the power of observation codes to predict future levels of distress or marital satisfaction.

Content validity. Content validity is established when test items are shown to reflect adequately the content domain of interest. For the marital observation studies, content validity is most relevant when the objective is to sample relevant marital behaviors in order to describe marital interaction. There are two different types of content validity problems that should be considered. First, do individual codes reflect adequately the domain of marital interaction of interest to the investigator, that is, communication and problem-solving behaviors? Since the marital observation systems were developed for this purpose, their content validity defined in this manner is generally accepted.

This does not mean, however, that marital observation systems have content validity for other domains of interest. For example, do the individual and summary codes reflect adequately the subtleties of marital interaction in which we are really interested? While behavioral codes are necessarily descriptive and relatively noninferential, we wonder if marital satisfaction is associated with phenomena which we are missing or which cannot be easily coded by our current observational systems. Perhaps we are like early phrenological researchers, charting the shape of a couple's communication, coding bumps, lumps, and smooth areas, to arrive at an understanding of the "character" of the relationship.

The point here is that content validity needs to be considered for each individual usage of marital observation systems. For example, the marital observation systems may have content validity for the purposes of describing communication behaviors in problem-solving situations, but not for describing projective identifications in other situations.

The second content validity question is how well do the individual codes, which are typically combined to form summary codes, represent the content described by the summary code? The basic issue here concerns the formation of the summary codes (see Table 15.2). As noted earlier, all marital observation systems use summary codes rather than individual codes as the basic unit of analysis. Typically, the individual categories are used to code the data and then they are combined to form summary codes, rather than having the coders use the summary categories in coding. While there are good reasons to use summary codes, including ease of data analysis and increasing reliability, the methods used to form these codes must be evaluated. Summary codes are generally formed by combining codes that are conceptually similar in the eyes of the investigator. For example, Birchler et al. (1975) decided that MICS codes represented positive, negative, or neutral social reinforcement, and formed summary codes on this basis. Similarly, we formed summary codes, such as problem solving, for the CISS by combining codes that we judged to focus on the problem-solving process (for example, plan). Bernstein and Neitzel (1980) contrasted this approach, which they call the rational approach, with the empirical approach, which involves combining codes that are empirically related through procedures such as cluster or factor analysis.

Although these methods may be face valid, research is needed to assess the extent to which the individual codes actually reflect the summary categories. To date there is little available evidence for the content validity of summary codes. Several strategies are available to evaluate the content validity of summary codes. First, judges can rate the individual codes on the dimensions reflected by the summary codes. For example, Jones et al. (1975) had mothers rate the extent to which individual behavioral codes represented the summary code of deviant behaviors.[7]

Another strategy is to use tests of sequential dependencies (Bakeman, 1978) to assess whether two individual codes in the same summary category function in a similar way in the stream interaction. If they do, support is provided for the content validity of the summary code (Gottman, 1979).

A third possibility is to use a cluster or factor analytic strategy to assess empirically which individual codes are similar. Such strategies can also be used to test the content validity of existing summary codes by comparing the set of individual codes, which form a factor, with the set of codes included in the summary code.

Finally, Resick et al. (Notes 12 and 13) have used multiple regression procedures to determine which set of individual codes are the best predictors of MAT scores. This type of procedure circumvents the formation of summary codes altogether.

Construct validity. Construct validity of the marital observation systems becomes relevant when the researcher's purpose is to test constructs or conceptualizations about marital distress based on marital observation data. The basic issue here is this: Do the summary codes (such as positive social reinforcement, coercion) adequately measure the construct they are intended to measure (that is, social reinforcement, coercion)? For example, Birchler et al. (1975) and Vincent et al. (1975) predicted, based on social learning theory, that the interaction of distressed couples, as compared to nondistressed couples, would be characterized by more negative reinforcement and fewer problem-solving behaviors. The MICS summary codes were used to evaluate these predictions. The researchers classified the 28 MICS codes into 3 categories: positive social reinforcement, negative social reinforcement, and problem-solving. No evidence or statement concerning content validity was provided. The results indicated that the interaction of distressed, as compared to nondistressed, couples was characterized by higher rates of negative and lower rates of positive behaviors and problem-solving behaviors. However, no evidence was presented to support the implicit contention that the summary codes really measured social reinforcement or problem solving. As noted by Jacobson et al. (in press) in a review of construct validity of the MICS: "There is no evidence that the frequency of any MICS code is associated with effective problem-solving . . . communication or exchange of reinforcement and punishment between spouses."

Our intent here is not to be overly critical of the Birchler et al. and Vincent et al. studies, but to use these pioneering studies as examples of problems in interpreting the results of marital interaction studies due to a paucity of attention to issues of construct validity. Unfortunately, the same criticism can be made of other studies and other observational systems. For example, Gottman et al. (1977) use CISS codes to measure communication skills and Raush et al. (1974) use CSIC codes to measure coercion, without supporting evidence for content or construct validity.

In order to provide guidelines for assessing construct validity, we will briefly describe several types of data which offer evidence for the construct validity of summary codes in particular and behavioral observation systems in general. As we will see, some work on construct validation has already begun in the marital interaction literature. There are three types of investigations that are typically used to provide construct validity of a test:

(1) Correlate measures of constructs obtained by observational methods with measures of the same construct obtained by maximally different procedures. This type of data reflects the classical example of construct validation proce-

dures (Campbell & Fiske, 1959; Cronbach & Meehl, 1955). In terms of Olson's assessment framework, described earlier (Table 15.1), this involves measuring two or more constructs using assessment procedures sampled from the four cells. It is encouraging to note that several researchers have recently attempted to compare observation data with other sources of information about the marital relationship (see Floyd, Note 15; Gottman, 1979; Margolin, 1978a; Royce & Weiss, 1975). Another promising procedure gaining popularity in the assertion literature is the social validation technique (Romano & Bellack, 1980; Kazdin, 1977). Briefly, this involves having an interaction sample rated by both trained observers using an observation system (such as MICS) and by untrained judges using global ratings on criteria of interest to the researcher (such as levels of assertive behavior). Significant correlations are considered as evidence for the construct validity of the codes. In addition, the content of cues judges use can be compared to the content of codes. In the only marital study using this procedure, Royce and Weiss (1975) compared frequency of MICS codes with cues untrained observers used to judge levels of distress. The results indicated that the content of five MICS codes significantly overlapped with the content of the judges' cues. This is an innovative method for evaluating the construct validity of codes from marital observation systems.

(2) Compare different criterion groups on behaviors of interest to assess the power of summary codes to discriminate between groups (Jacobson et al., in press; Jones et al., 1975). This strategy is also used to establish concurrent validity. Thus the strong evidence for the concurrent validity of marital observation data also provides evidence for construct validity.

(3) Demonstrate that patterns of codes change following interventions designed to change the constructs measured by the codes (Jones et al., 1975). For example, Jacobson, in a series of well-controlled studies (Jacobson, 1977, 1978, 1979), found that after behavioral marital therapy, treated couples showed more positive and less negative MICS summary codes as compared to control couples.

One study by itself, or one type of evidence for construct validity, is not sufficient to establish the construct validity of the summary codes. Accumulation of evidence for construct validity is obtained by numerous studies that provide support for a "network of propositions" which implicitly define the construct of interest (Cronbach & Meehl, 1955).

PROBLEMS WITH THE DESIGN
OF MARITAL OBSERVATON STUDIES

There are several design issues, which we will briefly summarize, that limit the conclusions we can draw from marital interaction studies.

Reactivity of the observational setting. As noted above, one of the advantages of using marital observation systems is that we can capture interaction in naturalistic settings. However, with the exception of a few studies conducted in the home (see Gottman, 1979; Robinson & Price, 1980; Steinglass, 1979) we have typically studied our couples in laboratory settings. To be sure, we strive to provide a "living room" atmosphere in our labs; however, most actual living rooms do not have video cameras and/or two-way mirrors! While we find that couples adjust quickly to this setting, we doubt that most couples completely lose sight of the fact that they are being observed as they become involved in our tasks. The basic issue here is this: How *reactive* are the observation settings that we are investigating and how representative is our interaction data? Even in home settings, the couple knows that they are being observed, and this probably affects their interaction. Since there have been many excellent discussions of the reactivity of the observation situation (Bernstein & Neitzel, 1980; Johnson & Bolstad, 1973; Lipinski & Nelson, 1974), we will refer interested readers to these sources. We will turn to research that attempts to document the types of effects due to reactivity.

While several studies with children and families (for example, Johnson & Lobitz, 1974) have attempted to document the specific types of effects observation has on behavior, until recently there has been no systematic research on the effects of observation on marital interaction. In a preliminary study, Markman et al. (Note 16) assessed the effects of being videotaped on marital interaction. The results indicated that husbands tended to be more positive in the videotape as compared to nonvideotape conditions, while wives did not seem to alter their communication patterns. Vincent et al. (1979) took a somewhat different approach to investigate reactivity. These researchers reasoned that if couples can respond to instructions to fake positive or negative behaviors, as reflected by MICS codes, then it is possible that couples could manage impressions if they desired to do so. Three very interesting findings emerged. First, both distressed and nondistressed couples changed their behaviors according to instructional sets. Second, the amount of change was equal for each group. Finally, verbal behaviors were more sensitive to instructional conditions than were nonverbal behaviors.

Taken together, these two studies indicate that demand effects do operate, although they may do so equally across distressed and nondistressed couples. However, a recent study by Cohen and Christensen (1980) found no evidence for demand effects using a design similar to Vincent et al. These studies represent the type of investigations needed to understand our research settings so that we can partition variance attributable to reactivity variables from variance attributable to effects of interest.

Finally, one additional method for addressing the issue of representativeness involves asking couples to "debrief" experimenters as to how representative the couples viewed their lab interaction (Billings, 1979). Increasing the dialog between researchers and couples can enhance the representativeness of the lab findings as well as provide potentially valuable input into the researcher's program.

Subject selection. A second major research design issue involves the genera-lizability of the results of the behavioral observation studies to the population of all married couples. The couples who decide to participate in marital interaction research are obviously select and nonrepresentative of couples in general. As seen in Table 15.2, the couples we study are young and relatively newly wed. This is consistent with O'Leary and Turkewitz's (1978) point that we tend to study YAVIS (young, attractive, verbal, intelligent, successful; Williams, 1956) couples. We add to this list White, nonhandicapped (e.g., deaf) and only moderately distressed couples. It is encouraging to note that there have been some recent efforts to extend the results of marital interaction studies to deaf (Ferraro & Markman, Note 17), Black (Baccus & Markman, Note 18), and severely distressed (Jacobson, 1979) couples.

PROBLEMS WITH DATA ANALYSIS STRATEGIES

We do not have space to provide a comprehensive critique of data analysis strategies (see Chapter 13, this volume, for a summary of typical data analysis strategies). However, we would like to summarize two issues that have not been adequately addressed in the marital interaction literature.

Low base-rate events. Low base-rate (that is, infrequent) events or behav-iors are typically discarded due to their lack of statistical predictability. Unfor-tunately, these rare events (such as metacommunication or a fleeting smile during an intense problem discussion) may be very important in influencing interaction patterns and determining marital satisfaction. Behavioral infrequen-cies may not be trivial phenonomologically, but may, in fact, be very relevant.

Nonindependence of husband and wife codes. Given the nature of marital interaction, husband behaviors are seen to influence wife behaviors, wife be-haviors to influence husband behaviors, and so on. This interdependency is a basic aspect of both the social learning and systems perspectives of marital relationships. However, the interdependence of husband and wife behaviors often carries important statistical implications when it comes to analyzing interactional data. The major problem arises when sex effects are of interest to the researcher. In general, the dependency of partners' behavior is controlled in analyses where sex is not the independent variable (Kraemer & Jacklin, 1979). As noted in Table 15.2, not all studies have evaluated sex effects. The rationale for not looking at sex as a variable of interest is that the basic unit of analysis is the couple. However, given the substantial data on sex effects in family studies in general (see Safilios-Rothschild, 1976), and some very interesting recent sex effects in the marital literature (see Floyd & Markman, Note 19), we feel that all studies should evaluate sex effects. However, sex effects should not be evalu-ated using an analysis of variance factorial design in which sex of partner is an independent variable. Since husband and wife behaviors are correlated, the observations in the cells of the ANOVA do not meet the important assumption of independence. The implication of this is that significance may be either overestimated or underestimated (Kraemer & Jacklin, 1979). Instead, a repeated measures ANOVA considering couples as subjects, and husband and wife as repeated measures, is recommended. As noted by Kraemer and Jacklin (1979), the logic here is the same as that for a matched pairs t-test.

SUMMARY AND CONCLUSIONS

The field of observation research in general, and observation research of marital interaction in particular, has emerged in the past decade and a half as a powerful force in studying complex interpersonal relationships. The techniques for observational study and the statistical analyses available for understanding data are among the most valuable contributions to the empirical study of marriage.

In this chapter we have placed marital observation in the context of behavioral assessment of couples, described four major marital observation systems, summarized the results and conceptual contributions of marital observation studies, and highlighted some of the important conceptual and methodological issues facing the field.

The application of observational methods to studying marriage has provided a technology to systematically describe and quantify marital interaction. It is a tool of many uses, which range from describing marital interaction to evaluating the outcome of couples' intervention programs. We expect that its heuristic value and theoretical grounding in behavioral assessment will lead many investigators to use marital observation systems in the future. We caution, however, against being seduced into becoming method-oriented researchers (Platt, 1964) who rely upon only one paradigm. Despite the impressive contributions of observational methods, the empirical investigation of marriage is only in its infancy. We have only scratched the surface in terms of what we need to know about marital interaction. Continued progress in the development of observational and other assessment methods needs to dovetail with increased conceptual sophistication about the nature of marital distress. Further, we would like to see the application of marital observation strategies to alternative conceptualizations of marital distress, in addition to the social learning perspectives.

We look forward to the significant methodological and theoretical contributions to come in the next decade as we learn more about the complexities of marital relationships.

NOTES

1. The Family Interaction Coding System (FICS) is the same as the Behavior Coding System (BCS) described by Jones et al. (1975). Personal communication, Roberta Ray, October 1980.

2. Wieder and Weiss (1980) present data on eight summary codes, however, three are combinations of the other five (such as total positive, total negative).

3. This construct has been used by Gottman et al. (1977) and Gottman (1979), and labeled context.

4. There were earlier attempts to code interaction (for example, Goodrich & Boomer, 1963), however, the authors of these early investigations do not present their coding systems in detail.

5. We have tried to be comprehensive in our review by including all the published studies which have used behavioral observation systems as well as a few unpublished papers. We hope we have not offended anyone whose work may have been missed in our review. We also did not include in Table 15.2 any evaluation studies that compare intervention and control groups at pre- and posttests using behavioral ratings as the dependent variable (for example, Harrell & Guerney, 1976; Jacobson, 1977, 1978; Patterson et al., 1975; Weiss et al., 1973).

6. A longitudinal study of premarital couples, conducted by the first author, is under way to evaluate the predictive validity of CISS codes.

7. This strategy is similar to the social validation procedures (Kazdin, 1977; Royce & Weiss, 1975) discussed in the following section on construct validity.

REFERENCE NOTES

1. MARKMAN, H. J., & NOTARIUS, C. I. *The Couples Interaction Scoring System (CISS): A method for the behavioral assessment of couples interaction.* Paper presented at the Conference on Family Observation, Behavioral Assessment and Intervention, Arizona State University, Center for Family Studies, February 1980.

2. MARKMAN, H. J. *A description of verbal and nonverbal communication in distressed and nondistressed marital dyads.* Unpublished master's thesis, Indiana University—Bloomington, 1976.

3. NOTARIUS, C. *A behavioral competency assessment of communication in distressed and nondistressed marital dyads.* Unpublished master's thesis, Indiana University—Bloomington, 1976.

4. OLSON, D. H., & RYDER, R. G. *The IMC Coding System.* Unpublished manuscript, University of Minnesota, 1973.

5. OLSON, D. H., & RYDER, R. G. *Marital and Family Interaction Coding System (MFICS).* Unpublished manuscript, University of Minnesota, 1977.

6. MARGOLIN, G. *The Verbal Interaction Coding System.* Unpublished manuscript, University of Southern California, 1978.

7. SMITH, R., & NOTARIUS, C. I. *The generalizability of observational coding systems for marital interaction.* Unpublished manuscript, Catholic University of America, 1981.

8. PATTERSON, G. R., RAY, R. S., SHAW, D. A., & COBB, J. A. *Manual for coding of family interactions.* Unpublished manuscript, University of Oregon, 1969.

9. SULLIVAN, M. *The effects of coercion on distressed and nondistressed couples.* Unpublished manuscript, Bowling Green State University, 1980.

10. MILLER, B., & OLSON, D. *Typology of marital interaction and contextual characteristics: Cluster analysis of the IMC.* Unpublished manuscript, University of Minnesota, 1980.

11. WIEDER, G. *The prediction of marital approach and avoidance conflict resolution.* Paper presented at the annual meeting of the Western Psychological Association, 1978.

12. RESICK, R. P., SWEET, J. J., KIEFFER, D. M., BARR, P. K., & RUBY, N. L. *Perceived and actual discriminations of conflict and accord in marital communication.* Paper presented at the Eleventh Annual Convention of the Association for the Advancement of Behavior Therapy, Atlanta, December 1977.

13. RESICK, P. A., WELSH, B. K., ZITOMER, E. A., SPIEGEL, D. K., MEIDLINGER, J. C., & LONG, B. R. *Predictors of marital satisfaction, conflict, and accord: A preliminary revision of the Marital Interaction Coding System.* Paper presented at the Twelfth Annual Meeting of the Association for the Advancement of Behavior Therapy, Chicago, November 1978.

14. MARKMAN, H. *The long-term effects of premarital intervention.* Unpublished manuscript, University of Denver, 1980.

15. FLOYD, F. *Insiders' and outsiders' perspectives of the communication of distressed and nondistressed married couples.* Unpublished manuscript, Bowling Green State University, 1980.

16. MARKMAN, H., FERRARO. B., WELLS, J., KOTANSKI, K., BACCUS, G., SULLIVAN, M., & FLOYD, F. *The reactivity of marital interaction in videotape vs. nonvideotape conditions.* Unpublished manuscript, Bowling Green State University, 1980.

17. FERRARO, B., & MARKMAN, H. *Application of the behavioral model of marriage to deaf marital relationships.* To be presented to the annual meeting of the Midwestern Psychological Association, Detroit, 1981.

18. BACCUS, G., & MARKMAN, H. *The behavioral model of marriage applied to the interaction of Black couples.* Unpublished manuscript, University of Denver, 1980.

19. FLOYD, F., & MARKMAN, H. *Insiders' and outsiders' assessment of distressed and nondistressed marital interaction.* Submitted to the annual meeting of the American Psychological Association, Los Angeles, 1981.

REFERENCES

American Psychological Association. *Standards for educational and psychological tests.* Washington, DC: Author, 1974

BAKEMAN, R. Untangling streams of interaction. In G. Sackett (Ed.), *Observing behavior* (Vol. 2): *Data collection and analysis methods.* Baltimore: University Park Press, 1978.

BERNSTEIN, D., & NEITZEL, M. *Introduction to clinical psychology,* New York: McGraw-Hill, 1980.

BILLINGS, A. B. Conflict resolution in distressed and nondistressed marital couples. *Journal of Consulting and Clinical Psychology,* 1979, *47,* 368-376.

BIRCHLER, G. R., WEISS, R. L., & VINCENT, J. P. A multimethod analysis of social reinforcement exchange between maritally distressed and nondistressed spouse and stranger dyads. *Journal of Personality and Social Psychology,* 1975, *31,* 349-360.

CAMPBELL, D. T., & FISKE, D. W. Convergent and discriminant validation by the multitrait-multimethod matrix. *Psychological Bulletin,* 1959, *56,* 81-105.

COHEN, R. S., & CHRISTENSEN, A. Further examination of demand characteristics in marital interaction. *Journal of Consulting and Clinical Psychology,* 1980, *48,* 121-123.

CONE, J. D., & HAWKINS, R. P. (Eds.). *Behavioral assessment: New directions in clinical psychology.* New York: Brunner/Mazel, 1977.

CROMWELL, R. E., OLSON, D. H., & FOURNIER, D. G. Diagnosis and evaluation in marital and family counseling. In D. H. Olson (Ed.), *Treating relationships.* Lake Mills, IA: Graphic, 1976.

CRONBACH, L. J., GLESER, C. G., NANDA, H., & RAJARATNAM, N. *The dependability of behavioral measures.* New York: John Wiley, 1972.

CRONBACH, L. J., & MEEHL, P. Construct validity in psychological tests. *Psychological Bulletin,* 1955, *52,* 281-302.

FINEBERG, B., & LOWMAN, J. Affect and status dimensions of marital adjustment. *Journal of Marriage and the Family,* 1975, *37,* 155-160.

GOLDFRIED, M.R., & KENT, R.N. Traditional versus behavioral personality assessment: A comparison of methodological and theoretical assumptions. *Psychological Bulletin*, 1972, *77*, 409-420.

GOLDFRIED, M.R., & LINEHAN, M.M. Basic issues in behavioral assessment. In A.R. Ciminero, K.S. Calhoun, & H.E. Adams (Eds.), *Handbook of behavioral assessment*. New York: John Wiley, 1977.

GOLDFRIED, M.R., & SPRAFKIN, J.N. *Behavioral personality assessment*. Morristown, NJ: General Learning Press, 1974.

GOODRICH, D., & BOOMER, D. Experimental assessment of modes of conflict resolution. *Family Process*, 1963, *2*, 15-24.

GOTTMAN, J.M. *Marital interaction: Experimental investigations*. New York: Academic, 1979.

GOTTMAN, J., MARKMAN, H., & NOTARIUS, C. The topography of marital conflict: A sequential analysis of verbal and nonverbal behavior. *Journal of Marriage and the Family*, 1977, *39*, 461-477.

GOTTMAN, J., NOTARIUS, C., GONSO, J., & MARKMAN, H. *A couple's guide to communication*. Champaign, IL: Research Press, 1976.

GOTTMAN, J., NOTARIUS, C., MARKMAN, H., BANK, S., YOPPI, B., & RUBIN, M.E. Behavior exchange theory and marital decision making. *Journal of Personality and Social Psychology*, 1976, *34*, 14-23.

HARRELL, J., & GUERNEY, B. Training married couples in conflict negotiation skills. In D.H.L. Olson (Ed.), *Treating relationships*. Lake Mills, IA: Graphic, 1976.

HAYNES, S.W., FOLLINGSTAD, D.R., & SULLIVAN, J.L. Assessment of marital satisfaction and interaction. *Journal of Consulting and Clinical Psychology*, 1979, *47*, 653-669.

HOPS, H., WILLS, T.A., PATTERSON, G.R., & WEISS, R.L. *Marital Interaction Coding System*. Eugene: University of Oregon and Oregon Research Institute, 1972.

HUTT, S.J., & HUTT, C. *Direct observation and measurement of behavior*. Springfield, IL: Charles C Thomas, 1970.

JACOBSON, N.S. Problem solving and contingency contracting in the treatment of marital discord. *Journal of Consulting and Clinical Psychology*, 1977, *45*, 92-100.

JACOBSON, N.S. Specific and nonspecific factors in the effectiveness of a behavioral approach to the treatment of marital discord. *Journal of Consulting and Clinical Psychology*, 1978, *46*, 442-452.

JACOBSON, N.S. Increasing positive behavior in severely distressed marital relationships: The effects of problem solving. *Behavior Therapy*, 1979, *10*, 311-326.

JACOBSON, N.S., ELWOOD, R., & DALLAS, M. The behavioral assessment of marital dysfunction. In D. Barlow (Ed.), *Behavioral assessment of adult dysfunction*. New York: Guilford, in press.

JACOBSON, N.S., & MARGOLIN, G. *Marital therapy: Strategies based on social learning and behavior exchange principles*. New York: Brunner/Mazel, 1979.

JACOBSON, N.S., WALDRON, H., & MOORE, D. Toward a behavioral profile of marital distress. *Journal of Consulting and Clinical Psychology*, 1980, *48*, 696-703.

JOHNSON, S.M., & BOLSTAD, O.D. Methodological issues in naturalistic observation: Some problems and solutions for field research. In L.A. Hamerlynck, L.C. Handy, & E.J. Mash (Eds.), *Behavior change: Methodology, concepts, and practice*. Champaign, IL: Research Press: 1973.

JOHNSON, S.M., & LOBITZ, G.K. Parental manipulation of child behavior in home observations. *Journal of Applied Behavior Analysis*, 1974, *7*, 23-32.

JONES, R.R., REID, J.B., & PATTERSON, G.R. Naturalistic observation in clinical assessment. In P. McReynolds (Ed.), *Advances in psychological assessment* (Vol. 3). San Francisco: Jossey-Bass, 1975.

KAZDIN, A. Assessing the clinical or applied importance of behavior change through social validation. *Behavior Modification*, 1977, *4*, 427-452.

KENT, R., & FOSTER, S. Direct observation procedures: Methodological issues in naturalistic settings. In A. Ciminero, K. Calhoun, & H. Adams (Eds.), *Handbook of behavioral assessment*. New York: John Wiley, 1977.

KIMMEL, D., & VAN DER VEEN, F. Factors of marital adjustment in Locke's marital adjustment test. *Journal of Marriage and the Family*, 1974, *36*, 57-63.

KOREN, P., CARLTON, K., & SHAW, D. Marital conflict: Relations among behaviors, outcomes, and distress. *Journal of Consulting and Clinical Psychology*, 1980, *48*, 460-468.

KRAEMER, H., & JACKLIN, C. Statistical analysis of dyadic social behavior. *Psychological Bulletin*, 1979, *86*, 217-224.

LAWS, J. L. A feminist review of the marital adjustment literature: The rape of the Locke. *Journal of Marriage and the Family*, 1971, *33*, 483-516.

LIPINSKI, D., & NELSON, R. Problems in the use of naturalistic observation as a means of behavioral assessment. *Behavior Therapy*, 1974, *5*, 341-351.

LOCKE, H., & WALLACE, K. Short marital-adjustment and prediction tests: Their reliability and validity. *Marriage and Family Living*, 1959, *21*, 251-255.

LOCKE, H., & WILLIAMSON, R. Marital adjustment: A factor analysis study. *American Sociological Review*, 1958, *23*, 562-569.

MARGOLIN, G. The relationships among marital assessment procedures: A correlational study. *Journal of Consulting and Clinical Psychology*, 1978, *46*, 1556-1558. (a)

MARGOLIN, G. A multilevel approach to the assessment of communication positiveness in distressed marital couples. *International Journal of Family Counseling*, 1978, *6*, 81-89. (b)

MARKMAN, H. J. The application of a behavioral model of marriage in predicting relationship satisfaction of couples planning marriage. *Journal of Consulting and Clinical Psychology*, 1979, *4*, 743-749.

MARKMAN, H., & FLOYD, F. Possibilities for the prevention of marital discord: A behavioral perspective. *American Journal of Family Therapy*, 1980, *8*, 25-48.

MISCHEL, W. *Personality and assessment*. New York: McGraw-Hill, 1968.

MITCHELL, S. Interobserver agreement, reliability, and generalizability of data collected in observational studies. *Psychological Bulletin*, 1979, *86*, 376-396.

O'LEARY, K., & TURKEWITZ, H. Methodological errors in marital and child treatment research. *Journal of Consulting and Clinical Psychology*, 1978, *46*, 747-758.

OLSON, D. Insiders' and outsiders' view of relationships: Research strategies. In G. Levinger & H. L. Raush (Eds.), *Close relationships*. Amherst: University of Massachusetts Press, 1978.

OLSON, D. H., & RYDER, R. G. Inventory of marital conflicts (IMC): An experimental interaction procedure. *Journal of Marriage and the Family*, 1970, *32*, 443-448.

PATTERSON, G. R., & HOPS, H. Coercion, a game for two: Intervention techniques for marital conflict. In R. E. Ulrich & P. Mountjoy (Eds.), *The experimental analysis of social behavior*. New York: Appleton-Century-Crofts, 1972.

PATTERSON, G. R., HOPS, H., & WEISS, R. L. Interpersonal skills training for couples in early stages of conflict. *Journal of Marriage and the Family*, 1975, *37*, 295-303.

PLATT, J. Strong inference. *Science*, 1964, *146*, 347-353.

RAUSH, H. L., BARRY, W. A., HERTEL, R. K., & SWAIN, M. A. *Communication, conflict, and marriage*. San Francisco: Jossey-Bass, 1974.

REVENSTORF, D., VOGEL, B., WEGENER, C., HAHLWEG, K., & SCHINDLER, L. Escalation phenomena in interaction sequences: An empirical comparison of distressed and nondistressed couples. *Behavior Analysis and Research*, 1980, *2*, 1-24.

ROBINSON, E. A., & PRICE, M. G. Pleasurable behavior in marital interaction: An observational study. *Journal of Consulting and Clinical Psychology*, 1980, *48*, 117-118.

ROMANO, J., & BELLACK, A. Social validation of a component model of assertive behavior. *Journal of Consulting and Clinical Psychology*, 1980, *48*, 478-490.

ROYCE, W. S., & WEISS, R. L. Behavioral cues in the judgment of marital satisfaction: A linear regression analysis. *Journal of Consulting and Clinical Psychology*, 1975, *5*, 15-26.

RYDER, R. G. Husband-wife dyads versus married strangers. *Family Process*, 1968, *7*, 233-238.

SAFILIOS-ROTHSCHILD, C. A macro- and micro-examination of family power and love: An exchange model. *Journal of Marriage and the Family*, 1976, *38*, 355-362.

SNYDER, D. K. Multidimensional assessment of marital satisfaction. *Journal of Marriage and the Family*, 1979, *41*, 813-824.

SPANIER, G. B. Measuring dyadic adjustment: New scales for assessing the quality of marriage and similar dyads. *Journal of Marriage and the Family*, 1976, *38*, 15-28.

STEINGLASS, P. The Home Observation Assessment Method (HOAM): Real-time naturalistic observation of families in their home. *Family Process*, 1979, *18*, 337-354.

STUART, R. B. Operant-interpersonal treatment for marital discord. *Journal of Consulting and Clinical Psychology*, 1969, *33*, 675-682.

THARP, R. Psychological patterning in marriage. *Psychological Bulletin*, 1963, *60*, 97-117.

VINCENT, J. P., FRIEDMAN, L. C., NUGENT, J., & MESSERLY, L. Demand characteristics in observations of marital interaction. *Journal of Consulting and Clinical Psychology*, 1979, *47*, 557-566.

VINCENT, J. P., WEISS, R. L., & BIRCHLER, G. R. A behavioral analysis of problem solving in distressed and nondistressed married and stranger dyads. *Behavior Therapy*, 1975, *6*, 475-487.

WEGENER, C., REVENSTORF, D., HAHLWEG, K., & SCHINDLER, L. Empirical analysis of communication in distressed and nondistressed couples. *Behavioral Analysis and Modification*, 1979, *3*, 178-188.

WEISS, R. L. The conceptualization of marriage from a behavioral perspective. In T. J. Paolino, Jr., & B. S. McCrady (Eds.), *Marriage and marital therapy: Psychoanalytic, behavioral, and systems theory perspectives*. New York: Brunner/Mazel, 1978.

WEISS, R. L., HOPS, H., & PATTERSON, G. R. A framework for conceptualizing marital conflict: A technology for altering it, some data for evaluating it. In F. W. Clark & L. A. Hamerlynck (Eds.), *Critical issues in research and practice: Proceedings of the Fourth Banff International Conference on Behavior Modification*. Champaign, IL: Research Press, 1973.

WEISS, R. L., & MARGOLIN, G. Assessment of marital conflict and accord. In A. R. Ciminero, K. S. Calhoun, & H. E. Adams (Eds.), *Handbook of behavioral assessment*. New York: John Wiley: 1977.

WIEDER, G. B., & WEISS, R. L. Generalizability theory and the coding of marital interaction. *Journal of Consulting and Clinical Psychology*, 1980, *48*, 469-477.

WIGGINS, J. S. *Personality and prediction: Principles of personality assessment*. Reading, MA: Addison-Wesley, 1973.

WILLIAMS, W. S. Class differences in the attitudes of psychiatric patients. *Social Problems*, 1956, *4*, 240-244.

WINTER, W. D., FERREIRA, A. J., & BOWERS, N. Decision-making in married and unrelated couples. *Family Process*, 1973, *12*, 83-94.

16

LOVE RELATIONSHIPS AMONG HEROIN-INVOLVED COUPLES: TRADITIONAL SELF-REPORT AND BEHAVIORAL ASSESSMENT

Robert A. Lewis
Erik E. Filsinger
Rand D. Conger
Philip McAvoy

The quality of marital and similar dyadic love relationships has been studied in a number of ways, such as marital adjustment, marital satisfaction, marital happiness, marital integration, and marital development. As with many concepts in the social sciences, there is no complete agreement about what constitutes high and low quality in love relationships. There is a growing belief, however, that it is the quality of most American marriages that is the primary determinant of whether they will remain intact or stable (see Lewis & Spanier, 1979). Concepts such as marital adjustment and marital satisfaction appear frequently in

AUTHORS' NOTE: This chapter is a revised version of a paper presented at the meetings of the First World Congress on Victimology, Washington, D.C., August 23, 1980. This research has been supported by Grant 1 R01 DA02286-01 from the National Institute on Drug Abuse: Robert A. Lewis, Principal Investigator. Special appreciation is extended to Dr. Thomas J. Glynn, NIDA, for his continual support of this research.

the family literature, but they have been criticized in terms of their definition and measurement (Spanier, 1976; Rollins & Galligan, 1978). This is true, in part, because they usually have been measured solely through self-reports. Several of the limitations of traditional self-reports are as follows:

(1) Self-reports force the subject to be the scientist, under the faulty assumption that each spouse can be objective enough to assess the quality of his or her own relationship.

(2) Few subjects are articulate enough to describe meaningfully something so complex as the qualitative dimensions of their relationships.

(3) Even though spouses' perceptions are important for understanding some aspects of their relationships (the value of subjective reality), responses are often distorted in order to conform with what the subject believes is socially desirable.

However, self-reports do help the researcher and the therapist become sensitized to the phenomenology of the spouses' experience of each other and of their relationship. That knowledge may be critical to careful handling and to insightful intervention strategies (see Margolin, Chapter 6, this volume).

Behavioral assessments of the quality of couples' relationships have been acclaimed by some researchers as needed replacements for, or as supplements to, self-reports (Olson & Ryder, 1970; Spanier & Lewis, 1980). In the behavioral mode, other researchers have suggested that marital adjustment may be operationalized as: (a) positive versus negative communication, (b) high exchanges of pleasing, as compared to displeasing, events, and (c) reliance on constructive rather than coercive methods for producing change in problem areas of couple relationships (Patterson et al., 1975).

A number of writers are asserting that family research and intervention that extends beyond self-reports will lead to more rigorous conceptualizations of complex phenomena, such as the quality of relationships and the interrelations between marital processes and outcomes. Aldous (1977) has noted that theoretical progress in understanding marital relationships will rely increasingly on actual observations of what people do rather than on what they say they do. Observation will extend our understanding of the behavioral processes that individuals go through, as well as outcomes.

The importance of identifying behavioral processes for couples through direct observation is multifaceted. For instance, whenever dysfunctional patterns are identified for couples (Gottman et al., 1976), they can be targeted for change. Indeed, changing behavior may be the most important means for remediating not only undesirable outcomes that certain styles of interaction produce, but for improving negative cognitive states, such as low self-esteem, which sometimes accompany such outcomes. Moreover, when the behaviors to be altered are identified, they may provide a reliable means for assessing the effects of intervention across time.

Furthermore, the behavioral approach enables one to sample the criterion behaviors directly and with fewer inferences (Goldfried & Kent, 1972). Behavioral assessments therefore are able to predict couple behavior and interaction more adequately and validly than self-reports, which are further removed from the criterion behaviors.

Even though there is little agreement among family researchers, interventionists, and family theorists as to which concepts best epitomize marital/couple quality, a number of writers suggest that it should be assessed by more than one methodology (see chapters by Allred, Cromwell, and Margolin). Several studies have investigated the relationship between self-report and behavioral measures of marital states. Generally their findings have been negative. For example, in one study of the relationship between traditional self-report measures of marital quality and behavioral measures, Margolin (1978) found that among 27 couples self-referred for marital counseling there was no relationship between the Locke-Wallace Marital Happiness Score and either positive or negative behaviors on the Marital Interaction Coding System.

The purpose of this study was to discover convergences that may exist between various indices of marital/couple quality obtained both through behavioral assessments of couples' interaction and global self-reports of the relationship by the partners. The belief was that more positive results could be found if more measures of marital quality were employed. Our goal was to identify those indices that might provide a more dynamic conceptualization and better predictors of the qualitative dimensions in marriage and other couple relationships.

METHODOLOGY

SAMPLE

These findings are based upon a sample of 35 heroin-involved couples. They are predominantly white couples, with some mixed marriages, in which either the male or both partners are or have been addicted to illegal opiates. The mean length of their relationship is 4 years; 21 couples are married, the remainder live together. The mean age of the men is 31 years, of the women, 27. The modal educational level for both sexes is "some college."

Of the 70 people in the sample, 50 are employed outside the home; only 6 of the women describe themselves as housewives. The modal annual income for males is in the $10,000 to $13,000 range; for the women it is in the $7,000 to $10,000 range. Some persons in the sample are unemployed, make their livings "by their wits," and have to hitchhike to travel anywhere.

PROCEDURES

These data were collected over two evenings. On the first evening, the Research Associate gathered background data and data on current drug use from each couple. Data gathering on the second evening took place in a family observation laboratory and included observation of the partners in interaction with each other.

The couples were asked to complete the Inventory of Marital Conflicts (IMC; Olson & Ryder, 1970). The IMC has nine vignettes describing marital situations. On some vignettes the version the male reads puts the onus of the blame upon the wife in the story, and vice versa for the version the female reads. The behavioral task requires the couple to reach a joint decision as to who is more responsible for the problem described in each vignette. The couple is encouraged to make their decisions in about twenty minutes.

Two coders, using the Dyadic Interaction Scoring Code (DISC), recorded the behaviors on Datamyte Data Collectors (Filsinger, Chapter 9, this volume). They carried out their observations from behind a two-way mirror. The sessions were also videotaped when the couples gave permission.

MEASURES

Self-Report measures. The Dyadic Exclusiveness Scale, from the Dyadic Formation Inventory (DFI; Lewis, 1973), measures the extent to which pair members exclude third persons from their dyadic relationships. The degree to which the partners orient themselves to the relationship itself was measured by the Couple Identity Index, also derived from the DFI (Filsinger & Lewis, Note 1). The degree to which partners agree or disagree about nine areas of values

TABLE 16.1   Zero-Order Correlations Between Self-Report and Behavioral
              Measures of Couple Quality (N = 35)

	Facilitative Behaviors (male)	Facilitative Behaviors (female)	Dysfunctional Behaviors (male)	Dysfunctional Behaviors (female)
Dyadic Exclusiveness (male)	.33	.34*	−.21	−.31
Dyadic Exclusiveness (female)	−.11	.19	−.17	−.19
Value Consensus (male)	.23	.22	−.34*	−.29
Value Consensus (female)	.29	.23	−.31	−.31
Couple Identity (male)	.08	.28	−.12	−.19
Couple Identity (female)	.18	.18	−.09	−.27
Dyadic Trust (male)	.29	.17	−.20	−.22
Dyadic Trust (female)	−.12	.24	−.04	−.04
Couple Happiness (male)	.16	.05	−.33	−.01
Couple Happiness (female)	.35*	.24	−.21	−.38*

*p less than .05.

was operationalized by the Value Consensus Scale (Locke & Wallace, 1959). Pair trust was measured for this study through an eight-item Dyadic Trust Scale, developed by Larzelere and Huston (1980) to assess the degree to which partners perceive each other's particularized honesty and sincerity (trust) toward the attributor. Finally, couples' happiness was assessed by Locke's one-item happiness question (Locke, 1951).

Behavioral measures. Facilitative behaviors were defined as the sum of the behavioral rates (the individual rates = number of occurrences/session length, or behaviors per minute) of back-channel comments, agreements, complies compromise, positive affect toward self, positive affect toward partner, goal directions, start gazing, laughs, and positive physical contacts. Dysfunctional behaviors were defined as the sum of interruptions, disagreements, requested changes in partner, negative self-statements, requests for information, negative affect toward partner, and negative physical contact. Interrater reliability, as measured by the Efficient Percentage Agreement (Hartmann, 1977), was .77.

FINDINGS

Table 16.1 contains the zero-order correlations between the measures. While many of these bivariate correlations were not statistically significant, the pattern of positive correlations for facilitative behaviors and negative correlations for dysfunctional behaviors is striking.

In order to determine whether or not the self-report and behavioral measures of marital quality tapped a common underlying dimension of couple quality, a principal component analysis was performed. The same five self-report variables were entered into the principal component analysis along with the positive and negative behavioral measures. Since the strategy was again to use both husband and wife variables as descriptive of the couple, the results were based on an analysis of the principal components of fourteen variables (seven variables for each of the sexes). The prior estimates of the communalities were all one. Due to the choice of principal component analysis, as opposed to factor analysis, no rotation was imposed.

Table 16.2 shows the loadings of the 14 measures on the first principal component. The eigenvalue for the first principal component was 4.06, and it explained 29% of the variance. The remaining eigenvalues were: 1.64, 1.49, 1.31, 1.14, 0.95, 0.73, 0.62, 0.54, 0.49, 0.38, 0.27, 0.20, and 0.15. Although the first principal component did not explain as much variance as might be liked, the jump between 4.06 and 1.64 was considerable and was felt to justify examination of the first component.

These results indicate that, except for the female's perception of the pair's Dyadic Exclusiveness, all of the variables loaded on the first principal compo-

TABLE 16.2   The Principal Component of Self-Report and Behavioral
              Measures of Marital Quality (N = 35)

Variables	Loadings
Dyadic Exclusiveness (male)	0.38
Dyadic Exclusiveness (female)	0.15
Value Consensus (male)	0.60
Value Consensus (female)	0.72
Couple Identity (male)	0.43
Couple Identity (female)	0.46
Dyadic Trust (male)	0.62
Dyadic Trust (female)	0.44
Couples' Happiness (male)	0.49
Couples' Happiness (female)	0.70
Facilitative Behaviors (male)	0.52
Facilitative Behaviors (female)	0.52
Dysfunctional Behaviors (male)	−0.61
Dysfunctional Behaviors (female)	−0.64

nent. The loadings are consistently fairly high, with the highest loadings occurring for female's Value Consensus and Couple Happiness. As hypothesized, the Facilitative behaviors load positively, and the Dysfunctional behaviors negatively.

DISCUSSION AND CONCLUSIONS

The principal component analysis suggests that both the self-report and the behavioral measures are tapping basically one underlying construct of couple quality, which for no better reason can be thought of as quality of the relationship. This is one of the first instances recorded in the literature in which there is as good a fit between traditional self-report and behavioral measures. However, a cautionary note should be added: A sample of 35 is actually quite small for principal component analysis.

It is interesting and perhaps significant that, for these couples, paper-and-pencil measures seem to be tapping the same core of couple qualities as do the behavioral measures. The implications of these findings suggest to us that there is value in using self-reports of couple relationships, as well as in observing couples and assessing their behaviors, since both contribute to our understanding of the richness and complexity of these interpersonal relationships. This precedent, of course, has been set already by researchers such as Weiss and his students at Oregon, whose studies of marriages utilize assessment packages that include both self-reports and behavioral assessments.

REFERENCE NOTE

1. FILSINGER, E. E., & LEWIS, R. A. *A new method to measure couple identity: The Couple Identity Index.* Unpublished manuscript, Arizona State University, 1980.

REFERENCES

ALDOUS, J. Family interaction patterns. *Annual Review of Sociology,* 1977, *3,* 105-135.

GOLDFRIED, M. R., & KENT, R. N. Traditional versus behavioral personality assessment: A comparison of methodological and theoretical assumptions. *Psychological Bulletin,* 1972, *77,* 409-420.

GOTTMAN, J. M., NOTARIUS, C., MARKMAN, H., BANK, S., YOPPI, B., & RUBIN, M. E. Behavior exchange theory and marital decision making. *Journal of Personality and Social Psychology,* 1976, *34,* 14-23.

HARTMANN, D. P. Considerations in the choice of interobserver reliability estimates. *Journal of Applied Behavior Analysis,* 1977, *10,* 103-116.

LARZELERE, R. E., & HUSTON, T. L. The Dyadic Trust Scale: Toward understanding trust in close relationships. *Journal of Marriage and the Family,* 1980, *42,* 586-604.

LEWIS, R. A. The Dyadic Formation Inventory: An instrument for measuring heterosexual couple development. *International Journal of Sociology of the Family,* 1973, *2,* 207-216.

LEWIS, R. A., & SPANIER, G. B. Theorizing about the quality and stability of marriage. In W. Burr et al. (Eds.), *Contemporary theories about the family* (Vol. 1). New York: Macmillan, 1979.

LOCKE, H. J. *Predicting adjustment in marriage: A comparison of a divorced and a happily married group.* New York: Holt, Rinehart & Winston, 1951.

LOCKE, H. J., & WALLACE, K. M. Short marital-adjustment and prediction tests: Their reliability and validity. *Journal of Marriage and Family Living,* 1959, *21,* 251-255.

MARGOLIN, G. Relationships among marital assessment procedures: A correlational study. *Journal of Consulting and Clinical Psychology,* 1978, *46,* 1556-1558.

OLSON, D. H., & RYDER, R. G. Inventory of Marital Conflicts (IMC): An experimental interaction procedure. *Journal of Marriage and the Family,* 1970, *32,* 443-448.

PATTERSON, G. R., HOPS, H., & WEISS, R. L. Interpersonal skills training for couples in the early stages of conflict. *Journal of Marriage and the Family,* 1975, *37,* 295-302.

ROLLINS, B. C., & GALLIGAN, R. The developing child and marital satisfaction of parents. In R. M. Lerner & G. B. Spanier (Eds.), *Child influences on marital and family interactions: A lifespan perspective.* New York: Academic, 1978.

SPANIER, G. B. Measuring dyadic adjustment: New scales for assessing the quality of marriage and similar dyads. *Journal of Marriage and the Family,* 1976, *38,* 15-28.

SPANIER, G. B., & LEWIS, R. A. Marital quality: A review of research in the seventies. *Journal of Marriage and the Family,* 1980, *42,* 825-839.

PART V

ISSUES AND CHALLENGES
IN BEHAVIORAL ASSESSMENT

17

PROTECTING HUMAN SUBJECTS IN OBSERVATIONAL RESEARCH: THE CASE OF FAMILY VIOLENCE

Murray A. Straus

There are three main issues or questions whenever human beings are the subjects of research: informed consent, safety, and confidentiality.[1] This chapter uses research on physical violence within the family to illustrate what is involved in each of these three problems. I chose physical violence because I have been studying this issue for the past ten years, and because it poses particularly acute ethical problems. However, my remarks are not intended to be a balanced review or weighing of the ethical issues involved in observing family group interaction. Instead, I have three main objectives.

The first part of this chapter presents a critique of the system used to protect research subjects up to February 1981, when revised regulations were issued (Department of Health and Human Services, 1981, p. 8386). I will suggest that

AUTHOR'S NOTE: This chapter is one of a series of publications of the Family Violence Research Program, supported by the University of New Hampshire and by NIMH Grants MH27557 and T32 MH15161. A program bibliography and list of available publications will be sent upon request. I would like to express my appreciation to the members of the Family Violence Research Program seminar for 1979-1980, who, as always, provided extremely valuable suggestions and criticisms; specifically, Barbara Carson, Diane Coleman, Jane Dingman, Linda Harris, Campbell Harvey, Susan Herrick, David Finkelhor, Robert Larzelere, and Kersti Yllo.

many of the restrictions imposed by this system were unnecessary impediments to research, and that they actually served to expose subjects to *greater* risk than would otherwise be the case. The revised regulations remove the most burdensome restrictions from interview studies and from studies that observe behavior in public places. However, they have not altered the situation in respect to laboratory or home observational research.

Aside from the problems associated with the formal regulatory system, if observational methods are to be used to study family violence, special techniques are needed. Consequently, the second part of the chapter describes three strategies for doing this.

In the last analysis, some system of review and control is needed, but one which avoids the excesses and harm of the present system. The third part of the chapter proposes new procedures for protecting research participants.

PROBLEMATIC ASPECTS OF THE PRESENT SYSTEM

Each organization sponsoring federally funded research must appoint a committee to review and monitor research involving human subjects. In a number of instances these "institutional review boards" (IRBs) have interpreted their task in a way that has threatened to bring a great deal of family research to a halt. Many of the problems are not with the regulations, but with the tendency to take the most narrow and restrictive interpretation of these regulations. Moreover, it is difficult to locate the source of these restrictive interpretations. IRBs view themselves as responding to federal pressures; federal officials state that it is up to the IRBs. There seems to be an implicit collusion to take the most restrictive course. The reasons for choosing this "conservative" (that is, restrictive) approach often have little to do with protecting human subjects. The real purpose is most often to minimize the chance that HEW or the institution will be criticized or sued. It is for the protection of the institution, rather than protection of human subjects. In addition, there is sometimes a subtle kind of censorship because the topic of the research is threatening to an institution (as when prison wardens suddenly become concerned with the rights of prisoners) or threatening to the personal values of one or more members of the board (as when the research is on power and violence in families). In the process, it is easy to lose sight of the rights of the researcher, freedom of inquiry, and, indeed, the right of subjects to engage in behavior of their own choosing.

In addition to unwarranted interference with research, there are instances in which IRBs set requirements that expose subjects to additional risks. This is particularly true of direct observation research. Let us look first at the question of informed consent to understand the basis for these concerns.

INFORMED CONSENT

The "informed consent" criterion refers to whether those participating in the study understand the nature and risks of participation, and whether their participation is truly voluntary.

That is an admirable principle. However, a problem arises when it is considered a moral absolute. This is because, sooner or later, all moral principles come into conflict with other valid moral principles. The IRBs are intended to provide the flexibility needed to deal with such conflicting values, and some do. Unfortunately, there are an increasing number of instances in which the requirement of informed consent is administered as a moral absolute, with resulting harm not only to research, but also an increased risk of harm to the subjects.

An example in which the requirement of full disclosure actually creates the possibility of harm which would not otherwise exist comes from some of the research using the SIMFAM technique (Straus, 1968; Straus & Tallman, 1971). SIMFAM is a puzzle in the form of a game played with balls and pushers. It is a highly engrossing game that permits one to observe many aspects of family interaction, such as power relationships, communication, and interpersonal support. In one experiment, the game was structured so that a random half of the families continued to obtain better and better scores from beginning to end. This was intended to permit observation of family interaction when everything is going well and the family has a sense of achievement and accomplishment.

It certainly produced the intended effect, as we discovered in the first few postexperimental debriefings. When we explained that the scores were deliberately arranged so that every family would get high scores, the typical reaction was disappointment. We therefore decided that the most ethical way to conduct this research was to *not* disclose this information. This permitted all the families to leave the experiment with a feeling of competence and accomplishment.

That, however, was 15 years ago. Both the current and previous federal regulations permit these procedures. However, many IRBs would not now give permission for this study because the very nature of the experimental treatment requires that the subjects not know that the scores are entirely artificial. But let us assume that permission is given for the experiment, provided that all subjects are *fully* informed about the exact nature of the experimental manipulations. This means that, instead of allowing subjects to leave with a good feeling about themselves and their families, we must provide information which was not requested and which is of no value, but which leaves many participants with a feeling of disappointment, and, in some cases, anger. That is an example of hurting subjects in the name of protecting them.

CONFIDENTIALITY

I doubt that anyone would disagree with the principle that research data must be kept confidential in order to safeguard the privacy of subjects. But the actual implementation of that principle reveals some ironic and dangerous aspects. This time the danger is to science, because unthinkingly rigid implementation of the federal regulations would prevent a great deal of important family research, without providing any needed protection to research subjects. Let us consider as examples research using videotape recordings of family interaction and longitudinal studies of family developmental processes.

Videotaped interaction. Federal regulations require that research data be maintained in a way that prevents identification of the subjects. This is an important safeguard. However, there is no way of disguising a family whose interaction is videotaped. Consequently, if an IRB interprets the privacy requirement this literally, research based on analysis of videotapes is ruled out. This would be a serious loss to family research because some important issues can only be analyzed by doing a detailed act-by-act analysis of videotapes. Moreover, it would also be an infringement of the rights of a citizen to participate in the research. Assuming that subjects are informed that there will be a videotaping, it is an unwarranted intrusion in the rights of the citizen and rights of the researchers for an IRB to deny them the opportunity.

Longitudinal studies. Longitudinal research poses a similar problem. If one is to be able to follow subjects over a period of time, there must be a record of names and addresses. It is true that exceptions can be and have been made to permit longitudinal research, but these involve seeking exceptions to the rules. The procedure is so long and intimidating that it has discouraged a number of people who might otherwise have done longitudinal studies.

This is exactly what happened in the case of my national Family Violence Survey (Straus et al., 1980). Getting permission to do that research took eight months of detailed negotiation with both the committee at my own university and with officials at NIHM. I felt that the situation was so precarious that if I also requested permission to maintain a file of names the entire project would have been turned down. I now very much regret that decision, because many issues have come up which, without longitudinal data, cannot be answered. We have therefore lost an important opportunity to advance understanding of the causes and consequences of a crucial family problem.

SAFETY

The obligation of a researcher to avoid harming the participants in research is clearly an important ethical principle. But IRBs have drifted toward an interpretation that will prevent or seriously interfere with research that poses no danger to the safety of the subjects. The root of the problem is an inappropriate transfer of a sound principle from medical research to the social sciences, coupled with an assumption that participants in research are extraordinarily fragile.

The medical model applies only if the research is designed to alter the physical, psychological, or social status of the subject. Such "intervention research" is a special category. I will deal with it briefly in a later section. The thrust of this chapter, however, is not with research designed to change families, but with research that is simply intended to find out something about the way families operate and why families are organized and operate the way they do.

The "fragility of subjects" problem stems from what seems to be a tendency of IRBs to assume that those we study might suffer psychotic episodes if they are asked questions on "sensitive" topics, such as whether they feel depressed, or how often they have sex, or how often they have hit another member of the family. Is there an empirical basis for this assumption? I have been unable to find evidence of harm being caused to research subjects because of (1) the "sensitive" nature of the questions asked, (2) the behavior observed, or even (3) experimental manipulations to test a theory (as opposed to clinical intervention research).

For example, one might expect that some of the subjects who participated in Milgram's (1974) famous experiments on conformity had been harmed by the experience. But even the extremely stressful experience to which they were exposed apparently produced no harm beyond the stress experienced during the experiment itself. A questionnaire study of the participants showed that only 1.3% expressed regret at participation. However, the testimony of participants is not adequate evidence. Fortunately another evaluation was done by a psychiatrist a year after the experiment. He examined the 40 participants who showed the most extreme signs of stress during the experiment, and reported that he found no evidence of any traumatic reactions. A few accepted responsibility for their actions and described their distress when faced with their willingness to inflict pain on another human being. "They felt that as a result of the experiment they had learned something valuable about themselves" (Errera, cited in Reynolds, 1980, p. 129).

THE NORMAL RISK CRITERION

I have not brought up the Milgram experiment to defend Milgram or other studies that expose subjects to a high degree of stress. That is a complicated issue. A decision on whether to proceed with such a study must take many things into account (see Reynolds, 1980). Rather, I am concerned with typical research in the social sciences. These are studies the research procedures of which do not impose any greater stress or risk than one encounters in the course of ordinary day-to-day activities.

The point of introducing Milgram's study—which goes beyond the stresses and risks of everyday life—is to show that robustness and resistance to change, rather than fragility, are typical of research participants. Of course, it is possible that a subject will take offense at being asked his or her frequency of feeling blue, or frequency of sex, or frequency of hitting or hugging a spouse. It is also possible that being asked about these things will have an adverse effect on the subject. However, neither of these possibilities makes the research unethical.

On the contrary, such studies are ethical because they do not expose the subjects to any greater risk of harm than do the kinds of issues that come up in the normal everyday life of people, and because the subjects are participating in the research on the same voluntary basis as their participation in other activities.

This is a very different situation from that encountered in medical research. Social scientists do not administer new drugs that might be dangerous. Nor do they try out new surgical techniques that might be fatal. In fact, in research on family therapy—which is closest to the medical research that gave rise to these regulations—the main problem is not that of producing injurious changes, but of producing any change at all.

We cannot judge the safety of research by whether it exposes subjects to *any* risk. That would end all research, and also life itself, because risk is an inherent part of life. About 4000 Americans die each year from choking on food. Just getting to the research laboratory exposes subjects to the risk of car accidents. Must we therefore prohibit research that requires subjects to eat sandwiches or leave their homes? Since the answer to this rhetorical question is "no," some other standard is needed. Instead of trying to evaluate research on the basis of whether it poses "any risk," the standard of comparison should be whether the research exposes subjects to greater risk than an average person encounters in his or her day-to-day life.

Does this seem like a novel standard? When the first draft of this chapter was written, I thought so. It turns out, however, that this was exactly the criterion given in the federal regulations for protection of human subjects (DHHS, 1981). These regulations stated that IRBs shall first determine if a research places a subject "at risk." Only if this were the case did the IRBs have any obligation to regulate the conduct of the research. The definition of being "at risk" is as follows: "Exposed to the possibility of injury, including physical, psychological, or social injury as a consequence of participation in any research . . . which increases the ordinary risks of daily life, including the recognized risks inherent in a chosen occupation or field of service." In short, the criterion is not that there be no risk, only that it not be greater than the ordinary risks of daily life.

IRBs typically ignored this criterion. In fact, most verged on acting as if the criterion was "no risk." It is essential that this trend be reversed. To be more specific, one must cease judging research by either of the following:

(1) Whether anyone might take offense to the study. People take offense to all kinds of things. For example, to this day, some people object to courses teaching the "theory" of evolution. It is a gross violation of freedom of speech and

academic freedom to use that as a criterion for judging either a course or research. Yet that seems to be the direction in which things are moving. I know of four projects at three different universities that were either seriously delayed, altered in ways that weakened the research, or stopped, for this reason. In each of these instances there was informed consent, privacy of the data, and no harmful procedures. But in each case there was concern about possible adverse public reaction to the study, or concern that the investigator might be sued. As important as it may be to protect the university and the investigator, this is not an appropriate function of a committee charged with protecting human subjects.

(2) Research should not be judged, either, on the basis of whether anyone might possibly have an adverse reaction to being a participant. People can have adverse reactions to almost anything. For example, a former employee broke into tears when I asked for her evaluation of a prospective new employee. The risk that someone will take offense at some aspect of an interview, or that someone will break into tears in response to having to evaluate a new employee, are all part of the "normal risks" of life and should not be a basis for rejecting a research project.

Why is a university willing to permit courses that some people find objectionable, and to permit faculty to talk to the staff, even though that might precipitate nervous breakdowns? The answer is that the university could not exist (at least in the form we know it) if these things were not permitted. These are the normal risks of operating a university.

It is essential that the same "normal risk" criterion be applied to research. That is, the content of the research must be protected by the same principles of free speech and academic freedom that apply to the content of teaching. No more, but certainly no less. Similarly, judgment of risks of harm must be based on the same principles that govern any other aspect of social interaction, rather than on the basis of whether anyone might conceivably have an adverse reaction.

What about research that involves observing the interaction of family members with each other? Most such research falls well within the "normal risk" criterion. After all, families perform in front of others almost every day of their lives. Sometimes they do things that are embarrassing or that they wish they had not done. That is the way life is. And since that is the way life is, there should be no objection to research which does nothing more.

On the other hand, research that requires or induces a family to act contrary to prevailing social standards for example, by physically or verbally assaulting each other, does not fall within the "normal risk" range. If observational or experimental studies are to be done on such issues, one must design them so that, despite the topic, participants are not exposed to a greater than normal risk of injury. The sections that follow suggest three strategies by which this can be accomplished.

STRATEGIES FOR ETHICAL OBSERVATIONAL
STUDY OF FAMILY VIOLENCE

STRATEGY A:
OBSERVE THEORETICALLY RELEVANT BEHAVIOR

The first of the three strategies is based on the somewhat ironic principle that the most important thing to observe about violent families is *not* usually their acts of violence. This is because the violence is not what is problematic. We know it exists. Usually, it is also a matter of secondary importance to know if he punches her or kicks her, or if she hits him with a rolling pin or a lamp. The crucial thing for either research or therapy is the pattern of interaction which eventuates in violence, not the violence itself.

Once this principle is grasped, we can see that direct observational study of violent families does not usually require that we observe the physical violence. What we want to observe is not the violence, but some aspect of family behavior which is theoretically important for understanding violence (or diagnostically important if the therapist is to help the family avoid violence in the future).

It follows that the critical need is not for ingenious techniques of observing the violence. What is needed are insightful theories about what produces violence, and techniques for observing the type of behavior that the theory suggests is the cause of the violence. Similarly, for clinicians, the critical thing is not to be able to observe a couple physically assaulting each other, but to be able to observe and diagnose what it is in their system of interaction that has brought them to blows.

STRATEGY B:
DEFINE THE EXPERIMENTAL TASK AS A GAME

Despite the importance of Strategy A, there are certain issues for which direct observation of family conflict or violence is necessary. The so-called catharsis theory is an example. This theory asserts that, to the extent that there are "outlets" for aggression which do minimal harm, the likelihood of expressing aggression in truly harmful ways—such as a physical assault—is reduced.

There has been considerable research on the catharsis theory, including well-designed laboratory experiments and interview surveys. These studies are just about unanimous in showing the exact opposite of what is predicted by the catharsis theory. However, even though the research findings are almost entirely contrary to the theory, each of the studies fails to meet one or the other of two criteria that are essential before the idea of catharsis can be finally dismissed from family therapy and family life education.

The *laboratory studies* have all been based on ad hoc groups. Therefore, defenders of the idea of catharsis can and do argue that the results do not necessarily apply to families. In *interview studies* of the presumed cathartic effect of verbal aggression on family violence, the causal direction is not established. Thus, an adequate test of the idea of catharsis (as it applies to families) requires either interview studies, which gather data on the sequence of events that led up to the violence, or laboratory experiments, in which the subjects are family groups. Since the focus of this book is on direct observation, I will confine my remarks to suggesting a strategy for a laboratory experimental study of catharsis.

The SIMFAM laboratory experimental method mentioned earlier studied the effects of a simulated crisis on the balance of power in the families, and the interpersonal supportiveness of family members (Kolb & Straus, 1974; Straus & Tallman, 1971; Straus, 1968). What made it possible to subject families to a frustrating experience, observe them in the throes of frustration, and at the same time not only avoid any negative reaction, but find that almost all participating families enjoyed their participation? I suggest that it was because the experimental task was in the form of a game, which has the following results:

(1) Games *legitimize* frustration because, by definition, games involve chance or other things over which the player has no control and which can cause the player to do well or poorly.

(2) What goes on in a game is *culturally defined* as unimportant. Games and puzzles are what Moore calls an "autotelic" activity (1971). That is, they contain their own goals and motivations. At the same time, the rewards and punishments connected with failure to play the game well are restricted by these cultural norms to the intrinsic features of the game itself, and do not generally carry over to other aspects of life. Thus, a scientist may be a miserable golfer or monopoly player without damaging his or her self-esteem or reputation as a scientist.

I suggest that the norms which restrict the consequences of a game to the game itself provide a strategy that has wide applicability for direct observational research on families. If the experimental task is cast in the form of a game, these norms insulate the family from regarding the behavior that occurred during the course of the game as reflecting what the family is really like. Consequently, poor performance in the game will not affect the way family members think about their real-life performance, and changes in family interaction brought about as a result of the experimental treatment will not carry over to situations outside the game context. But, even though families define or experience game behavior as not reflecting their real behavior, there is evidence that what goes on in the game does, in fact, reflect their behaviors in natural settings (Straus, Note 1).

STRATEGY C: ROLE PLAYING

The third strategy is role playing. Paradoxically, I do not think one should usually use actual family groups as the subjects in role playing experiments on issues such as family violence. This is because it does not provide as great an opportunity as the game format to regard what is done in the course of the role playing as "not real." But the very fact that the research technique is role playing frees us from the need to use actual family members in order to study the family.

The basic strategy is to have one group of subjects engage in the experimental task with instructions that they are to act as though they are the members of a family. Another group participates in the experiment, but as a typical ad hoc experimental group. Differences between the two groups can be interpreted as representing the unique characteristics of family groups as compared to nonfamily groups.

One of the most puzzling aspects of family violence is that outside the family, women are much less violent than men, but within the family, women are about as violent as men. That is, wives assault their husbands at about the same rate as husbands assault wives (Straus, 1980). The paper just cited describes a number of different factors that account for the discrepancy between the violence rate of women within the family and outside the family. One of these factors is the existence of a largely unperceived social norm which tolerates family members hitting each other under certain conditions. The marriage license is, in effect, a hitting license. However, the data supporting this explanation is far from conclusive. There is, therefore, an obvious need to test the theory by other methods.

One method of directly testing the hypothesis that the marriage license is an implicit license to hit is to have couples engage in mock fights with foam plastic bataca clubs rigged with sensing devices to relay frequency and intensity of attack. The subjects could be unmarried college students. A random half of the couples would be instructed to role play a couple who have been married two years. The other couples would receive no such instruction. A better design would use students who are married. They would have the experiences of their current marriages as well as experience in their parents' families to use as models.

The role playing strategy could be applied to the techniques used by Richardson (Note 2). She conducted laboratory experiments using mixed-sex pairs to investigate the conditions under which women would be victims of male aggression. In most other aggression experiments, male subjects are reluctant to aggress against females. But Richardson introduced several elements to make her experimental situation more isomorphic with real-life relations between the sexes. For example, she manipulated things so that some men performed more poorly than their female partners. Another manipulation involved verbal aggression against the male subject. Both these variables produced high rates of aggression by the men against their female partners. Richardson argues that this is parallel to what goes on between husbands and wives. I think she is correct. But the results would be even more convincing if a random half of the couples were instructed to role play a married couple, and if the results showed that the greatest amount of male aggression against women for the couples occurred among those who are role playing married couples.

ALTERNATIVES

THE THREAT TO SCIENCE
AND ACADEMIC FREEDOM

The three strategies just described will permit a great many direct observation studies and, at the same time, protect the participating families. Unfortunately, many IRBs will not approve research using these strategies, and that is unlikely to change under the new regulations. These regulations exempt most interview research from committee review. But observational research (except in public places) is not exempt. Moreover, the new regulations omit the wording that exempts studies which pose no greater risks than those ordinarily encountered in daily life. Consequently, under the guise of protecting human subjects:

(1) Research which could benefit humanity (either because of its direct applicability, or indirectly because it contributes to a better understanding of the family) will continue to be blocked. How much desirable research is prevented, or not even proposed, because of these regulations is itself an important issue to investigate.

(2) The informed consent rule will continue to be interpreted in a way that sometimes harms rather than helps subjects. This can occur when rigid interpretations of the rule forces investigators to impose on subjects information about the study that is not necessary or helpful, but which can cause embarrassment or disappointment.

(3) Scientific freedom will continue to be restricted because, under the guise of protecting human participants in research, IRBs inevitably evaluate the worthiness of the purpose of the research and the adequacy of the methods. The history of science indicates that this can be disastrous, even if the danger no longer includes being burned at the stake. However, my experience suggests that it does include conscious or unconscious censorship of projects that one or more committee members (and especially university administrative representatives) feel might be dangerous to the reputation of the institution. This usually means that it deals with a topic that the objecting member believes should not be studied because it is a "private" matter—for example, topics such as male dominance in families and wife beating.

(4) When research is carried out with grant funds, the grantor has the right to control the uses to which the funds are put. This does not mean that universities must accept such restrictions. In fact, I do not believe they should. A university would not accept funds for an endowed chair of biology if the grantor required

that the holder of the chair refrain from teaching or doing research on evolution. Unfortunately, while a university can afford to decline a specific private gift of this type, the dependence of universities on federal funds has reached the point where "practical" considerations seem to override the issues of academic freedom.

Moreover, the impact of these restrictions is not confined to those who receive federal funds. Although the revised federal regulations apply only to research directly funded by the government, some IRBs immediately assumed the opposite. At the University of New Hampshire, for example, I was informed that the rules apply to all research, whether federally funded or not. Since I could find no mention of this, I asked for the reference. I was told, "Well, it's indirect—sort of by innuendo." When I persisted in asking for the reference, it turned out to be a summary of the hearings, not the regulations themselves. When I pointed this out, I was told that even though the regulations do not require IRB review of unfunded projects, in fact, "If we submit a plan [for protection of human subjects] and it doesn't include review of unfunded projects, it won't have a chance of being approved." The real fact is that there is no such requirement, beyond a statement of principles for human subjects protection (DHHS, 1981: 8387, 46.103, section b.1).

The section just cited is consistent with our legal system. But as Pool (1979) has eloquently noted, an interpretation that requires prior approval of unfunded projects is a violation of the constitutional rights of students and faculty who do not have (and may not want) federal funds. It is a "prior restraint" in direct contradiction to the constitutional guarantee, and one which provides the basis for the type of subtle censorship and curtailment of academic freedom to which I have already referred.

The problems listed above, together with others, have been analyzed elsewhere in greater depth than is possible in this chapter (see, for example, LaRossa et al., in press; Seiler & Murtha, 1980; Cassell & Wax, 1980; *Society,* 1980). My experience, and that of many of the authors in the works just cited, suggests these problems will increase rather than decrease because the main difficulties arise over protection of the institution, or over research that an IRB member believes to be "offensive," even though the issue, ostensibly, is protection of human subjects.[2]

AN ALTERNATIVE TO THE PRESENT SYSTEM

Intervention research. The alternative I suggest starts by distinguishing "intervention research" from all other research. By intervention research, I mean investigation of a procedure intended to change the biological, psychological, or social status of persons participating in the study. All intervention research should be subject to prior review by an IRB. But all other research involving human subjects—which might be 90% of social science research—should be free of a required prior review.

The same idea is the central point of the letter sent by the executive officers of eleven social science organizations in response to the draft of the new regulations. They urged that the revised regulations include the following statement:

> These regulations do not apply to research using legally competent subjects that involves neither deceit nor intrusion upon the subject's person nor denial or withholding of accustomed necessary resources [Society, 1980, p. 22].

Responsibilities of researchers. Second, this proposal imposes large but appropriate responsibilities on researchers.

(1) Researchers would have the obligation to be familiar with the current regulations and to act in accordance with such regulations, just as journalists have the obligation to be familiar with the laws on slander and libel and to act in accordance with those laws. The researcher assumes the liability for any untoward events resulting from the research.

(2) Researchers would have the responsibility for submitting a statement evaluating the risks to subjects of the proposed research, and the procedures that will be used to protect privacy, safety, and the right to voluntary participation.

Responsibilities of the IRB. The responsibilities and orientation of IRBs should be transformed from the present roles of censor and adversary to one of expert consultants and advisors. This would involve the following:

(1) The IRB would *not* have the responsibility or right to approve or disapprove research, except for "intervention research."

(2) IRBs should emphasize providing whatever advice or suggestions they feel would help the subjects and/or the researchers. They could, if they wished, advise researchers against going ahead with particular studies.

(3) To maximize the advising and consulting function, an IRB would be prohibited from the present typical practice of meeting without the investigator. Investigators must be invited to attend when their proposals are being considered. This gives the researcher an opportunity to explain aspects of the study that may not be clear to the committee.

(4) IRBs would be prohibited from refusing permission to conduct research on the grounds of protecting *the university* from the risk of embarrassment because of the nature of the research, or protecting investigators from the risk of legal action by subjects who participate in the research. The former is a violation of academic freedom—as serious as refusing permission to include unpopular materials in a course. The latter is a paternalistic infringement on the rights of the researcher to engage in activities which he or she considers to be legal and ethical. When an IRB feels that a study exposes the researcher to the risk of suit, it should make the services of a university attorney available to the investigator. The researcher would then have appropriate information on which to base a decision.

The advantages of the alternatives just described, compared to the current system, include the following:

(1) The simple requirement to draw up an evaluation of the extent to which the subjects' right to privacy, safety, and voluntary participation are protected will prevent the largest single source of danger to subjects—failure to even think about the problem.

(2) By rejecting prior review of social science research (except for intervention research), universities avoid placing themselves in the position of appearing to endorse or approve the content or purpose of studies for which they lack enthusiasm or to which they may even be opposed.

(3) The administrative cost, frustration, stifling of needed research, unnecessary risk of harm to subjects, infringement on the rights of researchers as citizens, and the threat to freedom of inquiry which have characterized the review system will be greatly reduced.

(4) The transformation of the committee from one which controls and censures to one which advises and helps will contribute to eliminating the adversary relationship that often now prevails. Much more important, however, is the greater likelihood that, with IRBs in the role of advisors and consultants working with researchers, creative solutions to problems involving protection of human subjects will be found.

NOTES

1. The same issues also apply to use of direct observation for clinical diagnoses—perhaps in an even more direct way. This is because of the vulnerability of families seeking help from a therapist, and because the results of the observation do not simply form the basis for statistics. The lives of the client families can depend on the results of diagnosis using direct observation.

2. A colleague who read this said, "What's wrong with the IRB protecting subjects against offensive projects?" What is wrong is that, first, the definition of what is offensive is essentially "political." It differs from person to person, from group to group, and from one historical time to another. Not everyone will agree on what is offensive. Second, as noted earlier, we do not require that faculty exclude material on topics that some find offensive, as long as the material is germane to the course. The same principle of academic freedom must apply to research. Third, and also as noted earlier in the chapter, even if we assume that the topic is universally regarded as offensive, the rights of subjects should include the right to give informed consent to participate in such studies, just as it includes the right to possess and read "offensive" books.

REFERENCE NOTES

1. STRAUS, M. A. *Exchange and power in marriage in cultural context: A multimethod and multivariate analysis of Bombay and Minneapolis families*. Paper presented at the annual meeting of the Association for Asian Studies, New York, 1977.

2. RICHARDSON, D. The theoretical significance of laboratory research for understanding family violence. Paper presented at the meeting of the American Society of Criminology, Philadelphia, November 1979.

REFERENCES

CASSELL, J., & WAX, M. L. (Eds.). Ethical problems of fieldwork. *Social Problems*, 1980, *27*, special issue, 259-377.

DHHS (Department of Health and Human Services). Code of Federal Regulation, Title 45, Part 46, as amended. *Federal Register*, 1981 (January 26, 46, No. 16, 8386-8392.)

KOLB, T. M., & STRAUS, M. A. Marital power and marital happiness in relation to problem-solving ability. *Journal of Marriage and the Family*, 1974, *36*, 756-775.

LaROSSA, R., BENNETT, L. A., & GELLES, R. J. Ethical dilemmas in qualitative family research. *Journal of Marriage and the Family*, in press.

MILGRAM, S. *Obedience to authority*. New York: Harper & Row.

MOORE, O. K., & ANDERSON, A. R. Some principles for the design of clarifying educational environments. In J. Aldous, T. Condon, R. Hill, M. Straus, & I. Tallman (Eds.), *Family problem solving*. Hinsdale, IL: Dryden, 1971.

POOL, I. Prior restraint. *New York Times*, December 16, 1979, p. E19.

REYNOLDS, D. P. *Ethical dilemmas and social science research*. San Francisco: Jossey-Bass, 1980.

SEILER, L. H., & MURTHA, J. M. Federal regulation of social research using "human subjects": A critical assessment. *American Sociologist*, 1980, *15*, 146-157.

Society. Institutional review boards. Special issue, 1980, November/December, 22-51.

STRAUS, M. A. Communication, creativity, and problem-solving ability of middle-class families in three societies. *American Journal of Sociology*, 1968, *73*, 417-430.

STRAUS, M. A. Leveling, civility, and violence in the family. *Journal of Marriage and the Family*, 1974, *36*, 13-29.

STRAUS, M. A. Victims and aggressors in marital violence. *American Behavioral Scientist*, 1980, *23*, 681-704.

STRAUS, M. A., GELLES, R. J., & STEINMETZ, S. K. *Behind closed doors: Violence in the American family*. New York: Doubleday, 1980.

STRAUS, M. A., & TALLMAN, I. SIMFAM: A technique for observational measurement and experimental study of families. In J. Aldous, T. Condon, R. Hill, M. Straus, & I. Tallman (Eds.), *Family problem solving*. Hinsdale, IL: Dryden, 1971.

YOUNG, D. M., BEIER, E. G., BEIER, P., & BARTON, C. Is chivalry dead? *Journal of Communication*, 1975, *28*, 57-64.

18

ISSUES OF BEHAVIORAL ASSESSMENT: FINAL REFLECTIONS

Hal Arkowitz
Leanne K. Lamke
Erik E. Filsinger

The chapters presented in this book are of a very timely nature. They represent the most recent work in the study of marital interaction. Moreover, they constitute major contributions to the general area of behavioral assessment. The emphasis on direct behavioral observation technique is a well-placed and much needed one. There needs to be increased knowledge about the nature of marriage problems before effective treatments can be developed. Many therapists and researchers see the "action" as being in intervention, with assessment often viewed as a tedious undertaking, to be tolerated. This is unfortunate. Unless more is known about the dimensions of the problem to be treated, we are left with a "hit or miss" approach to intervention. By contrast, a good assessment leads to a more precise treatment plan directed at the determinants of the problems. The emphasis on assessment in the present volume is a healthy indication of progress in the field.

The more specific emphasis on direct observation procedures provides one of the most exciting and productive approaches to the assessment of marriage and family interaction. Assessment using direct observation is a relatively new field, and as such, it contains several issues that need to be addressed in further research and practice. The purpose of this chapter is to help identify and remediate problems in an area that has already yielded important results and is likely to be even more fruitful in the future.

SELECTION OF TARGET BEHAVIORS

There is one point about direct observational approaches that is often overlooked. These approaches are essentially *methods* to measure behavior. They do not tell us what behaviors to measure. The direct observational technology basically tells us how to proceed to measure behavior once we know what behaviors we wish to measure. Thus, the question of *what behaviors to code* becomes a crucial one—one for which the technology of direct observation provides no answer. This question is quite distinct from questions relating to the reliability or validity of categories in a coding system, or the reactivity of direct observation techniques. These issues are methodological ones, which relate to the technology of measurement in direct observation. The question of what behaviors to code is a conceptual and theoretical one, for which the technology itself provides no guidance.

Consider the example of a couple seeking help for marital distress. We know that they are experiencing distress and unhappiness. We can potentially measure an incredibly large number of their interactional behaviors and generate a behavioral description of how the two people interact. This is what the direct observation technology allows us to do. However, the technology does not in any way tell us what specific behavioral patterns might be contributing to their distress. The direct observation technology allows only a way of describing behavior. It does not tell us which behaviors we should measure or which behaviors might be most related to the distress.

There are several related directions that can be helpful in determining what behaviors to code. One approach is theoretical. Psychoanalytic theories suggest some directions, systems theories suggest other directions, and behavioral theories suggest still other directions. While there may be some overlap among the theories in terms of what patterns of behavior are viewed as important, there are many significant differences. The more support we have for our theories, the more assurance we have that they will direct us to the correct places when we observe behavior. However, the main point is that theory is really crucial for the direct observation of behavior in marital and family interaction. It is theory that tells us where to look. Our theories can point to the important dimensions of interpersonal interaction. Theories provide ways of organizing information and ways of viewing the world. In this respect, theory development is an extremely important direction for marriage and family research and practice. The development and refinement of our theories will, we hope, merge with the technology of direct observation so that we will not only know *how* to measure interactions, but also *what* aspects of marriage and family interactions to measure. Indeed, as was discussed by Filsinger and his colleagues in Chapter 1, behavioral techniques may open up new conceptual avenues for understanding marital interaction. Social competence and reciprocity are two such concepts that are particularly suited to behavioral assessment.

A number of recent developments in theories of marriage can be cited. Behavioral views (for example, Weiss, Chapter 2, this volume; Jacobson & Margolin, 1979) have become increasingly sophisticated over the past several years and seem to be capturing more of the complexity of marital interaction than did earlier behavioral theories. For example, Weiss (1978) argues that marriage consists of twelve basic sectors of activity: companionship, affection, consideration, sex, communication process, coupling activities, child care and parenting, household management, financial decision making, employment education, personal habit and appearance, and self and spouse independence. These dimensions could provide a basic framework for selecting behaviors to measure. Similar dimensions have been used to structure the Spouse Observation Checklist (Weiss et al., 1973). Perhaps the dimensions could also be used to sample behaviors from a greater number of life domains than just problem solving or conflict resolution in a clinical setting, which is most typical of current observational studies. As such, not only would the behaviors to code be selected, but the generalizability of findings on marital interaction would be extended beyond laboratory-contrived situations.

While theory development is a long, hard route, there are statistical procedures that can help considerably with the question of what behaviors to observe, although they cannot completely answer the question. Multiple regression analysis can help determine what behaviors contribute to a global subjective criterion. For example, Royce and Weiss (1975) used multiple regression analyses to determine those behavioral cues which contributed to ratings of marital satisfaction with some interesting results. Another technique that can be used is factor analysis. Lewis and his colleagues (Chapter 16, this volume) use a principal component analysis to determine if self-report and behavioral measures of marital quality tap a common underlying dimension of couple quality.

A somewhat different strategy would be to employ the behavioral-analytic model of assessing competence (Goldfried & D'Zurilla, 1969) in order to empirically determine behavioral correlates of marital satisfaction. The behavioral-analytic model consists of five steps: (a) situation analysis; (b) response enumeration; (c) response evaluation; (d) development of measuring instrument format; and (e) evaluation of the measure. Each process will be elaborated in terms of a hypothetical assessment of marital competence.

Situation analysis involves a comprehensive survey of relevant situations facing the couple, with which they must cope. According to Goldfried and

D'Zurilla (1969, p. 164), these situations are "those specific but meaningful situations with which most individuals . . . must cope effectively in order to be considered competent." Weiss's (Chapter 2, this volume) twelve areas of marriage might provide the initial framework for selecting the relevant situations. The next step, response enumeration, involves sampling the possible responses. Situations that elicit only a few responses may be dropped. The response enumeration will also help to clarify the situations, for example, cases in which ambiguous situations lead to qualified responses that indicate a number of interpretations are possible. It may be useful to observe subjects in each situation and to note the actual responses they make.

Response evaluation entails judging the effectiveness of each response in the situations. Goldfried and D'Zurilla (1969, p. 166) define effectiveness: "whether or not the response is likely to resolve the problematic nature of the situation and avoid possible negative consequences." A panel of judges can be used to evaluate the effectiveness of the responses. If the judges cannot agree on the evaluation of responses to a given situation, the situation can be dropped. As a result, a fairly large number of situations should be gathered initially.

We would argue that the measurement format should be observation of real-life situations, particularly because of the questions that have arisen concerning the validity of role-play procedures (Bellack et al., 1978). Evaluation of the measure should follow standard psychometric standards of reliability and validity.

In addition, we would suggest that the behavioral-analytic model, as well as other empirical procedures, continue to be used in conjunction with samples that represent both distressed and nondistressed couples. In much of our research we focus rather extensively on dysfunctional relationships. It would appear unwise to assume that dysfunctional relationships are mirror images of functional relationships. For example, knowing that unhealthy relationships are characterized by conflict does not mean that healthy relationships are conflict free. We believe that the study of healthy relationships would provide a more complete empirical basis for theory building.

A final strategy that would perhaps provide a great deal of information concerning important relationship behaviors to measure would be a comparison of the different behavioral coding schemes. Although this comparison would necessarily be time consuming, given the number of hours required to code behavioral interactions, it may be a more efficient use of time than developing additional behavioral coding strategies. A comparison of the various coding schemes would help clarify the relative efficacy of the behavioral codes in identifying distressed and nondistressed relationships. Furthermore, such a comparison would provide a means of identifying a common set of behaviors or patterns of behaviors that, across codes, can reliably discriminate between qualitatively different relationships. This would provide valuable empirical information concerning important behavioral correlates of marital quality regardless of theoretical basis. On the other hand, this same multitrait-multimethod approach can be helpful from a theoretical perspective. Given that a coding scheme is theoretically based, the extent to which it can more accurately predict relationship quality, as compared to other coding systems, may be viewed as providing comparative support for a particular theoretical framework. For these reasons, then, it would appear advantageous to make an assessment of where we are, rather than to develop new and different coding schemes. A comparison across behavioral coding systems would provide a more accurate basis from which new coding schemes can be developed.

METHODOLOGICAL ISSUES

In addition to the concerns already raised, there are several specifically methodological issues that need to be taken into account by researchers and clinicians involved with direct behavioral observation. One issue concerns methodological limitations related to coding behavioral interactions which may mitigate against including theoretically important behaviors in a coding system. For the most part, behaviors that are included in coding schemes include those behaviors that are nonreactive, can be coded reliably, and will occur during a specified time period, under specified conditions, and at a rate that warrants the use of data analysis techniques. This is not to imply that such behaviors are not theoretically or empirically useful, but rather that certain behavioral correlates of marital quality may go undetermined because they do not meet these criteria. Steinglass and Tislenko (Chapter 8, this volume), for example, have acknowledged that the reactivity of certain behaviors places limitations on what can be assessed. Their strategy for dealing with this issue is to select behaviors that are deemed nonreactive. While this technique is certainly one way of dealing with the issue of generalizability, it would seem unwise at this point to assume that reactive behaviors are unrelated to marital satisfaction. A similar logic applies to eliminating certain behaviors because observer reliability is low. Reliability is clearly a necessary condition for accuracy and generalizability (see Hartmann & Gardner, Chapter 12, this volume); but, again, the possibility exists that such behaviors may be theoretically important indicators of marital satisfaction.

Additional nontheoretical factors that may determine what behaviors are coded involve the resources available to researchers and/or clinicians. Such resources include amount of time that can be allocated to coding the data, money available for coders, and the level of coder sophistication. Coding gazing for speaking turns, for example, may prove too complex to be included solely on the basis of coder capabilities (see Filsinger, Chapter 9, this volume).

In short, there are a number of reasons to suspect that methodological issues place limitations on the ability of behavioral assessment procedures to accurately and comprehensively identify conceptually relevant behavioral correlates of marital satisfaction.

There are, however, methodological issues that are not inherent limitations of behavioral assessment strategies of marital interaction. One issue clearly addressed in this book, but not yet characteristic of the field, relates to the fact that many coding systems yield *frequency counts* of the output of certain behaviors or behavior chains. There are verbal content categories like "complaints" or "problem-solving statements," and nonverbal categories like "smiles" and "head-nods." Almost all coding systems deal with the output of behaviors and counting these behaviors. There are some real problems with this approach. Simple frequency counts obscure some very important issues relating to the timing, sequencing, and context of the behaviors.

Frequency counts of behavioral output are really quite gross estimates of what is happening in an interaction. There are times when such measures may be useless or misleading. As an example, consider the following incident, which occurred with a subject in an experiment. The experiment involved having the male subject interact with a woman for 10 minutes while we coded his various behaviors during the interaction. The man had never met the woman before he was introduced to her in the laboratory. One category coded was the number of self-disclosures during the 10-minute interaction. The man began his conversation with a vivid description of his recent hernia operation. As a result, he received high scores for frequency of self-disclosure. However, we might well question the appropriateness of these self-disclosures in the context of meeting a woman for the first time. From the expression on the woman's face during his description, it appeared that she was having a rather strong negative reaction to the man and his behavior. However, the same self-disclosure to a family member, or perhaps later on in the interaction with the woman, might have had a very different impact. However, in each case, the man would receive the same "score" for frequency of self-disclosure. Such a frequency count neglects the context and timing of the behavior. Similarly, a person who continually smiled would receive high scores of frequency of smiling. However, the impact of that behavior would be different depending on whether the partners were talking about pleasant and entertaining matters or some personal tragedies which had occurred. Once again, simple frequency counts used to measure interaction obscure some very important issues in the measuring of interaction through direct observation techniques. Thus, we need ways to take into account the *context* and *timing* of the behavior.

There are a number of ways of dealing with this issue. Systems theorists, for example, address the context of behavior by examining the different levels of systems within the family (see Cromwell & Peterson, Chapter 3, this volume).

The parent-child interaction is different in context from the husband-wife inter-action, although these subsystems have impact on each other. This has been noted as a major issue in studies on the family life cycle.

Another means of taking into account the timing and context of behavior is by analyzing behavior sequences through the use of conditional probabilities and time-series analyses (see Notarius and colleagues, Chapter 13, this vol-ume). This technique views the behaviors of the partner as one aspect of the content of an action that helps us understand what meaning the behavior actu-ally has. However, even this is just a beginning. Analysis of the timing and sequence of behavior needs to be addressed more fully before our direct obser-vation techniques can really capture more of the complexity and reciprocal nature of social interaction.

There is one other problem with simple frequency counts in coding systems. Usually, coding systems for marital interaction assume that the more of a "good" behavior, the better, and the less of a "bad" behavior, the better. For example, in coding marital interaction there seems to be an implicit assumption that the more "problem-solving statements" the better and the fewer "com-plaints" the better. However, there can be too much of a good thing and too little of a bad thing. A relationship characterized by an extremely high level of problem solving to the exclusion of other behaviors may still be far from ideal. Similarly, most people would agree that a certain amount of complaining to others may be a positive and desirable characteristic of an interaction. The point is that there may be *optimal levels* of certain behaviors that we need to deter-mine. The implicit assumption that the more of "good" behaviors, the better, and the less of "bad" behaviors, the better, may not be entirely correct.

Another methodological issue concerns the cognitive aspects of behavior. Our coding systems based on direct observational techniques do not tap more cognitive dimensions relating to the meanings of behaviors and how behaviors are perceived and processed by the individuals involved. This may be a particu-larly important consideration in the area of marital interaction, where people develop rather complicated attributions and interpretations of each other's be-havior. In marriage counseling, for example, many problems relate to how one spouse interprets the behavior of the other, rather than the actual behavior of the spouse. Thus, an apparently simple statement by one spouse to the other may evoke a powerful reaction based on the recipient's interpretation of the spouse's statement and the intentions behind it.

To illustrate some of these points, we provide this example. A husband may ask his wife if she has been having any affairs lately. First, this would probably be coded as a "request for information" in most of our existing coding systems. While this is a correct description, it also obviously misses the affective quality of the interchange. Further, that same question may be asked in a number of different ways that give it altogether different meanings. It may be done in a serious and angry way, or it may not be meant at all seriously and be done in a teasing, provocative way. "Request for information" captures only a very limited quality of this interchange.

It would be an interesting task to take our behavioral coding schemes and apply them to the interactions between Richard Burton and Elizabeth Taylor in the movie *Who's Afraid of Virginia Woolf?* We suspect the result of such an assessment would be less than satisfying. Much of the reason for this reflects the present inability of our coding systems to assess the perceptions, meanings, and interpretations of behaviors which can so radically influence the impact of the behavior. The issue seems particularly important in martial distress, where misperceptions, distorted meanings, and misinterpretations seem to be very much a part of the nature of the difficulties. For example, Weiss (Note 1) has suggested that a more accurate description of the pleasing/displeasing aspects of behavior can be obtained by having the spouses indicate on a panel of lights the affective value of ongoing behavior. This form of data provides a sequential measure of affective reactions.

Markman and Notarius (Note 2) have used a "communication box" to assess the impact of messages sent and received. They found that the discrepancy between the meaning of the intended message and the meaning received was one of the best predictors of marital distress. A partner in a distressed relationship may not be able to track his or her partner's behavior and accurately ascribe meaning to it. Without accurate tracking, neither partner would be able to make discriminations of the other's behavior and might even experience a high level of noncontingency in his or her behavior. The partners would not be able to build expectations concerning the likely response to their behaviors. These examples indicate that in order for direct observation measures to provide an accurate assessment of the complex phenomenon of marital interaction, they must begin to take into account the cognitive dimensions of behavior.

FUTURE CHALLENGES

As was noted above, one of the biggest problems for the future of observational research is the challenge of establishing the comparative validity of coding systems. This is especially true given the various sources of differences between coding systems, such as how an observed unit is defined, what behaviors are to be observed and how they are defined, the observational setting employed, the equipment and procedures used, the training and chosen reliability for the coders, and the purpose of the research. Riskin and Faunce (1972), for example, have reviewed how various behaviors are operationalized differently in several of the early coding schemes.

One feature, however, of the growing state of the art is the fundamental linkage between several of the major coding systems. For example, the MICS was developed from earlier efforts at Oregon on the Family Interaction Coding System (Patterson et al., 1969). The CISS, the MFICS, and the DISC all owe much to the MICS. Many of the differences are matters of emphasis. The CISS separates the coding of content from the coding of affect. The MFICS is inherently tied by its definitions to the Inventory of Marital Conflict, as well as to prior work with the Revealed Differences Test (Olson, 1969) and the Color Matching Test (Ryder & Goodrich, 1966).

It remains paramount, however, that the reader place findings in the context of the particular coding system employed, the situation in which behaviors were observed, and the exact procedures employed to collect the data. Hopefully, the comment of Riskin and Faunce (1972), concerning the serious problem in the lack of reporting such details for behavioral assessment, will not hold when the next decade of research is reviewed.

The use of standard research paradigms (such as the IMC) helps comparability. But even if the codes are similarly defined and even if the situations and coders are equivalent, the very fact that the behaviors are part of a larger coding system which contains other behaviors probably results in differences due to the contextual effects of those alternative behaviors existing alongside the behavior to be compared. When any element of the assessment package differs, comparison becomes more complex and problematic.

It may be possible in some cases to establish empirically the validity of one set of procedures over another. For example, Newtson et al. (1977) provide an impressive justification for focusing on the distinctive changes in behavioral states rather than on action unit boundaries. Consistent with that framework, some of the coding systems (such as the CISS) stress the importance of coding changes in behavior rather than coding strictly in terms of time-bracketed units.

Another likely development in the future that is closely related to the behavioral analytic approach is the use of social validation procedures in establishing the validity of behavioral assessment procedures (Kazdin, 1975), perhaps even by married persons themselves. In an example from the social skills literature, Romano and Bellack (1980) used a panel of subjects to rate social skill in the responses of twenty women. These ratings were compared with the scoring of the women's behaviors by trained raters. The ratings that were most highly associated with the panel's judgments could be thereby socially validated and emphasized in future research. Precursors of this technique exist in the marital literature. The caution should be added that in one case undergraduate judges were not able to predict marital satisfaction from marital distress at a high level of confidence (Royce & Weiss, 1975).

It should be noted, as well, that neither theorists nor therapists have necessarily done a very good job of identifying the major components of successful relationships. Markman and his colleagues (Chapter 15, this volume) found in their review of literature that certain behaviors with a long background in the therapy literature, such as expression of feeling, mind reading, and summarizing the other (reflective listening), do not seem to be important in distinguishing distressed and nondistressed relationships. However, it should also be noted that even observing the "appropriate" behaviors may not be necessary. Lowman (Chapter 4, this volume), for example, argues that a relatively simple assessment of emotional predispositions within the family gives very critical information.

CONCLUSION

We have attempted to provide additional direction for future work in the area of direct behavioral assessment of marital interaction. In total, the chapters included in this book contain many valuable substantive findings. They have provoked thoughts and questions which will serve as important catalysts for research and practice in the coming years. To the extent that the chapters are representative of the field, we can look forward to exciting developments in the very near future in marriage theory, research, and practice.

REFERENCE NOTES

1. WEISS, R. L. *Recent theoretical developments in the behavioral-systems approach to marriage.* Paper presented at the annual meetings of the National Council on Family Relations, Portland, Oregon, October 1980.

2. MARKMAN, H. & NOTARIUS, C. I. *Behavioral assessment of couples interaction from the couples perspective: The Communication Box.* Paper presented at the Conference on Family Observation, Behavioral Assessment and Intervention, Tempe, Arizona, February 1980.

REFERENCES

BELLACK, A. S., HERSEN, M., & TURNER, S. M. Role-play tests for assessing social skills: Are they valid? *Behavior Therapy,* 1978, *9,* 448-461.

GOLDFRIED, M. R., & D'ZURILLA, T. J. A behavioral-analytic model for assessing competence. In C. D. Spielberger (Ed.), *Current topics in clinical and community psychology.* New York: Academic, 1969.

JACOBSON, N. S., & MARGOLIN, G. *Marital therapy: Strategies based on social learning and behavior exchange principles.* New York: Brunner/Mazel, 1979.

KAZDIN, A. E. Assessing the clinical or applied importance of behavior change through social validation. *Behavior Modification,* 1975, *4,* 427-452.

NEWTSON, D., ENGQUIST, G., & BOIS, J. The objective basis of behavior units. *Journal of Personality and Social Psychology,* 1977, *35,* 847-862.

OLSON, D. H. The measurement of family power by self-report and behavioral methods. *Journal of Marriage and the Family,* 1969, *32,* 545-550.

PATTERSON, G. R., RAY, R. S., SHAW, D. A., & COBB, J. A. A manual for Coding Family Interactions. 1969 Revision. Document #01234, ASIS/NAPS c/o Microfiche Publications, 305 East 46th Street, New York, NY 10017, 1969.

RISKIN, J. M., & FAUNCE, E. E. An evaluative review of family interaction research. *Family Process,* 1972, *11,* 365-455.

ROMANO, J. M., & BELLACK, A. S. Social validation of a component model of assertive behavior. *Journal of Consulting and Clinical Psychology,* 1980, *48,* 478-490.

ROYCE, W. S., & WEISS, R. L. Behavior cues in the judgment of marital satisfaction: A linear regression analysis. *Journal of Consulting and Clinical Psychology,* 1975, *43,* 816-824.

RYDER, R. G., & GOODRICH, D. W. Married couples' responses to disagreement. *Family Process,* 1966, *5,* 30-42.

WEISS, R. L. The conceptualization of marriage from a behavioral perspective. In T. J. Paolino & B. S. McCrady (Eds.), *Marriage and marital therapy: Psychoanalytic, behavioral and systems theory perspective.* New York: Brunner/Mazel, 1978.

WEISS, R. L., HOPS, H., & PATTERSON, G. P. A framework for conceptualizing marital conflict: A technology for altering it, some data for evaluating it. In F. W. Clark & L. A. Hamerlynck (Eds.), *Critical issues in research and practice.* Champaign, IL: Research Press, 1973.

ABOUT THE AUTHORS

G. HUGH ALLRED is Professor of Marriage and Family Therapy at Brigham Young University.

HAL ARKOWITZ is an Associate Professor of Psychology at the University of Arizona and Associate in Psychiatry at the University of Arizona School of Medicine.

RAND D. CONGER is an Associate Professor of Human Development and Family Ecology at the University of Illinois—Urbana-Champaign.

RONALD E. CROMWELL is an Associate Professor of Family Studies at the University of Tennessee at Knoxville.

ERIK E. FILSINGER is an Assistant Professor of Family Studies in Home Economics at Arizona State University.

WILLIAM GARDNER is a graduate student in developmental psychology in the mathematical-statistics program at the University of Utah.

JAMES M. HARPER is an Assistant Professor of Marriage and Family Therapy at Brigham Young University.

DONALD P. HARTMANN is a Professor of Psychology at the University of Utah in Salt Lake City.

RICHARD A. HOLM is a Research Associate at the Department of Psychology, University of Washington, and President of Observational Systems, Inc., Seattle, Washington.

LOWELL J. KROKOFF is currently completing his doctoral studies at the University of Illinois—Urbana-Champaign.

LEANNE K. LAMKE is Assistant Professor of Family Studies in Home Economics at Arizona State University.

ROBERT A. LEWIS is Professor and Head of Child Development and Family Relations at Purdue University.

JOSEPH LOWMAN is Associate Professor of Psychology at the University of North Carolina at Chapel Hill.

PHILIP McAVOY received his M.S. in 1981 from Arizona State University, where he worked as Research Associate on a grant from the National Institute on Drug Abuse.

GAYLA MARGOLIN is an Assistant Professor of Psychology at the University of Southern California.

HOWARD J. MARKMAN is an Assistant Professor of Psychology at the University of Denver, and Director of the Denver Center for Marital and Family Studies.

CLIFFORD I. NOTARIUS is Assistant Professor of Clinical Psychology at the Catholic University of America in Washington, D.C.

DAVID H. OLSON is Professor of Family Social Science at the University of Minnesota.

GARY W. PETERSON is an Assistant Professor of Family Studies at the University of Tennessee at Knoxville.

RANDELL J. SMITH is currently a doctoral candidate in clinical psychology at the Catholic University of America.

STEVENS S. SMITH is a Research Associate at the University of Georgia.

PETER STEINGLASS is Professor of Psychiatry and Behavioral Sciences and Associate Director of the Center for Family Research at the George Washington University School of Medicine.

TIMOTHY STEPHEN is an Assistant Professor of Speech Communication at Bowling Green State University.

MURRAY A. STRAUS is Professor of Sociology and Director of the Family Violence Research Program at the University of New Hampshire.

LYDIA TISLENKO is a Research Associate at the Center for Family Research, George Washington University School of Medicine.

REX A. WADHAM is Associate Professor of Elementary Education at Brigham Young University.

ROBERT L. WEISS is Professor of Psychology and Director of the Marital Studies Program at the University of Oregon.

BRUCE H. WOOLLEY is Professor of Applied Pharmacology and Therapeutics in the College of Nursing at Brigham Young University.